UNFIT
COMMANDER

BUSH, GEORGE W., 2LT

UNFIT COMMANDER

TEXANS FOR TRUTH

TAKE ON GEORGE W. BUSH

GLENN W. SMITH

1❂ ReganBooks
Celebrating Ten Bestselling Years
An Imprint of HarperCollins*Publishers*

Also by Glenn W. Smith

The Politics of Deceit

HarperCollins books may be purchased for educational, business, or sales promotional use. For information please write: Special Markets Department, HarperCollins Publishers Inc., 10 East 53rd Street, New York, NY 10022.

FIRST EDITION

Designed by E. Grotyohann

Printed on acid-free paper

Library of Congress Cataloging-in-Publication Data has been applied for.

ISBN 0-06-079245-0

04 05 06 07 08 RRD 10 9 8 7 6 5 4 3 2 1

*To my brothers and sisters—Patty, Mack, Janice, and Rick.
We don't always agree, but we speak our minds, and our love
for one another is never threatened.*

So it should be with the family of America.

CONTENTS

I

UNGUARDED

THE UNFIT COMMANDER
AND THE NATIONAL GUARD

At this writing, the security and future of the United States are in the hands of a president who refused to serve his country in combat during the Vietnam War, and who then shirked his commitment to alternative service in the National Guard. This same man, George W. Bush, has gone to great lengths to present himself as a martial president, a military commander first and a civil authority second.

In much the same way one might treat a G.I. Joe doll, Bush's handlers dress him in military drag, in flight suits and leather airmen's jackets. They've changed the course of an aircraft carrier to allow the staging of a telegenic jet landing upon its deck, as if to suggest that Bush himself had flown to the front lines of battle. They've gleefully watched him assume a soldierly gait, his arms swinging in march time as he struts to his airplane or his helicopter. They watch as he holds his hands at his side, palms flattened and fingers held tightly together, as though the need to salute might arise at any moment.

In their vision, his natural language deficiencies are turned to strengths. He's a down-home guy, an Audie Murphy or Sergeant York. A man of action, not of words. His inarticulate, halting speaking style becomes a badge of authenticity, a medal to replace those he never earned on the front lines.

As president, George W. Bush has spoken of creating in America a "responsibility culture." Yet when he was younger, he acted as though his responsibility to the National Guard was somehow beneath a person of his economic privilege and social standing. And today he deftly sidesteps any accountability for the consequences of his own actions—a dangerous habit in a president who is proud to act but skeptical of thinking.

American soldiers are dying in combat in Iraq today because Bush told us that Saddam Hussein had weapons of mass destruction. What happened when no weapons were found? It was the fault of the British, or of inadequate intelligence. Bush took credit for the action, but not the consequences. Helpless prisoners have been tortured at the American-run Abu Ghraib prison. What happened when the torturers were exposed? Bush, more Pilate than pilot, washed his hands of the brutality. Bush's massive tax cuts for the wealthy failed to produce the promised economic prosperity. What happened when the results started coming in? He simply shrugged and told us the economy was doing better than it looked.

This latter dodge reminds me of nineteenth-century American humorist Bill Nye's comment that "Wagner's music is better than it sounds." The remark is often incorrectly attributed to Mark Twain. But in his own essay on Wagner, Twain did have something to say that illuminates the subject at hand. Writing of the different ways Europeans regard their princes and our American presidents, he observed that the former were held to be "of no more blood and kinship with men than are the serene eternal lights of the firmament with the poor dull tallow candles of commerce that sputter and die and leaving nothing behind but a pinch of ashes and a stink." Today, in modern America, Bush aspires to (and, from some quarters, receives) the very kind of royal treatment Twain felt was so alien to our New World culture.

Bush has managed to position himself far above the muck and confusion of everyday American life. That he has not earned any such position simply makes him all the more likely to expect it, as royals will do. Like Bush, princes inherit their status, from the genes and bank accounts of their fathers and their fathers' courts. This is what Bush's opponents find so dismaying: Why is he given credit for being what he is not? This may help explain the religious zeal of his followers: Bush's poor resume, his earthly failures, his bumbling talk, his obvious shortcomings, all serve to bolster his supporters' confidence that he's touched—not by madness but by something divine. The Transcendent Leader must surely receive his authority from a Transcendent Source.

Twain understood the pathology. Comparing the English fascination with their princes to their disregard for American presidents, he said of President Ulysses S. Grant: "The general who was never defeated, the general who never held a council of war, the only general who ever commanded a connected battle-front twelve hundred miles long, the smith who welded together the broken parts of a great republic and re-established it where it is quite likely to outlast all the monarchies present and to come, was really a person of no consequence to these people. To them, with their training, my General was only a man, after all, while their Prince was clearly much more than that. . . . "

And now, in today's America, we have a president who does little else but hold councils of war, who wouldn't know a battlefront from a boutonniere, who holds shards of the great republic in his hands while claiming he didn't break it—he just found it this way, and wants to put it back together again. The rest of the world, a world we used to mock for its royal inclinations, now thinks of us what Twain once thought of them: "Perhaps the essence of the thing is the value which men attach to a valuable something which has come by luck and not been earned," Twain wrote. "A prince picks up grandeur, power, and a permanent holiday and gratis support by a pure accident, the accident of birth, and he stands always before the grieved eye of poverty and obscurity a monumental representative of luck. And then—supremest value of all—his is the only high fortune on earth which is secure."

Bush and his team have gone to great lengths to create the impression that their man is a military hero, a fighter pilot and active-duty veteran with the courage to stand up to America's known and unknown threats.

Bush himself has altered the principles of our foreign policy to include preemptive, unprovoked military strikes on other nations. The philosophy, rhetoric, and imagery of his administration may well make America less secure, not more so.

Yet when it came time for him to serve his country, where was George W. Bush?

When millions of his fellow Americans were sent off to fight and die overseas, this modern faux-Alexander, pseudo-Caesar, and Neo-Napoleon managed to avoid military service in Vietnam. Indeed, he failed to fulfill even the far less daunting obligations of service in the National Guard.

And ever since he began his quest for public office decades ago, Bush has misrepresented his military past, emphasizing the danger he faced while flying training missions, and claiming at various times to have served on active duty in the U.S. Air Force, and to have continued flying long after he actually stopped showing up for duty. Of course, many Americans want to believe these things are true. Some, who simply agree with his conservative ideology and would like his policies to triumph, overlook the deceptions and the irresponsibility and dishonor that mark their president's past and present. Others cling to Bush's heroic image the way a child might refuse to see or understand a parent's errors. Authority is their guiding light, and maintaining that authority is more important than knowing the truth about their heroes.

I do not believe it is appropriate to mock or misunderstand either kind of Bush supporter. They have their reasons, and they are the reasons of human beings trying their best to build a future for themselves and for their country. They are misguided, but ridicule will not change their minds. As someone who has lived through the Bush ascendancy, first in Texas and then nationally, I'm often asked what it has been like to witness the surprising rise of this young man, whose only strengths seem to be his remarkable good luck, his privileged family background, and his ability to communicate to a confused and hero-hungry middle America. My answer is that it was disturbing. Some of my close friends and working colleagues turned their backs on their progressive pasts and joined the Bush effort. Watching them, I felt something like Baron von Trapp in *The Sound of Music,* who was confused and alarmed at his countrymen's enthusiastic support of reunification with Germany. (And no, I don't mean to imply a parallel between Bush and Nazi leaders. I simply point to my own dismay that anyone could be attracted to someone like George W. Bush.)

In launching Texans for Truth, of course, I am acting upon my own convictions. But in presenting the arguments and documents collected in this book, I hope as well that those Americans who are confused by the daily flood of news, spin, and counter-spin will gain a deeper understanding of Bush's character and his past—even though the message is carried by someone who has made up his mind. Thomas Paine did not apologize for his criticism of King George III, and while I do not pretend to the talent, eloquence, or historical reach of a Paine, neither do I apologize for my perspective on Bush. Too much is at stake in this election year for any of us to be a captive of timidity or tepid neutrality. Though his supporters may view this book as just another instance of Bush-bashing, I hold no personal hatred for George Bush. I simply believe that he has used illusion, deceit, and manipulation to gain power—and used that power, in turn, to lead our nation into a less secure future, one that will provide refuge for the privileged and lasting hardship and danger for the poor and the middle class.

I believe that the George W. Bush who occupies the White House today, and pursues those selfish and dangerous policies, is very much the same man who believed in the Vietnam War . . . so long as he and his privileged brethren could hide from danger while others risked their lives for the country he would one day lead. To ignore the lessons of Bush's past behavior, in the spirit of "putting Vietnam behind us," is no better than to discard the Declaration of Independence out of a need to put the Revolutionary War behind us. We live with the consequences of those years just as we live with the blessings of American independence.

Texans for Truth was created to help Americans understand the falsity of George W. Bush's claims to an honorable military past. As the 2004 campaign enters its final days, many questions about that past persist. There are questions about how Bush got into the Guard in the first place and about how he got out. And, of course, there are questions about his apparently cavalier attitude toward his commitment to the military, from the beginning to the end of his time there. Why was he grounded as a pilot in 1972? Was it because he failed to take the required flight physical? Why didn't he take that physical? Why did he return to flying a trainer jet not long before he quit flying altogether? Where did he go when he was missing from the 187th Tactical Recon Group in Montgomery, Alabama, where he had transferred from the Texas guard? Why was he never seen at drills there?

Bush's father was a congressman in Houston when George W. was admitted to the Texas Air National Guard in May 1968. More than three decades later, former Texas House speaker and lieutenant governor Ben Barnes has now confessed to pulling strings on behalf of the Bush family, strings that allowed the young Bush to jump ahead of a substantial waiting list for the Guard. "I would describe it as preferential treatment," Barnes said recently. "It's not something I'm necessarily proud of. . . . I'm very, very sorry." Barnes had admitted as much in a sworn deposition some years before, but in 2004 his unequivocal confession and apology—first made in May to a small group at a political rally in Austin, Texas, and then on network TV—reinvigorated public interest in the story as the president's reelection campaign entered its final stages.

At first, Bush seems to have been an enthusiastic pilot. Yet in 1972, as Richard Nixon was coasting to a reelection victory over George McGovern, Bush disappeared from his service in the guard. As the *Boston Globe* reported, "Bush's discharge papers list his service and duty station for each of his first four years in the Air Guard. But there is no record of training listed after May 1972, and no mention of any service in Alabama." Like the famous eighteen-minute gap on Nixon's Watergate tapes, this long lapse in Bush's military paper trail—focused largely on the time he was supposed to be reporting to Dannelly Air Force Base in Alabama—is a disturbing lapse in the historical record.

At the time, the reason that Bush gave for wanting to transfer to Alabama was to work on the U.S. Senate campaign of a family friend, Winton "Red" Blount. Questions remain, however, about whether what he really wanted was to go to Alabama, or just to get out of Texas, where his partying was reaching legendary levels. So off to Alabama he went, leaving Texas, and apparently his Guard responsibilities, behind him. According to workers in the Blount campaign, his partying ways came with him to the Deep South.

Former National Guard lieutenant colonel Bob Mintz, a career pilot who served years in the 187th, has no recollection of Bush ever appearing on the base. During the 2000 presidential campaign, when Mintz first heard Bush claim that he had served there, he wondered how he could have missed him. "Really? That was my unit. And I don't remember seeing you there," Mintz remembers thinking. "So I called my friends and said, 'Did you know that George Bush served in our unit?' And everyone said, 'No, I never saw him there.' It would be impossible to be unseen in a unit of that size."

I met Mintz in late August 2004, while traveling the country on tour for my book, *The Politics of Deceit: Saving Freedom and Democracy from Extinction*. The Swift Boat Veterans had recently launched their campaign against John Kerry, and it seemed that everyone I met knew the details of their attack. Far fewer remembered very much about George Bush's check-ered military record, or about the questions that have dogged Bush since he first ran for governor of Texas. Politics is often burlesque, but this was ridiculous. Here was a man who had dodged the draft, and failed to fulfill his obligations to his country as a young man, attacking the war record of a decorated hero—and getting away with it.

The Bush campaign has denied any foreknowledge of the Swift Boaters' efforts. But to anyone familiar with Texas politics, the connec-tions would be easy to recognize. The Swift Boat Veterans' PR representa-tive, Merrie Spaeth, worked for the Reagan/Bush White House, and in August 2004 Bush's national counsel, Benjamin Ginsberg, resigned after it was revealed that he had advised the Swift Boaters. But O'Neill's un-founded, and now largely discredited, attacks on John Kerry were serving a key purpose in the Bush reelection strategy: They were casting doubt upon one of Kerry's strongest selling points, his courageous service in the military. At the same time, they were reducing their own vulnerability on an issue they knew could hurt Bush's chances for reelection.

Bob Mintz was also disturbed by the Swift Boat phenomenon. He'd spoken up earlier in the year, telling a reporter from a Memphis newspaper that he didn't remember seeing Bush on the Alabama base. The story hadn't found much traction with political writers, but when I returned home from one leg of my book tour, I came across it while searching the Web for people who had made statements regarding Bush's poor service record. I called him, and he said he would be happy to talk about his years in the 187th. In fact, he said, he would feel less than a responsible citizen if he failed to speak out.

A couple of days later, we met at a local Austin restaurant. His simple, credible account was powerful. Unlike the Swift Boaters who attacked Kerry, Mintz wasn't making a claim that conflicted with available records. One medic claimed to have treated Kerry's wounds, which he described as too minor to justify a purple heart, but his name is nowhere on the medical records. Mintz, on the other hand, simply told me he had been there in Alabama, and that he had never seen Bush—even though he had been told to look out for the politically connected pilot who was transferring to the base.

It was Mintz's honest bearing and forthright account that persuaded me to proceed with the creation of Texans for Truth. American voters simply had to be informed about Bush's fakery, his irresponsibility, his lack of honorable service. In the wake of 9/11, Bush had positioned himself to take advantage of our shared national anxiety. His White House had used fear like a weapon against opponents; his grandiose War on Terror has become the quintessential Orwellian never-ending war. Stories like those of Bob Mintz and Ben Barnes promised to cut through all the bluster with real evidence of George W. Bush's character. As we launched Texans for Truth—and the long-anticipated Barnes interview aired on CBS the same day—the questions surrounding Bush's middle years finally reentered the news.

George W. had been down this road before. In fact, less than five years after his discharge, it was Bush himself who had first introduced the subject to public discourse. In 1978, while living in West Texas, Bush decided to run for Congress. One of his advertisements during that campaign claimed that he had served in the United States Air Force. Now, Bush may have considered his days of active duty training as Air Force rather than Air National Guard service. But they were not. Bush did not serve in the Air Force. A Pentagon spokesperson later confirmed that Air Guard trainees are not considered members of the active-duty Air Force. "Air Force" may have sounded better than "National Guard" to the aspiring congressman, but the voters weren't fooled: He lost the election.

That was only the first of a long line of dishonest accounts of his military service. In his 1999 autobiography, *A Charge to Keep,* Bush said that he had continued to fly with his unit for several years after he was turned down in 1970 for a program that might just have taken him to Vietnam. But the truth is that Bush was grounded in 1972. At this writing it is unclear whether he was grounded because he missed a required flight physical, or whether he skipped the physical because he had been grounded. But one thing is quite clear: After 1972, George Bush was no longer flying planes for the Guard.

The issue of Bush's spotty service record first surfaced publicly during his father's reelection campaign in 1992. The senior Bush's vice president, Dan Quayle, had also joined the National Guard; Bill Clinton's running mate, Al Gore, had served in Vietnam. Bush had defended Quayle's decision, and in turn reporters raised the subject of the younger Bush's service. Here's how the *Houston Chronicle* reported it on October 10, 1992: "George Bush's oldest son, George W. Bush, also avoided the draft by enlisting in the Texas National Guard after receiving student deferment while he attended Yale University. The younger Bush secured a place in the Texas National Guard in 1968 despite a lengthy waiting list because he volunteered for pilot duty, according to Texas National Guard spokesman Lt. Col. Edmond Komandosky."

The *Washington Post,* on October 13, 1992, also put a reasonably good spin on Bush's service. "The president's eldest son, George W. Bush, was born in 1946—as was Clinton—and got a student deferment that was reviewed four times while he studied at Yale University. He then served in the Texas Air National Guard, learned to fly jet fighters and signed up for a program that rotated some pilots to Vietnam, but he was never sent." But Bush admitted later that he was turned down for the program—which was shut down just a week after Bush qualified as a pilot. Meaning, of course, that it was the perfect kind of program for someone who wanted to be able to say he had volunteered for a program that could have taken him to Vietnam, while remaining certain that he wouldn't be sent. Bush's just-so stories, in other words, flew better than he did.

The trajectory of the media coverage of Bush's military exploits is instructive. Sometimes political journalists can behave more like Don

Quixote's Sancho Panza than like protectors of the public's access to the truth. Indeed, this may be true in more ways than one: Quixote's fantastic tales served to revive the morale of those who believed in them with him—but Quixote's magic wouldn't have worked if he himself hadn't believed his own fictions and shared them with others. They would merely have been lies—and Cervantes's brilliant exploration of the inspiring power of fiction would have become another piece of propaganda.

On occasion, Bush's temper has been known to overcome his discretion. During his run for governor of Texas in 1994, Bush was asked by the magazine *Texas Monthly* if he had joined the Guard to avoid Vietnam. "Hell, no," Bush answered. "Do you think I'm going to admit that? You are out of your mind. Let me give you the political answer, Mr. Reporter." The magazine goes on to report that Bush bragged that he had volunteered for a Guard program that could have taken him to Vietnam—the program that terminated a week after Bush inquired about it—and that he continued to fly with his colleagues for several years after he actually did.

From the beginning, Bush's tales of his military service begin to take on the aura of Pecos Bill, the legendary character said to have roped and ridden a tornado. It must have been a heady experience for George W. Bush to watch as audience after willing audience fell for his construction of his own mythic past. Just as he blithely claimed to have served in the Air Force, Bush could come within a hair's breadth of saying he'd volunteered for Vietnam—and suddenly the credulous voters would believe in his courage. It's hard to say what is more unsettling—the boldness and ease with which Bush embroidered his history, or the public's willingness to believe whatever he told them.

Ever since Ronald Reagan confused his own movie history with real history, the modern political tall tale has been met with a kind of shrugging acceptance as an effective leadership stratagem. Of course, Reagan hardly invented the practice of presidential mythmaking. But Bush may have taken his lead from his role model's dubious tales of inspiration; when he entered the political sphere, he took the art to a new level, demonstrating that in American politics simply telling a good story about oneself passes all too often for legitimate campaigning.

During Bush's 1994 race, quietly and off the record, many people with knowledge of Bush's shadowy National Guard history urged others of their number to step forward with the truth. No one did. One of the ways a politician's secrets remain secret, especially if the politician is the son of a former U.S. president with powerful business connections in your state, is by punishing those who betray them. In those years Texas political culture was a culture of fear, and the Bush family wasn't above finding a way to make their wrath known to those they considered traitors. It was a time of political transition in Texas; once dominated by Democrats, the state was fast becoming a Republican stronghold. Most of those in a position to tell the truth about Bush's National Guard record simply couldn't afford to do so. (Others took a different path: One man, who had been very active in quietly spreading the Guard story on behalf of Richards, quit spreading such tales once he found a new home in the Bush regime. Power can taketh away, but it also giveth.)

The questions about Bush's National Guard record would have remained largely unexplored in 1994, if it hadn't been for television journalist Jim Moore. Late in October of that year, in a debate between Governor Ann Richards and Bush, Moore asked: Had Bush's father used his influence to secure his son a coveted and safe spot in the National Guard?

Bush energetically denied the suggestion. "Putting an F-102 jet in afterburner in a single-seat, single-engine aircraft was a thrill, but it also wasn't trying to avoid duty," Bush said. "Had that engine failed, I could have been killed. So I was at risk." Richards refused to engage, taking the opportunity to congratulate anyone who had served in the National Guard. Her decision was probably for the best; Bush had successfully hidden the details of his military record from public scrutiny for years, and they weren't likely to be uncovered or reported in the closing days of that gubernatorial campaign. Questioning Bush's service might just as likely have backfired, making Richards look anti-military.

The question of how Bush entered the Guard resurfaced briefly not long after Bush was sworn in as governor, but it soon faded, and in his 1998 reelection campaign it remained largely offstage. The story didn't surface again until 1999, when Bush began to gear up for the 2000 presidential contest.

"He said he wanted to fly just like his daddy." That's how Col. Walter "Buck" Staudt remembered his encounter with the young Bush in an interview with the *Los Angeles Times* that ran on July 4, 1999. It was the kind of stuff presidential dreams are made of: In one sentence, Staudt had managed to merge a son's desire to follow his father's flight path to the White House with the National Guard entry on W's own resume.

According to the *Times* story, Bush's campaign denied that he had received any preferential treatment in getting a place in the Guard. But they offered no explanation for how the young Bush managed to get accepted ahead of a hundred thousand other men then on waiting lists around the country. The newspaper reported Sen. John McCain's joke that, as a prisoner of war in North Vietnam, he slept better knowing that Bush was protecting Texas from invasion. The story also noted a cryptic but intriguing observation by Ike Harris, a Republican who had served almost three decades in the Texas legislature. Of the use of political influence to avoid the Vietnam draft, Harris said, "There were all sorts of different things that were going on."

The *Los Angeles Times* story also quoted a bizarrely lighthearted press release sent out by the Guard during Bush's service, touting his first solo flight. "George Walker Bush is one member of the younger generation who doesn't get his kicks from pot or hashish or speed," read the piece. "Oh, he gets high, all right, but not from narcotics." (Bush would later refuse to answer questions about drug use, although he did admit to excessive use of alcohol.) Bush himself was quoted in the piece: The flight "was really neat," he said. "It was fun, and very exciting. I felt really serene up there."

A week after the Los Angeles story appeared, the *St. Petersburg Times* would declare, "In past elections, Dan Quayle and Bill Clinton were under fire for months about Vietnam and the draft and how they avoided both. But when questions were raised a week ago about how George W. Bush wound up as a pilot in the Texas Air National Guard in 1968, the issue came and went as quickly as a late-afternoon thunderstorm. Without the thunder."

The St. Petersburg story is informative. It reports that on the Tuesday following the holiday weekend, the Bush campaign reported receiving just two calls. Said the paper: "Campaign spokesman David Beckwith said one came from an editorial writer at a newspaper that wanted to defend Bush. The other came from Salon, the hip online magazine with an attitude.

Tuesday evening, none of the major television networks mentioned the story on their nightly news."

In hindsight, the newspaper's assertion that there "is nothing to indicate Bush has misrepresented his intentions or his record" seems laughable. Just about everything Bush had ever said or done on the subject has misrepresented his service in one way or another. And yet at the time Bush and his campaign were credited with addressing the issue honestly and effectively. Comparing the Bush story to the military draft controversies that dogged Dan Quayle and Bill Clinton, the paper said, "Perhaps even more revealing about the accounts is the way the Bush camp addressed the questions. Bush was well-prepared for the issue, and there are no indications so far that he has shaded the truth. In a broader sense, this may mark the end of an era in which the type and length of military service was a litmus test for candidates for president."

Meanwhile, the *Los Angeles Times* was apparently being swamped with complaints about its story on Bush. "According to hundreds of our readers, this political season's 'gotcha journalism' was launched in the *Times* on July 4 with a front-page story on GOP presidential candidate George W. Bush's service in the Texas Air National Guard."

Hundreds of readers? Very few newspaper stories get that kind of spontaneous reaction, especially stories that in the end don't really make any incendiary accusations. One wonders whether fears of irreparable damage might have spurred the campaign to start mobilizing letter writers, sending a signal to other media outlets about the consequences if they should pursue the story. From Florida to California, the Bush campaign spun itself out of trouble on the issue of the National Guard. In Florida, the story was treated as an old one with no legs. In California, it was slammed as unfair by a deluge of alleged reader outcry.

At the same time, though, the *Washington Post* was investing considerable time and energy into its own exploration of Bush's past. In the most thorough investigation of the future president undertaken until that time, on July 28, 1999, the *Post* published an extensive story called "The Life of George W. Bush." In a bit of news that would go largely unexplored by the media, the *Post* described how Barnes, his chief of staff Robert Spelling, and Barnes aide Nick Krajl (also a top aide to Guard General Jim Rose) remembered forwarding to Rose the names of young men interested in getting into the Guard. Barnes maintained that no one "in the Bush family" had asked him to do the favor for George W. When asked whether someone had asked on behalf of the family, however, he didn't answer—at least not at first.

Bush told the *Post* that he'd decided to apply to the Air National Guard because he wanted to be a pilot, not because he wanted to avoid service in Vietnam. But his actual words spoke volumes. "I'm saying to myself, 'What do I want to do?'" he was quoted as saying. "I think I don't want to be an infantry guy as a private in Vietnam."

The story also detailed the party atmosphere at the Chateaux Dijon, the apartment complex where Bush and his crowd lived and spent time during his days at the Ellington Field air base south of Houston. From this account and others, one gets the picture of a group of young men who were proud that partying took precedence over duty. The atmosphere was like that of a college fraternity house without advisers, or the dean, or any rules at all. When Bush and his friends reported for drills in their expensive cars—Jaguars, Corvettes, Mercedes—they shared a parking lot with the full-time Guard staffers. (If there had been Humvees back in those days, no doubt they would have filled the lots.) The contrast between the Volkswagens of the full-timers and the sleek rides of the wealthy could not have been greater.

The *Post* story also mentions Bush's move to Alabama in 1972. But it drops the thread of the National Guard story that was later to become big news. "Bush moved to Alabama and worked until November as political director for [Winton M.] Blount against longtime incumbent John J. Sparkman," the story recounted, glossing over the question of whether Bush was fulfilling his service obligations in Alabama.

In September 1999, the *Dallas Morning News* broke the story that Barnes was telling friends that Houston oilman and Bush family friend Sid Adger had asked Barnes to find a spot for George W. in the National Guard. Both Bushes, the young presidential hopeful and the former president, denied asking Adger to make such a request. But then, in late September, Barnes repeated the claim in a deposition in a lawsuit involving a former client of Barnes's. It had been alleged that the client had been allowed to keep a lucrative contract in Texas in return for Barnes's silence about Bush and the Guard; Barnes confirmed in a statement that the friend in question was Sid Adger.

Right on cue, newspapers around the country began weighing in against continued coverage of the story. Just as had happened in July after the appearance of the *Los Angeles Times* piece, editors began scolding their colleagues for reporting the story, accusing them of trash journalism. Such spontaneous anti-combustion is possible, one supposes. But isn't it at least as likely that the Bush campaign was rallying editorial opposition to coverage of Bush's National Guard experiences?

Witness the tone of the *Austin American-Statesman*'s piece: "It's been most curious, this press mini-frenzy about Gov. George W. Bush's service in the National Guard in the late 1960s. . . . Gasp. The scion of a wealthy and politically connected family derived a break from those in a position to help. As we have said before, it would be news if he hadn't gotten a break. Maybe now that Barnes has confirmed the obvious, this non-issue will subside."

Or the dry wit of the *Oregonian:* "This time the critics are picking at the bleached-out bones of George W. Bush's military record, which is this: he flew F-102 fighters for the National Guard and may have gotten the benefit of his father's influence and connections to get the appointment. . . . It's OK, Lieutenant Bush. Most of us would have done the same thing."

The Associated Press reported on October 3, 1999, that questions "about whether family friends greased the wheels for George W. Bush's admission into the National Guard during the Vietnam War seem to be drawing more yawns than outrage from Texans." On November 11, the Newhouse News Service used the same tired image: The "electorate, it seems, is yawning at the issue even as presidential candidates go out of their way to recount their war stories or explain their lack of them."

Bush got another good break on November 16 from the *New York Post*. The lead to its story: "Republican 2000 front-runner George W. Bush says in his new autobiography that he wanted to go to Vietnam as a pilot—but was told he hadn't logged enough flight hours." The headline was even better. "Bush: I Was Denied Viet Wings: Bio Says He Was Short on Flight Time." The *Post*'s enthusiasm for this heroic account seems to contradict the growing media opinion that the story was of little concern to voters. If the voters didn't care about Bush's service one way or another, why would the *Post* editors (or the Bush campaigners who no doubt solicited the story) bother to portray him as *volunteering* for Vietnam?

Miami Herald columnist Fred Grimm remained skeptical about public concern over Bush's service. Grimm wrote on November 26 that "Once a month, for six long years, George W. and I tugged on our black boots and our olive fatigues and braved heat and humidity and mosquitoes and other discomforts of wartime military service. We would've taken on the enemy too, if those gutless Viet Cong had tried to invade East Texas or the Mississippi Delta."

The *Richmond* [Virginia] *Times Dispatch,* in a December 8 editorial, said that "A possible analysis of the George W. Bush/National Guard flap could be as follows: A man should be barred from public office if he served in the National Guard or Army or Navy Reserve, ran to Canada, or just waited for a call from the draft board. This indicates that only those who were on active duty could run for public office." To the *Times Dispatch,* in other words, it appeared that Bush was being held to an absurd standard.

From July 4, 1999, until December of that year, questions about Bush's National Guard experience—most of them concerning how he got into the Guard in the first place—persisted at some level. But as 2000 approached, the Bush campaign appeared to have accomplished its goal: It had raised doubts about the issue's legitimacy, mocked those who continued to bring it up, and redefined the issue as a question not about Bush's past, but about the character of those who would ask the question in the first place. It is a pattern the campaign would rely on, with great success, throughout the coming year.

For the next few months the Guard story languished, until the *Boston Globe* revealed the long gaps in Bush's service record. In that story, the man who would have been Bush's commander in Alabama, Lieutenant Colonel William Turnipseed, said he didn't remember Bush being on the base. His personnel chief, Kenneth K. Lott, later told *Newsweek* he'd never spotted Bush there either: "I never saw the man, I never met the man."

And on June 18, the *Sunday Times* of London hit the streets with the following headline: "Bush Flies Into An Air Force Cocaine Cloud." Here's how the newspaper began its account of this startling charge: "The Republican frontrunner for the White House, George W. Bush, was suspended from flying as a young pilot for failing to take a medical examination that included a drug test. Documents obtained by the *Sunday Times* reveal that in August 1972, as a 26-year-old subaltern in the Air National Guard, Bush was grounded for failing to 'accomplish' an annual medical that would have indicated whether he was taking drugs." It was a sensational allegation, one that has yet to be fully investigated or proven—but which would resurface years later, during Bush's 2004 reelection campaign. The *Sunday Times* also raised the question of Bush's attendance in Alabama: "There is no evidence in his record, however, that once there he ever attended the periodic drills required by part-time guardsmen."

The accumulating doubts, questions, and revelations caused a scramble in the Bush camp. "Bush Campaign Is Searching for Records on Guard Service," ran the headline over an Associated Press story that ran (among other places) in the *Chattanooga Times Free Press* on June 25, 2000. "Gov. George W. Bush's campaign workers have concluded that no documents exist showing he reported for duty as ordered in Alabama with the Texas Air National Guard in 1972. They are looking for people who served with him to verify his story that he did."

Responding to questions about his failure to report to the Alabama air base and the failure to find records confirming that he reported for duty, Bush himself was quoted in the AP story: "I was there on temporary assignment and fulfilled my weekends at one period of time. I made up some missed weekends." In the story, Bush spokesman Dan Bartlett repeats that the campaign was focusing its attention on trying to locate people who served with Bush in late 1972, when he was supposed to be in Alabama. As of then, they had failed to find anyone to fit that bill. (In 2004, a man named John B. Calhoun did turn up claiming that Bush had put in his time—but Calhoun's claim fell apart when he specified that he remembered Bush being there from May to October 1972 . . . and Bush didn't even apply to perform equivalent service there until September 5.)

But once again interest waned as the 2000 campaign neared the home stretch. Covering criticism of Bush's record in the days before the election, the *Washington Post* would call Bush's National Guard service "a dormant issue." Somehow this emerging picture—that one of the two major-party presidential candidates had disappeared from military service before fulfilling his obligations, and was alleged to have missed a military physical for untoward reasons—was eclipsed in the national press by sniping about whether Al Gore claimed to have invented the Internet or to have been the inspiration for the book *Love Story.*

All candidates believe that lingering negative questions will be erased by victory in November. For George W. Bush, of course, that victory didn't come until December—and then, of course, it gave birth to more bad memories than it erased. Weakened by the loss of the popular vote and the Florida election debacle, Bush spent the early months of his presidency floundering.

Then came September 11, 2001. In the wake of the terrorist attacks, Americans went searching for a symbol of strength. And then, of necessity—and after some time for planning and preparation—a new George W. Bush arrived to assume the role. His bearing suddenly grew more military, his speech more forceful. The straight-talking Western hero, the courageous man of action: In the blink of an eye the martial presidency was born. Bush brandished a go-it-alone foreign policy, presenting preemptive war as a new foundation for international relations. And on that premise he sent American military personnel to war, first in Afghanistan, and then, disastrously, in Iraq. For roughly two years the erstwhile draft dodger was suddenly transformed into a military hero, and Bush's popularity soared. It seemed to matter little to the American media that this was the same man whose family had called in favors to help him avoid Vietnam, who had never adequately explained the gaps and contradictions in the stories of his own National Guard service.

But the unanswered questions never completely disappeared. And in 2004 the Democratic presidential primary gave the issue another boost. This time, two Democratic candidates with strong military credentials of their own—General Wesley Clark and Senator John Kerry—began to raise questions about Bush's National Guard record. With the Iraq war backfiring on the Bush administration, and Clark and Kerry emerging as true military men, the contrast between Bush the commander in chief and Bush the no-show Guardsman suddenly took on new resonance. The National Guard document wars began in earnest.

Once again the *Boston Globe* led the reporting, after two new documents emerged early in 2004. As the *Globe*'s Walter V. Robinson wrote on February 10, the documents, which showed that Bush had performed minimal service in the critical period from May 1972 to May 1973, "seem unlikely to resolve questions about whether Bush shirked his duty during his tour as a fighter-interceptor pilot for the Texas Air Guard during the Vietnam War. That is because some of the dates on the service list fell during a period in the fall of 1972 when Bush was reassigned to a guard unit in Alabama. The commander of the Alabama unit has said Bush did not appear for duty at his assigned unit there."

Dan Bartlett, Bush's White House communications director, explained that Bush had earned credits for attending drills in January and April 1973, drills that were probably conducted back in Houston. However, the *Globe* reported, "Bush's two commanders at Ellington Air Force Base wrote that they could not evaluate his performance for the prior 12 months because he had not been there. Two other Bush superiors said in interviews four years ago that they do not believe Bush ever returned to his Houston base from Alabama."

Under pressure from Democrats, on the day the *Globe* stories appeared the White House released eighteen months of Bush's National Guard payroll records, claiming that the records proved Bush had met his obligations. The documents themselves, however—copied from hard-to-read, thirty-year-old microfiche files—told a different story. "The records that were unearthed from a Colorado records facility show Bush appeared for training on nine occasions, for 25 days, during the contested 12 months." Yet Robinson notes that nothing in Bush's public military records actually confirms that he performed any service between April 16, 1972, and May 1, 1973. "Nor did he appear for monthly training in December 1972 or in February or March of 1973," he reported. And after releasing the records, the White House press secretary, Scott McClellan, could not explain why, if Bush appeared for duty on the days listed in the documents, Bush's superiors wrote on May 2, 1973, that he had not been seen at his Houston air base for the previous twelve months.

As the *Globe* reported, the records showed that "Bush may not have met the minimum-service requirement expected of most Guard members, according to National Guard officials." The newspaper quoted the judgment of retired Col. Earl W. Lively, operations officer for the Texas Air National Guard at the time, that Bush's performance fell short "of what everyone was expected to do."

The White House had expected that the new documents would settle the question of Bush's service between 1972 and 1973. And despite a standing invitation that had been in place for years, the Bush machine had still not found anyone to confirm the president's earlier claims that he remembered reporting for duty in Alabama. In late February *Doonesbury* cartoonist Garry Trudeau got into the act, offering to donate $10,000 to the USO if anyone stepped forward with proof that Bush had fulfilled his Guard duty in Alabama during the period in question. And in September 2004 Texans for Truth upped the ante, offering $50,000 for original information proving whether Bush performed duties in the Air National Guard between May 1972 and May 1973 at Dannelly Air National Guard Base in Alabama. As of this writing, no one has taken either prize.

The flurry of document releases, which fanned the flames of old questions, also raised some new ones. How had Bush lost his flying status? Was he grounded because he failed to take the required physical? Under Air Force regulations in effect at the time, the grounding should have demanded an investigation. As had happened so many times before, though, the story of Bush's military records dropped from the headlines after a few days—this time subsumed by coverage of the Democratic presidential primary. As John Kerry's wins in Iowa and New Hampshire brought the brief drama to a close, and spring arrived, the presidential race moved on to other matters.

But not among two new groups of constituents: the families of American soldiers who had lost their lives in Iraq, and the new counterculture of the Internet, where grassroots political inquiry had found a new life in the form of Web logs (or "blogs"). In the blogging culture, an issue like the controversy over Bush's military service could take on a life of its own—completely unimpeded by the media's reluctance to pursue the story. The explosion of blogs, the participation of thousand of amateur news gatherers sharing their opinions and analyses on the Web, kept the National Guard issue alive throughout 2004, when it otherwise might have disappeared into the Alabama mists.

And then, conveniently timed to break just before the Republican National Convention, the Right launched the Swift Boat Veterans for Truth offensive. Led by longtime John Kerry nemesis John O'Neill, the group initiated an attack on the Massachusetts senator's military record—an attack that mirrored a similar tactic from Bush's 2000 Republican primary contest against another Vietnam hero, Sen. John McCain. It was the second time that this man who avoided Vietnam has tried to neutralize the issue by casting doubts on the wartime heroics of his opponents.

The effects on McCain and Kerry alike were immediate. Like George Foreman when he was tormented by Muhammad Ali in Zaire, both men seemed so astounded by the attack that they momentarily lost their campaign footing.

John O'Neill, leader of the swift boat pack, had been hired by Richard Nixon in 1971 to debate Kerry, who had returned from Vietnam opposed to the war. Kerry had proven himself a credible, articulate spokesman against the war, and Nixon wanted a clean-cut veteran to counter him. O'Neill fit the bill. But Kerry wiped the floor with him in a televised debate, and to O'Neill's acquaintances in Houston it seemed clear that he never forgave Kerry for the humiliation. He also blamed Democrats for his failure to receive a judicial appointment from Bush's father. Whatever the motivation, the swift boaters were armed and dangerous. They had money from some of the biggest GOP donors in the nation, and a president happy to see others fighting his fight for him. They had a book *(Unfit for Command)*, a handy television network (Fox News), and an army of right-wing radio hosts and bloggers of their own to spread the message that Kerry had faked his heroics, injured himself so he could receive Purple Hearts, and misled his men and the nation about his exploits.

I was stunned by the viciousness of the Bush machine's attacks, especially given what I knew of Bush's own military record. And it soon became clear that I wasn't alone. Because I live in Austin, I am often called by journalists asking for my take on Bush-related subjects. Throughout the summer of 2004, I noticed that many of the reporters I talked to were still interested in the Guard stories. But they wanted new angles. Jim Moore, who had first raised the question with Bush during the 1994 debate, was continuing to press the issue, detailing some of the mysteries in his 2004 book, *Bush's War for Reelection*. And when an Associated Press lawsuit turned up a host of new Bush National Guard records on September 7—the very week Texans for Truth was launched, and Ben Barnes apologized on national TV for helping Bush get special treatment—the story suddenly became dinner-table conversation across America . . . for all the right reasons, and a few wrong ones as well.

On September 8, the same night Barnes made his public confession, Dan Rather announced the discovery of a series of memos allegedly written by the late Jerry Killian, Bush's Texas Air National Guard supervisor. The memos, four in all, described pressure from Killian's superiors to let Bush off the hook, despite his poor service record.

Almost from the start, though, it was apparent that something was wrong with the story. Before the broadcast was over, right-wing bloggers were already dissecting the memos, questioning their authenticity through detailed analyses of the typeface in which they were written, which appeared to be a computer-generated proportionally spaced font rather than a monospaced typewriter font. On September 20, after a week of further investigation, Rather was forced to admit that the source of the memos, former Texas Air National Guard official Bill Burkett, had misled his team about how he had come by the documents, and announced that CBS could not vouch for their authenticity.

For the White House, it was like a life preserver in a storm: As CBS and the rest of the mainstream media went into a bout of righteous self-excoriation, the right-wing propaganda machine did everything it could to conflate the entire National Guard controversy with the scandal over four pages that had quite evidently come from a different source than the rest of Bush's indisputable military record. As the president's defenders gleefully declared victory, some wondered whether it might not have been some especially crafty *conservative* player who fabricated the documents in the first place, to create just such a dodge and diversion. And national reporters temporarily forgot about Bush, dazzled by the new story—which had everything to do with the media chasing its own tail, and nothing to do with the character or behavior of the president of the United States. Whatever the explanation, what may be the most troubling aspect of this mini-scandal is how easily the press were distracted from the real story of

Bush's military service—a story that remains absolutely unchanged regardless of those four pages.

And that is the real reason for publishing *Unfit Commander:* Because in the swirl of charge and counter-charge, it is imperative that Americans not lose sight of the real question, which is, quite simply, *How did George W. Bush choose to serve his country during the Vietnam era?* In this book, for the first time, we have collected more than 260 pages of the official documents from Bush's National Guard service, as culled from the Guard's own records and released to the public over the years by the White House and the Pentagon. These records—*not one of which is in dispute*—offer the clearest picture we have to date of Bush's record, the gaping holes in that record, the unanswered questions. They are the best available evidence of what is known, and what remains concealed, about Bush's past.

The story starts on May 27, 1968, when George W. Bush enlisted in the 147th Fighter-Interceptor Group of the Texas Air National Guard. He did so just days before graduating from Yale and thus becoming eligible for the draft. Had he failed to enlist before receiving a draft notice, he would not have been able to choose an alternative service. He could have been sent to Vietnam. As part of his Guard service, Bush was selected to receive pilot training.

At the time Bush was admitted, there was a waiting list of some one hundred thousand young American men seeking entrance into the National Guard. It was this hurdle that Ben Barnes, then the speaker of the Texas House, managed to clear for the young George W., propelling him to the top of that list as a favor for the Bush family.

On that day Bush also signed a pledge promising to live up to his duties and responsibilities in the National Guard or face being called for active duty. "I understand that I may be ordered to active duty for a period not to exceed 24 months for unsatisfactory participation," Bush pledged. As detailed in the statement, satisfactory participation meant twenty-four days of weekend duty per year, usually involving one weekend per month. Also required were fifteen days of annual active duty. This was the point that the White House had hoped to put to rest with its massive release of documents in February 2004. But the records actually demonstrated that

Bush eventually fell far short of performing the duty he pledged to complete when he signed up in 1968.

On July 12, 1968, after completing basic airman's training, Bush received a direct commission as a second lieutenant from a three-member board of officers. Two days later, Bush began six weeks of basic training at Lackland Air Force Base in Texas. Examinations of Bush's records and the two systems used to measure a Guardsman's performance—the point system used for calculating retirement, and the number of training sessions attended each year of a member's commitment—show that Bush fell far short of the necessary service requirements.

On September 4, 1968, after he had received his full commission as a second lieutenant, Bush took an eight-week leave to work on a Senate campaign in Florida.

From November 25, 1968, to November 28, 1969, Bush attended flight school at Moody Air Force Base in Georgia. He graduated from flight school on November 28. From there Bush moved on to Houston, where he trained as an F-102 pilot at Ellington Air Force Base and lived at the notorious Chateaux Dijon apartments.

From July 1970 until April 16, 1972, Bush participated in drills and alerts at Ellington. On the surface, there is little about his service during this time that seems exceptional. In early 1972, however, serious questions about his service and his commitment to his responsibilities begin to emerge.

According to Bush's flight logs, released to the Associated Press after the agency's lawsuit, in February 1972 Bush quit flying the more sophisticated F-102 and abruptly shifted back to a T-33 training jet. He had graduated from that aircraft several years earlier.

Even though he had logged more than two hundred hours in the one-seat F-102A, the records suggest that Bush was no longer flying at peak performance. On two occasions he was unable to land an F-102 and a flight simulator on his first attempt. Military experts have speculated that Bush's downgrade could have been the result of many factors. Perhaps it wasn't that he was losing his skills; perhaps he was beginning to train for a new position. There is no record, however, of such a change. And his downgrade immediately preceded his abrupt request to transfer to Alabama.

Bush left Texas for Alabama in May 1972. He had failed to take a scheduled physical on May 14. After arriving in Alabama, where he joined Winton Blount's U.S. Senate campaign, on May 24 Bush asked for transfer to an Air Reserve squadron. But that squadron had no aircraft or regular drills, and his request was turned down.

In September, Bush applied for transfer to a Ready Reserve Unit in Montgomery. His application was accepted. The commander of that unit, the 187th, is Lieutenant Colonel William Turnipseed, and both he and his personnel officer, Kenneth K. Lott, have said repeatedly that they have no recollection of Bush showing up for duty. No other credible witness recalls Bush fulfilling his obligations to the National Guard in Alabama. (As noted, the one supposed witness who has stepped forward gave dates that failed to jibe with the military record.)

The Associated Press contacted a dozen members of the 187th. No one had seen Bush serving as he had pledged to do. Lieutenant Colonel Bob Mintz, who later became part of the Texans for Truth organization by speaking up about Bush's absence, says it would have been impossible for so many people to have missed Bush if he had been there.

Records released by the White House indicate that Bush saw a dentist at Alabama's Dannelly Air Force Base, where the 187th was stationed, in January 1973. Bush's spokesmen have offered this as proof that he was serving during that time. As will be detailed below, it proves nothing of the kind.

In November 1972, Bush returned to Houston. While in Alabama, he had been removed from flight service because of his failure to take the required physical the previous year. Back in Houston, Bush's superior officers—who had written commendatory evaluations of his performance in previous years—proved unable to complete his annual review. On May 1, 1973, they wrote that Bush had not been observed on the base during the period in question. There was no Lt. Bush to evaluate.

After examining Bush's records, both the *Boston Globe* and *U.S. News & World Report* have published detailed analyses of this disputed period. As many have noted, there are two methods of evaluating a pilot's performance in such a situation: number of points earned toward retirement, or number of drills attended each year. Despite White House denials, though, the *Globe* and *U.S. News* concur: Whichever standard is used, Bush fell far short of his service requirements in 1972 and 1973. For whatever reason, Bush appears to have lost interest in his obligation to the nation's military.

On July 30, 1973, the formal records tell us, Bush signed another pledge to the United States military. Having received permission to move to Boston so he could attend Harvard Business School, Bush acknowledged: "It is my responsibility to locate and be assigned to another Reserve forces unit or mobilization augmentation position. If I fail to do so, I am subject to involuntary order to active duty for up to 24 months."

Bush spokesman Dan Bartlett had told the *Washington Post* in 1999 that Bush completed his National Guard service at a Boston area Air Force Reserve Unit. But there is no record of Bush ever reporting to a Boston-area unit, and even Bartlett has retracted this contention: "I must have misspoke," he told the *Boston Globe* in a 2004 interview.

Bush appears to have left the National Guard in much the same way he entered it: with preferential treatment. Somehow, despite his failure even to approach completing his service requirements, George W. Bush received an honorable discharge from the Air National Guard on October 1, 1973.

These are the simple facts, but a number of important questions remain—questions that would reward serious investigation for anyone looking to establish the truth about Bush's military service, his honesty about his record, and his commitment to defending his country.

How did George W. Bush gain admission into the Texas Air National Guard?

In doing so, he vaulted ahead of one hundred thousand other young men on waiting lists around the United States—including, by one Guard source's estimate, roughly five hundred on the Texas waiting list.

Colonel Buck Staudt, who commanded the 147th air wing at Ellington Air Force Base in Houston, and Texas Guard commander and adjutant general James Rose, were both seasoned and savvy officers. Both would have seen the value in having the sons of wealthy and political people in

their units. Bush was moved up to the top of the waiting list when Texas
House Speaker Ben Barnes was contacted by Houston businessman
Sidney Adger, one of George H. W. Bush's closest friends. Known
throughout Texas as a longtime and well-connected Bush associate, Adger
also got his two sons into the same Texas Guard unit. It is completely im-
probable that Adger called on Barnes without the Bush family having
knowledge of his intentions.

Why was Bush promoted prematurely to 2nd Lieutenant?

There is no rational answer to this question. Bush's promotion, which
he received shortly after completing his flight training at Moody AFB in
Georgia, appears to have been unprecedented. He was not qualified to be
2nd Lieutenant, a rank reserved for enlistees with extensive ROTC background or who have been through the rigorous discipline of Officer Candidate School. A National Guard historian told the *Los Angeles Times* that
the only people promoted to Bush's rank as quickly as Bush were flight
surgeons, enlistees who come into the Guard as practicing MDs. Bush's
promotion was certainly fast enough to bolster suspicions of special treatment by the Guard.

What kind of a pilot was George W. Bush?

One of the oddest things about Bush's military record is that he would
walk away from his Guard service when, by all accounts, he started out so
strongly. In the first half of his six-year requirement, the Texas Air National Guard records demonstrate, Lieutenant Bush was an exemplary
pilot. This may have come as something of a surprise to anyone familiar
with his initial aptitude scores, which found him scoring a dismal 25 out
of 100 for pilot aptitude—just barely acceptable for enrollment in pilot
training. Pilot training and qualification took more than eighteen months,
which is why the guard required a six-year agreement.

Yet Bush seems to have grown uninterested in flying less than two years
after becoming a fully qualified pilot. TXANG records released in 2004
show that in 1972 Lieutenant Bush was unable to land his aircraft, an F-

102A fighter jet, on a simulator. He required several passes. The same records show Bush stopped flying the highly technical jet shortly after these difficulties and began flying a two-seat training jet, the T-33. The reasons for his sudden disengagement from flying remain shrouded in mystery.

Was there anything wrong with Bush's request for transfer to Alabama?

No, at least in principle. Guard members frequently got permission to transfer because of job relocations. In this case, however, the records suggest that Bush was trying not just to transfer his Guard service to another location, but to abandon the Guard altogether by transferring to an air reserve unit where he couldn't possibly fulfill his duties. On May 24, 1972, in an "Application for Reserve Assignment," he requested a transfer to the 9921st Air Reserve unit in Alabama. Yet this was a postal unit with no regular training or any flying responsibilities—a clear indication that Bush was trying to end his career as a pilot.

Bush's commanders should have known he wouldn't be eligible to transfer to such a unit. Yet Major Rufus G. Martin of the Texas Air National Guard and Major Charles K. Shoemake, the Texas ANG's Chief of Military Personnel, both signed off on the idea. When Bush's request reached the 9921st, a commander named Reese Bricken also signed off on it—but included a bizarre note to Bush that suggested how unusual the request was: "You already understand that this is a Training Category G, Pay Group None, Reserve Section MM proposition. The continuation of this type unit is uncertain at this time and may last 3 months, 6 months, a year or who knows! With this in mind, if you are willing to accept assignment under these circumstances, welcome! We're glad to have you."

Bush may have been "willing to accept" the assignment, but apparently the Air Force didn't take Bush's left-field request so lightly. In an undated memo, Gwen L. Dallin, chief of the Reserve Assignments Branch in the Air Force's Directorate of Personnel Reserves in Denver, rejected the application, noting that "an obligated Reservist" like Bush "can be assigned to a specific Ready Reserve position only. Therefore, he is ineligible for assignment to an Air Reserve Squadron" such as the 9921st. Not only did Guard regulations require Bush to continue reporting to his air wing at Ellington, then—he had received specific orders from Denver to do so.

Yet during all this time, Bush was making no effort to fulfill his duties—at Ellington or any other Air National Guard unit. Published accounts agree that Bush left Texas for Alabama to work on Blount's campaign in the spring of 1972. Yet it wasn't until three months later, on September 5, that he wrote his superior in Texas, Jerry Killian, requesting permission to perform equivalent duty at the 187th Tac Recon Group in Montgomery, for the months of September through November. This is the unit where Bush claims to have done his time.

Did Bush ever perform any service in Alabama?

There is nothing in Bush's military records that proves conclusively that Lieutenant Bush ever reported to the 187th for duty. By the time Bush's request to perform equivalent duty in Montgomery was approved on September 15, he'd already missed his chance to participate in the unit's September 9–10 Unit Training Assembly. In his memo approving Bush's request, Captain Kenneth Lott noted that Bush "should report to LtCol William Turnipseed," and that the unit's remaining UTAs were scheduled for October 7–8 and November 4–5, 1972. He also notes that "Lieutenant Bush will not be able to satisfy his flight requirements with our group"—having been suspended from flying the previous month.

Turnipseed and Lott, then, would have had specific reason to register Bush's appearance at the Alabama unit—which makes it especially telling that both men have since told reporters that they had no knowledge of Bush ever appearing at the unit.

Bush's best hope of convincing anyone that he ever appeared in Alabama are the payroll records, which suggest that Bush was credited with performing several weeks of substitute training during the period when he supposedly served in Alabama. Yet in his analysis of these records—certainly the most exhaustive study of the subject to date—researcher Paul Lukasiak presents persuasive evidence that those credits may not reflect real time served. "Other than the fact that he was paid for training," Lukasiak notes, "there is no evidence that [Bush] ever performed any training whatsoever after April 16, 1972. There is no evidence that he was ever authorized to perform any of the substitute training he is supposed to have accomplished in Alabama, and no one, not even the personnel officer that would have had to process the paperwork that accompanied six months worth of monthly training, recall[s] him training in Alabama."

Moreover, even if Bush actually had performed the training for which he was paid during these periods, a troubling question remains: What was Bush doing between May and October 1972? The records released by the White House confirm that during this period he performed absolutely no service for the Texas National Guard—or any equivalent service at the 187th, a location where he didn't even ask to serve until September. Even in the most generous reading of the record, then, there is no question that, despite the pledge of regular service he had made to the Guard, Bush went at least five months after his flight suspension in May 1972 without performing a single duty for the Air National Guard.

Did Bush ever return to his unit in Houston?

The president has said that he returned to Ellington AFB in late 1972, after completing work on Blount's campaign in Alabama. This assertion, however, contradicts the evidence in his files. Bush's unit had been issued orders for training from January through April 1973, and his file shows that he was credited with some points for those training assemblies. But Bush's annual review was due in May, because that was the anniversary date of his enlistment. On the OER (Officer Effectiveness Rating) form, Bush's commanders checked "not observed" on every last one of his rating categories.

On the second page of that form, which was dated May 1, 1973, they wrote, "Lt. Bush has not been observed at this unit during the period of report"—that is, from May 1, 1972 to April 30, 1973. Bush has claimed that he was back in Texas doing training during this same time when his commanders reported he was not observed, a claim belied by this record. He has also claimed that he was no longer flying, and was in a back office doing administrative duties. Yet there were only two dozen pilots in the unit, and Bush was too high-profile to be missed. This was the son of a congressman; his enlistment and promotion had been the subject of news conferences and photos, his character celebrated in press releases. If Bush had returned to Houston at that time, he would have been noticed—and yet, as in Alabama, no one has ever said they saw him back at Ellington in the spring of 1973. Bush was also given credit for weekend duties in April, May, and June of that year, but no one in his unit, including his commanding officers, has ever said they saw him present.

Was Bush punished in any way for his failure to appear for training?

Apparently not. Most of the records suggest that Bush's behavior put his commanders in an awkward and embarrassing position. After Houston commanders sent the OER on Bush to Denver, they received a response on August 23, 1973 from Master Sergeant Daniel Harkness. In this document, a "Notice of Missing or Correction of Officer Effectiveness/Training Report," Harkness sought answers to Bush's whereabouts and his performance as an officer. "Ratings must be entered on this officer," Harkness wrote, "so that this officer can be rated in the position he held. This officer should have been reassigned in May 1972 since he no longer is training in his AFSC (Air Force Service Code) or with his unit of assignment." Their response, on AF Form 77a: "Report not available for administrative reasons."

Don't Bush's Alabama dental records prove he served there?

The White House would have us believe they do, but no. The only thing they prove is that Bush got dental x-rays at the base in Montgomery on January 6, 1973. Bush was also paid for that date, according to points records released by the White House. Unfortunately, this January dental appointment creates an inconsistency in Bush's own account of his travels during this period: It contradicts his own contention that he returned to Texas to train at Ellington after the November 1972 election. If he had already reported back to Ellington, as he has claimed, what was he doing back in Alabama?

Don't the points records prove Bush qualified for an honorable discharge?

Points records are difficult and arcane documents, and the White House has consistently argued that Bush's records prove that the president performed his required service. Yet, as mentioned, both the *Boston Globe* and *U.S. News & World Report* have concluded independently that the records prove quite the opposite. To quote from the *U.S. News* story by Kit R. Roane, published on September 8, 2004:

- The White House used an inappropriate—and less stringent—Air Force standard in determining that President Bush fulfilled his National Guard duty.
- Even using this lesser standard, the president did not attend enough drills to complete his obligation to the Guard during his final year of service.
- During the final two years of his service obligation, Bush did not comply with Air Force regulations that impose a time limit on making up missed drills. Instead, he took credit for makeup drills he participated in outside that time frame. Five months of drills missed by the President in 1972 were never made up, contrary to assertions made by the White House.

Bush would have needed a minimum of 50 points each year to fulfill his requirement. This is not a taxing requirement for an active pilot: Even pilots with average attendance often accumulate 75 points annually. Bush would have needed to attend a minimum of 13 active duty training days each year, as well as 44 inactive sessions, known as unit training assemblies. In the analysis cited by the White House, Bush was apparently judged according to a less stringent Air Force points standard—and yet, even then, we know that in 1972 he performed no duty from April until at least October; it was impossible for him to meet even the Air Force's minimal standards during that time period.

Is there any missing document that might resolve the unanswered questions about Bush's Guard service?

Yes. Perhaps the most important missing link would be the document known as a "grounding and counseling statement." It was no minor event for a pilot to miss a physical and lose his flight status. Regulations would have required that a board of inquiry be convened to examine the causes of the suspension. As part of that investigation, a report should have been issued describing the reasons that Bush was grounded. It would also include a counseling statement, which is a recommendation from commanders to the pilot on how he can rehabilitate himself and/or regain his flight status. Such a document might well also reveal the underlying cause of Bush's sudden disaffection from the service—and whether it was related to drug or alcohol abuse (as the *Sunday Times* hinted), or some arrest and community service requirement (as Helen Thomas suggested in a 2004 White House briefing), or some combination of the two.

Anything as provocative as a grounding and counseling document would surely cause the Bush administration grave concern. Such documents may still exist in microfiche form, at either the Air Reserve Personnel Center in Denver, Colorado, or the National Personnel Records Center in St. Louis, Missouri. After all, even after several high-profile elections, Freedom of Information Act requests, lawsuits, and other forms of public pressure, "overlooked" documents were still being discovered as late as September 2004. But it would take extraordinary pressure to have the most revealing documents released: The president has still not permitted the public release of all his records (including medical records), and at this writing it was unclear whether a federal judge's order would succeed in uncovering the complete record.

At the end of the day, what is the point of all this investigation? Is it merely a matter of Bush-bashing, as the president's followers doubtless believe? Or is it a matter of legitimate public concern?

My own feelings about the issue are deeply personal. I received my draft number as a senior in high school. As a secondary school student I was not yet eligible, and the draft had ended some months after I graduated. I was never called. But I agonized over the possibility. Mine must be a very, very common story. I was opposed to the war. It was my first strongly held political position. But if I were drafted, I decided, I would have to go, because I could not live with the thought that one of my brothers or one of my friends would die in my place in Vietnam. I never had to make the choice, so I get no credit for courage. But I know what I thought was right.

Yet for me the purpose of examining Bush's own behavior during the Vietnam era—the purpose of launching Texans for Truth—is broader than any question of how any of us felt about the war. It is to establish, once and for all, whether our American leaders can still be held to the highest standards of judgment, responsibility, and honesty.

There is something profound at stake in this election. The presidency of George W. Bush has come to exemplify an unhealthy and undemocratic trend in our country, a trend that has us accepting the Imaginary over the Real, the fables of propagandists and ideologues over the evidence of our own eyes.

In 2004, we will decide whether we would rather accept that a sputtering economy means "growth," or rise up and do what it takes to fix an ailing economy.

We will decide whether we are content to be reassured by the vague promises of a "compassionate conservative," or whether we want to live again as good neighbors in a challenging world.

We will decide whether a man should be judged by the patriotic oaths he takes—or by the judgment and character he shows in fulfilling them.

Bush's supporters protest that this election is about a president's strength in the War on Terror, not his poor choices as a young man a long time ago. At home and abroad, though, Bush's poor judgment has come back to haunt us in the twenty-first century. He has deceived us about the imminent threats of the future, as surely as he deceived us about the mistakes of his past. He has disregarded his own commanders, just as he once disregarded the orders of his superiors. And yet he asks our young men and women to take him at his word, and step into harm's way to "defend their country"—a country he could not be bothered to defend when it was his turn to serve.

I hope that America has not yet decided it prefers the tragically flawed prince, the illusion of transcendent authority, to character of an honest and human leader, who can look us in the eye and earn our respect by confronting the difficult choices that lie ahead.

We know what to expect from President George W. Bush.

The election of 2004 is about what we expect from ourselves.

II

THE WHITE HOUSE AND
THE PRESS FACE OFF: 2004

The Bush military records controversy reached a critical point early in the 2004 election season, as the White House came under pressure to settle the unanswered questions about the president's National Guard service. Bush himself fueled public curiosity with his comments to Tim Russert on a February 8 *Meet the Press* appearance. Asked how he responded to charges that he didn't fulfill his duty to the Guard, Bush tried everything he could to bat the question down. "Political season is here," he observed to Russert. "I was—I served in the National Guard. I flew F-102 aircraft. I got an honorable discharge. I've heard this—I've heard this ever since I started running for office. I—I put in my time, proudly so." He scolded the interviewer, telling him "I would be careful to not denigrate the Guard"—which of course Russert hadn't done. He parroted his spokespeople's specious party line: "There may be no evidence, but I did report; otherwise, I wouldn't have been honorably discharged." And when asked why he was allowed to leave the Guard early, his answer hinted at the kind of special arrangement his detractors long suspected: "I was going to Harvard Business School and worked it out with the military."

But the real headline was Bush's promise on *Meet the Press* to "authorize the release of everything," as Russert put it, to help quell the story. Again, though, Bush hedged, telling Russert his records would be released "if we still have them, but I—you know, the records are kept in Colorado, as I understand, and they scoured the records."

Less than a week later, roughly four hundred pages of Bush's military record were released to the press. The file was rife with duplications and omissions, which illuminated some questions and raised others. The following pages, taken from the White House's own transcripts, show press secretary Scott McClellan's unconvincing attempts to parry the media's persistent questions on the subject. At a series of daily press briefings in February, and then again in the fall, McClellan takes a page from Bush's own playbook, repeating the same reductive responses ("these documents demonstrate that the President fulfilled his duties"), trying to deflect the questions with empty political rhetoric ("This race is about the future and the choices that the American people face") and dismissing the Guard issue altogether as "the same old recycled attacks" while accusing the press of "trolling for trash."

Amid these exchanges, one deserves special note: the excerpt from a February 13 press gaggle involving veteran White House correspondent Helen Thomas. Though transcripts of many of these informal morning briefings are posted at www.whitehouse.gov, this one is not—perhaps because of Thomas's bold suggestion that Bush may have been required to do "community service" during his time in the Guard. As yet, no proof of this allegation has ever been offered in public. Yet the transcript makes suggestive reading: Joined by several colleagues, Thomas gives McClellan every chance to rebut the story; at one point someone even asks, "Why does a simple 'yes' or 'no' elude you on this?" Yet not once during this protracted and difficult exchange does McClellan take the opportunity to deny that the allegation.

Scott McClellan
White House Press Secretary

11:31 A.M. CST

Q I've got to ask you, too, about military records. The President committed yesterday to releasing additional records. Is there any effort by the White House, the RNC, the campaign to come up with new records, new notes—

MR. McCLELLAN This issue, as the President pointed out, goes back to his first campaign for governor, it goes back to the 2000 campaign. You know, we made everything we had available during the 2000 campaign. I think that one of the things you can look at that will help address these questions is the annual retirement point summaries. And we previously made those available during the 2000 campaign. They show that the President fulfilled his duties, and that is why he was honorably discharged.

Q Every point summary is available—payroll stubs—

Q Russert asked a more specific question, tax returns and payroll stubs, and the President's answer to that was, yeah.

MR. McCLELLAN I don't think—I think the President, like most Americans, does not have his tax returns from thirty-three years ago. In terms of pay stubs, during the 2000 campaign we checked with the Texas National Guard and they informed us that they did not have them. Obviously, if there's anything additional, we'll keep you posted.

Q You checked during the 2000 campaign, or you checked in recent days?

MR. McCLELLAN We checked during the 2000 campaign, yes.

Q It's your interpretation, though, that everything that could be released has been released?

MR. McCLELLAN Well, everything we had we made available. And like I said, if there's more, we'll do our best to keep you updated on that.

Q But you're not looking for anything else at this point?

MR. McCLELLAN Well, if there's more that comes to our attention, we'll make sure we make that available.

Scott McClellan
White House Press Secretary

12:53 P.M. EST

Q On the attendance records of the National Guard, it said he had fifty-six out of a required fifty points. Is that considered a good attendance record, do you know? Or do you know what the maximum number of points you can get—

MR. McCLELLAN First of all, we were pleased to be able to provide you all with these additional records that just recently came to our attention. These documents clearly show that the President fulfilled his duties. And we had previously released some of the point summaries that you are referencing. There is more complete information relating to those point summaries that document the fact that the President of the United States fulfilled his duties when he was serving in the National Guard back in the early seventies.

Q Scott, a couple of questions I have—the records that you handed out today, and other records that exist, indicate that the President did not perform any Guard duty during the months of December 1972, February or March of 1973. I'm wondering if you can tell us where he was during that period. And also, how is it that he managed to not make the medical requirements to remain on active flight duty status?

MR. McCLELLAN John, the records that you're pointing to, these records are the payroll records; they're the point summaries. These records verify that he met the requirements necessary to fulfill his duties. These records—

Q That wasn't my question, Scott.

MR. McCLELLAN These payroll records—

Q Scott, that wasn't my question, and you know it wasn't my question. Where was he in December of '72, February and March of '73? And why did he not fulfill the medical requirements to remain on active flight duty status?

MR. McCLELLAN These records—these records I'm holding here clearly document the President fulfilling his duties in the National Guard. The President was proud of his service. The President—

Q I asked a simple question; how about a simple answer?

MR. McCLELLAN John, if you'll let me address the question, I'm coming to your answer, and I'd like—

Q Well, if you would address it—maybe you could.

MR. McCLELLAN I'm sorry, John. But this is an important issue that some chose to raise in the context of an election year, and the facts are important for people to know. And if you don't want to know the facts, that's fine. But I want to share the facts with you.

Q I do want to know the facts, which is why I keep asking the question. And I'll ask it one more time. Where was he in December of '72, February and March of '73? Why didn't he fulfill the medical requirements to remain on active flight duty status in 1972?

MR. McCLELLAN The President recalls serving both when he was in Texas and when he was in Alabama. And that is what I can tell you. And we have provided you these documents that show clearly that the President of the United States fulfilled his duties. And that is the reason that he was honorably discharged from the National Guard. The President was proud of his service.

The President spent some of that time in Texas. He was a member of the Texas Air National Guard, and he was given permission, on a temporary basis, to perform equivalent duty while he was in Alabama. And he performed that duty. And the payroll records, that I think are very important for the public to have, clearly reflect that he served.

Q Scott, when Senator Kerry goes around campaigning, there's frequently what they call "a band of brothers," a bunch of soldiers who served with him, who come forward and give testimonials for him. I see, in looking at our files in the campaign of 2000, it said that you were looking for people who served with him to verify his account of service in the National Guard. Has the White House been able to find, like Senator Kerry, "a band of brothers" or others who can testify about the President's service?

MR. McCLELLAN All the information that we have we shared with you in 2000, that was relevant to this issue. And all the additional information that has come to our attention we have shared with you. The President was asked about this in his interview over the weekend, and the President made it clear, yes, I want all records to be made available that are relevant to this issue; that there are some out there that were making outrageous, baseless accusations. It was a shame that they brought it up four years ago. It was a shame that they brought it up again this year. And I think that the facts are very clear from these documents. These documents—the payroll records and the point summaries verify that he was paid for serving and that he met his requirements.

Q Actually, I wasn't talking about documents, I was talking about people—you know, comrades-in-arms—

MR. McCLELLAN Right. That's why I said everything that came to our attention that was available, we made available at that time, during the 2000 campaign.

Q But you said you were looking for people—and I take it you didn't find any people?

MR. McCLELLAN I mean, obviously, we would have made people available. And we—Mr. Lloyd, who has provided a statement to put some of this into context for everybody, made some public statements during that time period to verify the records that the President had fulfilled his duties. And he put out an additional statement now to put this into context. He's someone with some technical expertise and someone that understands these matters, because he was in the National Guard at the time.

Q Scott, can I follow on this, because I do think this is important. You know, it might strike some as odd that there isn't anyone who can stand up and say, I served with George W. Bush in Alabama, or in Houston in the Guard unit. Particularly because there are people, his superiors who have stepped forward—in Alabama and in Houston—who have said in the past several years that they have no recollection of him being there and serving. So isn't that odd that nobody—you can't produce anyone to corroborate what these records purport to show?

MR. McCLELLAN David, we're talking about some thirty years ago. You are perfectly welcome to go back and talk to individuals from that time period. But these documents—

Q Hey, we're trying. But I would have thought you guys would have had a real good handle on—

MR. McCLELLAN —these documents make it very clear that the President of the United States fulfilled his duties—

Q Well, that's subject to interpretation.

MR. McCLELLAN No. When you serve, you are paid for that service. And these documents outline the days on which he was paid. That means he served. And these documents also show that he met his requirements. And it's just really a shame that people are continuing to bring this issue up. When—

Q I understand—

MR. McCLELLAN No, no, no, no. People asked for records to be released that would demonstrate he met his requirements. The records have now been fully released. The facts are clear—

Q Do you know that a lot of these payroll records are—

MR. McCLELLAN —the facts are clear—

Q —you can't read them. Have you looked at these? You can't—how are we supposed to read these?

MR. McCLELLAN Well, I think you can talk—one, we put it out on email. It's a lot easier to read, I think, on the email version because that was the—

Q Oh, you did put it on our email?

MR. McCLELLAN We are going to, if we haven't already. But it was sent to us in email form from the Personnel Center in Denver, Colorado.

Q One other thing on this. To corroborate these records, will the President do two things—one, will he authorize the relevant defense agency in Colorado to release actual pay stubs for the President? And if those don't exist, will the President file a form, as he can do at the IRS, to at least look for a '72 or '73 tax return that would corroborate what you claim are payroll summaries that he actually got paid for this duty?

MR. McCLELLAN Well, I think this information is his payroll records. It is my understanding this is the information that is available from his payroll records. And it shows the days on which he was paid. So that's the information that I understand is available. In terms of tax returns, the President, like most Americans, does not have his tax returns from some 30 years ago.

Q But it's possible that he could file a form requesting the IRS to search if they have a return for '72 or '73. Is he willing to do that?

MR. McCLELLAN Obviously, if there's any additional information that came to our attention that was relevant, we would make that information available.

Q Well, it could be relevant if he would file a form—

MR. McCLELLAN I think that these documents clearly show that the President of the United States fulfilled his duties. I mean, these were the documents that people questioned and said should be made available. And we went back to double-check. We thought we had all the information that existed previously, but we went back to double-check after the comments that were made over the weekend, to see if there was any additional information available. And when we contacted the Personnel Center in Colorado, it was our understanding that the Personnel Center in St. Louis and Colorado were already working to pull this information together, and that this is the information that they have that is relevant to this topic.

Q So it's your position and it's the President's position that these documents put this issue to rest, period?

MR. McCLELLAN Oh, I think these documents show that he fulfilled his duties. These documents show that he met his requirements.

Q Scott, two questions, one on the documents, one on the issue. There seems to be a discrepancy now in the President's record that I wondered if you could help me with. These documents that you're holding up show that the President showed up for duty in October and November of '72, January, April and May of '73. But the President's officer effectiveness report, filed by his commanders, Lieutenants Colonel Killean and Harris, both now deceased, for the period 01 May '72 to 30 April, '73, says he has not been observed at this unit, where he was supposed to show up and earning these points on these days. How do you square—

MR. McCLELLAN You're talking about which unit?

Q The Texas—at the Ellington Air Force Base.

MR. McCLELLAN From '72 to '73?

Q Correct. And certainly by—the President said he returned to Texas in November of '72. So some of these dates of service, which are in these records, ought to have been noted by his commanding officers, who, nevertheless, said, twice, he has not been observed here. Can you explain that?

MR. McCLELLAN I'm not sure about these specific documents. I'll be glad to take a look at them. But these documents show the days on which he was paid for his service. And the President—as I've said, and we previously said during the 2000 campaign—recalls serving both in Texas and in Alabama during the time period you're bringing up.

Q So he served, but his commanding officers didn't know it?

MR. McCLELLAN Again, I don't know the specific documents you're referring to. If you want to bring those to me, I'll be glad to take a look at them and get you the answers to your questions.

Q Okay. Then on the general issue, Senator Kerry has said that the National Guard was one way for people to avoid service in Vietnam. The President and the White House have taken umbrage at that, saying that's denigrating the National Guard. In 1994, the President told the *Houston Chronicle,* in relation to his joining the National Guard, "I was not prepared to shoot my eardrum out with a shotgun in order to get a deferment, nor was I willing to go to Canada, so I chose to better myself by learning how to fly airplanes." It sounds like the President, himself, acknowledged that he went into the National Guard because he didn't want to go to Vietnam.

MR. McCLELLAN The President—again, Terry, this issue has been addressed fully. Now we're trying to change into different issues here. The President was proud of his service in the National Guard. He fulfilled his duties; he was honorably discharged. I think there are some that we're now seeing are not interested in the facts. What they are interested in is trying to twist the facts for partisan political advantage in an election year. And that's unfortunate.

Q It is a partisan issue. I'm not doubting that, I'm trying to explore it. One of the reasons the Democrats are raising it is because they've got a guy who was in Vietnam.

MR. McCLELLAN Now it's—he didn't serve, now it's a different issue—when the facts clearly show that he did serve, he did fulfill his duties, he did meet his requirements, he was honorably discharged.

Q But he didn't want to go to Vietnam.

MR. McCLELLAN I think the facts are clear. It's clear that some are not interested in the facts. It's clear that some may be more interested in using this for partisan political advantage.

Q Scott, these are very hard to read, these payroll documents. Are you saying that every date listed on document five is a day that the President was actually—showed up, he was suited up, he was flying planes—that's what that means? Because there are, you know, points for active duty, points for inactive duty. What, exactly, are these?

MR. McCLELLAN Well, and that's why we put out the statement from Mr. Lloyd, so you could put that in context. He's someone with the technical expertise that understands those matters and can explain what those points mean. And I think that his statement does that. In terms of the payments, you are paid for the days on which you serve.

Q The days on which you serve, meaning he was actually there on these dates listed, he was actually there—

MR. McCLELLAN You are paid for the days you serve.

Q Is that what document five is, the dates he served?

MR. McCLELLAN Again, there was a time period when he was in Alabama, and he recalls serving in Alabama. He was still a member of the Texas Air National Guard at that time. What he was doing was performing equivalent duty, because he was working in Alabama at the time. And he also remembers serving in Texas, as well.

Q Scott, so, for example, in January '73, the President served, according to this, on January 4th, January 5th, January 6th in either Texas or Alabama—according to document five. Is that correct?

MR. McCLELLAN You are paid for the days you serve. You have the documents right in front of you. These are documents straight from the Personnel—

Q Is that "yes"?

MR. McCLELLAN —straight from the Personnel Center in Colorado.

Q Is that "yes"?

MR. McCLELLAN I said you are paid for the days in which you serve. And, again, we're talking about thirty years ago, Elisabeth. The President recalls serving in Alabama. He also recalls serving in Texas. That's what he recalls. And that's why—

Q But, again,—I know you're going to bat this down, but there are people who—

MR. McCLELLAN You know, there were a lot of people calling for these records to be released. We finally came across these records. They have been released, and these documents reflect the fact that the President met his requirements and fulfilled his duties.

Q And the fact that some of his officers don't recall ever seeing him, are you suggesting that they just don't remember after thirty years?

MR. McCLELLAN Well, I think I'll let them speak for themselves. I'm not sure that they exactly said it in that way. Some different ones said different things.

Q They have. They have spoken for themselves. They don't remember.

Q What is your answer to them about why they don't remember seeing the President?

MR. McCLELLAN That the President recalls serving. I just said that.

Q But why are they saying this?

MR. McCLELLAN And if you look at the records, if you look at these records, these records document that the President fulfilled his duties. These records reflect that he met his requirements, both in point summaries and that he was paid for the days in which he served.

Q Scott, can you just clarify, back to Elisabeth's question here on document five? For example, in February and March of '73, there are no dates that appear, meaning he didn't show up then, or what—

MR. McCLELLAN Well, look, I mean, we're talking about thirty years ago, again. And these documents show the dates on which he was paid, which means those are the days on which you serve.

Q Does that mean, then, that he—

MR. McCLELLAN I don't have—Roger, I'm sorry, I don't have an hour-by-hour itemization of everything he was doing thirty years ago.

Q Are you able to make out any of the paid amounts? How much did he get? I can't read the letters.

MR. McCLELLAN And again, this is going to be put out in the email version, as well, and you're welcome to contact the Personnel Center. I'm sure that they will be glad to help you, as well.

Q Scott, may I re-ask Dana's question? You keep saying he served—he fulfilled his duty, he met his requirements. You're not saying, he drilled, he showed up, he attended. Is that intentional?

MR. McCLELLAN No, he recalls performing his duties, both in Alabama and Texas. I said that in response to Elisabeth's question.

Q Define that.

MR. McCLELLAN Well, again, I don't have a minute-by-minute break-down of every single thing he did throughout that time period.

Q What did he do?

Q You keep saying the word, "serve." Define "serve."

MR. McCLELLAN He met—he served both in Alabama, and he served both in Texas.

Q Doing what? Did that period—can you at least tell us the difference be-tween inactive—because it's not clear in these documents.

MR. McCLELLAN No, I think that I'll leave it to those who can explain these documents to do the explaining. That's why we put the statement from Mr. Lloyd, who was in the National Guard at the time; he was some-one that had the expertise to explain to you what these points mean. And that's why we provided that statement. Obviously, the Personnel Center can tell you more about what everything means on these documents. We just received these late yesterday.

But the one thing that these documents clearly show is that the Presi-dent of the United States fulfilled his duties when he was in the National Guard. He met his requirements and he was honorably discharged because he fulfilled his duties.

Q Just so I can be sure that I'm interpreting this crystal-clearly—you're not making any claim here that the President attended, showed up, drilled on these days?

MR. McCLELLAN I'm telling you that he did—he does recall showing up and performing his duties. And you're paid for the days on which you serve. And that's what these documents reflect.

Q Scott, is it your—

MR. McCLELLAN We're going to stay on this topic, and then we'll jump to other topics.

Q It's your position that these documents specifically show that he served in Alabama during the period 1972, when he was supposed to be there. Do they specifically show that?

MR. McCLELLAN No, I think if you look at the documents, what they show are the days on which he was paid, the payroll records. And we previously said that the President recalls serving both in Alabama and in Texas.

Q I'm not interested in what he recalls. I'm interested in whether these documents specifically show that he was in Alabama and served on the days during the latter part of 1972—

MR. McCLELLAN And I just answered that question.

Q You have not answered that question. You—

MR. McCLELLAN No, I said—no, I said, no, in response to your question, Keith.

Q No, so the answer is, "no"?

MR. McCLELLAN I said these documents show the days on which he was paid. That's what they show. So they show—they show that he was paid on these days.

Q Okay, but they do not show that he was in Alabama when he was supposed to be—

MR. McCLELLAN These are payroll records, and they reflect the fact that he was paid on the days on which he served.

Q Do any of them show that he was paid on days that he served in the latter part of 1972 when he was in Alabama? I don't see any dates for that.

MR. McCLELLAN It just kind of amazes me that some will now say they want more information, after the payroll records and the point summaries have all been released to show that he met his requirements and to show that he fulfilled his duties.

Q But these documents do not show that. They do not show that he was in Alabama and served at that time. I don't even see any pay dates during that period.

MR. McCLELLAN They show payments. No, they show pay dates during that fall of 1972 period.

Q They do?

MR. McCLELLAN There's October on there, there's November on there, and then there's January on there, as well, in '73. There's some pay dates on there.

Q Okay, so then, do they specifically show that he served in Alabama during that time?

MR. McCLELLAN They show payments in October; they show payments in November.

Q But just because he's paid doesn't mean that he served and worked there, does it?

Q Come on.

MR. McCLELLAN You know, like I said, people call on us to release the records. We didn't even know they still existed until just the other day. Now we've released the records, which document that the President fulfilled his duties. And now people are trying to move the goalpost even more.

Q You said in Alabama that he had served equivalent duty.

MR. McCLELLAN That's right.

Q Can you describe what that was, and what—why did he need to move to Alabama? What was—

MR. McCLELLAN Like I said, Greg, you're asking me to kind of break down hour-by-hour what he was doing during 1972 and 1973. What these documents show is that he was serving in the National Guard and he was paid for that service. And they show that he was serving in the National Guard and that he met the requirements necessary to fulfill his duties.

Q But his equivalent duty, does he mean that there was a base there he was flying out of? Is that what he recalls?

MR. McCLELLAN I'd have to go back and double-check, but he remembers serving during that period and performing his duties, both in Alabama and in Texas.

And these are—look, these are questions we addressed all during the campaign. The issue that came up recently was some were trying to make an outrageous, baseless accusation. If I recall, some were using the comment, "deserter" or "AWOL." I mean, that is outrageous; it is baseless. The President of the United States fulfilled his duties, he was honorably discharged. And now there are some that are not—are clearly not interested in the facts. They're clearly more interested in twisting the facts to seek a partisan political advantage in the context of an election year. And that's just really unfortunate that some would stoop to such a level.

Q Scott, what is it that took him to Alabama?

MR. McCLELLAN I'm sorry?

Q —that took him to Alabama?

MR. McCLELLAN It was a campaign, a senatorial campaign.

Q Scott, we all know people who tomorrow may not show up for work and will be paid. And their payrolls will show they were paid.

MR. McCLELLAN Well, again, when you're serving in the National Guard you're paid for the days on which you serve. I mean, it's specifically related to the service.

Q Could you walk us through the sequence of events in the last few days that led to the production of these records?

MR. McCLELLAN Sure, sure.

Q And did those efforts begin after or before the interview with—

MR. McCLELLAN No, it was after. The questions came up in the interview on "Meet the Press," and the President made it very clear, some of what I'm saying here. And he said, yes, I want all records out there. And it was our belief, it was our impression that all the records that existed that were relevant were already released. Back in the 2000 campaign, we went to the Texas Air National Guard to ask for records so that they could be released, and it was our understanding that the payroll records—it was our impression at the time that the payroll records didn't exist.

Then after this weekend, after the interview, we contacted the National Guard here and asked them where would one go, if these records existed, to find them. We were just going back and double-checking. And we were put in touch with the Personnel Center in Denver, Colorado. So we contacted the Personnel Center in Denver, Colorado. It was our understanding at that time that the Denver and St. Louis offices were already working to pull this information together at the time that we contacted them—

Q On their own?

MR. McCLELLAN That's correct. They could explain more about why they were doing that.

Q Did you contact them on Monday, Scott?

MR. McCLELLAN I'll double-check. I believe it would have been probably Monday before we were able to reach them. So, yesterday—yes, yesterday. I know there were conversations yesterday.

Q Who initiated the conversations?

MR. McCLELLAN Oh, Dan Bartlett, from here, Communications Director.

Anyway, so he contacted them and found out that there was, indeed, additional payroll records. And the President authorized that those be made available, as he said he was going to do. He said he wanted all the records released that existed, that were relevant. And to our knowledge, this is all the records that exist that are relevant to this topic.

Q The letter from Colonel Lloyd says that he assessed the records. Did— there's no indication that he had any direct oversight of President Bush. Did he?

MR. McCLELLAN I'm sorry?

Q That Lt. Colonel Lloyd, did he have any direct oversight over President Bush at the time he served?

MR. McCLELLAN I think he could address those questions, in terms of what his role was at the time in the National Guard. But he was certainly someone that had the technical expertise to be able to explain what the point summaries mean, in terms of the numbers, and what they reflect. So that's what he did. And he stated—he made some comments back during the 2000 campaign; I'm sure you can go back and look at those, as well.

Q Just to be clear, what he's saying today is that his assessment of the records is that the requirements were fulfilled.

MR. McCLELLAN That the requirements were met. His own words are in his statements so I would refer you straight back to his words.

Q When did Lloyd make this memorandum?

MR. McCLELLAN This one?

Q Yes.

MR. McCLELLAN In the last day. I think we received it yesterday from him.

Q —one date that I was—

MR. McCLELLAN Yes.

Q Are you ready to take questions on a different subject?

MR. McCLELLAN We're still on this topic, right?

Q Since there have been so many questions about what the President was doing over thirty years ago, what is it that he did after his honorable discharge from the National Guard? Did he make speeches alongside Jane Fonda, denouncing America's racist war in Vietnam? Did he testify before Congress that American troops committed war crimes in Vietnam? And did he throw somebody else's medals at the White House to protest a war America was still fighting? What was he doing after he was honorably discharged?

MR. McCLELLAN We've already commented on some of his views relating back to that period the other day. And, obviously, this was a time period also when he was going to get his MBA at Harvard. But the President was certainly proud to serve in the National Guard.

Q And would the White House consider those actions by Senator Kerry, that Jeff mentions fair game in the political season?

MR. McCLELLAN Terry, I think—I know that that's a way to try to draw us into a Democratic primary that is ongoing.

Q You're there, my friend. (Laughter.)

MR. McCLELLAN Well, this is an important matter that some have chosen—some have chosen to twist the facts. And it's important that the facts are clear. And I think that these documents clearly show that the President met his requirements and fulfilled his duties. But, look, we'll let the Democratic primary continue. They can work out their differences. I think if you have questions to address to people that made certain accusations, you should direct them to those individuals. Because now, in light of these documents, this is new information that clearly shows otherwise to what they were suggesting.

Q Scott, the President said clearly—

MR. McCLELLAN Let me keep going. I'll come back to you.

Q Wait a second—

MR. McCLELLAN We have a few in the back. I'll come back to you, I promise. But let me try to get to everybody in the room. I promise I'll come back to you. Ben I think had one, and then April. And did you have another one, Ron? Kind of slipped one in there.

Q The records show, between April 16, 1972 and October 28th there was no pay period, he wasn't paid. That was when he was in Alabama. Now, you said some of the payroll records were lost, but that you know he didn't serve. And was this the President remembering he didn't serve?

MR. McCLELLAN I think it was for the fall period, when he—and again, I'd have to go back and look at the exact dates of when he was in Alabama. But it was during the fall that he made a request to perform equivalent duty in Alabama again. That was still a period when he would be a member of the Texas Air National Guard. But I'd have to go back and double-check those exact dates that he was in Alabama.

Q —wouldn't have been paid for equivalent duty?

MR. McCLELLAN I'm sorry?

Q You wouldn't be paid for equivalent duty.

MR. McCLELLAN You're paid for serving. And equivalent duty is performing your duties for the Texas Air National Guard.

Q But the summary sheets state that he did not perform service in the third quarter of—

MR. McCLELLAN These are not our summary sheets, these are the summary sheets from the Personnel Center in Colorado.

Q —payroll records were lost, but also, we know he didn't perform service in that third quarter.

MR. McCLELLAN You are paid for the days on which you serve.

Q So when he was in Alabama during that quarter, he didn't perform service—

MR. McCLELLAN Well, again, I'm not sure that he was in Alabama during that whole period you are talking about. I'd have to go back and look. He requested—I know that he requested to perform equivalent duty during that fall time period when he was in Alabama. You are going back further than that. I'd have to double-check.

Q He left in May, I believe—

MR. McCLELLAN I'd have to double-check the time period in which he was there.

Q Is this cumulative, the sort of thing you don't have to perform every month, it's just a matter of, out of the course of a year, you get your fifty points?

MR. McCLELLAN You know, I'm not—there are people that have technical expertise in these matters. I think they're the National Guard. You can direct those questions to those individuals. I'm sure that they would be glad to try to help you out.

Q You keep saying this is a shame, and you're talking partisan politics, but don't you think the American public, as well, particularly the U.S. military, who has been tested right now with the fact that they went to war on faulty intelligence, possibly, and now finding out that their Commander-in-Chief possibly tried to avoid going to the Vietnam War—don't you think that the American public is owed a little bit more than photo copies that we can't see things of? Don't you think the military is owed a little bit more than just, "he served"?

MR. McCLELLAN April, I'm really sorry that you phrased that question the way you did, some of it, when you were saying that they're owed more than the documents that show that he served during that time period. Now, let me go back—

Q But wouldn't someone know what he did?

MR. McCLELLAN And the President—we have previously said, going back to the 2000 campaign and even before that, that he recalls performing his duties, both in Alabama and in Texas, during the time period that some have questioned. So let's be very clear about that. Let's be very clear about the facts. Because the American people should have the facts, and the facts are right here in these documents. The facts are right here in these documents.

Q We can't see facts. We can't see—these facts are very messed up, they're blurred.

MR. McCLELLAN April, I mentioned earlier that we were going to be putting this out on email, if we haven't already, because it was sent to us in email form. You are also welcome to contact the Personnel Center in Denver, Colorado. I am sure that they will be glad to walk you through this.

Q You're saying that this is political—this is all politics and everything and people are obscuring in putting the facts up. But people are not able to stand up for the President. There are dates that aren't accounted for. You can't even tell us what kind of drills or what-have-you. What do you say to the U.S. military—

MR. McCLELLAN No, we addressed all those questions back during the 2000 campaign fully. Let me be very clear: The issue that came up recently was an outrageous, baseless accusation suggesting that the President did not serve and did not meet his requirements. People called on us to release records that might be available to show that he, indeed—that he, indeed, did meet his requirements and serve and fulfill his duties. The records have been released. These records document that the President fulfilled his duties. Now people are wanting to go further than that. And these are the records that reflect his service.

Q You can detail your job. You can detail what you do as Press Secretary—

MR. McCLELLAN And we did. During the 2000 campaign, we talked about this issue fully. You're now going to a different issue. These issues—

Q It's still the same issue—

MR. McCLELLAN Let me be very clear here about this. There are some that made some very outrageous accusations about the President's time in the National Guard. There was a call for us to release payroll records. The payroll records have been released, as they just came to our attention and we shared them with you very quickly. The point summaries showing that he met his requirements have been released. Those were records that were—that some called on us to release. We didn't know that some of these records previously existed. Obviously, if they had, we would have been glad to share them with everybody at the time.

This issue was addressed fully four years ago. Like I said, it was really a shame that it came up four years ago, and it's really a shame that it's being brought up again this year. The facts are clear. Now, there may be some out there that are not interested in the facts. And those people clearly are simply more interested in trying to seek a partisan political advantage in an election year, than the facts. That's unfortunate.

Q I don't really have a question that goes to the politics of this. I just want to ask a question about a contradiction, and a question about a specific record. After all of the things you repeated here, you cannot explain this contradiction, the fact that his payroll records indicate he was paid for a period of time for fulfilling service, and yet his commanding officers at that time wrote that he was not observed. Can you or can you not explain that contradiction?

MR. McCLELLAN If you're talking about the question that Terry brought up, I said I would glad to go back and look at the document that he's referencing. I have not—

Q You know the document he's referencing. Everybody does. His commanders—

MR. McCLELLAN No, I have not—I have not seen the document he's referencing.

Q —are quoted repeatedly for years—

MR. McCLELLAN You're talking about quotes—you're talking about quotes from individuals. And we said for years, going back four years ago, that the President recalls serving and performing his duties.

Q I understand that, but his commanders do not recall it. And, in fact, they say, that he was not observed. So can you explain the contradiction, or can't you?

MR. McCLELLAN I've seen some different comments he's—no, I've seen some different comments made over the recent time period.

Q I haven't seen any different—different comments from Brigadier General Turnipseed, not from his Ellington commanders, who said he was not observed. Can you explain the contradiction?

MR. McCLELLAN Look, I can't speak for those individuals. I can speak for the President of the United States. And I can speak—

Q —the documents—

MR. McCLELLAN And I can speak for the fact that the documents that—as far as we know, all the documents that are available relevant to this issue demonstrate that the President fulfilled his duties. Are you suggesting these documents do not reflect that?

Q I'm not suggesting—I'm asking, that's all I'm doing. Here's the second point, the President said to Tim Russert, very specifically, on Sunday, that he would be willing to provide pay stub records and tax return records to corroborate—

MR. McCLELLAN And we addressed this situation previously.

Q —wait a second—to corroborate—

MR. McCLELLAN It's the second time you've asked this question.

Q Right, and I'll ask it until we maybe get something—which is to corroborate these payroll records that are coming from one source. Will he request that all the records are released, from Denver and from St. Louis, to prove that he actually received money, not just that they say he did?

MR. McCLELLAN These are the payroll records that we understand are available. This is it.

Q —all that's there—

MR. McCLELLAN It is our understanding that these are the payroll records that are available, yes.

Q Just out of curiosity, how much money does a person get paid for each day's service, and is there any evidence that George W. Bush might not have accepted the money, might have turned it down?

MR. McCLELLAN Oh, Connie, you'd have to go back and ask at the time what the pay was. Again, it shows the dates on which he was paid. And I think this goes into some of the amounts here on these papers.

Q Scott, new subject?

MR. McCLELLAN Same subject?

Q Yes.

MR. McCLELLAN Go ahead.

Q Am I wrong in reading document five that he didn't perform any days of service between April 16 and October 28—

MR. McCLELLAN Yes, we've been through this. Again, the documents—

Q I want to make sure that's correct.

MR. McCLELLAN:—well, those are the documents. You have them right in front of you. I'm not disputing these documents. In fact, I'm saying that these documents demonstrate that the President fulfilled his duties. These are the payroll records.

Q Which of these dates refers to days he served in Alabama?

MR. McCLELLAN I'm sorry?

Q Which of the dates in document five—

MR. McCLELLAN If you look at the fall time period, that was a time period that he was in Alabama. Again, Keith asked this question earlier, and asked if it shows exactly where he was serving when he was paid. And I said, no. I said, what these documents show is that he was paid for the days on which he was—served. These are the payroll records that reflect the days on which he served.

Q On what date did he come back, did he return from Alabama?

MR. McCLELLAN I think we've been through some of these issues previously. I don't know the exact date off the top of my head. We'll be glad to look back and try to get you that information. But those were all questions that were addressed previously. The relevant issue that was brought up by some recently was whether or not the President had served. The documents clearly show that the President served and met his requirements and fulfilled his duties.

Q Scott, could you just tell us, are these all the documents you got, you received, here at the White House, from Colorado, or have you kept some in reserve? And also—

MR. McCLELLAN No, these—

Q —do you expect any additional documents from St. Louis or from Colorado?

MR. McCLELLAN Well, as always, I said that we would—if there is additional information that comes to our attention, we will make sure to get you that information. This is the information that we understand is available from the Personnel Center in Denver, Colorado.

Q And that's all that they sent you, this is the extent of all the documents?

MR. McCLELLAN Yes, this is what they sent us. And we just put it in our own email and sent it out for you all.

Q Scott, Dan Bartlett told the Associated Press, in June of 2000, that he traveled to the Air Reserve Personnel Center and reviewed President Bush's military file. He said, "I've read it, and there is nothing earth-shattering." Did he see these documents when he reviewed the file? Did he see any other documents when he reviewed the file? And was there anything in the file—

MR. McCLELLAN Well, that's a broad question about other documents. All the relevant documents relating to his service have been released—

Q So has Dan Bartlett ever seen these documents?

MR. McCLELLAN:—as we said. And as I said yesterday, everything that we had we released in 2004—I mean, 2000, at the time, or during the 2000 campaign. It might have been '99.

Q There may be documents that were in that file—

MR. McCLELLAN No, this is the first time this information has come to our attention.

Q So Dan Bartlett didn't see these documents—

MR. McCLELLAN Again, I think I've answered this question up here, and I've answered it back for you.

Q I've got one more—

MR. McCLELLAN We're going to keep moving. Any more on this topic? Do you have this topic, this topic? Then Wendell is a new subject. We're off this topic.

Scott McClellan
White House Press Secretary

12:30 P.M. EST

Q Scott, you used some pretty tough language this morning about those who are saying that the President has not answered all of the questions about the National Guard. You accused them of gutter politics and trolling for trash. As you know, back in the '92 campaign, then Governor Clinton's Vietnam-era history came up. And near the end of the campaign, then President Bush, this President's father, in a speech used the words "Slick Willie," talking about Governor Clinton then, and talked about the controversy, that the Governor had promised to release all his draft records, but had not. And he said, "He ought to level with the American people on the draft." He referred again to the records controversy, and he said, "He ought to level on these kinds of things." Is that trolling for trash?

MR. McCLELLAN John, we released documents showing that the President fulfilled his duties. Some people are calling on us to release documents. The documents spell out that the President fulfilled his duties. I think that you expect the garbage can to be thrown at you in the eleventh hour of a campaign, but not nine months before election day. And I certainly hope that this level of discourse is not a reflection of what the American people can expect from the Democratic Party over the duration of the campaign.

Q You also mentioned this morning that the Pentagon had requested the full personnel file, and that you expected it to be shared by the White House—

MR. McCLELLAN By the way, on that time period, there are—a lot of people said things that are one way and certainly saying other things these days.

Q I understand that to be the case, and I assume that will all come up in the campaign, as well. When you get the President's full file, what will be the standard for deciding whether additional information will be released?

MR. McCLELLAN Well, one, we would have to see if there is any new information in that. Like I said yesterday, we thought we had all the information that was relevant to this issue. So we haven't even seen that information at this point.

Q Again, when this controversy came up ten years ago, the then Bush-Quayle campaign, on October 15, 1992, put out a press release saying that because of the controversy and the questions, that Governor Clinton should release all documents relating to his draft status, and went on to list letters to the Selective Service system, to the Reserve Officer Training Corps, the Army, the Navy, the Air Force, the Marines, the Coast Guard, the Departments of State and Justice, any foreign embassy or consulate. Was that a fair standard?

MR. McCLELLAN This is 2004, I would remind you. But let me point out to you that the issue that was before us was whether or not the President had served. There had been some who made an outrageous accusation that the President was AWOL, or that he was a deserter. Just outrageous and baseless accusations. And there was a call for more documents to be released, specifically payroll records. We didn't know that they previously existed still. But we found out that they did, and we provided that documentation. That documentation clearly shows that the President fulfilled his duties.

I think what you're seeing now is that some are not interested in the facts. Some are more interested in trolling for trash for political gain. And that's just unfortunate that we're seeing that this early in an election year. This is nothing but gutter politics. The American people deserve better.

We are facing great challenges in this nation, and the President is focused on acting decisively to meet those challenges.

Instead of talking about the choices we face in addressing our highest priorities, some are simply trolling for trash for political gain. The American people deserve better. The American people deserve an honest debate about the choices we face. The American people deserve an honest discussion about the type of leadership their Commander-in-Chief is providing in a time of war, at a time when we are confronting dangerous new threats. I began this briefing by talking about the importance of confronting the spread of weapons of mass destruction, about the importance of stopping the spread of weapons of mass destruction. This President, from very early on in his administration, has made it a high priority to confront the dangerous new threats we face in this day and age. These are threats that did not come to us overnight. But September 11th taught us that we must confront these threats. Let's have an honest discussion about the type of leadership people are providing to confront those threats. That's what the American people deserve.

Q On "Meet the Press," the President was asked, "When allegations were made about John McCain or Wesley Clark on their military records, they opened up their entire files. Would you agree to do that?" And the President replied, "Yeah." Is that still your position?

MR. McCLELLAN The President—the specific question was about service, whether or not he had served in the military, if you go back to look at the context of the discussion. And the President said, if we have them, we'll release them, relating to that issue. We have released what additional documents came to our attention.

Scott McClellan
White House Press Secretary

10:03 A.M. EST

Q In your words, what do the dental records show or prove?

MR. McCLELLAN Well, there were some that raised the question about his service during his time in Alabama. And this document further demonstrates the President fulfilling his duties and serving while in Alabama. I suppose some might now try to suggest that, well, this is only his teeth, this doesn't show that he was there. (Laughter.)

Q If you guys are so interested in putting out all the explanations you could possibly give to say, you know, he was there, he fulfilled his duties, why won't you talk about why he didn't show up for his physical, which is a question that persists still?

MR. McCLELLAN No, I don't think it is; we answered that question four years ago. The reason—well, he was on—first of all, you're saying he didn't show up. He was on—he moved to Alabama for a civilian job and he was on non-flying status while in Alabama. There was no need for a flight exam.

*   *   *.

Q Joe Allbaugh says that it is hogwash, the report from one person who was in Texas, that some documents were thrown away a couple of years ago—I guess during the governor's years—having to do with the records. Is anyone from the White House checking or double-checking to make sure no documents were discarded?

MR. McCLELLAN Ann, I think it wasn't just Joe Allbaugh, it was several individuals that were—that charges were leveled against. All of them said how ridiculous that accusation was. And I noticed an article in one of the papers today that had a graphic with information that was blacked out. And it was—it's interesting to see the conspiracy theories that are out there, because there are certain privacy issues always involved when the National Guard or any government agency releases information.

Let me tell you what was in that blacked out part. I've got it here right with me. This is from what was in the paper today. It says, "Have you ever been arrested, indicted or convicted for any violation of civil or military law?" This was the President's application for a commission. And he was providing personal history there. On here it says—and you all can see it right here with me, this is the part that was in the paper this morning—misdemeanor, New Haven, Connecticut, December 1966, charge dismissed. Well, this was a widely-reported prank that the President was involved in while at Yale University.

Q The wreath—

MR. McCLELLAN The wreath, that's exactly right. Two speeding tickets, July '64 and August '64, $10 fine, Houston traffic court. Two collisions, July '62 and August '62, $25 fine, Houston traffic court. I'm just amazed by the kinds of conspiracy theories that some have chosen to pursue. The facts are very clear. But there are some that are simply not interested in the facts. And the American people deserve better. They deserve an honest discussion about leadership in a time of war. They deserve an honest discussion about leadership in a time when our economy is growing strong, but there is more to do.

Q Scott, just to keep trolling for a minute. This sheet that's in your hand and the blackout that was in one of the newspapers—

MR. McCLELLAN This is the exact thing in the newspaper.

Q Who did the blackout that showed up in the—

MR. McCLELLAN You'd have to ask the people who released those documents.

Q Okay. So what you have is something that came from the same source, that was not blacked out?

MR. McCLELLAN I think that you all recognize that when government agencies or people like the National Guard release information, there are privacy issues involved. And I expect that they follow those—

Q But the White House got a copy that did not have the blackout.

MR. McCLELLAN The President's records, that's correct.

Q Glad we asked.

MR. McCLELLAN Anything else? Thank you.

Scott McClellan
White House Press Secretary

This transcript does not appear on the official White House website.

Q Did the President ever have to take time off from Guard duty to do community service?

MR. McCLELLAN To do community service? I haven't looked into everything he did thirty years ago, Helen. Obviously, there is different community service he has performed in the past, including going back to that time period—

Q Can you find out if he actually had—

MR. McCLELLAN Helen, I don't think we remember every single activity he was involved in thirty years ago.

Q No, this isn't an activity. Was he forced to do community service at any time while he was on—

MR. McCLELLAN What's your interest in that question? I'm sorry, I just—

Q Lots of rumors. I'm just trying to clear up something.

MR. McCLELLAN Rumors about what?

Q Pardon?

MR. McCLELLAN Rumors about what?

Q About the President having to do community service while he was in the National Guard, take time out for that.

MR. McCLELLAN I'm not aware of those rumors. But if you want to—

Q Could you look it up? Would you mind asking him?

MR. McCLELLAN That's why I'm asking what's your interest in that? I just don't understand your interest in that.

Q It's what everybody is interested in, whether we're getting the true story on his Guard duty.

MR. McCLELLAN Well, you have the documents that show the facts.

Q I'm asking you to try to find out from the President of the United States.

MR. McCLELLAN Like I said, it's well known the different jobs he had and what he was doing previously, that we know. That goes back to—

Q I didn't say "previously." I said, while he was on Guard duty.

MR. McCLELLAN But you're asking me about thirty years ago. I don't think there's a recollection of everything he was doing thirty years ago.

Q Well, he would know if he had to take time out.

MR. McCLELLAN Again, I mean, the issue that was raised was whether or not the President was serving while he was in Alabama. Documents reflect that he was—

Q Well, this is another issue.

MR. McCLELLAN:—hold on—that he was serving in Alabama. That was the issue that was raised. We went through, four years ago, other issues related to this.

Q So you won't answer the question or you won't try to find out?

MR. McCLELLAN Well, I'm asking you, what's your interest in that question? I'm just curious, because rumors—

Q Did he have to do any community service while he was in the National Guard?

MR. McCLELLAN Look, Helen, I think the issue here was whether or not the President served in Alabama. Records have documented—

Q I'm asking you a different question. That's permissible.

MR. McCLELLAN Can I answer your question? Sure it is. Can I ask you why you're asking it? I'm just—out of curiosity myself, is that permissible?

Q Well, I'm interested, of course, in what everybody is interested in. And we have a very—

MR. McCLELLAN Let me just point out that we've released all the information we have related to this issue, the issue of whether or not he served while in Alabama. Records have documented as false the outrageous—

Q I asked you whether he had to do any community service while he was in the National Guard.

MR. McCLELLAN Can I walk through this?

Q It's a very legitimate question.

MR. McCLELLAN And I want to back up and walk through this a little bit. Let's talk about the issue that came up, because this issue came up four years ago, it came up four years before that—or two years before that, it came up four years before that—

Q Did my question come up four years ago, and was it handled?

MR. McCLELLAN Helen, if you'll let me finish, I want to back up and talk about this—

Q Don't dance around, just give us—

Q It's a straightforward question.

Q Let's not put too fine a point on it. If I'm not mistaken, you're implying that he had to do community service for criminal action, as a punishment for some crime?

Q There are rumors around, and I didn't put it in that way. I just—

Q Could you take that question? I guess apparently that's the question, that he had to take time out to perform community service—

MR. McCLELLAN That's why I wanted to get to this because—

Q —as a sentence for a crime.

MR. McCLELLAN No, that's why I wanted to get to this because I want to step back for a second. I want to go back through a few things. Look, the—I think we've really exhausted the issue that came up. The issue that came up was related to whether or not he had served while he was in Alabama. Records have documented as false the outrageous, baseless accusation that he did not serve while in Alabama. The conspiracy theory of one individual, that the National Guard cleansed documents, has been discredited.

Q How so?

MR. McCLELLAN Read the *Boston Globe* today.

Q Well, we want answers from you, not—

MR. McCLELLAN Read the *Boston Globe*. No, the answers are from the people that would have knowledge of that. But read—

Q Why do you think this person made those allegations?

MR. McCLELLAN Hang on, hang on.

Q What? Just read the *Boston Globe*—

MR. McCLELLAN Just read the *Boston Globe*. Read the *Boston Globe*. I would draw your attention to that. What I think we're seeing now is just politics. And we're not going to engage in it, because there are great challenges facing our nation, and there should be an honest discussion of the actions the President is taking to make our world safer and better and make America more prosperous and secure.

You want me to go—

Q —the personal record of a President is—

MR. McCLELLAN No, hang on, Helen, hang on. I've said from this podium, if we have new information that comes to our attention that relates to this issue, we have made it clear we will share that information. You're asking me to go and chase rumors. There was a conspiracy theory—

Q I think—

MR. McCLELLAN Hold on, hold on, Helen. There was a conspiracy theory made by one individual, when everybody he accused of being involved in that said, it's ridiculous, didn't happen.

Q This is not based on a conspiracy theory.

MR. McCLELLAN And there was a lot of attention given to this individual, and he's been discredited. There's a *Boston Globe* article on it this morning. And there are some—

Q That says what? Your point—

MR. McCLELLAN You can go read it. I mean, we've got other things to move on to. I mean, you can go read it. But there are some, unfortunately, who simply are not interested in the facts. Again, the documents—the records document that he did serve while in Alabama. And now there are people that are bringing up issues that were addressed four years ago.

Q But you still haven't answered Helen's question. She asked you a simple question.

MR. McCLELLAN There are people that want to replay the 2000 campaign all over again, Bill, and—

Q You still haven't answered her question about community service.

MR. McCLELLAN —there are too many important—there are too many important policies and decisions that are being made that we need to discuss.

Q Why does a "yes" or "no" elude you on this?

MR. McCLELLAN I didn't say that. I said that these were all issues addressed four years ago. If there's additional information—

Q This issue quite obviously wasn't addressed four years ago.

MR. McCLELLAN Oh, issues—these issues were addressed four years ago.

Q This issue was? The community service issue was addressed four years ago?

MR. McCLELLAN The issues—the issues that we're going to here—

Q I don't recall—

MR. McCLELLAN This is called chasing a rumor. And I'm not going to engage in this kind of politics, Bill.

Q —finding out whether a rumor is true or false.

MR. McCLELLAN No, this issue, absolutely—

Q Why can't you say whether or not he performed community service?

MR. McCLELLAN Absolutely, this issue came up four years ago. And if you all want to play politics, then go call the RNC, call the campaign.

Q The best defense is offense. We know that. Just, all you've got to say is you don't know.

MR. McCLELLAN Helen, it was—this issue was addressed four years ago. I think people that were involved in the campaign will know—

Q —if they know—

MR. McCLELLAN —that the issue that you're trying to bring up was addressed four years ago. It's about chasing rumors.

Q It isn't a question of four years ago. The issue has come up now, very large.

MR. McCLELLAN I'm not going to get into chasing rumors.

Q Headlines.

MR. McCLELLAN I'm not going to get into chasing rumors.

Q So you refuse to answer the question?

MR. McCLELLAN You're saying that people said he was forced to do something, and you're asking me to chase a rumor.

Q Everything is politics today, of course.

Q She asked you a "yes" or "no" question.

MR. McCLELLAN Look, if you all want to—this is just politics. That's what this is. And if there's any more information I have to share with you all, I will always—I will do that.

Q Scott, I have a question of this individual, and I confess, I haven't read the Boston article. But who—what do you believe was this person's motivation, that if they have been discredited, for making these allegations?

MR. McCLELLAN Just—I would read the *Boston Globe*. Everybody that he accused of being involved in this has said it was totally ridiculous. And there are others that—

Q So are you saying—was it politically motivated?

MR. McCLELLAN There are others that are quoted in the *Boston Globe* today, that you might want to see what they said.

Q Speaking of politics, has the President authorized his campaign—

MR. McCLELLAN And we've got to—

Q —to release a video attacking Senator Kerry?

MR. McCLELLAN You need to talk—you need to talk to the campaign. But let me go to the week ahead because we've used up more than 15 minutes.

Q So the President did authorize—

Q Scott, I've got—

MR. McCLELLAN I'm going to go to the week ahead.

Scott McClellan
White House Press Secretary

12:30 P.M. EST

Q Can I ask you a question, Scott? I just want to be absolutely clear on something here. The records that you released earlier this week on the President's Guard service state that he did not perform any Guard service in the third quarter of 1972. That's correct?

MR. McCLELLAN Well, you have the records in front of you, and they state the dates on which he was paid. And you are paid for the days on which you serve.

Q So they state that between April 16th of 1972 and October 28th of 1972 he did no Guard duty.

MR. McCLELLAN We've been through these issues, John, and we've provided you with the documents that show his service.

Q And do you believe that's correct, that he did no duty between April 16th and October 28th?

MR. McCLELLAN John, I don't know why we need to go through this again. This issue we've been through earlier this week.

Q Well, the reason I bring up the question is that John Calhoun, who claims he was the person in charge of making sure that President Bush reported for duty at the 187th Tactical Recon Group, says that he saw the President several times on the base between May and October of 1972, yet there is no record of him being there, in terms of what you released earlier this week.

MR. McCLELLAN I don't speak for him. You would have to talk to Mr. Calhoun. I do not know him.

Q We did talk to Mr. Calhoun, and Mr. Calhoun said that he saw the President several times between May and October of 1972.

MR. McCLELLAN And like I've said—

Q So I was just wondering, can you explain that discrepancy?

MR. McCLELLAN And like I've said, the President doesn't recall the specific dates on which he performed his duties. He does remember serving both in Alabama and in Texas. During that entire period, he was a member of the Texas Air National Guard.

Q But the records that you released do recall quite specifically the days that the President served on. There's no record of his being there—

MR. McCLELLAN Actually, these are National Guard records that document the President did serve during that time period. And that was an issue that was raised earlier this week.

Q Right. But the records clearly recall that he did no Guard duty between April 16th and October 28th. Yet, Mr. Calhoun says he saw him on the base at the 187th between May and October of '72. So there's a discrepancy here. I'm wondering if you can explain it?

MR. McCLELLAN John, again, we've provided you with the records and the facts are in the records that we have.

Q A good point. Could the records be incomplete?

MR. McCLELLAN I'm sorry?

Q Could the records be incomplete?

MR. McCLELLAN Direct that question to the National Guard. These are the personnel records that we've received.

Q Scott, have you been through the entire personnel file now? And have you released everything you're going to release?

MR. McCLELLAN Well, like I said, that if there is additional information that comes to our attention that is relevant to the issue, we will certainly provide you with that information. That's a commitment that we've made.

Q But have you seen the entire file? That sounds like a reasonable question.

MR. McCLELLAN Have I seen the entire file? I don't know the answer to that question at this point, because there is a possibility—we have expected to receive additional documents from the National Guard. I think we just very recently received some additional documents, but I'm not sure if any of those documents are new. We're going to take a look at those. We'll take a look at those, and if there's new information relevant to the issue, then we will certainly provide you with that information.

Q Saturday, during the taping of the Tim Russert program, *Meet the Press,* the President said something at the end—many thought it was a very confident statement, at the least—that he would not lose this election. That was Saturday. At 12:35 p.m. today, Friday, does he still feel that same way in the midst of all of this controversy, polls showing that he's at his lowest rating ever?

MR. McCLELLAN Absolutely. You know, one, that's not something that he pays great attention to. What he's focused on is the decisions that we are making on behalf of the American people. And the decisions that the President is making are the right decisions for the American people. They are decisions that are making our country more secure and more prosperous and they are decisions that are leading to a safer and better world.

Q But a follow up. Apparently, he does feel that this is a problem, the AWOL story, the alleged AWOL story, and some of the other—

MR. McCLELLAN Which has now been documented to be false.

Q Well, there are still some discrepancies. But apparently he's fighting these stories, so that's saying that the President realizes there is a problem for this campaign, correct?

MR. McCLELLAN I'm sorry? That there is—

Q I made my point clear.

MR. McCLELLAN That may be your interpretation. This President is confident that the decisions that we are making are the right policies for the American people, and he is confident that the American people are supportive of the decisions that we are making.

Q Putting out paper, you're giving out paper—

MR. McCLELLAN Look, April—

Q —you're directing us to the *Boston Globe* article—

MR. McCLELLAN Let me finish the question there that you asked. There is going to be plenty of time to talk about the campaign. Right now this President is going to remain focused on the great challenges that we are working to meet. And we are meeting them in a number of different ways, but there is more to do.

But this President is acting decisively to make America more secure, to make America more prosperous, to make America a more compassionate place. And he's acting to make the world a safer and better place.

Q Well, then why would you give us this information, then, if he's not worried about it?

MR. McCLELLAN I'm sorry?

Q Why would you give us this information, direct us to the *Boston Globe* story today? Why would you give us—

MR. McCLELLAN Why would you ask those questions?

* * *

Q I'd like to come back to the records one more time, if I could. Forgive me if I'm beating a horse that you would rather see depart this world. (Laughter.) But the President, in his—

MR. McCLELLAN I think most of the American people believe that this issue has kind of run its course.

Q The President, in his interview on Sunday, was asked the first question about possible release of records, the first question about possible release. He was asked, when there were questions about Senator John McCain's record, Wesley Clark's record, they authorized the release of their entire file. The President was asked, would he do that? And he replied, "Yeah." So why is the President reneging on that pledge?

MR. McCLELLAN John, do you want to continue on and go through the rest of that questioning?

Q Because that was the first question to which he answered in the affirmative—don't try to parse it out.

MR. McCLELLAN John, here's the question, quote from Tim Russert. "But you will allow pay stubs, tax records"—

Q Let's go with the first question. You're parsing.

MR. McCLELLAN No, I think you are, because the issue that Tim Russert raised was whether or not he had served while he was in Alabama.

Q Read the first question, Scott.

MR. McCLELLAN "But you will allow pay stubs, tax records, anything to show that you were serving during that period." "Yes. If we still have them." We have provided you with that information, and we will continue to.

Q Read the first question.

MR. McCLELLAN I just—you read the first question. I read this question. It was the—

Q Right. It was the very first question—

MR. McCLELLAN The context of this discussion—

Q The very first question, when he said, "entire record," the President said, "Yeah."

MR. McCLELLAN Oh, John, let's look at the context of the discussion. The context of the discussion was clear about whether or not he had served while he was in Alabama. It was very clear.

Q The first question was about entire—

MR. McCLELLAN We can agree to disagree on this issue, but I think it was very—

Q We're going to end up on *The Daily Show* again with this one.

MR. McCLELLAN:—very clear about the context of the question.

Scott McClellan
White House Press Secretary

Q Will the Commander-in-Chief insist that his Pentagon get to the bottom, find every last document of the National Guard service?

MR. McCLELLAN I think that's what the President directed back in February.

Q Are you frustrated, or is he, that more documents are surfacing?

MR. McCLELLAN All the personnel, payroll, and medical records have been made public, and the President directed back in February that the Department of Defense do a comprehensive search and make all the documents available, and we had assurances that they had done that and, unfortunately, we have since found out that it was not as comprehensive as we thought. So they've continued to go and look for additional documents.

Q Is the President frustrated, irritated by this?

MR. McCLELLAN See, that's why I pointed out that all the personnel, payroll and medical records have been released.

Q How do you know that?

MR. McCLELLAN They've assured us that all those records are out, and in fact, you have those records.

Scott McClellan
White House Press Secretary

11:53 A.M. EDT

Q Why did the President defy a direct order to get a physical in 1972?

MR. McCLELLAN Scott, these are the same old recycled attacks that we see every time the President is up for election. It's not surprising that you see a coordinated effort by Democrats to attack the President when Senator Kerry is falling behind in the polls. And we had a very successful convention, and that's what this is about. It was well known that the President was going to work in Alabama and seeking a transfer to perform equivalent duty in a non-flying status. And that's what he was doing.

Q Did he decline to take it because he was moving to Alabama?

MR. McCLELLAN He was transferring to a unit in Alabama to perform equivalent duty in a non-flying status. That is nothing new.

Q This was a direct order he defied, right? I mean, he did have a direct order that he defied?*

MR. McCLELLAN John, these issues have come up every year. This was all part of the records—that he was seeking to transfer to a unit in Alabama because he was going there to work in a civilian capacity. And he was granted permission to do so. And he was proud of his service and he was honorably discharged in October '73, after meeting his obligations.

*The memos that were released, in fact, show the President was working with his commanders to comply with the order.

Q Do you think that the Kerry campaign was behind these allegations surfacing again now?

MR. McCLELLAN I think you absolutely are seeing a coordinated attack by John Kerry and his surrogates on the President. The polls show Senator Kerry falling behind, and it's the same old recycled attacks that we've seen every time the President has been up for election.

Q Do you think it's retaliation for the Swift Boats attacks on Kerry?

MR. McCLELLAN I think it's—I think it's in response to Senator Kerry falling behind in the polls and a successful convention that we had last week in New York.

Q Scott, even if these are old and recycled, and he was—

MR. McCLELLAN This—there—

Q I'd like to ask—

MR. McCLELLAN I would like to finish my answer.

Q But I didn't ask my question yet.

MR. McCLELLAN But I haven't finished my answer to Steve. This race is about the future and the choices that the American people face. And there are clear differences on the issues. And I don't—Senator Kerry will do anything he can to avoid defending his record and talking about the clear choices that the American people face. And this President—the President will continue to focus on his agenda for the future. And that's what the American people want this election to be focused on. And that's where our focus has been and where it—well, where it will continue to be.

Q Scott, I'm just wondering, even if these were old charges, and even if the President was honorably discharged, did he or did he not defy an order to get that physical?

MR. McCLELLAN Holly, again, these are the same kind of recycled attacks that the Democrats are trying to engage in. The President fulfilled all his obligations, and that is why he was honorably discharged from the National Guard in October, 1973. He was given permission to perform equivalent duty in Alabama, and he met his obligations, and he met his obligations when he returned to Texas. And he met his obligations when he was in Texas, prior to going to Alabama.

Scott McClellan
White House Press Secretary

Q Scott, on the National Guard documents, do you have any suspicions about their authenticity?

MR. McCLELLAN We don't know whether the documents were fabricated or are authentic. You know, the media has talked to independent experts who have raised questions about the documents. CBS has not disclosed where the documents came from. But, regardless, it does not—the documents do not change the facts. The President met his obligations and was honorably discharged. And the one thing that is clear is the timing and the coordination going on here. There is an orchestrated effort by Democrats and the Kerry campaign to tear down the President because of the direction the polls are moving. And it's not surprising that we're seeing the same old recycled attacks. The Democrats are determined to throw the kitchen sink at us, and I suspect this is just the beginning.

Q When you use the word "coordination," it seems to suggest in a legal sense that the Kerry campaign is illegally coordinating with the 527—

MR. McCLELLAN It's clear. I mean, look at the media reports, they've documented the coordinated efforts by Democrats to tear down the President here, because they're falling behind in the polls. You look at the—the *Washington Post* had a story about it today, talking about the multi-front effort by the Democratic National Committee, other Democrats. You have outrageous comments being made by Senator Harkin. You have the Democratic National Committee using the term "Operation Fortunate Son." *Fortunate Son* was the name of a book by an ex-convict that was widely discredited in the 2000 campaign.

Q But what I'm saying is, you're essentially accusing Mr. Kerry of violating McCain-Feingold, it sounds like.

MR. McCLELLAN What I'm saying is that the Democrats are seeing the direction the polls are moving and they are now—and they are determined to tear down the President, they are determined to throw the kitchen sink at us.

We're focused—the President is focused on his agenda for the future and where he wants to lead this country. The Democrats are focused on tearing down the President with the same old recycled attacks, because they're falling behind.

Q Are you guys doing a—are you doing an analysis of your own about the documents, to see if they're fake or not?

MR. McCLELLAN No. I don't know that we have any way to verify that. I mean, these are serious allegations and they are being looked into by others.

Q Two questions. Does the White House regret handing out those documents, taking CBS's word on their authenticity, without checking them, themselves?

MR. McCLELLAN No, we—you know, we released all the President's personnel—or made available publicly all the President's personnel, medical and payroll files in their entirety. The Department of Defense has continued to go back and look for additional documents that weren't in those files. It was an issue of openness. CBS provided us with those documents and—

Q Did you ask—

MR. McCLELLAN Well, we did ask, and CBS did not disclose to us, either, where they obtained those documents from. We wanted to be open about it, so we provided that information, as we have other documents to the media.

Q Were you duped, do you think?

MR. McCLELLAN Bill, that's assuming a lot of things. Like I said, we don't know whether the documents were fabricated or authentic.

Q Have you been in contact with CBS since this question about their authenticity has arisen, in terms of their internal investigation, et cetera?

MR. McCLELLAN In terms of their internal investigation?

Q Have they notified you—

MR. McCLELLAN CBS put out a statement yesterday, I noticed. So you all are very aware of the—

Q But have they contacted you directly and said, we may have given you bogus documents?

MR. McCLELLAN No, not that I'm aware of. You all were very well aware of what their position is. They put a statement out.

III

THE RECORDS

1968

By far the greatest number of pages in Bush's available military records come from the year of his enlistment, 1968. The lion's share of these date to May, and comprise a majority—but apparently not a complete set—of the documents from Bush's "enlistment packet" (inventoried on 99). These documents establish several notable points about Bush's background, and about his commitment to the Guard. In his Enlistment Contract (100–1), Bush agrees in a legally binding document to "incur a service obligation of six (6) years." His Application for a Commission (102–3) notes his dismal 25 rating for pilot aptitude, and five run-ins with the law (one dismissed misdemeanor charge in New Haven, and two speeding tickets and two "negligent collisions" in Houston; he paid small fines for all four traffic violations). In his Application for Extended Active Duty (104–5), when asked about his area assignment preferences, he checked "DO NOT VOLUNTEER FOR OVERSEAS"—a clear confirmation that Bush had no intention of volunteering for Vietnam. A crucial document is his Statement of Understanding (106–7), in which Bush agrees to "perform assigned duties at 48 scheduled inactive duty training periods and 15 days' field training . . . annually," and agrees that "if I fail to participate, I may be involuntarily ordered to perform 45 days' active duty and/or be certified for induction." He also acknowledges "that I may be ordered to active duty for a period not to exceed 24 months for unsatisfactory partic-ipation as presently defined in Chapter 41, AFM 35-3. Further, I under-stand that if I am unable to satisfactorily participate in the ANG, and have an unfulfilled military service obligation, that I may be discharged from the State ANG and assigned to the Obligated Reserve Section (ORS), AF Reserve, Denver, Colorado."

Bush's Statement of Personal History (108–11) was originally released with a redaction under Question 18; later, the uncensored version shown here revealed that the note gave details on Bush's 1966 disorderly conduct arrest at Yale, and promised that Yale's Security Director "will vouch for the insignificance of the prank." Also included are Bush's college tran-scripts, and a pledge that he belongs to no subversive organizations. Sev-eral documents pertain to his application for pilot training, including the Statement of Intent (126) in which he expresses his "goal of making flying a lifetime pursuit" and desire to serve "as a member of the Air National Guard as long as possible," and a certificate of understanding (127) noting that Bush can be discharged if he fails to complete his pilot training. An undated, handwritten note from Bush (128) may have accompanied NGB Form 21 (129), in which Bush confirms that his disorderly conduct charge was dropped, and an August 22 Waiver of Arrest (134) apparently settled the matter for the Guard's purposes.

Many of the remaining documents concern Bush's swift promotion to 2nd Lieutenant in August–September—including a memo (143) with the notation "PLEASE APPOINT IMMEDIATELY"; a September 4 Federal Recogni-tion Examining Board report (137–8) in which Walter Staudt, Jerry Kil-lian, and Frank Davis recommend Bush for the promotion; and Bush's signed oaths that same day (151–2). Bush's Airman Military Record (147–50) notes his service between enlistment and promotion. Further documents concern Bush's security clearance, his temporary transfer to Georgia, and his acceptance of commission in December.

2 9 MAY 1968

SPCR

Preview and Grade Determination

AGTEX-AP

1. Attached are documents comprising an application for preview and grade determination and federal recognition of GEORGE WALKER BUSH. It is desired to appoint this individual in the grade of Second Lieutenant with duty assignment as Pilot Trainee, AFSC 0006, 111th Fighter Interceptor Squadron, Ellington AFB, Texas.

2. Airman Bush will be designated a class assignment upon return from Basic Military Training.

3. Appointment is desired under the provisions of paragraph 15d, ANGR 36-02 and Ltr, NGB (NG-AFPO) 1 May 1968, Subj: FY 69 Pilot Trainees and AGTEX-AT 1st Indorsement of 1 May 1968 thereto.

4. A review of the attached documents indicate that Airman Bush meets all the requirements established for this appointment program.

WALTER B. STAUDT, Colonel, TexANG
Commander

15 Atch
1. AF Form 24
2. AF Form 56
3. AF Form 125 (Includes 5 yr agreement)
4. Certificate of Understanding
5. Certificate of AFOQT Results
6. College Transcripts
7. DD Form 98
8. AF Form 1145
9. DD Form 398
10. DD Form 1584
11. FD-258 (Fingerprint Cards)
12. SF 88 & 89 (Includes EKG & Dental Xrays)
13. NGB Form 63
14. Commander's Statement of Interview
15. Individual's Statement of Intent upon completion of Pilot Training

ENLISTMENT CONTR___ED FORCES OF THE UNITED STATES					Form Approved Budget Bureau No. 22-R016

(Also to be used by AFEES in conjunction with induction processing as a means of providing data for manpower information reporting systems.)

1. SERVICE NO.	2. HIGHEST SCHOOL GRADE COMPLETED	3. RATE/GRADE	4. BRANCH/CLASS AND COMPONENT	5. LAST NAME – FIRST NAME – MIDDLE NAME
AF26230638	15	E1AB 31	TX ANG–ResAF	BUSH, GEORGE WALKER

6. DATE OF ENL/INDUC.	7. TERM OF ENLISTMENT/INDUCTION	8a. MARITAL STATUS	8b. NO. DEPEND.	9. NAME & LOCATION OF ACTIVITY AFFECTING ENLISTMENT/ REENLISTMENT/INDUCTION
27 05 68	6 YEARS ☐ MINORITY	S	0	ELLINGTON AFB, TX

10. ___ SCORE	11. ENLISTED/REENLISTED/INDUCTED			12. AUTHORITY FOR ENLISTMENT/REENLISTMENT/INDUCTION
NA	☒ 1ST ENLIST. ☐ REENLISTMENT ☐ INDUCTION			ANGR 39-09

13. TERM OF ACDU (Reserve only)	14. ACTIVE/INACTIVE STATUS (Reserve only)			15. ACCEPTED AT
NA MONTHS	☐ RETAINED ON AD ☐ IMMED AD (within 24 hours) ☒ INACTIVE DUTY			ELLINGTON AFB, TX

16. DATE MIL OBLI INC	17. PMOS/AFS CODE/MOD	18. RELIGION	19. SSAN	20. CONTRACT DUTY LIMITATIONS
27 05 68	70230	E		NA

21. DATE OF BIRTH	22. CITIZENSHIP		COUNTRY (Specify)	23. PLACE OF BIRTH (City, State or country)
06 07 46	☒ US ☐ NAT US	☐		New Haven, CT

24. DATE OF TRANSFER	25. PHYSICAL PROFILE		26.	27. TRANSFER TO (Activity and location)	27a.
NA	111111A 1		71½" 180	NA	NA

28. DATE LAST DC/RAD	29. SVC FROM WHICH LAST DISCHARGED	30.	31.	32. TYPE OF LAST DISCHARGE	33.
NA	NA	NA	NA	NA	0

34. DATE OF RATE/GR	35. SELECTIVE SERVICE NO.	36. RATE/GR APT/RAPT	37. SELECTIVE SERVICE LOCAL BOARD (Board No., city and state)
27 05 68	41-62-46-1480	NA	#294 HOUSTON HARRIS TX

38. BAND/ADSG	39. TOTAL ACTIVE FEDERAL SERVICE	40. HOME OF RECORD
NA	NA YEARS ___ MONTHS ___ DAYS	HOUSTON, TX 44

41.	42. SPED/PERD	43. TOTAL INACTIVE FEDERAL SERVICE	44. MENTAL TEST SCORES
	27 05 68	NA YEARS ___ MONTHS ___ DAYS	

45. SEX	46. RACE	47. DATA PROCESSING CODE
A	NA	Yale Univ, 120SH, attending

48.

NA

49.

PRIOR SERVICE

BRANCH & CLASS/ ARMED FORCE & COMPONENT	SERVICE NUMBER	DATE ENL. IND. APT. AND/OR OAD	DATE OF DISCHARGE OR RELEASE	GRADE/ RATE OR RANK	TYPE OF DISCHARGE	REASON FOR DISCHARGE	TIME LOST (No. Days)
NA							

50. I know that if I secure my enlistment by means of any false statement, willful misrepresentation or concealment as to my qualifications for enlistment, I am liable to trial by court martial or discharge for fraudulent enlistment and that, if rejected because of any disqualification known and concealed by me, I will not be furnished return transportation to place of acceptance.

I am of the legal age to enlist. I have never deserted from and I am not a member of the Armed Forces of the United States, the US Coast Guard or any Reserve component thereof; I have never been discharged from the Armed Forces or any type of civilian employment in the United States or any other country on account of disability or through sentence of either civilian or military court unless so indicated by me in item 56, "Remarks" of this contract. I am not now drawing retired pay, a pension, disability allowance, or disability compensation from the government of the United States.

51. SECTION 5538 OF TITLE 10 OF THE UNITED STATES CODE is quoted: "(a) The Secretary of the Navy may extend enlistments in the Regular Navy and the Regular Marine Corps in time of war or in time of national emergency declared by the President for such period as he considers necessary in the public interest. Each member whose enlistment is extended under this section shall be discharged not later than six months after the end of the war or national emergency, unless he voluntarily extends his enlistment. (b) The substance of this section shall be included in the enlistment contract of each person enlisting in the Regular Navy or Regular Marine Corps."

52. SECTION 5540 OF TITLE 10 OF THE UNITED STATES CODE is quoted: "(a) The senior officer present afloat in foreign waters shall send to the United States by Government or other transportation as soon as possible each enlisted member of the naval service who is serving on a naval vessel, whose term of enlistment has expired, and who desires to return to the United States. However, when the senior officer present afloat considers it essential to the public interest, he may retain such a member on active duty until the vessel returns to the United States. (b) Each member retained under this section (1) shall be discharged not later than 30 days after his arrival in the United States; and (2) except in time of war is entitled to an increase in basic pay of 25 percent. (c) The substance of this section shall be included in the enlistment contract of each person enlisting in the naval service.".

53. I understand that, upon enlistment in a Reserve component of any of the Armed Forces of the United States, or upon transfer or assignment thereto, in time of war or National emergency declared by Congress, or when otherwise authorized by law, I may be ordered to active duty for the duration of the war or National emergency and for six months thereafter.

54. I have had this contract fully explained to me, I understand it; and certify that no promise of any kind has been made to me concerning assignment to duty, geographical area, schooling, special programs, assignment of government quarters, or transportation of dependents except as indicated   NA

DD FORM 4   REPLACES DD FORM 4, 1 OCT 63, WHICH IS OBSOLETE.

55. I swear (or affirm) that the foregoing statements have been read to me, that my statements have been correctly recorded and are true in all respects and that I fully understand the conditions under which I am enlisting.

SIGNATURE OF WITNESS....

DONALD DEAN BARNHART SGT

SIGNATURE OF APPLICANT (First Name - Middle Name - Last Name)

George Walker Bush

56. REMARKS

"I certify that the following statements are correct to the best of my knowledge:

The recruiter explained in detail all items of my enlistment contract to include the coding used and I understand them completely. I have furnished my latest DD Form 214, "Report of Transfer or Discharge" for previous military service and/or current information regarding reserve status, if any. The enlistment contract records my true name, date of birth, residence, school, and home of record. I am not a conscientious objector. I have been counseled and provided information on financial problems as a result of marriage while serving in the lower airman grade of E-4 with less than 4 years total service or below. I am not under orders for induction and my current Selective Service Classification is ___II-S___. I accept enlistment in the ANG (ResAF) in the grade of ___AB___. I understand that from this date, I incur a service obligation of six (6) years under USC 651."

57. OATH OF ENLISTMENT (For service in Regular or Reserve Component of the Armed Forces except National Guard or Air National Guard)

I, _____ (First Name - Middle Name - Last Name), do hereby acknowledge to have voluntarily enlisted under the conditions prescribed by law, this _____ day of _____, 19__, in the _____ for a period of _____ years unless sooner discharged by proper authority, and I do solemnly swear (or affirm) that I will support and defend the Constitution of the United States against all enemies, foreign and domestic; that I will bear true faith and allegiance to the same; and that I will obey the orders of the President of the United States and the orders of the officers appointed over me, according to regulations, and the Uniform Code of Military Justice. So help me God.

SIGNATURE

58. OATH OF ENLISTMENT (For service in National Guard or Air National Guard)

I do hereby acknowledge to have voluntarily enlisted this __27th__ day of __MAY__, 19__68__, in the (Army) (Air) National Guard of the State of __TEXAS__ and as a Reserve of the (Army) (Air Force) with membership in the (Army National Guard of the United States) (Air National Guard of the United States) for a period of __6 Years__ (Years - Months - Days) under the conditions prescribed by law, unless sooner discharged by proper authority.

I, __GEORGE WALKER BUSH__ (First Name - Middle Name - Last Name), do solemnly swear (or affirm) that I will support and defend the Constitution of the United States and of the State of __TEXAS__ against all enemies, foreign and domestic; that I will bear true faith and allegiance to them; and that I will obey the orders of the President of the United States and the Governor of __TEXAS__ and the orders of the officers appointed over me, according to law, regulations, and the Uniform Code of Military Justice. So help me God.

SIGNATURE

George Walker Bush

59. CONFIRMATION OF ENLISTMENT

The above oath was subscribed and duly sworn to before me this __27th__ day of __MAY__, 19__68__. To the best of my judgement and belief, enlistee fulfills all legal requirements, and in enlisting this applicant, I have strictly observed the regulations governing such enlistment. The above oath, as filled in, was read to the applicant prior to subscribing thereto.

TYPED NAME, GRADE/RANK, AND ORGANIZATION OF ENLISTING OFFICER

WILLIE J HOOPER JR, Capt, 147th Cmbt Spt Sq

SIGNATURE OF ENLISTING OFFICER

APPLICATION FOR A COMMISSION, FOR TRAINING LEADING TO A COMMISSION, OR FOR FLYING TRAINING IN OFFICER GRADE	DATE 28 May 1968	Budget Bureau No. 21–R0156 Approval Expires 13 May 1966

INSTRUCTIONS.—Answer all questions completely by checking boxes or entering the information required. Write "None" in any blank not applicable to you. Read certification at the end of this questionnaire before entering required data. If more space is needed make entry in "Remarks section" or add additional sheets.

1. LAST NAME—FIRST—MIDDLE INITIAL (Maiden name, if applicable)	SEX	STATUS	MILITARY ACTIVE
BUSH, GEORGE W.	Male	USAF X	MILITARY INACTIVE
	X ANG	CIVILIAN	

2. PRESENT ADDRESS (Civilian or military)	3. PERMANENT HOME ADDRESS	GRADE	AF SPECIALTY
5000 Longmont #8 Houston, Texas 77027	5000 Longmont #8 Houston, Texas 77027	RESERVE ANG	PRIMARY 70010
		TEMPORARY	ADDITIONAL

MARITAL STATUS	U.S. CITIZEN	NATURALIZED	SERVICE NO.	DATE ELIGIBLE FOR RETURN FROM OVERSEAS
Single		DATE N/A	AF 26230638	N/A
NO. OF DEPENDENTS 0	YES X NO	PLACE N/A	SOCIAL SECURITY NO.	BIRTHDAY (Day, month, year) 6 July 1946

4. APPLICANT FOR (Apply for only one of the following categories of training):

AVIATION CADET	OFFICER TRAINING SCHOOL (Indicate preference, 1, 2, 3)	COMMISSION UPON COMPLETION OF AFROTC TRAINING	FLYING IN OFFICER GRADE
USAF ANG	PILOT NAVIGATOR ADMIN. AND TECH.	PILOT NAVIGATOR	DATE COMMISSIONED OR TO BE COMMISSIONED
X PILOT		ADMINISTRATIVE AND TECH.	PILOT NAVIGATOR
NAVIGATOR			

5. HAVE YOU EVER PREVIOUSLY MADE APPLICATION FOR OR BEEN ENROLLED IN: (a) A PROGRAM LEADING TO A COMMISSION, (b) ENLISTMENT IN THE NAVY, MARINE CORPS, COAST GUARD, ARMY, AIR FORCE OR OF ANY COMPONENT THEREOF? (Include military, service academies, Federal and State Maritime Academies, all ROTC programs, officer candidate training, platoon leaders school, etc.)

☐ YES (If "YES" complete the following information below) X NO

NATURE OF APPLICATION OR ENROLLMENT	DATE	PLACE	RESULT			COMPLETED
			ACCEPTED	REJECTED	WITHDREW	YES NO
N/A						

6. EXPLAIN UNDER "REMARKS" REASONS FOR NONCOMPLETION OF ANY TRAINING LISTED BELOW

7. WERE YOU DISQUALIFIED AT ANY TIME FOR A SERVICE-CONDUCTED FLYING TRAINING COURSE?	8. HAVE YOU COMPLETED A COURSE OF INSTRUCTION IN A SERVICE FLYING SCHOOL LEADING TO AN AERONAUTICAL RATING?	DATE
☐ YES X NO	☐ YES X NO	
	A. TYPE OF TRAINING	B. AERONAUTICAL RATING NOW HELD

9. WERE YOU ELIMINATED FROM A COURSE OF INSTRUCTION IN A SERVICE FLYING SCHOOL LEADING TO AN AERONAUTICAL RATING?		DATE
☐ YES X NO		
A. TYPE OF TRAINING	B. REASON FOR ELIMINATION	C. NAME OF SCHOOL	D. CLASS

10. OTHER COURSES (Military and/or civilian) TAKEN IN FLIGHT, TRAINING, METEOROLOGY, NAVIGATION, MATHEMATICS, PHYSICS, ELECTRONICS

COURSE	NAME OF SCHOOL	INCLUSIVE DATES	CREDITS EARNED
None			

11. THIS SPACE FOR AFOQT SCORES. ONLY AIR FORCE TEST CONTROL OFFICERS OR ORGANIZATION COMMANDERS ARE AUTHORIZED TO ENTER APPLICANT'S TEST SCORE IN THIS SPACE. (Entries will be made in ink or by typewriter.)

AFOQT FORM		APTITUDE				INTEREST			
	PILOT	NAV. TECH.	O.O.	VERBAL	QUAN.	FLYING	TECH.	ADM.	QUAN.
DATE TESTED 19 Jan 1968	25	50	95	85	65				

12. EDUCATION

CIRCLE HIGHEST SCHOOL YEAR COMPLETED	☐ GRADUATE WORK	DEGREES EARNED	SCHOLARSHIPS, HONORS, AWARDS
GED ☐ 1 2 3 4 GED X 1 2 3 4 HIGH SCHOOL COLLEGE		BA – June 1968	

UNDER GRADUATE MAJOR SUBJECTS (College)	SEMESTER HRS.	GRADUATE MAJOR SUBJECTS (College)	SEMESTER HRS.
History	16		

AF FORM 56 MAR 64   PREVIOUS EDITION OF THIS FORM WILL BE USED UNTIL STOCK IS EXHAUSTED.

ATCH 2

13. OTHER TYPES OF TRAINING COMPLETED THAT REFLECT BACKGROUND QUALIFICATIONS OF VALUE TO THE AIR FORCE

None

14. CHRONOLOGICAL STATEMENT OF SERVICE AND TRAINING IN THE AIR FORCE, ARMY, NAVY, MARINE CORPS, OR ANY OF THE COMPONENTS THEREOF; UNITED STATES MILITARY OR NAVAL ACADEMY, OR RESERVE OFFICERS TRAINING CORPS.

DATES		HIGHEST GRADE	ORGANIZATION (Type and service)	DUTY	SERIAL NO.	ACTIVE OR INACTIVE
FROM	TO					
27 May 68	Present	Amn	147th Ftr Gp (TexANG)	Adm Spec	AF 26230638	Active

15. SELECTIVE SERVICE DATA

BOARD NUMBER	BOARD ADDRESS	CURRENT CLASSIFICATION	SELECTIVE SERVICE NO.
294	Room 413, 201 Fannin Street Houston, Texas 77002	I -D	41-62-46-1480

16. KNOWLEDGE OF FOREIGN LANGUAGE

LANGUAGE	HOW ACQUIRED (School, family, work, etc.)	READ			SPEAK			UNDERSTAND		
		EXC.	GOOD	FAIR	EXC.	GOOD	FAIR	EXC.	GOOD	FAIR
Spanish	School			X			X			X

17. HAVE YOU EVER BEEN ARRESTED, INDICTED OR CONVICTED FOR ANY VIOLATION OF CIVIL OR MILITARY LAW INCLUDING MINOR TRAFFIC VIOLATIONS? (If "YES" explain stating nature of offense, date, name and place of the court and disposition of the case.)

Misdemeanor - New Haven Conn - Dec 1966 - Charge Dismissed
Two Speeding Tickets - July 64 - Aug 64 - $10 Fine - Houston Traffic Ct
Two Negligent Collisions - July 62 - Aug 62 - $25 Fine - Houston Traffic Ck.

18. EMPLOYMENT RECORD (Start with your present position and work back).   DO NOT ENTER PART-TIME EMPLOYMENT OR EMPLOYMENT OF LESS THAN 60 DAYS DURATION

EMPLOYER	TYPE OF WORK	DATES: FROM-TO	SALARY	WHY TERMINATED
Baker, Botts, Sheppard, Coates	Messenger	6/6/62 - 21/8/62	200.00	Return to School
Jack Greenway, VV Ranch Williams, Arizona	Ranch Hand	6/6/64 - 21/8/64	200.00	Return to School
Circle Oil Co. Lake Charles, La.	Oil Field Wk	6/6/65 - 31/8/65	375.00	Return to School
Sears Roebuck, Houston, Texas	Salesman	1/6/66 - 25/8/66	212.00	Return to School
James L. Bayless, SW Int Bell Bk	Bookkeeper	1/5/67 - 25/8/67	250.00	Return to School

REMARKS:

19. I UNDERSTAND AND AGREE THAT:

A. Upon completion of the training course, I will accept an appointment as an officer in the Reserve of the Air Force in career reserve status.   Further, I agree to remain on active duty as a commissioned officer for the period prescribed in AFR 36-22 or 36-51 on the date of this application, unless sooner relieved by competent authority.

B. If, at the time I am about to be appointed an aviation cadet, or officer trainee, I am a member of the Air Force with less than 16 months remaining under my enlistment contract, I will extend my enlistment for the necessary period to include 16 months' service:

C. As an applicant for aviation cadet training, I am unmarried and, if selected for training, will remain unmarried until either my graduation or elimination therefrom.

I certify that the foregoing entries are true, correct and complete to the best of my knowledge and belief; and in signing this application I do so with the understanding that the veracity of all statements made may be investigated and if found incorrect I may be subject to such disciplinary action as appropriate.

DATE	TYPE NAME AND GRADE OF APPLICANT	SIGNATURE
28 May 1968	GEORGE WALKER BUSH, Amn	George Walker Bush

U.S. GOVERNMENT PRINTING OFFICE : 1964 OF—725—024

APPLICATION FOR EXTENDED ACTIVE DUTY WITH THE UNITED STATES AIR FORCE

(Read conditions and Instructions on reverse side before completing this application)

TO:			DATE
147th Fighter Group, Ellington AFB, Texas			28 May 1968
NAME (Last, first, middle initial)			BIRTH DATE
BUSH, GEORGE W.			6 July 1946

HOME ADDRESS (City, County, State and Zip Code)	MAIL ADDRESS (If other than home)	AFRES	ANGUS
5000 Longmont #B Houston (Harris) Texas, 77027	Same as home		X
		SERVICE NUMBER	
		AF 26230638	

RESERVE GRADE	TEMPORARY GRADE (Instruction 4)	PRIMARY AFSC:		SOCIAL SECURITY ACCT.NO
	N/A	70010		
AMN		2: 3:		SINGLE / MARRIED X

PRESENT ASSIGNMENT	LOCATION	DUTY AFSC	NO OF DEPENDENTS (Other than self)
Admin Apprentice	Ellington AFB, Texas	70230	0

I hereby volunteer for extended active duty (EAD) as prescribed in the directive checked below: I agree to the active duty agreement specified; and I certify all information furnished by me to be correct:

☐ AFR 45-13- (Air Force Participation in the Selective Service Program).
Submit application to CAC, Robins AFB, GA 31093; Angus officers must have consent of Governor or other appropriate State official.
I agree to remain on EAD with the Selective Service System (SSS) for an indefinite period unless sooner relieved by competent authority. I further understand that I may request release from EAD at any time and that such release will be dependent upon the requirements of the SSS at time of submission.

☐ AFR 45-21- (Voluntary Entry on EAD of Airmen of the Reserves of the Air Force.) (Notes 3 & 4)
I agree to serve on EAD for a period of four years unless sooner relieved by competent authority.

☐ AFR 45-22/ANGR 36-08- (Reserve Component Representation on Air Force Staffs.) (To fill 10 USC 265, 8033, or 8494 positions in HQ USAF; NGB, or MAJCOM HQS)
I understand that if I am ordered to EAD under AFR 45-22/ANGR 36-08, my tour of duty will be for a four year period unless sooner relieved by competent authority; and that I will be released from EAD upon completion of such tour unless my continuance on EAD is approved by HQ USAF.

☐ AFR 45-26- (Voluntary Entry on EAD of Commissioned Officers and Warrant Officers of the Air Reserve Forces.)

   ☐ Chaplains - I agree to serve on EAD for a period of three years unless sooner relieved by competent authority.

   ☐ Other than Chaplains - I agree to enter on EAD for an indefinite period in career reserve status and understand that I must serve a minimum of four years of active duty. I further understand that I may incur no additional active duty service commitment beyond the minimum four years as the result of training received, a permanent change of station, promotion, or for other reasons as prescribed in AFR 36-51. This agreement to enter on active duty for an indefinite period does not preclude my release or separation from active duty if required by a change in law, regulations, or policy.

☐ ANGR 11-02- (US property and fiscal officers.)
I agree to serve on active duty for an indefinite period unless sooner relieved by competent authority.

☒ AFR 51-4 (Flying Training in Officer Grade - ANG Pilot Trainee Retention Provisions.)
I agree to serve on active duty for the unexpired portion of my obligation, as stated in AFR 51-4, if deemed appropriate by my unit commander or the Secretary of the Air Force to be in the national interest, or if I wilfully violate the terms of my contract.

☐ Other

EDUCATION: (Highest level of education attained, including professional military schools)

TYPE OF SCHOOL	NAME OF SCHOOL	YEARS ATTENDED		MAJOR SUBJECT	NO.YRS. COMPL.	GRADUATE		TYPE OF DEGREE
		FROM	TO			YES	NO	
College	Yale University	1964	1968	History	4	X		BA

REMARKS (See Instructions 1, 3, and 5)

AF FORM 125 AUG 67 — PREVIOUS EDITIONS OF THIS FORM ARE OBSOLETE.

ATCH 8

PRESENT CIVILIAN OCCUPATION (*You may enter under REMARKS any prior periods of employment having a direct bearing to the specialty for which recall to EAD is being sought.*) **Not Employed**

DATES OF EMPLOYMENT (*Month, Year*)	TITLE		MONTHLY SALARY
FROM: TO PRESENT			

NAME AND ADDRESS OF EMPLOYER:

DESCRIPTION OF WORK:

SINCE THE DATE OF YOUR LAST ENTRY ON EAD, HAVE YOU EVER BEEN CONVICTED BY A CIVIL COURT OR ARE YOU AWAITING TRIAL BY A CIVIL COURT FOR ANY OFFENSE INCLUDING MINOR TRAFFIC VIOLATIONS? (*If Yes, explain fully under remarks.*) ☐ YES ☐ NO

WOMEN APPLICANTS ONLY (*Instruction 6*). I DO NOT HAVE PERSONAL CUSTODY AS A PARENT, STEPPARENT, OR LEGAL GUARDIAN OF ANY CHILD UNDER 18 YEARS OF AGE WHO RESIDES WITHIN MY HOUSEHOLD MORE THAN 30 DAYS A YEAR *Initials* ☐

FLYING STATUS AGREEMENT (*Officers Only*)

IF I AM SELECTED FOR RECALL IN A NON-FLYING CAPACITY, I HEREBY VOLUNTARILY REQUEST PERMANENT SUSPENSION FROM FLYING STATUS. ☐ YES ☒ NO

AREA ASSIGNMENT PREFERENCES

☐ I DO ☒ DO NOT VOLUNTEER FOR OVERSEAS.

UNITED STATES (*Number areas in order of preference*)

NORTHEAST	SOUTHEAST	NORTH CENTRAL	SOUTH CENTRAL	NORTHWEST	SOUTHWEST
6	2	4	3	5	1

OVERSEAS (*Number areas in order of preference*)

EUROPEAN AREA	PACIFIC AREA	ALASKAN AREA	CARIBBEAN AREA

I WILL BE AVAILABLE FOR ACTIVE DUTY ON (*Date*) ☐ I DO ☐ DO NOT REQUIRE THIRTY (30) DAYS NOTICE PRIOR TO MY ENTRY ON ACTIVE DUTY.

INSTRUCTIONS

1. All information should be typewritten or clearly printed in ink. Enter postal zip code for all addresses. When allotted spaces are insufficient, continue under remarks or on a separate sheet and complete appropriate explanation. Enter all dates in day, month, and year sequence.

2. Applications are valid for one (1) year from date thereof, except in the case of ANG pilot trainees under the provisions of AFR 51-4, which are valid for five (5) years.

3. Include any additional information you believe will be helpful in processing the application. Especially important are items of information which may not be contained in your military record.

4. Reservists who served on EAD in a temporary grade higher than the permanent reserve grade currently held will enter such higher temporary grade in this item.

5. Applicants serving on active duty in a warrant officer or enlisted status will enter in the remarks section the w/o or enlisted grade in which serving, service number, and unit of assignment.

6. Women applicants attest to this item by placing their initials in the block at end of statement. Applicants who cannot so attest are ineligible for EAD consideration.

7. Permanent home address shown on this application will be indicated in EAD orders. For purpose of computing mileage allowances upon relief from EAD, any changes in permanent home address reported after entry on EAD will not affect the permanent home address indicated in the active duty orders. If applicant is ordered to EAD from an address other than the permanent home address, such temporary address will also be indicated in the orders.

8. In addition to other documents specified in the directive under which applying, it is important that the following be attached:

   A. One copy of the orders relieving applicant from most recent tour of EAD. (This item is applicable to reservists who have previously served on EAD in a commissioned grade.)

   B. If rated, certified or photostatic copy of last page of AF Form 5 or 5A, Individual Flight Record, with tables I, II, and III completed. If personal copy not available, write: Dir of Aerosp Safety (AFIAS), Norton AFB CA 92409.

NOTES (*Continue*):

1. No action should be taken to close out personal affairs until actual receipt of competent orders or instructions. The Air Force cannot be held liable for any actions contrary to this condition.

2. No assurance of assignment to an area of choice may be given since selections for EAD are based on Air Force-wide requirements.

3. If a reserve airman is selected for assignment to an overseas unit, he will not be authorized travel by privately owned vehicle or transportation of dependents and household goods/house trailer to the base from which processed for overseas movement.

4. EAD under AFR 45-21 will be for four years only. Provisions for discharge for the purpose of immediate enlistment in the Regular Air Force are contained in AFR 39-9.

TYPE OR PRINT NAME	SIGNATURE
GEORGE WALKER BUSH	*George Walker Bush*

STATEMENT OF UNDERSTANDING

Date: 27 May 68

Place: Ellington AFB, Texas

In connection with my enlistment this date as a Reserve of the Air Force for service in the Air National Guard of the United States, I understand and agree that:

a. I will enter on active duty for training for _____120 days_____ or until I (tour length) have satisfactorily completed the training courses which I have elected.

b. I must enter on such active duty training within 120 days from date of my enlistment, unless I am otherwise qualified for delay under established criteria, but in no event later than 1 year from the date of my enlistment.

c. If selected for attendance at an Air Force Technical School the duration of which will extend my active duty for training beyond 4 months, I voluntarily agree to remain on active duty for training for the additional period required to complete satisfactorily the course of technical training for which enrolled.

d. If the AFSC for which enlisted requires OJT beyond 4 months, I voluntarily agree to remain on active duty for the additional period required to satisfactorily complete the prescribed specialty training.

e. I incur a military service obligation to remain a member of the Air National Guard and as a Reserve of the Air Force for a period of 6 years as required by law; if I am separated from the Air National Guard of the United States for any reason prior to completion of my enlistment, I will be transferred to the Air Force Reserve to complete the remaining portion of my military service obligation and will be subject to further Reserve training as determined by proper authority.

f. This enlistment in no way relieves me of my obligation to register with the Selective Service System. I understand the voluntary military service obligation which I am assuming will override any classification for which I may be eligible under the Selective Service System.

g. Provided I satisfactorily participate as a member of the Ready Reserve, I will be deferred from induction; if I fail to participate, I may be involuntarily ordered to perform 45 days' active duty and/or be certified for induction.

h. Satisfactory participation during my membership in the Air National Guard of the United States will be attendance and satisfactory performance of assigned duties at 48 scheduled inactive duty training periods and 15 days' field training (active duty for training) annually, unless excused therefrom by proper authority. It also includes successful completion of on-the-job upgrade training.

i. While I am retained as a member of the Ready Reserve, I am subject to involuntary entry into active duty in time of any future emergency proclaimed by the President of the United States or the Congress, or as otherwise provided by law.

j. "I have been counseled this date regarding the provisions of DOD Directive 1215.13, 23 February 1967. I understand that I may be ordered to active duty for a period not to exceed 24 months for unsatisfactory participation as presently defined in Chapter 41, AFM 35-3. Further, I understand that if I am unable to satisfactorily participate in the ANG, and have an unfulfilled military service obligation, that I may be discharged from the State ANG and assigned to the Obligated Reserve Section (ORS), AF Reserve, Denver, Colorado, and subject to active duty for a period not to exceed a total of 24 months considering all previous active duty and active duty for training tours."

k. "However, I also understand that the provisions for invoking the 45 day tour for a member who has a satisfactory attendance record but has failed to progress in specialty training will remain in effect. (Paragraph 41-7a, AFM 35-3.)"

WITNESSED BY:

WILLIE J HOOPER JR, Capt, Asst Admin Officer
(Unit Commander or Authorized
Representative)

(Signature of Enlistee)

George W. Bush
(Typed Name)

STATEMENT C PERSONAL HISTORY   28 MAY 65

INSTRUCTIONS: Read the certification at the end of this questionnaire before entering the required data. Print or type all answers. All questions and statements must be completed. If the answer is "None," so state. Do not misstate or omit material fact since the statements made herein are subject to verification. If more space is needed, use the Remarks section, item 20, and attach additional sheets if necessary. The information entered hereon is for official use only and will be maintained in confidence.

1. (Print) FIRST NAME—MIDDLE NAME—MAIDEN NAME (If any)—LAST NAME		2. STATUS
☐ MR. ☒ MRS. ☐ MISS GEORGE WALKER BUSH		☒ CIVILIAN MILITARY ON ACTIVE DUTY
3. ALIAS(ES), NICKNAME(S), OR CHANGES IN NAME (Other than by marriage) None	4. PERMANENT MAILING ADDRESS 5000 Longmont #8 Houston, Texas 77027	

5. DATE OF BIRTH (Day, month, year) 6 July 1946	PLACE OF BIRTH (City, County, State, and Country) New Haven, New Haven, Conn. USA	PLACE CERTIFICATE RECORDED Courthouse New Haven, Conn.

HEIGHT 71½	WEIGHT 130	COLOR OF EYES Hazel	COLOR OF HAIR Brown	SCARS, PHYSICAL DEFECTS, DISTINGUISHING MARKS Chest Scars - Appendix scar

6. DO YOU HAVE A HISTORY OF MENTAL OR NERVOUS DISORDERS? ☐ YES ☒ NO   ARE YOU NOW OR HAVE YOU EVER BEEN ADDICTED TO THE USE OF HABIT FORMING DRUGS SUCH AS NARCOTICS OR BARBITURATES? ☐ YES ☒ NO   ARE YOU NOW OR HAVE YOU EVER BEEN A CHRONIC USER TO EXCESS OF ALCOHOLIC BEVERAGES? ☐ YES ☒ NO   IF THE ANSWER TO ANY OF THE ABOVE IS "YES," EXPLAIN IN ITEM 20

7. U.S. CITIZEN	NATIVE ☒	IF NATURALIZED, CERTIFICATE NO.	IF DERIVED, PARENTS' CERTIFICATE NO(S).	DATE, PLACE, AND COURT
	YES ☐ NO			
ALIEN ☐	REGISTRATION NO.	NATIVE COUNTRY	DATE AND PORT OF ENTRY	DO YOU INTEND TO BECOME A U.S. CITIZEN? YES ☐ NO ☐

MILITARY SERVICE

8. ARE YOU PRESENTLY ON ACTIVE DUTY IN THE U.S. ARMED FORCES DRAWING FULL PAY? ☐ YES ☒ NO IF "YES," COMPLETE THE FOLLOWING:

GRADE AND SERVICE NO.	SERVICE AND COMPONENT	ORGANIZATION AND STATION	DATE CURRENT ACTIVE SERVICE STARTED

ARE YOU PRESENTLY A MEMBER OF A U.S. RESERVE OR NATIONAL GUARD ORGANIZATION? ☒ YES ☐ NO IF "YES," COMPLETE THE FOLLOWING:

GRADE AND SERVICE NO. AMN AF 26230636	SERVICE AND COMPONENT AF TexANG	ORGANIZATION OR STATION OR UNIT AND LOCATION 147th Combat Support Sq. Bldg. 1362 Ellington AFB, Texas

HAVE YOU PREVIOUSLY SERVED TOURS OF EXTENDED ACTIVE DUTY, DRAWING FULL PAY, FROM WHICH YOU WERE DISCHARGED OR SEPARATED TO CIVILIAN STATUS? ☐ YES ☒ NO IF "YES," COMPLETE THE FOLLOWING:

COUNTRY	SERVICE	COMPONENT	FROM (Date)	TO (Date)	TYPE DISCHARGES OR SEPARATIONS—GRADE AND SERVICE NO.

9. **EDUCATION** (Account for all civilian schools and military academies. Do not include service schools)

MONTH AND YEAR FROM	TO	NAME AND LOCATION OF SCHOOL		GRADUATE YES	NO	DEGREE
Sep 1955	Jun 1959	San Jacinto Jr. High	Midland, Texas	X		
Sep 1959	Jun 1961	The Kinkaid School	Houston, Texas	X		
Sep 1961	Jun 1964	Phillips Academy Andover	Andover, Mass	X		Diploma
Sep 1964	Jun 1968	Yale University	New Haven, Conn	X		

10. **FAMILY** (List in order given, parents, spouse, guardians, stepparents, foster parents, parents-in-law, former spouse(s) (if divorced give date and place), children, brothers and sisters, even though deceased. Include any others you resided with or with whom a close relationship existed or exists. If the person is not a U.S. citizen by birth, give date and port of entry, alien registration number, naturalization certificate number and place of issuance.)

RELATION AND NAME	DATE AND PLACE OF BIRTH	PRESENT ADDRESS, IF LIVING	U.S. CITIZEN YES	NO
FATHER George Herbert Walker Bush	June 12, 1924 Plymouth, Mass 22360	5000 Longmont #8 Houston, Texas 77027	X	
MOTHER (Maiden name) Barbara (nee) Bush, nee Pierce	June 8, 1925, New York, N.Y. Aka Mrs. George Herbert Walker Bush	5000 Longmont #8 Houston, Tex 77027	X	
SPOUSE (Maiden name) None				
OTHER (Specify) Brother: John Ellis Bush	Feb. 11, 1953 Midland, Texas 75217	5000 Longmont #8 Houston, Texas 77027	X	
Brother: Neil Mallow Bush	Jan. 22, 1955 Midland, Texas	5000 Longmont #8 Houston, Texas 77027	X	
Brother: Marvin Pierce Bush	Oct. 11, 1956 Midland, Texas	5000 Longmont #8 Houston, Texas 77027	X	
Sister: Dorothy Walker Bush	Aug. 18, 1959 Houston, Texas	5000 Longmont #8 Houston, Texas 77027	X	
Sister: Pauline Pierce Bush	Dec. 20, 1949 Bakersfield, Calif.	Deceased October 1953	X	

REPLACES EDITION OF 1 MAY 55 WHICH MAY BE USED.   Exception to Standard Form 86

11.	OTHER RELATIVES AND ALIEN FRIENDS LIVING IN FOREIGN COUNTRIES (*List grandparents, first cousins, aunts, uncles, brothers- and sisters-in-law, and other persons with whom a close relationship existed or exists*)				
	RELATIONSHIP AND NAME	AGE	OCCUPATION	ADDRESS	CITIZENSHIP
None					

12.	FOREIGN TRAVEL (*Other than as a direct result of United States military duties*)		
DATES		COUNTRY VISITED	PURPOSE OF TRAVEL
FROM	TO		
Aug 1959	Sep 1959	Scotland	Pleasure – vacation

13.	EMPLOYMENT (*Show every employment you have had and all periods of unemployment*)			
MONTH AND YEAR		NAME AND ADDRESS OF EMPLOYER	NAME OF IMMEDIATE SUPERVISOR	REASON FOR LEAVING
FROM	TO			
Jun 62	Aug 62	Baker, Botts, Shepard & Coates 809 Travis, Houston, Texas 77002	Baine P. Kerr	Return to School
Jun 63	Aug 63	IX Ranch Williams, Arizona	Mr. Jack Greenway	Return to School
Jun 65	Aug 65	Circle Oil Company Lake Charles, Louisiana	Mr. G. Wilcox	Return to School
Jun 66	Aug 66	Sears & Roebuck 1201 Main, Houston, Texas 77002	Mr. Jim Miles	Return to School
Jun 67	Aug 67	Rauscher, Pierce Securities 901 1st City Nat'l Bank, 1001 Main, Houston, Tex. 77002	Mr. James L. Bayless	Return to School
Aug 67	Present	Unemployed: May be verified by: Mr. Terry Johnson Holland Road Far Hills, N. J. 07301		

DID ANY OF THE ABOVE EMPLOYMENTS REQUIRE A SECURITY CLEARANCE? ☐ YES ☐ NO DO YOU HAVE ANY FOREIGN PROPERTY OR BUSINESS CONNECTIONS, OR HAVE YOU EVER BEEN EMPLOYED BY A FOREIGN GOVERNMENT, FIRM, OR AGENCY? ☐ YES ☒ NO HAVE YOU EVER BEEN REFUSED BOND? ☐ YES ☒ NO IF THE ANSWER TO ANY OF THE ABOVE IS "YES," EXPLAIN IN ITEM 20.

SOCIAL SECURITY NO. ▓▓▓▓▓▓

14.	CREDIT AND CHARACTER REFERENCES (*Do not include relatives, former employers, or persons living outside the United States or its Territories.*)				
	NAME (List 3 credit and 3 character)	YEARS KNOWN	STREET AND NUMBER (Business address preferred)	CITY	STATE OR TERRITORY
CREDIT	Baker, Botts Shepperd&Coats	9	809 Travis	Houston 77002	Texas
	Baine P. Kerr–Rauscher Pierce Securities	6 Yrs.	1001 Main	Houston 77002	Texas
	Houston Club	7	3 Potomac	Houston 77027	Texas
CHARACTER	Cathryn Lee Wolfman	5	5700 Tecumseh	Houston 77037	Texas
	Mr. Britton W. Kolar	5	1515 Yale Station	New Haven 06505	Conn.
	Mr. J. P. Kerr	5	203 Maple Valley	Houston 77063	Texas
	Mr. J. L. Bayless	5	241 Pine Hollow	Houston 77002	Texas
	Mr. Sam Chauncey	5	Yale University	New Haven 06505	Conn.

15.	LIST ALL RESIDENCES FROM 1 JANUARY 1937			
MONTH AND YEAR		STREET AND NUMBER	CITY	STATE OR COUNTRY
FROM	TO			
Dec 53	Dec 56	1412 West Ohio	Midland	Texas 79701
Dec 56	Jun 59	2703 Sentinel	Midland	Texas 79701
Jun 59	Jan 67	5925 Briar Dr	Houston	Texas 77027
Jan 67	Present	5000 Longmont #8	Houston	Texas 77027
		while attending College;	New Haven	06520
		1266 Yale Station		Connecticut
		I stayed in Boarding School on the following period:	Andover	Massachusetts
Sep 61	Jun 64	Phillips Academy		01810

16.	PAST AND/OR PRESENT MEMBERSHIP IN ORGANIZATIONS			MEMBERSHIP	
NAME AND ADDRESS	TYPE (Social, fraternal, professional, etc.)		OFFICE HELD	FROM	TO
Delta Kappa Epsilon 222 York St. New Haven, Conn. 06520	Fraternity		President	Oct 65	Jan 68

17.		
YES	NO	
	X	ARE YOU NOW OR HAVE YOU EVER BEEN A MEMBER OF THE COMMUNIST PARTY U. S. A., OR ANY COMMUNIST ORGANIZATIONS ANYWHERE?
	X	ARE YOU NOW OR HAVE YOU EVER BEEN A MEMBER OF A FASCIST ORGANIZATION?
	X	ARE YOU NOW OR HAVE YOU EVER BEEN A MEMBER OF ANY ORGANIZATION, ASSOCIATION, MOVEMENT, GROUP OR COMBINATION OF PERSONS WHICH ADVOCATES THE OVERTHROW OF OUR CONSTITUTIONAL FORM OF GOVERNMENT, OR WHICH HAS ADOPTED THE POLICY OF ADVOCATING OR APPROVING THE COMMISSION OF ACTS OF FORCE OR VIOLENCE TO DENY OTHER PERSONS THEIR RIGHTS UNDER THE CONSTITUTION OF THE UNITED STATES, OR WHICH SEEKS TO ALTER THE FORM OF GOVERNMENT OF THE UNITED STATES BY UNCONSTITUTIONAL MEANS?
	X	ARE YOU NOW OR HAVE YOU EVER BEEN AFFILIATED OR ASSOCIATED WITH ANY ORGANIZATION OF THE TYPE DESCRIBED ABOVE AS AN AGENT, OFFICIAL, OR EMPLOYEE?
	X	ARE YOU NOW ASSOCIATING WITH, OR HAVE YOU ASSOCIATED WITH ANY INDIVIDUALS, INCLUDING RELATIVES, WHO YOU KNOW OR HAVE REASON TO BELIEVE, ARE OR HAVE BEEN MEMBERS OF ANY OF THE ORGANIZATIONS IDENTIFIED ABOVE?
	X	HAVE YOU EVER ENGAGED IN ANY OF THE FOLLOWING ACTIVITIES OF ANY ORGANIZATION OF THE TYPE DESCRIBED ABOVE: CONTRIBUTION(S) TO, ATTENDANCE AT OR PARTICIPATION IN ANY ORGANIZATIONAL, SOCIAL, OR OTHER ACTIVITIES OF SAID ORGANIZATIONS OR OF ANY PROJECTS SPONSORED BY THEM; THE SALE, GIFT, OR DISTRIBUTION OF ANY WRITTEN, PRINTED, OR OTHER MATTER, PREPARED, REPRODUCED, OR PUBLISHED, BY THEM OR ANY OF THEIR AGENTS OR INSTRUMENTALITIES?

IF "YES," DESCRIBE THE CIRCUMSTANCES. ATTACH ADDITIONAL SHEETS FOR A FULL DETAILED STATEMENT. IF ASSOCIATED WITH ANY OF THE ABOVE ORGANIZATIONS, SPECIFY NATURE AND EXTENT OF ASSOCIATION WITH EACH, INCLUDING OFFICE OR POSITION HELD, ALSO INCLUDE DATES, PLACES, AND CREDENTIALS NOW OR FORMERLY HELD. IF "ASSOCIATIONS HAVE BEEN WITH INDIVIDUALS WHO ARE MEMBERS OF THE ABOVE ORGANIZATIONS, THEN LIST THE INDIVIDUALS AND THE ORGANIZATIONS WITH WHICH THEY WERE OR ARE AFFILIATED.

18. HAVE YOU EVER BEEN DETAINED, HELD, ARRESTED, INDICTED OR SUMMONED INTO COURT AS A DEFENDANT IN A CRIMINAL PROCEEDING, OR CONVICTED, FINED, OR IMPRISONED OR PLACED ON PROBATION, OR HAVE YOU EVER BEEN ORDERED TO DEPOSIT BAIL OR COLLATERAL FOR THE VIOLATION OF ANY LAW, POLICE REGULATION OR ORDINANCE (excluding minor traffic violations for which a fine or forfeiture of $25, or less was imposed?) . INCLUDE ALL COURT MARTIALS WHILE IN MILITARY SERVICE. ☐ YES-☐ NO IF "YES," LIST THE DATE, THE NATURE OF THE OFFENSE OR VIOLATION, THE NAME AND LOCATION OF THE COURT OR PLACE OF HEARING, AND THE PENALTY IMPOSED OR OTHER DISPOSITION OF EACH CASE.

Disorderly conduct — Dec 66 — New Haven, Conn. City Court — Charges were dropped. The Security Director of Yale, Mr. Powell will vouch for the insignificance of the prank.

DD FORM 398

19. ARE THERE ANY INCIDENTS IN YOUR LIFE NOT MENTIONED HEREIN WHICH MAY REFLECT UPON YOUR LOYALTY TO THE UNITED STATES OR UPON YOUR SUITABILITY TO PERFORM THE DUTIES WHICH YOU MAY BE CALLED UPON TO TAKE OR WHICH MIGHT REQUIRE FURTHER EXPLANATION? ☐ YES ☒ NO (IF "YES" GIVE DETAILS)

20. REMARKS

Courses taken: History

ITEM 13:
XX Ranch is located approximately 8 miles southeast of Williams, Arizona
Circle Oil Co in Lake Charles: I do not remember street address or part of town
it was located in.

Period Aug 63 - Jun 65: Unemployed. May be verified by: Mr. B. P. Kerr
283 Maple Valley
Houston, Texas 77023

Item 8. Enl in ANG - 27 May 68.

Immediate Supervisor's name and telephone: SSgt Oren W. McClure, HU 7-1400 Ext. 498

I CERTIFY THAT THE ENTRIES MADE BY ME ABOVE ARE TRUE, COMPLETE, AND CORRECT TO THE BEST OF MY KNOWLEDGE AND BELIEF AND ARE MADE IN GOOD FAITH. I UNDERSTAND THAT A KNOWING AND WILLFUL FALSE STATEMENT ON THIS FORM CAN BE PUNISHED BY FINE OR IMPRISONMENT OR BOTH (See U. S. Code, title 18, section 1001)

DATE: 28 May 1968
SIGNATURE OF PERSON COMPLETING FORM: George Walker Bush
TYPED NAME AND ADDRESS OF WITNESS: THOMAS M. SULLIVAN   9930 Tolman, Houston Tex 77080
SIGNATURE OF WITNESS: G Thomas M Shallhew

21. THIS SECTION TO BE COMPLETED BY AUTHORITY REQUESTING INVESTIGATION
BRIEF DESCRIPTION OF DUTY ASSIGNMENT AND DEGREE OF CLASSIFIED MATTER (top secret, secret, etc.) TO WHICH APPLICANT WILL REQUIRE ACCESS

Individual is applying for Pilot Training under the Air National Guard Program and
is required access to classified material up to and including SECRET, however prior
to entry into the Advanced Pilot Training Program, a Background Investigation is
required in accordance with Air Force Manual 50-5.

RECORD OF PRIOR CLEARANCES

DATE OF CLEARANCE	TYPE OF CLEARANCE	AGENCY THAT COMPLETED INVESTIGATION
None		

REMARKS
None

HEADQUARTERS
147TH FIGHTER GROUP (AD)
TEXAS AIR NATIONAL GUARD
Ellington Air Force Base, Texas

REPLY TO
ATTN OF: CBPO

27 May 68
(Date)

SUBJECT: Character Certification

TO: AGTEI

1. This is to certify that GEORGE W. BUSH who has applied for enlistment in this command has furnished the following persons as character references in his behalf.

NAME	ADDRESS	TELEPHONE
BAINE P. KERR	283 Maple Valley, Houston, Texas	NA 2-8949
JAMES L. BAYLESS	241 Pine Hollow, Houston, Texas	NA 1-1130
C. FRED CHAMBERS	38 North Wynden, Houston, Texas	NA 1-2057

2. Each of the above references has been contacted and has stated that he or she knew the applicant and belived him to be of good character and temperate behavior.

WILLIE J HOOPER JR, Capt, TEXANG

Asst Admin Officer
(Type Name, Grade, Orgn & Duty
Title of Enlisting Officer)

DEPARTMENT OF THE AIR FORCE
UNITED STATES AIR FORCE RECRUITING DETACHMENT 106 (ATC)
660 CHAPEL STREET
NEW HAVEN, CONNECTICUT 06510

REPLY TO
ATTN OF: OTO

SUBJECT: Request for AFOQT Scores

TO:

SS

1. Mr. _GEORGE W. BUSH_ was administered the Air Force Officers Qualification Test on _19 JAN 68_ using Test Form _66_ and obtained the following scores:

Pilot Aptitude: 25
Navigator Aptitude: 50
Officer Quality: 95
Verbal Aptitude: 85
Quantitative: 68

2. I certify that the above information pertaining to the AFOQT Scores of the OTS applicant indicated above to be true and correct as recorded on the AF Form 338 on file at this Headquarters in accordance with AF Regulation 53-27.

RALPH J. IANNUZZI, 1st Lt, USAF
Test Control Officer

22Jan68/200

YALE UNIVERSITY NEW HAVEN, CONNECTICUT

YALE COLLEGE
Office of the Registrar
Sheffield Hall

March 18, 1968

TO WHOM IT MAY CONCERN:

    This is to certify that _____George Walker BUSH_____ is currently enrolled in Yale College in the Class of 19_68_ and is pursuing the undergraduate program of study in _____History_____.

    Upon the successful completion of this curriculum, we anticipate he will be a candidate for the degree of Bachelor of _Arts_ in _June_, 19_68_.

ATTEST:

Grant Robley

Grant Robley
Registrar

GR:JT

(Seal)

ATCH

YALE UNIVERSITY NEW·HAVEN CONN.	Mr. George Walker Bush 5000 Longmont Apt. 8 Houston, Texas 77027			School YALE COLLEGE Class 1968 Major History Birthdate 7/6/46 Degree Date Awarded Admitted from: Phillips Academy, Andover, Mass.					
Course and No.		Jan.	June	Course and No.	Jan.	June	Course and No.	Jan.	Ju
1964-1965				1966-1967			1967-1968		
English 15				American Studies 59a			History 39a		
Philosophy 10a				Anthropology 25			History 85-1		
Political Science 11a				City Planning 10a			History 89		
Science II Geology				History 35a			Japanese 77		
Spanish 40				History 54a			Political Science 48		
Philosophy 15b				Classical Civil. 23b			History 36b		
Science II Astronomy				History 35b			History 56b		
Political Science 13b				History 54b					
				Philosophy 38b					
1965-66									
Economics 10									
History 32a, 32b									
History 58a, 58b									
Sociology 55a									
Spanish 41									
History 63b									

Year	1964-1965			1965-66			1966-67			Cumulative	Final					Jan.	June	Year	Final	Departmental Examination
Term	Jan.	June	Year	Jan.	June	Year	Jan.	June	Year		Jan.	June	Year							Pass
Average																				High Pass
Percentile																				Superior
Credits																				Failure
Degree Credits																				
Ranking Scholar																				
Dean's List																				

This record without the appropriate signature and imprint of the Seal is only a statement of the student's progress to date and is *not* an official transcript.

Grant Robley
Associate Dean or Registrar

3/19/68
Date

YALE COLLEGE—YALE UNIVERSITY

REGISTRAR'S OFFICE · 11 SHEFFIELD HALL
NEW HAVEN, CONNECTICUT

NUMBERING OF COURSES

In general, courses numbered from 10 to 19 are first-year subjects. Second-year or intermediate courses are numbered from 20 to 29. Subjects taken in the Junior and Senior years, particularly those in a student's major, are customarily numbered from 30 to 99. Graduate School courses are numbered 100 and above.

MARKING SYSTEM

The Yale College Faculty voted on November 30, 1967, that as of January 1968 the term grades for all undergraduates are to be designated

H—Honors
HP—High Pass
P—Pass
F—Fail

These grades have no numerical, letter, or grade-point equivalents.

Numerical Grades (prior to 1968)

Under this system grades were reported in units of one between 60 and 100 (with 60 being the minimum for passing). After July 1, 1963, a student's percentile standing was not recorded unless he specifically so requested. A survey of the grades for several years preceding, however, indicates that a student's average for a given term would rank him approximately as given below:

TERM AVERAGES

Numerical Range	Class Standing
85 and above	Top Quarter
81–84	Second Quarter
76–80	Third Quarter
75 and below	Fourth Quarter
60	Minimum passing grade

HONORS: Under the numerical system, if a student had no deficiencies on his record and if he ranked in the top ten per cent of his class at a given marking period he was designated a *Ranking Scholar*. Also, the man having no deficiencies and ranking in the top quarter of his class at a marking period was placed on the *Dean's Honor List*.

GRADUATION REQUIREMENTS

The Standard Major requires for graduation that 40 term courses be completed with grades of Pass or higher. If a student receives Advanced Standing (i.e., College Credits) for Advanced Placement work taken in secondary school, he may, with permission, use these credits to reduce the number of subjects required for his Yale degree.

The Intensive (or Honors) Major may be allowed to reduce his Junior and Senior year programs to four courses per term. In such instances, 36 courses completed with grades of Pass or higher satisfy the requirements for the degree. As in the case of the Standard Major, a student entering with Advanced Placement work may be permitted to reduce his Yale program accordingly.

With the above noted exceptions, a student's program normally consists of five subjects per term. Most courses meet three times a week for fifty minute periods and are equivalent to three semester hours. Laboratory sessions in which a separate grade is given may be exceptions, and, in such instances, do not usually count as a portion of the customary five-course program.

Starting with the class of 1968, the semester hours of credit for each subject are recorded in the column to the right of the term grades.

DIVISIONAL MAJORS—TITLES

Division I—History, the Arts, and Letters.
Division II—Political Science and Economics.
Division III—Culture and Behavior.
Division IV—Special—usually combining studies in two fields.

SCIENCE COURSES—TITLES

Science I—Chemistry and Physics.
Science II—Geology–Astronomy, Meteorology and Oceanography.

TRANSCRIPTS

Grade Symbols:

W—Withdrew	ABX, ABP—Absent Final Examination
WF—Withdrew Failing	SAT—Satisfactory
INC, INP—Incomplete	NS—Unsatisfactory

WF, INP, and ABP count as 50 in the term's average in the numerical system.
A grade of Superior on the Departmental Examination is equivalent to Honors.

Course Titles:

Course titles and complete descriptions of the content of each course are given in the Yale College Programs of Study Bulletin, which will be forwarded to you, promptly, upon request.

PRAESES ET SOCII
UNIVERSITATIS YALENSIS

IN NOVO PORTU IN RE PUBLICA CONNECTICUTENSI OMNIBUS
AD QUOS HAE LITTERAE PERVENERINT SALUTEM IN DOMINO
SEMPITERNAM NOS PRAESES ET SOCII HUIUS UNIVERSITATIS

George Walker Bush

PRIMI HONORIS ACADEMICI CANDIDATUM AD GRADUM
TITULUMQUE ARTIUM LIBERALIUM BACCALAUREI ADMISIMUS
EIQUE CONCESSIMUS OMNIA IURA PRIVILEGIA INSIGNIA
AD HUNC HONOREM SPECTANTIA

IN CUIUS REI TESTIMONIUM HIS LITTERIS UNIVERSITATIS
SIGILLO IMPRESSIS NOS PRAESES ET SCRIBA ACADEMICUS
SUBSCRIPSIMUS IV. ID. IUN. ANNO DOMINI MDCCCCLXVIII
ET UNIVERSITATIS YALENSIS CCLXVII

SCRIBA

PRAESES

ARMED FORCES SECURITY QUESTIONNAIRE

I.—EXPLANATION

1. The interests of National Security require that all persons being considered for membership or retention in the Armed Forces be reliable, trustworthy, of good character, and of complete and unswerving loyalty to the United States. Accordingly, it is necessary for you to furnish information concerning your security qualifications. The answers which you give will be used in determining whether you are eligible for membership in the Armed Forces, in selection of your duty assignment, and for such other action as may be appropriate.

2. You are advised that in accordance with the Fifth Amendment of the Constitution of the United States you cannot be compelled to furnish any statements which you may reasonably believe may lead to your prosecution for a crime. This is the only reason for which you may avail yourself of the privilege afforded by the Fifth Amendment in refusing to answer questions under Part IV below. Claiming the Fifth Amendment will not by itself constitute sufficient grounds to exempt you from military service for reasons of security. You are not required to answer any questions in this questionnaire, the answer to which might be incriminating. If you do claim the privilege granted by the Fifth Amendment in refusing to answer any question, you should make a statement to that effect after the question involved.

II.—ORGANIZATIONS OF SECURITY SIGNIFICANCE

1. There is set forth below a list of names of organizations, groups, and movements, reported by the Attorney General of the United States as having significance in connection with the National Security. Please examine the list carefully, and note those organizations, and organizations of similar names, with which you are familiar. Then answer the questions set forth in Part IV below.

2. Your statement concerning membership or other association with one or more of the organizations named may not, of itself, cause you to be ineligible for acceptance or retention in the

Armed Forces. Your age at the time of such association, circumstances prompting it, and the extent and frequency of involvement, are all highly pertinent, and will be fully weighed. Set forth all such factors under "Remarks" below, and continue on separate attached sheets of paper if necessary.

3. If there is any doubt in your mind as to whether your name has been linked with one of the organizations named, or as to whether a particular association is "worth mentioning," make a full explanation under "Remarks."

Organizations designated by the Attorney General, pursuant to Executive Order 10450, are listed below:

Communist Party, U. S. A., its subdivisions, subsidiaries and affiliates.

Communist Political Association, its subdivisions, subsidiaries and affiliates, including—
Alabama People's Educational Association.
Florida Press and Educational League.
Oklahoma League for Political Education.
People's Educational and Press Association of Texas.
Virginia League for People's Education.

Young Communist League.

Abraham Lincoln Brigade.
Abraham Lincoln School, Chicago, Illinois.
Action Committee to Free Spain Now.
American Association for Reconstruction in Yugoslavia, Inc.
American Branch of the Federation of Greek Maritime Unions.
American Christian Nationalist Party.
American Committee for European Workers' Relief.
American Committee for Protection of Foreign Born.
American Committee for the Settlement of Jews in Birobidjan, Inc.
American Committee for Spanish Freedom.
American Committee for Yugoslav Relief, Inc.
American Committee to Survey Labor Conditions in Europe.
American Council for a Democratic Greece, formerly known as the Greek American Council; Greek American Committee for National Unity.
American Council on Soviet Relations.
American Croatian Congress.
American Jewish Labor Council.
American League Against War and Fascism.
American League for Peace and Democracy.
American National Labor Party.
American National Socialist League.
American National Socialist Party.
American Nationalist Party.
American Patriots, Inc.
American Peace Crusade.
American Peace Mobilization.
American Poles for Peace.
American Polish Labor Council.
American Polish League.
American Rescue Ship Mission (a project of the United American Spanish Aid Committee).
American-Russian Fraternal Society.
American-Russian Institute, New York (also known as the American Russian Institute for Cultural Relations with the Soviet Union).
American Russian Institute, Philadelphia.
American Russian Institute of San Francisco.
American Russian Institute of Southern California, Los Angeles.

American Slav Congress.
American Women for Peace.
American Youth Congress.
American Youth for Democracy.
Armenian Progressive League of America.
Associated Klans of America.
Association of Georgia Klans.
Association of German Nationals (Reichsdeutsche Vereinigung).
Ausland-Organization der NSDAP, Overseas Branch of Nazi Party.

Baltimore Forum.
Benjamin Davis Freedom Committee.
Black Dragon Society.
Boston School for Marxist Studies, Boston, Massachusetts.
Bridges-Robertson-Schmidt Defense Committee.
Bulgarian American People's League of the United States of America.
California Emergency Defense Committee.
California Labor School, Inc., 321 Divisadero Street, San Francisco, California.
Carpatho-Russian People's Society.
Central Council of American Women of Croatian Descent (also known as Central Council of American Croatian Women, National Council of Croatian Women).
Central Japanese Association (Beikoku Chuo Nipponjin Kai).
Central Japanese Association of Southern California.
Central Organization of the German-American National Alliance (Deutsche-Amerikanische Einheitsfront).
Cervantes Fraternal Society.
China Welfare Appeal, Inc.
Chopin Cultural Center.
Citizens Committee to Free Earl Browder.
Citizens Committee for Harry Bridges.
Citizens Committee of the Upper West Side (New York City).
Citizens Emergency Defense Conference.
Citizens Protective League.
Civil Liberties Sponsoring Committee of Pittsburgh.
Civil Rights Congress and its affiliated organizations, including Civil Rights Congress for Texas, Veterans Against Discrimination of Civil Rights Congress of New York.
Columbians.
Comite Coordinador Pro Republica Espanola.
Comite Pro Derechos Civiles.
Committee to Abolish Discrimination in Maryland.
Committee to Aid the Fighting South.
Committee to Defend the Rights and Freedom of Pittsburgh's Political Prisoners.

Committee for a Democratic Far Eastern Policy.
Committee for Constitutional and Political Freedom.
Committee for the Defense of the Pittsburgh Six.
Committee for Nationalist Action.
Committee for the Negro in the Arts.
Committee for Peace and Brotherhood Festival in Philadelphia.
Committee for the Protection of the Bill of Rights.
Committee for World Youth Friendship and Cultural Exchange.
Committee to Defend Marie Richardson.
Committee to Uphold the Bill of Rights.
Commonwealth College, Mena, Arkansas.
Congress Against Discrimination.
Congress of the Unemployed.
Connecticut Committee to Aid Victims of the Smith Act.
Connecticut State Youth Conference.
Congress of American Revolutionary Writers.
Congress of American Women.
Council on African Affairs.
Council of Greek Americans.
Council for Jobs, Relief, and Housing.
Council for Pan-American Democracy.
Croatian Benevolent Fraternity.
Dai Nippon Butoku Kai (Military Virtue Society of Japan or Military Art Society of Japan).
Daily Worker Press Club.
Daniels Defense Committee.
Dante Alighieri Society (Between 1935 and 1940).
Dennis Defense Committee.
Detroit Youth Assembly.
East Bay Peace Committee.
Elsinore Progressive League.
Emergency Conference to Save Spanish Refugees (founding body of the North American Spanish Aid Committee).
Everybody's Committee to Outlaw War.

Families of the Baltimore Smith Act Victims.
Families of the Smith Act Victims.
Federation of Italian War Veterans in the U. S. A., Inc. (Associazione Nazionale Combattenti Italiani, Federazione degli Stati Uniti d'America).
Finnish-American Mutual Aid Society.
Florida Press and Educational League.
Frederick Douglass Educational Center.
Freedom Stage, Inc.
Friends of the New Germany (Freunde des Neuen Deutschlands).
Friends of the Soviet Union.

Garibaldi American Fraternal Society.
George Washington Carver School, New York City.
German-American Bund (Amerikadeutscher Volksbund).

DD FORM 98
1 Jun 59

PREVIOUS EDITION OF THIS FORM WILL
BE USED UNTIL STOCK IS EXHAUSTED.

Page 1

ATCH 7

German-American Republican League.
German-American Vocational League *Deutsche-Amerikanische Berufsgemeinschaft*.
Guardian Club.

Harlem Trade Union Council.
Hawaii Civil Liberties Committee.
Heimusha Kai, also known as Nokubei Heieki, Gimusha Kai, Zaibei Nihonjin, Heiyaku Gimusha Kai and Zaibei Heimusha Kai *(Japanese Residing in America Military Conscripts Association)*.
Hellenic-American Brotherhood.
Hinode Kai *(Imperial Japanese Reservists)*.
Hinomaru Kai *(Rising Sun Flag Society)—a group of Japanese War Veterans)*.
Hokubei Zaigo Shoke Dan *(North American Reserve Officers Association)*.
Hollywood Writers Mobilization for Defense.
Hungarian-American Council for Democracy.
Hungarian Brotherhood.

Idaho Pension Union.
Independent Party *(Seattle, Washington)*.
Independent People's Party.
Industrial Workers of the World.
International Labor Defense.
International Workers Order, its subdivisions, subsidiaries and affiliates.

Japanese Association of America.
Japanese Overseas Central Society *(Kaigai Dobo Chuo Kai)*.
Japanese Overseas Convention, Tokyo, Japan, 1940.
Japanese Protective Association *(Recruiting Organization)*.
Jefferson School of Social Science, New York City.
Jewish Culture Society.
Jewish People's Committee.
Jewish People's Fraternal Order.
Jikyoku Iin Kai *(The Committee for the Crisis)*.
Johnson-Forest Group.
Johnsonites.
Joint Anti-Fascist Refugee Committee.
Joint Council of Progressive Italian-Americans, Inc.
Joseph Weydemeyer School of Social Science, St. Louis, Missouri.

Kibei Seinen Kai *(Association of U. S. citizens of Japanese ancestry who have returned to America after studying in Japan)*.
Knights of the White Camelia.
Ku Klux Klan.
Kyffhaeuser, also known as Kyffhaeuser League *(Kyffhaeuser Bund)*, Kyffhaeuser Fellowship *(Kyffhaeuser Kameradschaft)*,
Kyffhaeuser War Relief *(Kyffhaeuser Kriegshilfswerk)*.

Labor Council for Negro Rights.
Labor Research Association, Inc.
Labor Youth League.
League for Common Sense.
League of American Writers.
Lictor Society *(Italian Black Shirts)*.

Macedonian-American People's League.
Mario Morganti Circle.
Marione Labor Committee to Defend Al Lannon.
Maryland Congress Against Discrimination.
Massachusetts Committee for the Bill of Rights.
Massachusetts Minute Women for Peace *(not connected with the Minute Women of the U. S. A. Inc.)*.
Maurice Braverman Defense Committee.
Michigan Civil Rights Federation.

Michigan Council for Peace.
Michigan School of Social Science.

Nanka Teikoku Gunyudan *(Imperial Military Friends Group or Southern California War Veterans)*.
National Association of Mexican Americans *(also known as Asociacion Nacional Mexico-Americana)*.
National Blue Star Mothers of America (not to be confused with the Blue Star Mothers of America organized in February 1942).
National Committee for the Defense of Political Prisoners.
National Committee for Freedom of the Press.
National Committee to Win Amnesty for Smith Act Victims.
National Committee to Win the Peace.
National Conference on American Policy in China and the Far East *(a Conference called by the Committee for a Democratic Far Eastern Policy)*.
National Council of Americans of Croatian Descent.
National Council of American-Soviet Friendship.
National Federation for Constitutional Liberties.
National Labor Conference for Peace.
National Negro Congress.
National Negro Labor Council.
Nationalist Action League.
Nationalist Party of Puerto Rico.
Nature Friends of America *(Since 1935)*.
Negro Labor Victory Committee.
New Committee for Publications.
Nichibei Kogyo Kaisha *(The Great Fujii Theatre)*.
North American Committee to Aid Spanish Democracy.
North American Spanish Aid Committee.
North Philadelphia Forum.
Northwest Japanese Association.

Ohio School of Social Sciences.
Oklahoma Committee to Defend Political Prisoners.
Oklahoma League for Political Education.
Original Southern Klans, Incorporated.

Pacific Northwest Labor School, Seattle, Washington.
Palo Alto Peace Club.
Partido del Pueblo of Panama *(operating in the Canal Zone)*.
Peace Information Center.
Peace Movement of Ethiopia.
People's Drama, Inc.
People's Educational and Press Association of Texas.
People's Educational Association *(Incorporated under the name Los Angeles Educational Association, Inc.)*, also known as People's Educational Center, People's University, People's School.
People's Institute of Applied Religion.
Peoples Programs *(Seattle, Washington)*.
People's Radio Foundation, Inc.
People's Rights Party.
Philadelphia Labor Committee for Negro Rights.
Philadelphia School of Social Science and Art.
Photo-League *(New York City)*.
Pittsburgh Arts Club.
Political Prisoners' Welfare Committee.
Polonia Society of the IWO.
Progressive German-Americans, also known as Progressive German-Americans of Chicago.
Proletarian Party of America.
Protestant War Veterans of the United States, Inc.
Provisional Committee of Citizens for Peace, Southwest Area.
Provisional Committee on Latin American Affairs.
Provisional Committee to Abolish Discrimination in the State of Maryland.
Puerto Rican Comite Pro Libertades Civiles (CLC).

Puertorriquenos Unidos *(Puerto Ricans United)*.

Quad City Committee for Peace.
Queensbridge Tenants League.

Revolutionary Workers League.
Romanian-American Fraternal Society.
Russian American Society, Inc.

Sakura Kai *(Patriotic Society, or Cherry Association composed of veterans of Russo-Japanese War)*.
Samuel Adams School, Boston, Mass.
Santa Barbara Peace Forum.
Schappes Defense Committee.
Schneiderman-Darcy Defense Committee.
School of Jewish Studies, New York City.
Seattle Labor School, Seattle, Washington.
Serbian-American Fraternal Society.
Serbian Vidovdan Council.
Shinto Temples *(Limited to State Shinto abolished in 1945)*.
Silver Shirt Legion of America.
Slavic Council of Southern California.
Slovak Workers Society.
Slovenian-American National Council.
Socialist Workers Party, including American Committee for European Workers' Relief.
Sokoku Kai *(Fatherland Society)*.
Southern Negro Youth Congress.
Suiko Sha *(Reserve Officers Association, Los Angeles)*.
Syracuse Women for Peace.

Tom Paine School of Social Science, Philadelphia, Pennsylvania.
Tom Paine School of Westchester, New York.
Trade Union Committee for Peace.
Trade Unionists for Peace.
Tri-State Negro Trade Union Council.

Ukrainian-American Fraternal Union.
Union of American Croatians.
Union of New York Veterans.
United American Spanish Aid Committee.
United Committee of Jewish Societies and Landsmanschaft Federations, also known as Coordination Committee of Jewish Landsmanschaften and Fraternal Organizations.
United Committee of South Slavic Americans.
United Defense Council of Southern California.
United Harlem Tenants and Consumers Organization.
United May Day Committee.
United Negro and Allied Veterans of America.

Veterans Against Discrimination of Civil Rights Congress of New York.
Veterans of the Abraham Lincoln Brigade.
Virginia League for People's Education.
Voice of Freedom Committee.

Walt Whitman School of Social Science, Newark, New Jersey.
Washington Bookshop Association.
Washington Committee to Defend the Bill of Rights.
Washington Committee for Democratic Action.
Washington Commonwealth Federation.
Washington Pension Union.
Wisconsin Conference on Social Legislation.
Workers Alliance *(since April 1936)*.

Yiddisher Kultur Farband.
Yugoslav-American Cooperative Home, Inc.
Yugoslav Seamen's Club, Inc.

III.—INSTRUCTIONS

1. Set forth an explanation for each answer checked "Yes" under question 2 below under "Remarks." Attach as many extra sheets as necessary for a full explanation, signing or initialing each extra sheet.

2. Title 18, U. S. Code, Section 1001, provides, in pertinent part: "Whoever . . . falsifies, conceals or covers up . . . a material fact, or makes any false . . . statements . . . or makes or uses any false writing . . . shall be fined not more than $10,000 or imprisoned not more than 5 years, or both." Any false, fraudulent or fictitious response to the questions under Part IV below may give rise to criminal liability under Title 18,

U. S. C., Section 1001. You are advised, however, that you will not incur such liability unless you supply inaccurate statements with knowledge of their untruthfulness. You are therefore advised that before you sign this form and turn it in to Selective Service or military authorities, you should be sure that it is truthful; that detailed explanations are given for each "Yes" answer under question 2 of Part IV below, and that details given are as full and complete as you can make them.

3. In stating details, it is permissible, if your memory is hazy on particular points, to use such expressions as, "I think," "in my opinion," "I believe," or "to the best of my recollection."

Page 2

IV.—QUESTIONS

(for each answer checked "Yes" under question 2, set forth a full explanation under "Remarks" below).

	YES	NO		YES	NO
1. I have read the list of names of organizations, groups, and movements set forth under Part II of this form and the explanation which precedes it.	✓		j. Have you ever contributed money to any of the organizations, groups, or movements listed?		✓
2. Concerning the list of organizations, groups and movements set forth under Part II above:			k. Have you ever contributed services to any of the organizations, groups, or movements listed?		✓
a. Are you now a member of any of the organizations, groups, or movements listed?		✓	l. Have you ever subscribed to any publication of any of the organizations, groups, or movements listed?		✓
b. Have you ever been a member of any of the organizations, groups, or movements listed?		✓	m. Have you ever been employed by a foreign government or any agency thereof?		✓
c. Are you now employed by any of the organizations, groups, or movements listed?		✓	n. Are you now a member of the Communist Party of any foreign country?		✓
d. Have you ever been employed by any of the organizations, groups, or movements listed?		✓	o. Have you ever been a member of the Communist Party of any foreign country?		✓
e. Have you ever attended any meeting of any of the organizations, groups, or movements listed?		✓	p. Have you ever been the subject of a loyalty or security hearing?		✓
f. Have you ever attended any social gathering of any of the organizations, groups, or movements listed?		✓			
g. Have you ever attended any gathering of any kind sponsored by any of the organizations, groups, or movements listed?		✓	q. Are you now or have you ever been a member of any organization, association, movement, group or combination of persons not on the Attorney General's list which advocates the overthrow of our constitutional form of government, or which has adopted the policy of advocating or approving the commission of acts of force or violence to deny other persons their rights under the Constitution of the United States, or which seeks to alter the form of government of the United States by unconstitutional means?		✓
h. Have you prepared material for publication by any of the organizations, groups, or movements listed?		✓			
i. Have you ever corresponded with any of the organizations, groups, or movements listed or with any publication thereof?		✓	r. Have you ever been known by any other lost name than that used in signing this questionnaire?		✓

REMARKS

none - GWB

REMARKS (Continued)

CERTIFICATION

In regard to any part of this questionnaire concerning which I have had any question as to the meaning, I have requested and have obtained a complete explanation. I certify that the statements made by me under Part IV above and on any supplemental pages hereto attached, are full, true, and correct.

TYPED FULL NAME OF PERSON MAKING CERTIFICATION	SERVICE NUMBER (If any)	SIGNATURE OF PERSON MAKING CERTIFICATION
GEORGE WALKER BUSH	AF 26230638	*George Walker Bush*
TYPED NAME OF WITNESS	DATE	SIGNATURE OF WITNESS
THOMAS M. SHELLSFEAR JR.	28 May 1968	*Thos. M. Shellsfear Jr.*

STAPLE HERE

NACC Use Only	DEPARTMENT OF DEFENSE	REQUEST DATE
	NATIONAL AGENCY CHECK REQUEST	28 May 1968

1. LAST NAME - FIRST NAME - MIDDLE NAME	2. SEX
BUSH GEORGE WALKER	Male

3. ALIAS(ES) AND ALL FORMER NAME(S)	4. SOCIAL SECURITY NUMBER
None	▓▓▓▓▓▓▓

5. MONTH, DAY, YEAR OF BIRTH	6. PLACE OF BIRTH	7. SERVICE NUMBER
July 6 1946	New Haven, New Haven, Conn. USA	AF 26230638

8. a. SECURITY PROGRAM
- ☐ MILITARY
- ☒ CIVILIAN
- ☐ INDUSTRIAL

RETURN RESULTS TO:

14TH AF (14CTG-S)
GUNTER AFB, ALABAMA 36114

b. ☒ LOCAL FILES CHECKED WITH FAVORABLE RESULTS

c. INITIATOR OF REQUEST

9. RELATIVES	10. DATE AND PLACE OF BIRTH	11. PRESENT ADDRESS	12. CITIZENSHIP
a. FATHER George Herbert Walker Bush	June 12, 1924 Plymouth, Mass 22360	5000 Longmont #8 Houston, Texas 77027	US
b. MOTHER (Full Maiden Name) Barbara (NMN) Bush, Nee Pierce AKA Mrs. George Herbert Walker Bush.	Jun 8, 1925, New York, N.Y.10025	5000 Longmont #8 Houston, Tex.77027	US
c. SPOUSE (Full Maiden Name) None			

13. RESIDENCES (List all from 18th birthday or during past 15 years, whichever is shorter. If under 18, list present and most recent addresses.)

a. FROM	b. TO	c. NUMBER AND STREET	d. CITY	e. STATE & ZIP
Dec 52	Dec 56	1412 West Ohio	Midland 79701	Texas
Dec 56	Jun 59	2703 Sentinel	Midland 79701	Texas
Jan 59	Jan 67	5525 Briar Dr	Houston 77027	Texas
Jan 67	Present	5000 Longmont #8	Houston 77027	Texas
Sep 61	Jun 64	Phillips Academy (Boarding School)	Andover 01810	Mass.
Sep 64	May 68	1385 Yale Station	New Haven 06520	Conn.

14. EMPLOYMENT (List all from 18th birthday or during past 15 years, whichever is shorter. If under 18, list present and most recent employment)

a. FROM	b. TO	c. EMPLOYER	d. PLACE
Jun 62	Aug 62	Baker, Botts, Sheppard & Coates,	809 Travis,Houston,Tex.77002
Jun 63	Aug 63	XX Ranch-located approx.	8 Mi.Southeast of Williams,Arizona
Jun 65	Aug 65	Circle Oil Co.	Lake Charles, Louisiana 70601
Jun 66	Aug 66	Sears & Roebuck	4201 Main, Houston, Tex.77002
Jun 67	Aug 67	Rauscher, Pierce Securities,	1001 Main, Houston, Texas 77002

15. LAST CIVILIAN SCHOOL

a. FROM	b. TO	c. NAME	d. PLACE
Sep 64	Present	Yale University	1385 Yale Station,New Haven, Conn. 06052

YES	NO	16. ("Yes" answers must be explained in Item 18, below.)
	X	a. Is the subject an alien or naturalized citizen?
	X	b. Has the subject any foreign connections, employment or military service?
X		c. Has the subject travelled or resided abroad other than for the U.S. Government?
	X	d. Has the subject had employment requiring a security clearance or investigation?
	X	e. Is the subject now or has he ever been in the Federal Civil Service or Armed Forces?
	X	f. Has the subject qualified DD Form 398, 98, 48-1, or similar security form?
	X	g. Has the subject ever been addicted to drugs?

17. REQUEST DATA

a. REQUESTER DESIGNATOR		b. REASON
ARMY	DASA	BASIC TRAINEE
NAVY	DCA	PRE-COMMISSION
☒ AIR FORCE	DCAA	NUCLEAR
OSD	DIA	BI
JCS	DSA	☒ SECRET
NSA	DISCO	CLEARANCE

18. REMARKS (If additional space is needed, continue on plain paper.)

ITEM 14: Aug 67-Present: Unemployed: May be verified by: Mr. Terry Johnson
Holland Road
Far Hills, N. J. 07391

ITEM 16: Aug 59-Sep 59 Individual was in Scotland on vacation.

DD FORM 1584
1 DEC 66

ATCH 10³

DEPARTMENTS OF THE ARMY AND THE AIR FORCE
NATIONAL GUARD BUREAU

APPLICATION FOR TRAINING

PART I
GENERAL INFORMATION
(To be completed by applicant)

1. LAST NAME FIRST NAME MIDDLE NAME	2. GRADE	3. AFSN	4. DATE OF BIRTH
BUSH GEORGE WALKER	AB	AF26230638	6 July 1946

5. MAILING ADDRESS
5000 Longmont #8
Houston, Texas 77027

6. UNIT OF ASSIGNMENT AND ADDRESS
147th Fighter Group
P. O. Box 34567
Houston, Texas 77034

7. TRAINING REQUESTED - COURSE NUMBER - TITLE
P-V44 -A (111103) - Undergraduate Pilot Training (T-31/T-37/T-38)

8. COURSE LOCATION Craig, Laredo, Laughlin, Moody, Randolph, Reese, Vance, Webb, Williams AF Bases

9. COURSE DURATION Approximately 53 Weeks.

10. DESIRE TO ENTER TRAINING (Date)
November 1968

11. WILL ACCEPT ANY DATE UNTIL (Date)
Released from consideration

12. AIRMEN ONLY
THE ABOVE REQUESTED COURSE IS PART OF PREVIOUSLY ALLOCATED NON PRIOR SERVICE QUOTA

13. YES | 14. NO
N/A

15. SIGNATURE OF APPLICANT
George Walker Bush

16. DATE
28 May 1968

PART II
(To be completed by custodian of Field Personnel Records)

17. CIVILIAN OCCUPATION	18. AIR TECHNICIAN	19. EDUCATIONAL LEVEL
Student	☐ YES ☒ NO	BA

20. AIRMAN QUALIFYING EXAMINATION (AQE)
G-85, A-95, M-40, E-60

21. PRIMARY AFSC DATE AWARDED
70010

22. ADDITIONAL AFSC'S
None

23. DUTY AFSC
70230

24. TMSD   TFCSD
27 May 1968

25. PAY DATE
27 May 1968

26. SECURITY CLEARANCE (Specify Interim or Final)
Pending

27. MARITAL STATUS
Single

28. NUMBER DEPENDENTS, (E-1 thru E-4)
None

29. OVER 4 YEARS ENLISTED SERVICE
(0-1 thru 0-3) ☐ YES ☒ NO

30. FLYING STATUS
☐ YES ☒ NO

31. AERO RATING
Non-Rated

32. FLYING HOURS

	JET	
CONV	
FIRST PILOT	

33. PHYSICAL PROFILE SERIAL (Airman) - DIAGNOSIS OF DEFECTS (If a digit other than '1' is recorded. Use block '46' if more space is needed)

P	U	L	H	E	S	SUFFIX
1	1	1	1	1	1	Y

34. SERVICE SCHOOLS ATTENDED   COURSE NUMBER   TITLE   DATE COMPLETED
Scheduled to attend BMT 14 July 1968

I certify to the accuracy of the above information and that all applicable provisions of AFM 50-5 and ANGR 53-05 have been complied with.

| 28 May 1968 | WILLIE J. HOOPER, CAPTAIN | |
| DATE | NAME, GRADE AND TITLE TYPED
TexANG, CHIEF, CBPO | SIGNATURE |

NGB FORM 85
31 OCT 66

(This Form replaces NGB Form 65, dated 22 Mar 64, which is obsolete and will not be used)

ATCH 13

PART III
(To be completed by Comptroller)

	CURRENT FISCAL YEAR	CARRY-OVER
35. PAY AND ALLOWANCES	6648.96	
36. FICA (Employers)	169.50	
37. STUDENTS TRAVEL A. MODE OF TRAVEL TP B.-NR DAYS ROUND TRIPS 1	57.42	
38. HOUSEHOLD GOODS OR EXCESS BAGGAGE		
39. DEPENDENTS TRAVEL		
40. CLOTHING	300.00	
41. OTHER (Identify)		
42. ESTIMATED NUMBER OF DAYS ACCRUED 30	468.20	
43. TOTAL COST	7644.08	
44. PAY AND ALLOWANCES PER MONTH (Including FICA)	(Per day if less than one month)	
45. VERIFICATION BY COMPTROLLER		

(SIGNATURE)

WILLIE J. HOOPER JR., Captain
TexANG, Chief, CBPO
(NAME AND RANK-TYPED)

46. REMARKS

None

FOR USE BY NGB

DOCUMENT NUMBER	DATE
AMOUNT-CURRENT FY $	

NGB FORM 65
31 OCT 66   (This Form replaces NGB Form 65, dated 22 Mar 64, which is obsolete and will not be used)

GPCR

Statement of Interview

Whom It May Concern

1. Pursuant to the authority contained in AFKR 36-02, an interview of George Walker Bush was conducted in my office on 27 May 1968.

2. Airman Bush was born 6 July 1946 in New Haven, Connecticut. He attends Yale University and is scheduled to graduate in June of this year.

3. Applicant is a quiet, intelligent young man who has the interest, motivation, and knowledge necessary to become a commissioned officer in today's Air Force and Air National Guard flying programs.

4. It is highly recommended that Airman Bush be accepted for pilot training.

WALTER B. STAUDT, Colonel, TexANG
Commander

STATEMENT OF INTENT

I, GEORGE WALKER BUSH, UPON SUCCESSFUL COMPLETION OF PILOT TRAINING
PLAN TO RETURN TO MY UNIT AND FULFILL MY OBLIGATION TO THE UTMOST
OF MY ABILITY. I HAVE APPLIED FOR PILOT TRAINING WITH THE GOAL OF
MAKING FLYING A LIFETIME PURSUIT AND I BELIEVE I CAN BEST ACCOMPLISH
THIS TO MY OWN SATISFACTION BY SERVING AS A MEMBER OF THE AIR NATIONAL
GUARD AS LONG AS POSSIBLE.

George Walker Bush
GEORGE WALKER BUSH

CERTIFICATE OF UNDERSTANDING

I, GEORGE WALKER BUSH, UNDERSTAND THAT FAILURE TO SATISFACTORILY
COMPLETE THIS ENTIRE COURSE OF PILOT TRAINING WILL RESULT IN MY
BEING DISCHARGED FROM APPOINTMENT AS A RESERVE OF THE AIR FORCE
AND WITHDRAWAL OF FEDERAL RECOGNITION.

George Walker Bush
GEORGE WALKER BUSH

Dear Sirs:

Thank you for your quick response —
I hope the following form is
adequate for reinvestigation —

Sincerely

[signature]

...TEMENT FOR ENLISTMENT IN THE NATIONAL G...

DATE	PLACE
27 May 68	Ellington AFB, Texas

1. In connection with my enlistment in the National Guard this date, the following is a complete and accurate record of all violations and offenses (including minor traffic violations) for which I have been arrested (regardless of the subsequent dispositions of my case) by civil law enforcement officials. (Prior service personnel list only those violations occurring during and/or subsequent to last period of honorable active service, except for offenses previously revealed. If none, so state.

(For each answer checked YES set forth a full explanation under REMARKS, Item 1e below)

YES NO

☒ ☐ a. Have you ever been arrested, charged or held by Federal, State or other law enforcement authorities for any violation of any Federal Law, State Law, County or Municipal law, regulation or ordinance?

☐ ☒ b. Have you ever been convicted of a felony or any other offense, or adjudicated a youthful offender or juvenile delinquent (including violations of local ordinance)?

☐ ☒ c. Have you ever been imprisoned, under sentence of any court?

☐ ☒ d. Are you now or have you ever been on suspended sentence, parole, probation or are you awaiting final action on charges against you?

e. REMARKS: (Enter full explanation for those questions answered "YES".)

REFERENCE ITEM	OFFENSE	DATE AND PLACE	DISPOSITION
a	Disorderly conduct	Dec66, Yale Univ.	Charges Dropped

2. Have you ever been rejected for enlistment or induction in any of the Armed Forces or been discharged from previous service under other than Honorable conditions, under personnel security regulations or by reason of unsuitability or undesirable habits or traits or character, or for medical reasons? YES ☐ NO ☒ (If answer is YES give details below).

SERVICE	DATE AND PLACE	CAUSE

3. I have read or had explained to me the following cited paragraphs of the directives indicated below which sets forth the criteria (or reasons) for discharge and types of discharges and certify that I have ☐ Have ☒ (initial one) engaged in disloyal or subversive activities as defined therein.

CHECK ONE	MILITARY SERVICE	PARAGRAPHS	DIRECTIVES
☐	Army National Guard	14 and 19	AR 604-10
☒	Air National Guard	6 and 7	AFR 35-62

4. Indicate below the number, relationship and age of persons dependent on you for support. If none so state

RELATIONSHIP	AGE
Single	

5. I certify that the recruiting officer has informed me that should I willingly conceal any information required above I may later be subject to disciplinary action or discharge upon it discovery.

TYPED FIRST, MIDDLE, LAST NAME	SIGNATURE
GEORGE WALKER BUSH	George Walker Bush
TYPED NAME UNIT COMMANDER OR AUTHORIZED REPRESENTATIVE (WITNESS)	SIGNATURE
WILLIE J HOOPER JR, Capt, Asst Admin Officer	

NGB FORM 21
17 AUG 66

APPLICATION & APPOINTMENT AS RESERVES OF THE AIR FORCE OR USAF WITHOUT COMPONENT

☐ APPOINTMENT AS A RESERVE OF THE AIR FORCE ☒ FEDERAL RECOGNITION AND APPOINTMENT AS A RESERVE OF THE AIR FORCE ☐ APPOINTMENT AS USAF WITHOUT COMPONENT

INSTRUCTIONS:
1. COMPLETE ON TYPEWRITER, IF PRACTICABLE, IF NOT, PRINT PROPER NAMES AND WRITE CLEARLY.
2. THIS FORM MUST BE EXECUTED IN TRIPLICATE AND EACH COPY MUST BE SIGNED.
3. CHECK THE TYPE OF APPOINTMENT, UNDER FORM TITLE, FOR WHICH YOU ARE APPLYING.
4. WHEN ALLOTTED SPACES ARE INSUFFICIENT, STATE ITEM NO. UNDER REMARKS AND COMPLETE APPROPRIATE EXPLANATION.

TO: 147th Fighter Group, Ellington AFB, Texas   DATE 28 May 1968

FROM: (Last name - first - middle)
BUSH, GEORGE WALKER

(For use by selecting and appointing authorities only)
SERVICE NO. | GRADE | AFSC

1. ADDRESS (Number, Street, City, State, Zip Code)
PERMANENT 5000 Longmont #8
Houston, Texas 77027

MAILING (If other than permanent)
Same as permanent

2. BIRTH: (Day, Month, Year; City, State, Country)
6 July 1946, New Haven Conn. USA

4. MARITAL STATUS (Check one)
☒ SINGLE ☐ MARRIED ☐ SEPARATED ☐ DIVORCED ☐ WIDOWED

5. DEPENDENTS (Number completely dependent upon you other than wife): 0

6. SOCIAL SECURITY NO.

3. SELECTIVE SERVICE NO. AND ADDRESS OF LOCAL SS BOARD
41-62-46-1480
Texas Local Board #294
Room 413, 201 Fannin St.
Houston, Texas 77002

7. CITIZENSHIP

A. U.S. CITIZEN
YES X | NO

B. HOW OBTAINED
BIRTH X | NATURALIZATION

C. IF YOU ARE A UNITED STATES CITIZEN BY OWN NATURALIZATION, STATE DATE, NUMBER OF CERTIFICATE, AND COURT
N/A

8. I UNDERSTAND I AM BEING CONSIDERED FOR APPOINTMENT:
☐ TO FILL AN ACTIVE FORCE REQUIREMENT AND AGREE TO REMAIN ON ACTIVE DUTY FOR THE PERIOD SPECIFIED IN APPROPRIATE REGULATIONS (AFR 45-36, AFR 45-48, and AFR 36-51).
MY GEOGRAPHICAL PREFERENCE OF ASSIGNMENT IS _____
I WILL BE AVAILABLE TO ENTER ACTIVE DUTY ON _____ , ☐ I DO ☐ I DO NOT
REQUIRE AT LEAST 30 DAYS NOTICE PRIOR TO ENTRY ON ACTIVE DUTY.
☒ TO FILL AN AUTHORIZED POSITION VACANCY IN THE READY RESERVE.

9. NAME, RELATIONSHIP, AND ADDRESS OF PERSON TO BE NOTIFIED IN CASE OF EMERGENCY
GEORGE H. W. BUSH (Father)
5000 Longmont #8, Houston, Texas 77027

EDUCATION

TYPE OF SCHOOL	NAME OF SCHOOL	DATES ATTENDED FROM (D/M/Y)	TO (D/M/Y)	MAJOR SUBJECT	NO. YRS. COMPL.	GRADUATE YES	NO	TYPE OF DEGREE
SECONDARY AND OTHER	Phillips Academy Andover	12/5/61	12/6/64	General	3	X		Diploma
COLLEGE	Yale University	12/9/64	12/6/68	History	4	X		Jun 68
POST-GRADUATE								
INTERN-SHIP								
RESIDENCY								
FELLOW-SHIP								
MILITARY								

11. OTHER SUBJECTS SPECIALIZED IN (Include certification by American Specialty Boards and Date of Certification).

N/A

12. PHYSICIANS ONLY
☐ I DO ☐ I DO NOT DESIRE TRAINING IN AVIATION MEDICINE

13. CHRONOLOGICAL STATEMENT OF SERVICE AND TRAINING IN THE AIR FORCE, ARMY, NAVY, MARINE CORPS, OR ANY OF THE COMPONENTS THEREOF, UNITED STATES AIR FORCE, MILITARY, OR NAVAL ACADEMY, OR RESERVE OFFICERS TRAINING CORPS.

DATES FROM–	TO–	HIGHEST GRADE	ORGANIZATION (Type and Service)	DUTY	SERVICE NO.	ACTIVE OR INACTIVE
27 May 68	Present		147th Fighter Gp, TexANG		AF25230638	Active

14. ARE YOU PRESENTLY A MEMBER OF ANY OF THE SERVICES ENUMERATED IN ITEM 13, ABOVE? ☒ YES ☐ NO. IF SO, STATE:
147th Fighter Group (TexANG)
Ellington AFB, Texas

15. WERE ALL DISCHARGES GRANTED UNDER HONORABLE CONDITIONS? ☐ YES ☐ NO   N/A

16. WERE YOU EVER REJECTED FOR ANY OF THE SERVICES ENUMERATED UNDER ITEM 13, ABOVE? ☐ YES ☒ NO

17. IF ANSWER TO ITEM 16 IS YES, STATE WHEN AND WHERE REJECTED, AND CAUSE.
N/A

18. CHRONOLOGICAL STATEMENT OF CIVILIAN EMPLOYMENT, INCLUDING PART TIME. IF ADDITIONAL SPACE IS REQUIRED, USE A SHEET OF PAPER THIS SIZE AND ATTACH TO APPLICATION.

(From–To) (Day, month, year)	EMPLOYED BY (Give name, street and number, city, and State)		MONTHLY SALARY
5/6/52 to 21/8/62	Baker Botts Sheppard, Coates, Esperson Bldg, Houston, Tex.		200.00
POSITION & DUTIES Messenger – Runner for Firm		REASON FOR TERMINATION Return to School	
6/6/63 to 21/8/63	Jack Greenway, XX Ranch, Williams, Arizona		200.00
POSITION & DUTIES Ranch Hand – Normal Ranch Duties		REASON FOR TERMINATION Return to School	
5/6/65 to 31/8/65	Circle Oil Co., Lake Charles, Louisiana		375.00
POSITION & DUTIES Roustabout – Oil Field Work		REASON FOR TERMINATION Return to School	
1/6/66 to 25/8/66	Sears Roebuck, 4201 Main, Houston, Texas		212.00
POSITION & DUTIES Salesman – Sold Sporting Goods		REASON FOR TERMINATION Return to School	

19. HAVE YOU EVER BEEN ARRESTED, INDICTED, OR CONVICTED FOR ANY VIOLATION OF CIVIL OR MILITARY LAW, INCLUDING MINOR TRAFFIC VIOLATIONS?
☒ YES ☐ NO. IF SO, STATE NAME AND PLACE OF COURT, NATURE OF OFFENSE, DATE, AND DISPOSITION OF CASE.
Arrested for misdemeanor in New Haven, Conn, December 1966, charge dismissed.
Two speeding tickets, two negligent collisions, Houston Traffic Court, Houston, Texas.

20. ARE YOU A CONSCIENTIOUS OBJECTOR?
☐ YES ☒ NO

21. ARE YOU NOW, OR HAVE YOU EVER BEEN AFFILIATED WITH ANY ORGANIZATION OR MOVEMENT THAT SEEKS TO ALTER OUR FORM OF GOVERNMENT BY UNCONSTITUTIONAL MEANS, OR SYMPATHETICALLY ASSOCIATED WITH ANY SUCH ORGANIZATION, MOVEMENT, OR MEMBERS THEREOF? ☐ YES ☒ NO. IF SO, DESCRIBE.

22. ARE THERE ANY OTHER UNFAVORABLE INCIDENTS IN YOUR LIFE WHICH YOU BELIEVE MAY REFLECT UPON YOUR LOYALTY TO THE UNITED STATES GOVERNMENT OR UPON YOUR ABILITY TO PERFORM THE DUTIES WHICH YOU MAY BE CALLED UPON TO UNDERTAKE?
☐ YES ☒ NO. IF SO, DESCRIBE.

REMARKS (Use additional sheet if necessary)
ITEM 18 Cont'd:
2/6/67 to 25/8/67: James L. Bayless, 901 First City Nat'l Bank, Houston, Texas
$250.00 – Bookkeeper – Return to School

I CERTIFY THAT THE ABOVE ANSWERS ARE TRUE AND CORRECT TO THE BEST OF MY KNOWLEDGE AND BELIEF:

PRINTED OR TYPE NAME (First, middle, and last names)
GEORGE WALKER BUSH

SIGNATURE (First, middle, and last names)
George Walker Bush

DISPOSITION FORM
(AR 340-15)

REFERENCE OR OFFICE SYMBOL	SUBJECT
AGTEX-AP	Pet Trainee application

TO	FROM	DATE	CMT 1
Maj Robinson Gen Rose	Sgt Bivens	5 Jun 68	

Approved / Disapproved

Sgt Bivens
to Personnel
Approved

DA FORM 2496 FEB 62 REPLACES DD FORM 96, EXISTING SUPPLIES OF WHICH WILL BE ISSUED AND USED UNTIL 1 FEB 63 UNLESS SOONER EXHAUSTED.

COORDINATION AND FILE COPY

Ltr, Hq 147th Ftr Gp, dtd 29 May 68, Subj: Preview and Grade Determination (BUSH, George Walker)

1st Ind (AGTEX-AF)   10 June 1968

OAC, State of Texas, Austin, Texas 78703

TO: NGB (NG-AFPMO).

Recommend Approval

FOR THE ADJUTANT GENERAL OF TEXAS

JAMES M. ROSE   15 Atch
Brig General, TexANG   1-15 n/c
Asst Adjutant General-Air

AIR MAIL

Name of Originator & Typist's Initials   Phone Ext. 71   Memo For Record ☑ None ☐ See Reverse   Date 10 June

Return in action agency for signature if checked.

AGTEX - ANG Form Nov 64 3

(AFPMRDS)   22 Aug 68

Waiver of Arrest

Chief, National Guard Bureau (NG-AFPMO)
Wash DC 20310

1. Waiver of arrest at New Haven, Connecticut, in Dec 66, is granted
to Amn George W. Bush, AF26230638, for the purpose of accepting an
appointment as a Reserve of the Air Force (ANGUS). The charge of
disorderly conduct was nol prossed.

2. Favorable BI, File 10D51-1793, was completed 20 Aug 68, by OSI
District 10, and is filed at Hq USAF (AFISISA4I), Bldg T-E, Wash DC
20333.

FOR THE CHIEF OF STAFF

DEE J. BUTLER, Lt Col, USAFa
Directorate of Personnel
  Resources & Distribution

DEPARTMENT OF THE AIR FORCE

HEADQUARTERS 31ST AIR DIVISION (ADC)

OKLAHOMA CITY AIR FORCE STATION

OKLAHOMA CITY, OKLAHOMA 73150

SPECIAL ORDER   12 July 1968
AA- 633

Under the provisions of Title 32, US Code, Section 307, and pursuant
to authority contained in ANGR's 36-02, 36-03, 36-04, as amended and
by the direction of the Secretary of the Air Force, a board of officers
is appointed to examine and report upon the fitness for Federal
Recognition and Promotion of such ANG personnel of the State of Texas
as may be properly brought before it. The following are appointed
members of this board:

BRIGGEN ROBERT L POU, JR, FG651005, Hq TexANG, Camp Mabry, Austin, Texas.
COLONEL NIVEN K. CRANFILL, FR8125, USAF, Hq 12th AF, w/perm duty stn 136th
Air Rflg Wg, Hensley Fld, Dallas, Texas (with concurrence of Commander
concerned).
COLONEL CHARLES A FRANCIS, FG923394, ANG, Hq TexANG, Camp Mabry, Austin,
Texas.
COLONEL CHARLES A QUIST, JR, FG670433, TexANG, Hq 149th Ftr Gp, Kelly
AFB, Texas.
COLONEL CECIL M SONNTAG, FG910097, NAG, Hq TexANG, Camp Mabry, Austin,
Texas.
COLONEL WALTER B STAUDT, FG686671, TexANG, Hq 147th Ftr Gp, Ellington,
AFB, Texas.
COLONEL (MC) MILTON TURNER, FG1690684, ANG, Hq TexANG, Camp Mabry, Austin,
Texas.
LT COLONEL HERMAN L EVANS, FG2070631, ANG, Hq TexANG, Camp Mabry, Austin,
Texas.
LT COLONEL BELISARIO DJ FLORES, FG2206231, TexANG, 149th Cmbt Spt Sq,
Kelly AFB, Texas.
LT COLONEL BILLIE G HOLLOWELL, FG190972, ANG, Hq TexANG, Camp Mabry,
Austin, Texas.
LT COLONEL MATTHEW F HEIMAN, FG722071, TexANG, 174th Cmbt Spt Sq, Ellington
AFB, Texas.
LT COLONEL FRANK DAVIS, JR, FV786076, USAF, 747 ACW Sq, Ellington AFB,
Texas (with concurrence of Commander concerned).
LT COLONEL EDWARD A ELBERT, JR, FR52123, 741 ACW Sq, Lackland AFB, Texas
(with concurrence of Commander concerned).
MAJ (MC) ROBERT W PARET, FG190502, TexANG, 194th USAF Dispensary, Kelly
AFB, Texas.
LT COLONEL EARL W LIVELY, FG1909172, ANG, Hq TexANG, Camp Mabry, Austin,
Texas.

AA-633

SO AA- 633, 12 Jul 68, Hq 31 Air Division (ADC) Okla City AFS, OK 73150

LT COLONEL ISAHMAEL E MCNEILL, FG871440, TexANG, Hq 149th Cmbt Spt Sq, Ellington AFB, Texas.

LT COLONEL PAUL D STRAW, FG690001, TexANG, Hq 149th Ftr Gp, Kelly AFB, Texas.

LT COLONEL FRANKLIN E THRAILKILL, FG225697, TexANG, Hq 149th Ftr Gp, Kelly AFB, Texas.

LT COLONEL DAVID K BARNELL, FG2222794, TexANG, 147th Consol Acft Maint Sq, Ellington AFB, Texas.

LT COLONEL ROBERT D GOODMAN, FG2259660, TexANG, 182d Ftr Intcp Sq, Kelly AFB, Texas.

MAJOR ERVIN C HERBER, FG2287300, ANG, Hq TexANG, Camp Mabry, Austin, Texas.

LT COLONEL BOBBY W HODGES, FG3003177, TexANG, Hq 147th Ftr Gp, Ellington AFB, Texas.

MAJOR CLAYBORNE E KRUCKEMEYER, FG3041196, TexANG, 149th Cmbt Spt Sq, Kelly AFB, Texas.

MAJOR CHARLES A BEASLEY, FG3039597, TexANG, 182d Ftr Intcp Sq, Kelly AFB, Texas.

LT COLONEL HARRY C DISLER, FG1903072, TexANG, 149th Consol Acft Maint Sq, Kelly AFB, Texas.

MAJOR IRA G SMITH, FG3037624, TexANG, 149th Supply Sq, Kelly AFB, Texas.

MAJOR RICHARD D VIA, FG3034264, TexANG, Hq 147th Ftr Gp, Ellington AFB, Texas.

MAJOR JERRY B KILLIAN, FG3022460, TexANG, 111th Ftr Intcp Sq, Ellington AFB, Texas.

MAJOR WILLIE J HOOPER, FG3088076, TexANG, 147th Cmbt Spt Gp, Ellington AFB, Texas.

MAJOR KENNITH L ROBINSON, FG3127516, ANG, Hq TexANG, Camp Mabry, Austin, Texas.

MAJOR LEROY THOMPSON, FG3127542, TexANG, Hq 147th Ftr Gp, Ellington AFB, Texas.

CAPTAIN KENNETH D ANDERSON, FG3060648, TexANG, 111th Wea Flt (Mbl/Fxd) Ellington AFB, Texas.

CAPTAIN (MC) MARSHALL J DYKE, FG3184572, TexANG, 147th USAF Dispensary, Ellington AFB, Texas.

CAPT MARK A HULBERT, FR75389, USAF, AFA to 272d GEEIA Sq, TexANG La Porte, Texas (with concurrence of Commander concerned).

FOR THE COMMANDER

JACK K. SNYDER
Chief, Administrative Services

DEPARTMENTS OF THE ARMY AND THE AIR FORCE
NATIONAL GUARD BUREAU

PROCEEDINGS OF A FEDERAL RECOGNITION EXAMINING BOARD

| CONVENED PURSUANT TO PARAGRAPH | SPECIAL ORDERS NO. | HEADQUARTERS 31st Air Div | DATED |
| 1 | AA - 633 | Okla City AFS ARMY | 12 July 1968 |

| PLACE | DATE | HOUR |
| Ellington AFB, Texas | 4 September 1968 | 1100 |

PRESENT: (All the members)

COLONEL WALTER B. STAUDT, President
LT COL FRANK DAVIS, JR., Member
MAJOR JERRY B. KILLIAN, Recorder

SSAN:
FG 3244754
(SERVICE NUMBER)

The order directing the applicant _____ George Walker Bush _____
(NAME IN FULL)

111th Ftr Intcp Sq _____ Air Force _____ Texas
(UNIT) (BRANCH) (STATE)

To report for examination to determine his qualifications for Federal recognition as _____ 2nd Lieutenant
(GRADE)

Air Force _____ and the orders convening the Board were read.
(BRANCH)

The applicant was asked if he objected to examination by any member of the Board, to which he replied in the negative.
The members of the Board and the Recorder were duly sworn.
The Board proceeded with the examination and finds that—

| HIS PHYSICAL QUALIFICATIONS ARE SATISFACTORY | HIS MORAL CHARACTER IS SATISFACTORY | HIS GENERAL QUALIFICATIONS ARE SATISFACTORY |
| [X] YES [ ] NO | [X] YES [ ] NO | [X] YES [ ] NO |

PROFESSIONAL QUALIFICATIONS

The Board then proceeded with the examination of the professional qualifications of the applicant and finds that—

1. In the opinion of the board, the candidate is qualified for promotion to the grade and position for which recommended.

2. The examination was conducted in accordance with paragraph 9 & 10, ANGR 36-03.

NGB FORM 89
1 OCT 57

PROFESSIONAL QUALIFICATIONS—Continued

MILITARY KNOWLEDGE QUALIFICATIONS ARE SATISFACTORY	ABILITY QUALIFICATIONS ARE SATISFACTORY
[X] YES ☐ NO GENERAL AVERAGE	[X] YES ☐ NO
NONMILITARY EDUCATIONAL QUALIFICATIONS ARE SATISFACTORY	CIVILIAN EXPERIENCE QUALIFICATIONS ARE SATISFACTORY
[X] YES ☐ NO	[X] YES ☐ NO

FINDINGS OF THE BOARD

THE BOARD FINDS THAT THE APPLICANT IS

PHYSICALLY— [X] QUALIFIED ☐ NOT QUALIFIED   GENERALLY— [X] QUALIFIED ☐ NOT QUALIFIED

MORALLY— [X] QUALIFIED ☐ NOT QUALIFIED   PROFESSIONALLY— [X] QUALIFIED ☐ NOT QUALIFIED

FOR THE APPOINTMENT SOUGHT, AND RECOMMENDS THAT HE BE (NOT) GRANTED FEDERAL RECOGNITION

DATE, EXAMINATION COMPLETED

4 September 1968

WALTER B. STAUDT, Colonel, TexANG
(PRESIDENT)

(RECORDER, GENERAL OFFICERS BOARD)

FRANK DAVIS, JR., Lt Col, USAF
(MEMBER)

(MEDICAL OFFICER, GENERAL OFFICERS BOARD)

JERRY B. KILLIAN, Major, TexANG
(MEMBER)
(Recorder)

INCLOSURES

CERTIFICATE OF ELIGIBILITY AND RECORD OF PERSONNEL SECURITY CLEARANCE

INSTRUCTIONS

1. A new form will be accomplished for each specific action (that is: interim clearance, final clearance, etc.).
2. Sections not used will be lined out in ink.

SECTION I.

BASIC INFORMATION

NAME (Last, first, middle initial)	MILITARY OR CIVILIAN GRADE	BRANCH OF SERVICE
BUSH, George Walker	AMN	X AIR FORCE / ARMY / NAVY
DATE OF BIRTH (Day, month, year) 6 July 1946	PLACE OF BIRTH (City, county, state, country) New Haven, New Haven, Connecticut USA	SERVICE OR SOCIAL SECURITY NO. AF26230638

SECTION II.

PERSONNEL SECURITY CLEARANCE

BASIS FOR CLEARANCE (Check one)	DATE OF REPORT (Day, month, year) 5 August 1968
BACKGROUND INVESTIGATION	AGENCY WHICH CONDUCTED INVESTIGATION
X LNAC	DOD, NAC Center, Fort Holabird, Maryland 21219
NAC PLUS 15 CONSECUTIVE YEARS SERVICE	LOCATION OF INVESTIGATIVE REPORT (Show specific OSI District or other location when appropriate, and case file number)
NAC PLUS WRITTEN INQUIRIES	201-3201
CHECK OF PERSONNEL RECORDS	DOD, NAC Center, Fort Holabird, Maryland 21219
HIGHEST CLASSIFICATION FOR WHICH CLEARANCE IS GRANTED ***SECRET***	(Check appropriate box) INTERIM X FINAL	DATE INVESTIGATION REQUESTED TO SATISFY FINAL CLEARANCE REQUIREMENTS (Day, month, year)

CERTIFICATION AND SIGNATURE OF CLEARING AUTHORITY

THIS IS TO CERTIFY THAT THE ABOVE NAMED INDIVIDUAL IS CLEARED UNDER THE PROVISIONS OF AFR 205-6 AND MAY BE AUTHORIZED ACCESS TO CLASSIFIED DEFENSE INFORMATION, AS INDICATED ABOVE, BY PROPER AUTHORITY IN THE PERFORMANCE OF OFFICIALLY ASSIGNED DUTIES.

ORGANIZATION AND LOCATION Adjutant General's Dept, Camp Mabry, Austin, Texas	DATE (Day, month, year) 9 September 1968
TYPED NAME, GRADE AND OFFICIAL POSITION KENNETH L. ROBINSON Maj, Tex ANG, Chief, Air Pers & Tng Branch	SIGNATURE Kenneth L. Robinson

SECTION III.

LIMITED EMERGENCY ACCESS PENDING COMPLETION OF CLEARANCE REQUIREMENTS

ACCESS TO (Insert whether Top Secret, Secret or Confidential) _____ INFORMATION BASED ON REVIEW

OF AVAILABLE RECORDS WAS AUTHORIZED ON (date) _____ INVESTIGATION TO SATISFY CLEARANCE

REQUIREMENTS WAS REQUESTED ON (date)

BRIEF DESCRIPTION OF INFORMATION INVOLVED AND DUTY ASSIGNMENT (Do not include classified information. If necessary use reverse)

CERTIFICATION AND SIGNATURE OF OFFICER AUTHORIZED TO GRANT CLEARANCES

THIS IS TO CERTIFY THAT IMMEDIATE ACCESS TO CLASSIFIED INFORMATION IS NECESSARY AND THAT DELAY CAUSED BY AWAITING INTERIM CLEARANCE WOULD BE HARMFUL TO THE NATIONAL INTEREST.

ORGANIZATION AND LOCATION	DATE (Day, month, year)
TYPED NAME, GRADE AND OFFICIAL POSITION	SIGNATURE

SECTION IV.

RECORD OF COMPLETION OF FAVORABLE INVESTIGATION

(This section to be used when clearance action is not required following completion of favorable investigation)

TYPE OF INVESTIGATION CONDUCTED	DATE OF REPORT (Day, month, year)	AGENCY WHICH CONDUCTED INVESTIGATION

LOCATION OF INVESTIGATIVE REPORT (Show specific OSI District, or other location when appropriate)

SIGNATURE OF AUTHORITY AUTHENTICATING FAVORABLE INVESTIGATION

ORGANIZATION AND LOCATION	DATE (Day, month, year)
TYPED NAME, GRADE AND OFFICIAL POSITION	SIGNATURE

¹ Applicable only when clearance is based on formal investigation.
² Complete only when interim clearance is granted.

AF FORM 47 APR 63 — REPLACES AF FORM 47, JUL 60, WHICH WILL BE USED.

AVPS SA OCT 66, 2000

DEPARTMENT OF THE AIR FORCE
HEADQUARTERS LACKLAND MILITARY TRAINING CENTER (ATC)
LACKLAND AIR FORCE BASE, TEXAS 78236

13 AUGUST 1968

RESERVE ORDER
252

UNDER PROVISIONS OF CHAP 33, AFM 35-3, FOLLOWING NAMED AB, PIPELINE
STUDENT FLT 6128, 3724 BASIC MILITARY TRAINING SQUADRON, THIS BASE,
ARE PROMOTED AS RESERVE OF THE AF TO THE GRADE OF AMN WITH DOR AND
EFFECTIVE DATE OF 23 AUG 68.

NAME	AFSN
BUSH GEORGE W	AF26230638
CRUTCHER JOHN M	AF26230488
DINOVO RUSSELL	AF23052708
DINSTHUL GARY E	AF25359605
DUNLAP RANDALL T	AF25359601
EPSTEIN STEVEN B	AF22047656
ESBAUGH DAVID M	AF24460989
HERIGODT RICHARD J	AF26373181
HOEY DENNIS C	AF25367538
HOLMES ROGERS B JR	AF24872628
HUGHES PAUL J JR	AF22038185
HURST DWIGHT E	AF24672829
JENSEN THOMAS W	AF21151089
LUDWIG RAYMOND H	AF22036216
MACEWEN LEE D	AF24672827
MCNEELY LARRY L	AF26373183
MEDLIN KENNETH L	AF24672824
PARTELOW GARRY R	AF22046738
PEINERT ROGER R	AF23616934
PORTER JAMES M	AF26230489
POWELL TOMMY B	AF26230142
ROGERS ROBERT A	AF29245349
ROGIN ALBERT N	AF21034070
SAND PAUL D	AF27392900
SIMMONS ROBERT H	AF26230143
STURGIS DANIEL B	AF21151087
TERHUNE DAVID A	AF23052713
THEVE ROBERT L	AF23614283
VERNON CARL R	AF23563857
WADE GORDON D	AF25367539
WESTFALL CHARLES W	AF23617080
WIGGINS LAWRENCE E JR	AF21151086
WILBOURNE RICHARD M	AF23616933
YOUNG JERRY	AF21805057

RO-252

RO-362, 13 AUG 68, DAF, HQ LACKLAND MIL TNG CEN, ATC, LACKLAND AFB, TEX 78236.

NAME:

ZETTLE DEAN E
ZAPCIC ROBERT G

AFSN:

AF23947727
AF23982619

G B GREENE, JR, MAJGEN, USAF
Commander

FRANK S SWALM, MAJOR, USAF
Director of Administration

DISTRIBUTION
R

1. LAST NAME - FIRST NAME - MIDDLE NAME		2. SERVICE NUMBER		3. SOCIAL SECURITY NUMBER	
BUSH, GEORGE WALKER		AF26230638			

4. DEPARTMENT, COMPONENT AND BRANCH OR CLASS			5a. GRADE, RATE OR RANK	5b. PAY GRADE	6. DATE OF RANK	DAY	MONTH	YEAR
AIR FORCE, ANGUS			Amn	E2			NA	

7. U. S. CITIZEN	8. PLACE OF BIRTH (City and State or Country)		9. DATE OF BIRTH	DAY	MONTH	YEAR
☒ YES ☐ NO	NA				NA	

10a. SELECTIVE SERVICE NUMBER	b. SELECTIVE SERVICE LOCAL BOARD NUMBER, CITY, COUNTY, STATE AND ZIP CODE	c. DATE INDUCTED		
41 62 46 1480	LB #62, 201 Fannin, Houston, Harris, Texas 77002	DAY	MONTH NA	YEAR

11a. TYPE OF TRANSFER OR DISCHARGE Release from Active Duty Training   **b. STATION OR INSTALLATION AT WHICH EFFECTED** Ellington AFB, Texas

c. REASON AND AUTHORITY Completion of AD Training (Non-Prior Service Ready Reservists), AFM 35-3.	d. EFFECTIVE DATE	DAY 25	MONTH Aug	YEAR 68

12. LAST DUTY ASSIGNMENT AND MAJOR COMMAND	13 a. CHARACTER OF SERVICE	b. TYPE OF CERTIFICATE ISSUED
NA	HONORABLE	NA

14. DISTRICT, AREA COMMAND OR CORPS TO WHICH RESERVIST TRANSFERRED	15. REENLISTMENT CODE
ANG, State of Texas	NA

16. TERMINAL DATE OF RESERVE/UNITED OBLIGATION			17. CURRENT ACTIVE SERVICE OTHER THAN BY INDUCTION	A. TERM OF SERVICE (Years)	c. DATE OF ENTRY		
DAY	MONTH	YEAR	SOURCE OF ENTRY:		DAY	MONTH	YEAR
	NA		☐ ENLISTED (First Enlistment) ☐ ENLISTED (Prior Service) ☐ REENLISTED ☒ OTHER Orders for AD Tng.	NA	14	Jul	68

18. PRIOR REGULAR ENLISTMENTS	19. GRADE, RATE OR RANK AT TIME OF ENTRY INTO CURRENT ACTIVE SVC	20. PLACE OF ENTRY INTO CURRENT ACTIVE SERVICE (City and State)
NA	NA	NA

21. HOME OF RECORD AT TIME OF ENTRY INTO ACTIVE SERVICE (Street, RFD, City, County, State and ZIP Code)	22. STATEMENT OF SERVICE		YEARS	MONTHS	DAYS
NA	a. CREDITABLE FOR BASIC PAY PURPOSES	(1) NET SERVICE THIS PERIOD	00	01	12
		(2) OTHER SERVICE	00	01	17
22a. SPECIALTY NUMBER & TITLE	23. RELATED CIVILIAN OCCUPATION AND D.O.T. NUMBER	(3) TOTAL (Line (1) plus Line (2))	00	02	29
70210 - Admin	NA	b. TOTAL ACTIVE SERVICE	00	01	12
Rlpx		c. FOREIGN AND/OR SEA SERVICE	00	00	00

24. DECORATIONS, MEDALS, BADGES, COMMENDATIONS, CITATIONS AND CAMPAIGN RIBBONS AWARDED OR AUTHORIZED
NA

25. EDUCATION AND TRAINING COMPLETED
Basic Mil Tng Crse AG800012 - Aug 68

26 a. NON-PAY PERIODS/TIME LOST (Preceding Two Years)	b. DAYS ACCRUED LEAVE PAID	27 a. INSURANCE IN FORCE (NSLI or USGLI)	b. AMOUNT OF ALLOTMENT	c. MONTH ALLOTMENT DISCONTINUED
No time lost	4 days	☐ NA ☐ NO $ NA	NA	NA
	28. VA CLAIM NUMBER C- NA	29. SERVICEMEN'S GROUP LIFE INSURANCE COVERAGE ☒ $10,000 ☐ $5,000 ☐ NONE		

30. REMARKS
AIR FORCE SERVICE ENLISTMENT PROGRAM. College - Completed 4 years. "Blood Type O Pos".

31. PERMANENT ADDRESS FOR MAILING PURPOSES AFTER TRANSFER OR DISCHARGE (Street, RFD, City, County, State and ZIP Code)	32. SIGNATURE OF PERSON BEING TRANSFERRED OR DISCHARGED
NA	*George Walker Bush*
33. TYPED NAME, GRADE AND TITLE OF AUTHORIZING OFFICER	34. SIGNATURE OF OFFICER AUTHORIZED TO SIGN.
LEE A. BURKE, SMSGT, USAF Air Force Advisor	*Lee A. Burke*

DD FORM 214   PREVIOUS EDITIONS OF THIS FORM ARE OBSOLETE.   ARMED FORCES OF THE UNITED STATES REPORT OF TRANSFER OR DISCHARGE   2

2nd Ind to Hq 147th Ftr Gp Ltr, 29 May 68, Preview and Grade Determination (AB George W. Bush)

DAAF, NGB (NG-AFPMO), Wash DC 20310   26 August 1968

TO: TAG Texas, PO Box 5218, Austin TX 78703

1. AB George W. Bush   is approved for appointment as
Pilot Trainee   , AFSC 0066   , provided otherwise qualified,
in the grade of 2dLt   , AFSN FG3244754   , SSAN ███████

2. TYSD: Eff date of appt
   PSD: Eff date of appt

( ) Flying Status is valid.
( ) Flying Status will be revalidated by this Bureau on the day Federal recognition orders are published. Individual is not authorised to fly prior to that date.
( ) The ( ) FEB ( ) ARB pertaining to above applicant is approved contingent upon his appointment as a Reserve officer of the AF and extension of Federal recognition. When officer signs his Oath (AF Form 133), request this Bureau (NG-AFPM, Mrs. Fairman, Ext 53219) be notified in order that USAF may publish orders rating him Pilot and placing him on flying status. Officer is not authorized to participate in flights until competent orders have been issued.

3. ( ) Favorable NAC completed   by and is on file at DOD NAC Center, PO Box 4, Ft Holabird Md 21219.
( ) Favorable BI completed 20 Aug 68 , File No 10B51-1793 , and is on file at Hq USAF (AFISISA4I), Bldg T-E, Wash DC 20333.

4. Application may be submitted in accordance with ANGR 36-02. If individual is not appointed please advise this office ASAP.

5. Additional remarks-PLEASE APPOINT IMMEDIATELY. Anticipated class entry date 26 Nov 68. Please submit evidence of degree with appointment papers.

Please withdraw attached phy exam for file in FIELD MEDICAL RECORDS. Cys have been retained here for Bureau use.

FOR THE CHIEF, NATIONAL GUARD BUREAU

G. L. Tunkliv Lt-Col.
RAYMOND J. HIGGINS
Chief, Air Personnel Division

8 Atch
1 n/c
2 & 3 w/d
4 thru 6 n/c
7 w/d
8 n/c
9 thru 11 w/d
12 n/c
13 w/d
14 & 15 n/c

STATE OF TEXAS
ADJUTANT GENERAL'S DEPARTMENT
Post Office Box 5218
Austin, Texas 78703

SPECIAL ORDER
ANG-A 146

28 August 1968

AMN GEORGE W. BUSH (FG3244754), TexANG, (Present address: 5000 Logmont #8, Houston, Texas 77027), is appointed 2D LT, TexANG, assigned Pilot Trainee, (AFSC, 0006, Functional Code 3110, vice original vacancy UMD grade vacancy Lt), 111th Fighter Interceptor Sq, TexANG, Ellington AFB, Texas. Individual will report at time and place designated by President of Examining Board, Ellington AFB, Texas, for examination for Federal Recognition in grade to which appointed. Authority: ANGR 36-02.

FOR THE GOVERNOR

E. C. HERBER
Major, TexANG
Air Administrative Officer

DISTRIBUTION
20 - AGTEX-AP
20 - Total

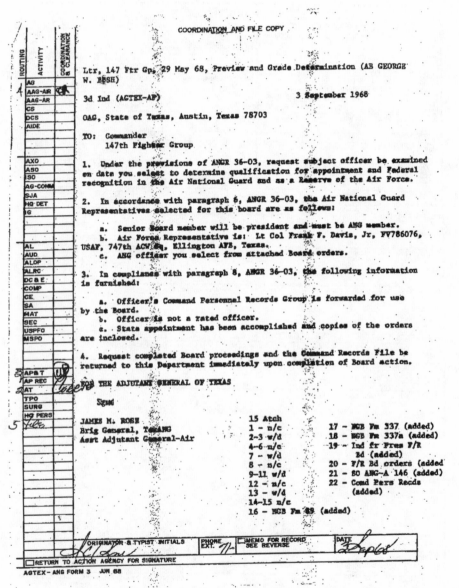

COORDINATION AND FILE COPY

Ltr, 147 Ftr Gp, 29 May 68, Preview and Grade Determination (AB GEORGE
W. BUSH)

3d Ind (AGTEX-AP)   3 September 1968

OAG, State of Texas, Austin, Texas 78703

TO: Commander
     147th Fighter Group

1. Under the provisions of ANGR 36-03, request subject officer be examined
on date you select to determine qualification for appointment and Federal
recognition in the Air National Guard and as a Reserve of the Air Force.

2. In accordance with paragraph 6, ANGR 36-03, the Air National Guard
Representatives selected for this board are as follows:

     a. Senior Board member will be president and must be ANG member.
     b. Air Force Representative is: Lt Col Frank F. Davis, Jr, FV786076,
USAF, 747th ACW Sq, Ellington AFB, Texas.
     c. ANG officer you select from attached Board orders.

3. In compliance with paragraph 8, ANGR 36-03, the following information
is furnished:

     a. Officer's Command Personnel Records Group is forwarded for use
by the Board.
     b. Officer is not a rated officer.
     c. State appointment has been accomplished and copies of the orders
are inclosed.

4. Request completed Board proceedings and the Command Records File be
returned to this Department immediately upon completion of Board action.

FOR THE ADJUTANT GENERAL OF TEXAS

Signed

JAMES M. ROSE
Brig General, TexANG
Asst Adjutant General-Air

15 Atch
1 - n/c
2-3 w/d
4-6 n/c
7 - w/d
8 - n/c
9-11 w/d
12 - n/c
13 - w/d
14-15 n/c
16 - NGB Fm 89 (added)

17 - NGB Fm 337 (added)
18 - NGB Fm 337a (added)
19 - Ind fr Pres F/R
     Bd (added)
20 - F/R Bd orders (added
21 - SO ANG-A 146 (added)
22 - Comd Pers Recds
     (added)

ORIGINATOR & TYPIST INITIALS   PHONE EXT: 71-   MEMO FOR RECORD SEE REVERSE   DATE 3 Sep 68

☐ RETURN TO ACTION AGENCY FOR SIGNATURE

AGTEX- ANG FORM 3   JUN 68

DEPARTMENTS OF THE ARMY AND THE AIR FORCE
NATIONAL GUARD BUREAU

REPORT OF SEPARATION AND RECORD OF SERVICE IN THE **AIR** NATIONAL GUARD OF **TEXAS**
AND AS A RESERVE OF THE **AIR FORCE**
TYPE OF DISCHARGE **HONORABLE**
(No erasures or alterations in this entry valid)

1. NAME (Last, first, middle initial)	2. SERVICE NO	3. GRADE	4. ARM OR SERVICE	5. TERM OF ENLISTMENT
BUSH, GEORGE W.	AF26230638	AMN	AF TEXANG	6 Years

6. ORGANIZATION 147th Cmbt Spt Sq	7. DATE OF DISCHARGE	8. PLACE OF DISCHARGE
HOME STATION Ellington AFB, Texas	2 Sep 68	Ellington AFB, Texas

9. PERMANENT ADDRESS FOR MAILING PURPOSES 77027 5000 Longmont, Apt #8, Houston, Texas	10. DATE OF BIRTH 6 Jul 46	11. PLACE OF BIRTH New Haven, Connecticut

12. CIVILIAN OCCUPATION (Include name and address of present employer, or if unemployed, the last employer)

None

13.	RACE		14.	MARITAL STATUS			15. U.S. CITIZEN	
WHITE	NEGRO	OTHER (Specify)	SINGLE	MARRIED	OTHER (Specify)		YES	NO
X			X				X	

16. COLOR EYES Hazel	17. COLOR HAIR Brown	18. HEIGHT 5 FT 11½ IN	19. WEIGHT 180 LBS	20. NO DEPENDENTS None

MILITARY HISTORY

21. DATE AND PLACE OF ENLISTMENT 27 May 68, Ellington AFB, Texas	22. MILITARY OCCUPATIONAL SPECIALTY AND NUMBER 70230 – Apr Admin Specl

23. MILITARY QUALIFICATION AND DATE (i.e. Infantry, Aviation, Marksmanship Badge, etc)

None

24. DECORATIONS, CITATIONS, MEDALS, BADGES, COMMENDATIONS, AND CAMPAIGN RIBBONS AWARDED OR AUTHORIZED (This period of service)

SAEMR

25. PRIOR SERVICE (Branch of service, inclusive dates, and primary duty with MOS)

None

26. LENGTH THIS SERVICE			27. TOTAL SERVICE FOR PAY PURPOSES			28. EDUCATION (Years)			29. HIGHEST GRADE HELD
YEARS	MONTHS	DAYS	YEARS	MONTHS	DAYS	GRAMMAR	HIGH SCHOOL	COLLEGE	
0	3	7	0	3	7	8	4	4	Amn

30. SERVICE SCHOOLS ATTENDED AND DATES
None

31. REASON AND AUTHORITY FOR DISCHARGE

Par 14b, ANGR 39-10: Commissioned as an Officer in the Tex ANG

32. REMARKS (This space for completion of above items or entry of other items specified in NG directive)

This airman has a 6 year service obligation under the provisions of the UMT&S Act, as amended, and has completed 0 years 3 months 7 days toward this obligation.

33. SIGNATURE OF PERSON BEING DISCHARGED (Full name) (NOT AVAILABLE FOR SIGNATURE)	34. SIGNATURE OF OFFICER AUTHORIZED TO SIGN (grade and organization) MATTHEW F. HEIMAN, Lt Col, 147th Cmbt Spt Sq

NGB FORM 22
15 JAN 58
1. Insert either Army or Air
2. Insert either Army or Air Force
REPLACES NGB FORM 22 DATED 15 NOV 49, WHICH IS OBSOLETE
☆ GPO : 1958 O—433889

1. LAST NAME—FIRST NAME—MIDDLE INITIAL—AFSN

BUSH, GEORGE W.   AF26230638

ENLISTMENT CATEGORY,

GRADE, *AMN*   COMPONENT, *ANGUS*

3. PERSONAL DATA

DATE OF BIRTH	RELIGION	BIRTHPLACE
6 Jul 46	Episcopalian	New Haven, Connecticut

MARITAL STATUS   PERMANENT MAILING ADDRESS

S-0   *5000 Longmont Apt 8*
Houston, Harris, Texas 77027

4. SERVICE DATES

DATE OF ENLISTMENT OR INDUCTION   *27 May 68*

DATE OF ORDER TO EAD

COMPLETION OF ENLISTMENT OR PERIOD OF INDUCTION   *26 May 74*

DATE OF COMPLETION OF SERVICE OBLIGATION   26 May 74

DATE TO BE RELEASED FROM AD OR EAD

TAPHSD   *As of 26 May 69*

THSD   *27 May 68*

5. GRADE DATA

TEMP. GRADE	PERM. GRADE	DATE OF RANK	AUTHORITY
	AB	27May68	ANGR 39-09
	AMN	23Aug68	RO362,13Aug68,INTG

PROFICIENCY PAY RATING

RATING	DATE	AUTHORITY

2. FOREIGN SERVICE

DATE DEPARTED	LOCATION	ACCOMPANIED OR UNACCOMPANIED	FSSD	ISOLATED AREA

FOREIGN SERVICE SUMMARY

DATE RETURNED 2b.

6. ASSIGNMENT LIMITATIONS

ON PCS. DISLOCATION ALLOWANCE

DEPARTED	PHYSICAL STATUS								DATE
	P	U	1	2	3		SUFFIX		24 May 68
	✓	✓	✓	✓	✓		B		

7. AIR FORCE SPECIALTIES

AFSC		SPECIALTY TITLE	AUTHORITY
	DESIGNATED		
70010	P	Admin Hlpr	SO P-23/147FG/20Jun68
70230	C	Apr Admin Specl	

AIRMAN MILITARY RECORD

AF FORM 7   PREVIOUS EDITIONS OF THIS FORM MAY BE USED.
JUN 66

2 / Ann

LAST NAME—FIRST NAME—MIDDLE INITIAL—AFSN
BUSH, GEORGE W.   AF26230638

8. IN-SERVICE SCHOOLS

COURSE TITLE AND AFSC	RATING	YEAR TERM
Bsc Mil Tng (ANG) AGM00012	Comp	1968

9. OTHER EDUCATION

NAME—LOCATION OF SCHOOL	DEGREE	YEAR COMPLETED
Yale Univ. New Haven, Conn.	BA(Hist)	68

10. AWARDS

AWARD	AUTHORITY	PRESENTED
SAEMR	AFM900-3	No

11. TEST RESULTS

APTITUDE   OTHER

12. PERSONNEL SECURITY CLEARANCE DATA

CLEARANCE	DATE GRANTED	INVESTIGATIVE DATA

13. FOREIGN LANGUAGES

LANGUAGE	DIALECT	RHTR.	TRANS.	U	R	W

14. COMBAT

13. CIVILIAN OCCUPATION

JOB TITLE	NO. MOS.	YEAR TERM
Office Work	3	6-7

MAIN
OTHER

16.				RESERVE DATA						LAST NAME—FIRST NAME—MIDDLE INITIAL—AFSN		
	ASSIGNED			QUALIFIED FOR (Pencil)			AVAILABILITY CODE			BUSH, GEORGE W. AF26230638		3
CATEGORY	STATUS	DATE		CATEGORY	DATE		CODE	DATE				
							AA			18.	REMARKS	
										SOCIAL SECURITY NO.		
										OTHER SERVICE NO.		
										SSAN 41-62-46-1480		

17. ITEM CONTINUATION

LAST NAME—FIRST NAME—MIDDLE INITIAL—AFSN

BUSH, GEORGE W.   AF26230638

19. CHRONOLOGICAL LISTING OF SERVICE

EDCSA	DAFSC	DUTY TITLE	ORGANIZATION AND STATION OF ASSIGNMENT
27May68	70230	Continuous Non-Extended Active Duty From 27 May 68	
6 Jul 1968	00010	Apr Admin Specl (Enlisted ANG) RATING ATTACHED	147thCmbtSptSq, EllingtonAFB Texas (TEXANG) 3724 BAMILTRARON LCCLLAND AFB TEX (ATC)
24Aug68	70230	Apr Admin Specl	147th CmbtSptSq, Ellington AFB TX (TEXANG)
25Aug68	70230	Rel fr AD for Tng (AFM 35-3)	147th CmbtSptSq, Ellington AFB TX (TEXANG)
26Aug68	70230	Apr Admin Specl	147th CmbtSptSq, Ellington AFB TX (TEXANG)
3Sep68	70230	Discharged fr ANG and as a ResAF	

20. PERFORMANCE REPORTS

DATE	TYPE

Oath of  Office

I, _____ George _____ Walker _____ Bush _____
(First name) (Middle name) (Last name)

do solemnly swear that I will support and defend the Constitution of the United States and the con-

stitution of the State of _____ Texas _____ against all enemies, foreign and domestic;

that I will bear true faith and allegiance to the same; that I will obey the orders of the President of the

United States and of the Governor of the State of _____ Texas _____; that

I make this obligation freely, without any mental reservation or purpose of evasion, and that I will well

and faithfully discharge the duties of the office of _____ 2nd Lieutenant _____, _____ USAF _____
(Grade) (Branch)

in the National Guard of the State of _____ Texas _____ upon which I am about to enter;

So help me God.

_____ George Walker Bush _____
2nd Lieutenant, TexANG
FG 3244754
(Grade) (Branch)

Sworn to and subscribed before me at _____ Ellington AFB, Texas _____

this _____ 4th _____ day of _____ September _____, 1968

_____ Rufus G. Martin _____
RUFUS G. MARTIN, Captain, TexANG
Personnel Officer

NGB FORM 337
15 MAY 53 (All previous editions of this form are obsolete)   16—48574-2 U. S. GOVERNMENT PRINTING OFFICE

OATH TO BE EXECUTED PRIOR TO EXTENSION OF TEMPORARY

FEDERAL RECOGNITION IN THE AIR NATIONAL GUARD

I, _____George Walker Bush_____, do solemnly swear (or
(First, middle, last name)

Affirm) that upon the extension of temporary Federal recognition to me pursuant

to the provisions of section 704, Armed Forces Reserve Act of 1952 in the grade

of _2nd Lieutenant_____
(Grade)

in the Air National Guard of the state of_____Texas_____, I will perform all
(State)

Federal duties and obligations required of me the same as though I were appointed

a Reserve Officer of the Air Force in the same grade, during such temporary Federal

recognition.

_____George Walker Bush_____
(Signature in full)
2nd Lieutenant, TexANG
FG 3244754, ▮▮▮▮▮▮▮
(Grade)

Sworn to and subscribed before me at Ellington AFB, Texas on this

day of 4 September , 19 68 .

_____Rufus G. Martin_____
RUFUS G. MARTIN, Captain, TexANG
Personnel Officer

NGB FORM 337 Air
5 JUNE 54

GPO 8781

DEPARTMENT OF THE AIR FORCE
HEADQUARTERS TENTH AIR FORCE (ADC)
RICHARDS-GEBAUR AIR FORCE BASE, MISSOURI 64030

REPLY TO
ATTN OF: 10CIG-S

4 September 1968

SUBJECT: Report of Completed Investigation

TO: TAG Texas

1. A favorable limited national agency check concerning the following members of the Air National Guard of your state has been completed by the DOD National Agency Check Center, Fort Holabird, Maryland, 21219, in accordance with paragraph 23c, AFR 205-6.

Name, AFSN, File Number	Date LNAC Completed
BUSH, George Walker, AF26230638, 201-3201	5 Aug 1968

///

2. If applicant(s) for a security clearance were on active duty and assigned to ADC, a clearance would be granted.

3. This information is provided for the use of the Adjutant General only and is not to be considered as a clearance. This letter will be destroyed after AF Form 47 has been completed.

FOR THE COMMANDER

GUY S. MIRICH, Major, USAF
Chief, Security Police Division

ᴴ⁻

STATE OF TEXAS

ADJUTANT GENERAL'S DEPARTMENT

Post Office Box 5218

Austin, Texas 78703

9 September 1968

REPLY TO
ATTN OF: AGTEX-AP

SUBJECT: Certificate of Clearance and Record of Personnel Investigation
BUSH, George Walker, AMN, AF26230638

TO: 147th Fighter Group, Tex ANG

1. Inclosed is final certificate of clearance indicating the
above referenced individual is eligible for access to information
and material classified SECRET. Access certificate must be issued
in accordance with AFR 205-6.

2. It is requested that the following action be taken:

    a. Make appropriate entry in Item 12, Officer's AF Form 11,
(Reference Chapter 8, Para 64, AFM 35-9), and Item 12 of airman's
AF Form 7 (Reference Para 38, AFM 35-12).

    b. Forwarded for inclusion in the individual's unit personnel
records group.

FOR THE ADJUTANT GENERAL OF TEXAS

ROGER V. BIVENS
1st Lt, TexANG
Personnel Staff Officer

1 Atch
AF Fm 47

HEADQUARTERS
147TH FIGHTER GROUP (AD)
TEXAS AIR NATIONAL GUARD
ELLINGTON AIR FORCE BASE, TEXAS

SUBJECT: Request for Clearance Certificate

13 Sep 1968
(Date)

TO: AGTEX-AP

1. Request Clearance Certificate be issued for the following individual based on prior security investigation as outlined below:

a. Name: GEORGE WALKER BUSH   AFSN: FG3244754

b. Grade: 2D Lieutenant

c. Date of Birth: 6 July 1946

d. Place of Birth: New Haven, Conn.

e. Degree of Clearance Required: SECRET

f. Date of last investigation: 20 Aug 1968

g. Type of last investigation: Background Investigation

h. Investigation accomplished by: Hq USAF (AFISISA4I), Bldg. T-E Washington, D.C., 20333   File #10D51-1793

i. Reason for clearance and DAFSC: This officer requires access to Information up to and including SECRET. AFSC: 1125D

2. This individual has had no break in service of more than 6 months since date of security investigation indicated above. Copies of AF Form 47 and page 4, AF Form 7 or AF Form 11 (BTMR) (are not) attached.

3. An investigation of unit personnel records reveals no adverse information concerning this individual.

FOR THE COMMANDER

RUFUS G. MARTIN, Captain, TexANG
Personnel Officer

_____ Atch

DEPARTMENTS OF THE ARMY AND THE AIR FORCE
NATIONAL GUARD BUREAU
WASHINGTON, D.C.   20310

SPECIAL ORDERS
NUMBER   196M   27 September 1968

1. By dir of the SAF announcement is made of the ext of Fed recog to the fol
ANG offs in grade, State and on date indc, such offs having qual under the
provisions of 32 USC 305 and 307:

					DATE OF
GRADE	NAME	SN	UNIT	STATE	FED RECOG
CAPT ROBERT L WILLIAMS		FG2098980	163 Tac Ftr Sq	IN	28 Aug 68
2DLT RICHARD A KEEHFUS		FG3235243	108 Tac Ftr Sq	NY	7 Jun 68
CAPT JOHN H OCONNOR JR		FG3069761	137 Mil Alft Sq	NY	7 Aug 68
2DLT BARRY C FAWCETT		FG3244757	269-1 Mbl Comm Sq	OH	8 Sep 68
2DLT EDWARD B BOWERS JR		FG3244740	157 Ftr Intcp Sq	SC	20 Sep 68
2DLT GEORGE W BUSH		FG3244754	111 Ftr Intcp Sq	TX	4 Sep 68
2DLT MICHAEL H EDEN		FG3244755	182 Ftr Intcp Sq	TX	13 Sep 68

2. By dir of the SAF announcement is made of the ext of Fed recog of the prom of the
fol ANG offs in grade, State and on date indc, offs having qual for prom under the
provisions of 10 USC, 8374, 8379 and ANGR 36-04:

GRADE	NAME	SN	UNIT	STATE	EFF DATE
MAJ LAWRENCE C CAERINHA		FG3059130	199 Ftr Intcp Sq	HI	5 Sep 68
LTCOL(DC) ARNOLD J GIVEN JR		FG999329	Hq WV ANG	WV	21 Aug 68

BY ORDER OF THE SECRETARY OF THE ARMY AND THE AIR FORCE:

OFFICIAL

C. BOATWRIGHT
Colonel, NGB
Executive, National Guard Bureau

DISTR:

WINSTON P. WILSON
Major General
Chief, National Guard Bureau

15 ea State for ea Off
2 ea Off listed in Para 1 to HQ ARPC (RPCA-3) plus 4 cys
1 USAFMPC (AFPMDS) Randolph AFB TX
1 USAFMPC (AFPMAJB1) Randolph AFB TX
1 NGFA
1 NGB MSS
100 NG-AFFMO

OATH OF OFFICE *(MILITARY PERSONNEL)*

INSTRUCTIONS

This form will be executed in full upon acceptance of a commission or appointment in the Air Force. Typewriter will be used, if available.

FOR THE EXECUTION OF THE OATH OF OFFICE

1. Whenever any person is elected or appointed to an office of honor or trust under the Government of the United States, he is required before entering upon the duties of his office, to take and subscribe the oath prescribed by 5 USC 3331.

2. 10 USC 8312, 8394 and 8451 eliminates the necessity of executing oath on promotion of officers.

3. Oaths of office of Air Force officers should be taken before some civil officer who is authorized by the laws of the United States or by the local municipal law to administer oaths or before any commissioned officer of any component (including the Reserve component) of any of the Armed Forces of the United States, whether or not on active duty, or before a warrant officer who is serving as the adjutant, assistant adjutant, or personnel adjutant of a command, or before a warrant officer of the

Air Force who is serving as a Director, Deputy, or Chief of Administrative Services, Administrative Officer, or similar title.

4. If the oath is administered by a warrant officer of the Air Force serving in one of the positions mentioned in 3 above, his title and a statement will be added to the signature element as follows: "Authorized to administer oaths and act as a notary under 10 USC 936 and AFR110-6." If the oath is administered by a civil official, the oath must bear the official seal of the person administering the oath, or if he does not use a seal, his official capacity to administer oaths must be certified to under seal by clerk of court or other proper local official. The date of expiration of commission as notary must be indicated. Notary public must affix seal. Return the AF Form 133 to the headquarters tendering the appointment.

Commission Mailed   2 5 OCT 1968

INDICATE TYPE OF COMMISSION BY PLACING X IN PROPER BLOCK

	REGULAR AIR FORCE
	UNITED STATES AIR FORCE *(Temporary)*
XX	RESERVE AIR FORCE

I, _____George Walker Bush_____   FG 3244754
(First name - middle name - last name)   (AFSN)   (SSAN)

having been appointed a _____Second Lieutenant_____, United States Air Force,
(Grade)

do solemnly swear (or affirm) that I will support and defend the Constitution of the United States against all enemies, foreign and domestic; that I will bear true faith and allegiance to the same; that I take this obligation freely, without any mental reservation or purpose of evasion; and that I will well and faithfully discharge the duties of the office upon which I am about to enter, SO HELP ME GOD.

TYPE OR PRINT NAME, GRADE, AND ORGANIZATION	SIGNATURE
GEORGE WALKER BUSH 2d Lt , ResAF (ANGUS)	*George Walker Bush*

Sworn to and subscribed before me, at   Ellington AFB, Texas

this   12   day of October , 19 68   * Acceptance recorded
as of 4 Sep 68 ,

TYPE OR PRINT NAME, GRADE, ORGANIZATION AND OFFICE OF OFFICIAL ADMINISTERING OATH	SIGNATURE
BOBBY W. HODGES, Lt Col, TexANG Deputy Commander, Operations 147th Fighter Group	*Bobby W. Hodges*

AF FORM 133   PREVIOUS EDITIONS OF THIS FORM
FEB 68   MAY BE USED UNTIL 1 JAN 69.   GPO 943-982

DEPARTMENT OF THE AIR FORCE
HEADQUARTERS UNITED STATES AIR FORCE
WASHINGTON, D.C.

USAFMPC (AFPMRDC)
RANDOLPH AFB TEXAS 78148   7 October 1968

SUBJECT: Appointment as a Reserve Officer of the Air Force

TO: The Adjutant General, State of Texas

2d Lt George Walker Bush, FG3244754, ResAF (ANGUS)   AFSC: 0006
5000 Longmont #8   TYSD: 4 Sep 68
Houston TX 77027   PSD: 4 Sep 68
IN TURN   TFCSD: 4 Sep 68

1. The Secretary of the Air Force has directed me to inform you that,
by direction of the President, you are tendered an indefinite term
appointment as a Reserve officer of the Air Force. Grade and service
number are shown in the address above.

2. Request you execute and return the inclosed oath of office at once.
This action constitutes acceptance of your appointment and no other
evidence is required. Failure to execute and return the required oath
of office will result in cancellation of this appointment and withdrawal
of Federal recognition in the Air National Guard.

3. Upon acceptance, this appointment will become effective on the date
of temporary Federal recognition in the Air National Guard, State of
Texas, 4 September 1968.   You will be discharged from any appointment
you may hold in this or another service.

4. You will not perform the duties of an officer under this appointment
until specifically ordered by competent authority.

5. Authority for this appointment is Sections 593 and 8351b, Title 10,
U. S. Code.

FILE IN MASTER
PERSONNEL RECORDS
Initials _____ Jm
Office Symbol AFPMRDS
Date ____ 25 Oct 68

DEE J. BUTLER, Lt Col, USAF   3 Atch
Directorate of Personnel   1. AF Form 133
Resources & Distribution   2. Certificate of Commission
                                      (Instruction Sheet)
                                   3. DAF Self-Addressed Envelope

Cy to: NG-AFPO

Favorable BI (File 10D51-1793) completed 20 Aug 68 by OSI Dist 18
& is filed at HQ USAF (AFISISA4I) Bldg T-E, Wash DC 20333.

AFPMRD-FL-14

Ltr, NGB (NG-AFPS), dtd 16 October 1968, Subj: Air National Guard School
Attendance for Duration of One Year or More (2d Lt George W. Bush FG3244754)

1st Ind (AGTEX-AT)   28 October 1968

OAG, State of Texas, Austin, Texas 78703

TO: 147th Fighter Group
     Attn: CBPO Manday Control Officer

1. Basic communication forwarded for your information and obligation of
mandays.

2. On the basis of basic communication this department will prepare
and distribute orders at the earliest possible date.

3. Mandays will be issued on an NGB Form 40 within 10 days.

FOR THE ADJUTANT GENERAL OF TEXAS

KENNITH L. ROBINSON   cc: AGTEX-ALM/C
Major, TexANG
Chief, Pers & Tng Branch

REQUEST AND AUTHORIZATION FOR ACTIVE DUTY TRAINING ACTIVE DUTY TOUR O-201

TO: AGTEX-XO   FROM: AGTEX-AT

1. [X] BY ORDER OF THE SAF (VOLUNTARILY & WITH CONSENT OF THE GOVERNOR)

2. GRADE, LAST NAME, FIRST, MIDDLE INITIAL, AFSN
2DLT BUSH, GEORGE W.   FG3244754   SSAN: ▮▮▮▮

3. PAFSC
70010

4. PRESENT ADDRESS
5000 Longmont, #8
Houston, Texas 77027

5. ON FLYING STATUS
☐ YES   [X] NO

6. AERO RATING
Non-rated

7. IS ORDERED TO ACTIVE DUTY FOR 405 DAYS PLUS REQUIRED TRAVEL TIME

8. PURPOSE (Type)
☐ ANNUAL TOUR   [X] SCHOOL TOUR   ☐ SPECIAL TOUR OF ACDUTRA   ☐ SPECIAL TOUR OF AD
TITLE (Indicate specific school course or special tour title): Sec 505, USC 32

9. PRESENT ASSIGNMENT
ANG 147th Fighter Group, Ellington AFB,
Houston, Texas

10. UNIT OF ATTACHMENT
NOT APPLICABLE

		HOUR	DAY	MONTH	YEAR
11. INDIVIDUAL WILL REPORT TO 3615th Student Squadron Craig AFB, Alabama			25	Nov	1968
12. INDIVIDUAL WILL BE RELEASED FROM ORGANIZATION ATTACHED/ ASSIGNED FOR ACTIVE DUTY TRAINING ON			2	Dec	1969

13. INDIVIDUAL [X] IS ☐ IS NOT AUTHORIZED TO PARTICIPATE IN FLYING ACTIVITIES DURING THE PERIOD OF ACTIVE DUTY COVERED BY THIS ORDER.

14. AUTHORITY
See Item 18 (Remarks)

15. INDIVIDUAL WILL PROCEED FROM PRESENT ADDRESS IN SUFFICIENT TIME TO COMPLY WITH REPORTING TIME AND DATE.

16. MODES OF TRANSPORTATION [X] AUTHORIZED ☐ DIRECTED [X] TPC
MILITARY [X] AIRCRAFT   COMMERCIAL ☐ AIRCRAFT   ☐ RAIL   [X] BUS

17. PCS TON, PAV, ALLOWANCES, AND TRAVEL CHARGEABLE TO: FY 69 5793850 569 4156 P523.01 (P&A) 523.04 (UG) P523.08 (TVL) 5594700 FY 70 5703850 560 4156 P523.01 (P&A) P523.04 (see reverse)

18. REMARKS Security Clearance SECRET   Series No. 45-69-35
To Attend: Undergraduate Pilot Training-in-Grade Course P-V4A-A, Class 70-04
Copy of paid vouchers will be furnished BAO, TexANG Ellington AFB, Texas
NGB (NG-AFPS) Ltr, Air National Guard School Attendance for Duration of One Year or
More dated 4 October 1968. (see reverse)

19. DATE
16 Oct 1968

20. PHONE NO.
Ext 71

21. APPROVING OFFICIAL (Typed Name and Grade)
KENNITH L. ROBINSON, Major, TexANG
Chief, Pers & Tng Branch

22. SIGNATURE
Kennith L. Robinson

23. DESIGNATION AND LOCATION OF HEADQUARTERS
DEPARTMENT OF THE AIR FORCE
STATE OF TEXAS
ADJUTANT GENERAL'S DEPARTMENT
Post Office Box 5218
Austin, Texas 78703

24. ORDER NO.
ANG-T 1102

25. DATE
16 October 1968

26. FOR THE GOVERNOR

27. DISTRIBUTION
1 — AGTEX-ALM/C
2 — AGTEX-AT
1 — ANG Liaison Off, LMTC, OPA
1 — NGB (NG-AFCB)
50 — Unit of Assignment 147th FG
5 — BAO, TexANG Ellington AFB, Texas
5 — 3615 Stu Sq, Craig AFB, Alabama
65 — Total

28. SIGNATURE ELEMENT OF ORDERS AUTHENTICATING OFFICIAL
E. C. HERBER
Major, TexANG
Air Administrative Officer

AF FORM 938 FEB 67   DIRECT ENTRY TECH TNG - OFFICER

.17. continued: (UG) P523.08 (Tvl) S594700.

18. continued: Transporation of dependents and shipment of household goods will
be in accordance with Chapters 7 and 8, Joint Travel Regulations.. (Officer
due initial clothing allowance $200.00 and active duty clothing allowance $100.00).

REQUEST AND AUTHORIZATION FOR CHANGE OF ADMINISTRATIVE ORDERS
(If more space required, continue on reverse, identify items by number)

TO: AGTEX-AXO

FROM: AGTEX-AT

ORDERS PERTAINING TO THE INDIVIDUAL (S) LISTED IN ITEM 3 ARE ☐ REVOKED ☐ RESCINDED ☒ AMENDED AS SHOWN IN ITEM 4

1. IDENTIFICATION OF ORDER BEING AMENDED (Issued by this Headquarters unless otherwise stated in item 5.)

A. PARA	B. ORDER (Type and No.)	C. DATE	D. EDCSA	E. RELATING TO (TDY, PCS, Short Tou of AD, etc.)
	ANG-T 1102	16 October 68	- - - - - - - -	Initial Tour of Active Duty

2. PREVIOUS AMENDMENTS ISSUED BY THIS HEADQUARTERS.

A. PARA	B. ORDER (Type and No.)	C. DATE

3. IDENTIFICATION OF INDIVIDUAL(S) TO WHOM CHANGE ACTION PERTAINS

A. GRADE	B. LAST NAME, FIRST, MIDDLE INITIAL	C. AFSC OR POSITION TITLE (Civilian)	D. ORGANIZATION
2D LT	BUSH, GEORGE W.	FG3244754 SSAN: ▅▅▅▅	111th Fighter Interceptor Sq

4. AMENDMENT (Identify item in order being amended)

A. ITEM	AS READS	IS AMENDED TO READ
11	3615th Student Squadron Craig AFB, Alabama	3550th Student Squadron Moody AFB, Georgia
9	147th Fighter Group, Ellington AFB, Houston, Texas	111th Fighter Interceptor Sq, Ellington AFB, Houston, Texas

B. ITEM | IS AMENDED TO INCLUDE

5. REMARKS.

6. DATE	7. APPROVING OFFICIAL (Typed name, grade and title)	8. SIGNATURE	9. PHONE NO.
17 Oct 68	KENNITH L. ROBINSON, Maj, TexANG, Ch, Pers & Tng Br	*Kennith L. Robinson*	Ext 71

10. DESIGNATION AND LOCATION OF HEADQUARTERS.
DEPARTMENT OF THE AIR FORCE
STATE OF TEXAS
ADJUTANT GENERAL'S DEPARTMENT
Post Office Box 5218
Austin, Texas 78703

11. ORDER (Type and No.)	12. DATE
ANG T 1110	17 Oct 68

12. FOR THE GOVERNOR

13. SIGNATURE ELEMENT OF ORDERS AUTHENTICATING OFFICIAL

[signature]

E. C. HERBER, Major, TexANG
Air Administrative Officer

14. DISTRIBUTION
1 - AGTEX-ALM/C
1 - AGTEX-AT
1 - ANG Liaison Officer, LMTC-OPA
1 - NGB (NG-AFCB)
50 - Unit of Assign, 147th FG
5 - BAO, TexANG, Ellington AFB, Texas
5 - 3615 Stu Sq, Craig AFB, Alabama
65 - Total

AF FORM 973 FEB 67

B-28128

REQUEST AND ~~~HORIZATION FOR CHANGE OF ADMINIST~~ TIVE ORDERS
(If more space i. .equired, continue on reverse, identifying .iems by number)

TO:	FROM:
AGTEX-AXO	AGTEX-AT

☐ REVOKED   ☐ RESCINDED
☒ AMENDED AS SHOWN IN ITEM 4

ORDERS PERTAINING TO THE INDIVIDUAL(S) LISTED IN ITEM 3 ARE

1. IDENTIFICATION OF ORDER BEING AMENDED (Issued by this Headquarters unless otherwise stated in item 5.)

A. PARA	B. ORDER (Type and No.)	C. DATE	D. EDCSA	E. RELATING TO (TDY, PCS, Short Tou of AD, etc.)
	ANG-T 1102	16 October 68	- - - - - -	School Tour

2. PREVIOUS AMENDMENTS ISSUED BY THIS HEADQUARTERS.

A. PARA	B. ORDER (Type and No.)	C. DATE

3. IDENTIFICATION OF INDIVIDUAL(S) TO WHOM CHANGE ACTION PERTAINS.

A. GRADE	B. LAST NAME, FIRST, MIDDLE INITIAL	C. AFSN OR POSITION TITLE (Civilian)	D. ORGANIZATION
2d Lt	BUSH, GEORGE W.	FG3244754 SSAN: ▮▮▮▮▮	111th Fighter Interceptor Sq

4. AMENDMENT (Identify item in order being amended)

A. ITEM	AS READS	IS AMENDED TO READ
9	147th Fighter Group, Ellington AFB Texas	111th Fighter Interceptor Sq, Ellington AFB, Texas
11	3615th Student Sq, Craig AFB, Ala.	3550th Student Sq, Moody AFB, Georgia

B. ITEM	IS AMENDED TO INCLUDE

revoked ANG-T 1145 30 Oct 68

B. REMARKS

6. DATE	7. APPROVING OFFICIAL (Typed name, grade and title)	8. SIGNATURE	9. PHONE NO.
28 Oct 68	KENNITH L. ROBINSON Maj, TexANG, Ch, Pers & Tng Br	Kenneth L. Robinson	Ext 71

10. DESIGNATION AND LOCATION OF HEADQUARTERS	11. ORDER (Type and No.)	12. DATE
DEPARTMENT OF THE AIR FORCE STATE OF TEXAS ADJUTANT GENERAL'S DEPARTMENT Post Office Box 5218 Austin, Texas 78703	ANG - T 1140	28 Oct 68

13.

FOR THE GOVERNOR

15. SIGNATURE ELEMENT OF ORDERS AUTHENTICATING OFFICIAL

E. C. HERBER, Major, TexANG
Air Administrative Officer

14. DISTRIBUTION
1 - AGTEX-ALM/C; Master 201 File
2 - AGTEX-AT
1 - ANG Liaison Officer, LMTC-OPA
1 - NGB (NG-AFCB)
50 - Unit of Assign., 147th FG
5 - BAO, TexANG, Ellington AFB, Texas
5 - 3615th Stu Sq, Craig AFB, Ala.
30 - 3550th Stu Sq, Moody AFB, Georgia

97 - Total

R-25126

O-201

REQUEST AND THORIZATION FOR CHANGE OF ADMINIS TIVE ORDERS
(If more space i.. required, continue on reverse, identifying items by number)

TO:	FROM:
AGTEX-AXO	AGTEX-AT

ORDERS PERTAINING TO THE INDIVIDUAL(S) LISTED IN ITEM 3 ARE

[X] REVOKED   [ ] RESCINDED
[ ] AMENDED AS SHOWN IN ITEM 4

1. IDENTIFICATION OF ORDER BEING AMENDED (Issued by this Headquarters unless otherwise stated in item 5.)

A. PARA	B. ORDER (Type and No.)	C. DATE	D. EDCSA	E. RELATING TO (TDY, PCS, Short Tour of AD, etc.)
	ANG T 1140	28 October 68	- - - - - - -	School Tour

2. PREVIOUS AMENDMENTS ISSUED BY THIS HEADQUARTERS.

A. PARA	B. ORDER (Type and No.)	C. DATE

3. IDENTIFICATION OF INDIVIDUAL(S) TO WHOM CHANGE ACTION PERTAINS

A. GRADE	B. LAST NAME, FIRST, MIDDLE INITIAL	C. AFSN OR POSITION TITLE (Civilian)	D. ORGANIZATION
2d Lt	BUSH, GEORGE W.	FG3244754 SSAN: ███████	111th Fighter Interceptor Sq

4. AMENDMENT (Identify item in order being amended)

A. ITEM	AS READS	IS AMENDED TO READ

B. ITEM	IS AMENDED TO INCLUDE

5. REMARKS

6. DATE	7. APPROVING OFFICIAL (Typed name, grade and title) KENNITH L. ROBINSON, Maj, TexANG, Ch, Pers & Tng Br	8. SIGNATURE *Kennith L. Robinson*	9. PHONE NO. Ext 71
30 Oct 68			

10. DESIGNATION AND LOCATION OF HEADQUARTERS
DEPARTMENT OF THE AIR FORCE
STATE OF TEXAS
ADJUTANT GENERAL'S DEPARTMENT
Post Office Box 5218
Austin, Texas 78703

11. ORDER (Type and No.) ANG T 1145	12. DATE 30 Oct 68

13. FOR THE GOVERNOR

15. SIGNATURE ELEMENT OF ORDERS AUTHENTICATING OFFICIAL

E. C. HERBER, Major, TexANG
Air Administrative Officer

14. DISTRIBUTION
1 - AGTEX-ALM/C, Master 201 file
2 - AGTEX-AI
4 ANG Liaison Officer, LMTC-OPA
1 - NGB (NG-AFCB)
50 - Unit of Assign, 147th FG
5 - BAO, TexANG, Ellington AFB, Texas
5 - 3615th Stu Sq, Craig AFB, Ala.
30 - 3550th Stu Sq, Moody AFB, Georgia
97 - Total

B-25125

AF FORM 973
FEB 67

~~147th Cmbt Spt Sq~~
(Unit of Assignment)
TEXAS AIR NATIONAL GUARD
ELLINGTON AIR FORCE BASE, TEXAS

SUBJECT: ~~Incoming~~/outgoing* Clearance   ~~1 Nov 68~~
                                                              (Date)

1. All personnel of this group will be required to execute this clearance upon initial assignment and upon discharge or transfer.

2. Upon completion of clearance, individual concerned will sign and turn in to unit first sergeant. Clearance will then be hand carried to Group Personnel for necessary action.

3. Personnel Data:

   a. Name: ~~BUSH, GEORGE W.~~   Rank: ~~Amn~~   AFSN ~~AF XXXXXXX~~

   b. Reason for discharge, if applicable ~~commissioned as an officer~~

   c. Source, if initial assignment ~~NA~~

   d. Mailing address ~~5000 Longmont, # 8, Houston, Texas 77027~~

   e. Marital Status: ~~Single~~   Number of dependents:

   f. Civilian Occupation: ~~None~~   Company Name

   AND ADDRESS

4. Following sections will be cleared as required:

REQUIRED

(X)   Unit First Sergeant   (X)   Unit Supply
(X)   Section Supervisor   Base Supply
        OJT Trainers Name   Training
        Classified Documents   Personal Equipment
        Security Termination   (X)   Finance (Personnel)
        AF Form 47a/b   Civilian Personnel Office
(X)   Personnel   Air Tech Insurance
        I. D. Card   Operations
        Photo Lab   Motor Pool
(X)   Security Pass   Credit Union
        Auto Registration   NCO Club
(X)   Dispensary   Officer's Club
        Blood Type   ANG Auto Parking
        Records   (X)   ANG Coffee Shop
        Shots   AGAT
        AFR 35-9 Screening

        2 Jan 64   (Signature)
    (Date completed)

*Strike out non-applicable word.
DISTRIBUTION: Original to individual (outgoing only)
              One copy to Personnel

147th Cmbt Spt Sq

Texas Air National Guard

Ellington AFB, Texas

REPLY TO
ATTN OF: SQCR

12 Nov 68

SUBJECT: Application for Discharge

TO: 147th Ftr Gp

1. Request the following airman be discharged from the Texas Air
National Guard under provisions of paragraph __1hb__, ANGR 39-10.

    a. Name __George W. Bush__   SN AF26230638

    b. Present Rank __Amn__

    c. Enlistment Date __27 May 68__   Nr of Years Enlisted __6__

    d. Authority for Discharge Par 1hb, ANGR 39-10: Acceptance of
      Commission on 4 Sep 68. Request Amn be discharged eff 3 Sep 6

    e. Military behavior __Excellent__   Performance of Duty __Excellent__
                                              77027

    f. Current Mailing Address: __5000 Longmont, Apt#8, Houston, Texas__ 77

    g. TIM/PTI __43h__   MSO __26 May 74__

2. I certify that __George W. Bush__ has been cleared of all
property issued to him by this organization and that there is no
indebtness to the Government for the loss or damage of property.

3. Facts, circumstances, investigations and results thereof involved
concerning this case.

Airman has accepted a commission in the ANG. Request that he be dischar

from this unit eff 3 Sep 68.

4. The Selective Service Status and Obligations of individual have
been explained.

5. Subject (will) (willnot) reenlist in grade. Date of reenlistment
NA

Confirming
Case I 438
Disch - 3 Sep 68

MATTHEW F. HEIMAN, Lt Col, TEXANG
Commander

1 Atch
Clearance Sheet

STATE OF TEXAS
ADJUTANT GENERAL'S DEPARTMENT
Post Office Box 5218
Austin, Texas 78703

SPECIAL ORDER   21 November 1968
ANG-P 143

1. The following airmen, Tex ANG, are relieved from assignment indicated and
honorably discharged from Tex ANG and as a Res of the AF effective dates as
shown. NGB Form 438 will be furnished. Authority: Par 13 (Expiration of
Term of Svc), ANGR 39-10. TIN Code 430.

GRADE NAME AFSN SSAN UNIT	EFF DATE
SSGT CLARENCE R. CAFFEY, AF26006569, ▮▮▮▮▮▮▮ 147th Supply Sq, Ellington AFB, Tex	6 Dec 68
TSGT EDWARD J. DWORSKY, AF26006567, ▮▮▮▮▮▮▮ 147th Supply Sq, Ellington AFB, Tex	6 Dec 68
SGT GARY L. GOODNER, AF26006568, ▮▮▮▮▮▮▮ 147th Cmbt Spt Sq, Ellington AFB, Tex	6 Dec 68
SSGT WALTER N. JACKSON JR, AF26006563, ▮▮▮▮▮▮▮ 147th Consol Acft Maint Sq, Ellington AFB, Tex	22 Nov 68
SGT ERNEST E. KUBALA, AF26006565, ▮▮▮▮▮▮▮ 147th Consol Acft Maint Sq, Ellington AFB, Tex	29 Nov 68
SSGT COY D. LEWIS, AF26006566, ▮▮▮▮▮▮▮ 147th Supply Sq, Ellington AFB, Tex	29 Nov 68
SSGT FRANK S. LOTT JR, AF26006564, ▮▮▮▮▮▮▮ 147th Consol Acft Maint Sq, Ellington AFB, Tex	22 Nov 68
SGT WILBOURN B. McADAMS, AF26006571, ▮▮▮▮▮▮▮ 147th Cmbt Spt Sq, Ellington AFB, Tex	6 Dec 68
TSGT JAMES D. McSPADDEN, AF26006573, ▮▮▮▮▮▮▮ 147th Supply Sq, Ellington AFB, Tex	13 Dec 68
SSGT WILLIAM E. SMITH, AF26006572, ▮▮▮▮▮▮▮ 147th Consol Acft Maint Sq, Ellington AFB, Tex	13 Dec 68
SSGT RALPH WITTNER, AF26006574, ▮▮▮▮▮▮▮ 147th Consol Acft Maint Sq, Ellington AFB, Tex	13 Dec 68

2. The verbal orders of the CinC Tex ANG on 15 Nov 68 directing the relief
of SSGT ALFRED P. MUECK, AF26006561, ▮▮▮▮▮▮▮, from assignment 147th
Consol Acft Maint Sq, Ellington AFB, Tex and honorable discharge from Tex ANG
and as a Res of the AF effective 15 Nov 68 are confirmed, exigencies of the

Par 2, SO ANG-P 143, AGTEX, 21 Nov 68   (CONT'D)

service having been such as to preclude issuance of competent written orders in advance. NGB Form 438 will be furnished. Authority: Par 13 (Expiration of Term of Svc), ANGR 39-10. TIN Code 430.

3. The verbal orders of the CinC Tex ANG on 3 Sep 68 directing the relief of AMN GEORGE W. BUSH, AF26230638, SSAN: ████████, from assignment 147th Cmbt Spt Sq, Ellington AFB, Tex and honorable discharge from Tex ANG and as a Res of the AF effective 3 Sep 68 are confirmed, exigencies of the service having been such as to preclude issuance of competent written orders in advance. NGB Form 438 will be furnished. Authority: Par 14b (Accepted a Commission as an Officer in the Tex ANG), ANGR 39-10. TIN Code 434.

4. The verbal orders of the CinC Tex ANG on 18 Nov 68 directing the relief of SGT REX B. CARR, AF18627598, SSAN: ████████ from assignment 147th Consol Acft Maint Sq, Ellington AFB, Tex and honorable discharge from Tex ANG and as a Res of the AF effective 18 Nov 68 are confirmed, exigencies of the service having been such as to preclude issuance of competent written orders in advance. NGB Form 438 will be furnished. Authority: Par 15 (Resignation-Own Convenience), ANGR 39-10. TIN Code 432.

FOR THE GOVERNOR

E. C. HERBER
Major, Tex ANG
Air Administrative Officer

DISTRIBUTION
192 - AGTEX-AP

O-2

REPORT OF	☐ ARNGUS ☒ ANGUS	DATE
☐ ACTIVE DUTY ☒ ACDUTRA	☐ USAR ☐ AFRes	26 Nov 68

TO:
Chief NGB
Washington D.C. 20305

FROM:
3550 Plt Tng Wg
Moody AFB, Ga. 31601

1. LAST NAME – FIRST NAME – MIDDLE INITIAL	2. SERVICE NO.	3. GRADE	4. BRANCH	5. EYE
Bush, George W	FG3244754	2d Lt	USAF	

	DAY	MONTH	YEAR
6. EFFECTIVE DATE OF ENTRY ON ACTIVE DUTY/ACDUTRA (Determined by personnel officer at first duty station IAW criteria outlined in AR 37-104 or AFM 35-3)	25	Nov	68
7. REPORTING DATE (Date specified in orders or the actual reporting date if subsequent thereto)	25	Nov	68
8. DATE DEPARTED FROM DUTY STATION FOR HOME			
9. DATE TOUR OF DUTY TERMINATED (Include allowable travel time time for return to home)			

10. AUTHORITY LTR ORDER PAR ANG-T1102
HQ TRI Austin Tx DATED 16 Oct 68

11. LENGTH OF TOUR (Last than 90 days if ARNGUS or USAR)

12. (ARMY USE ONLY) UPON MOBILIZATION THIS ITEM WILL BE FILLED IN FOR MEMBERS OF UNITS OF RESERVE COMPONENTS OF THE ARMY AND COPIES OF ORDERS WILL NOT BE ATTACHED TO THIS FORM

ENTERED ON AD AS A MEMBER OF _____ (Unit and Unit Home Station)

ORDERED TO AD FROM (Home of Record or Home Address) _____

13. (ARMY USE ONLY) DA FORM 67-5 (Officer Efficiency Report) OR DA FORM 1059 (Academic Report) PREPARED AND FORWARDED
☐ YES – FORWARDED TO _____ DATE _____
☐ NO – REPORT WILL BE FORWARDED ON OR ABOUT (date) _____ ☐ NOT APPLICABLE

14. (ARMY USE ONLY) DATE OF RANK (for officers and warrant officers ordered to AD for 12 or more months) (enter computation on other side)

15. (AIR FORCE USE ONLY) DATE OF RANK
☐ AF FORM 352 (Computation of Date of Rank upon entry on EAD) PREPARED (See AFR 35-54)

16. REMARKS (explain reason for delay, if any, in complying with orders) ☐ SEE OTHER SIDE ☐ NONE	17. TYPED NAME AND GRADE LAWRENCE D. McDONALD 2d Lt USAF Chief Data Control	SIGNATURE (Adjutant or other officer representing CO) Lawrence M. Donald

18. STATEMENT OF PHYSICAL CONDITION

STATEMENT NO. 1 (In lieu of medical examination) I, THE UNDERSIGNED, UNDERWENT A COMPLETE MEDICAL EXAMINATION FOR MILITARY SERVICE ON OR ABOUT
24 May 68 WHICH WAS ACCOMPLISHED AT WESTOVER AFB, MASS
AND SINCE THAT TIME—

☒ I HAVE NOT BEEN TREATED BY CLINICS, PHYSICIANS, HEALERS OR OTHER PRACTITIONERS.

☐ I HAVE BEEN TREATED BY _____ DURING THE PERIOD FROM _____

TO _____ FOR _____

☐ I WAS HOSPITALIZED IN _____ HOSPITAL – ATTENDING PHYSICIAN WAS _____

DIAGNOSIS WAS _____

☒ DO/DO NOT BELIEVE THAT I AM NOW MEDICALLY QUALIFIED TO PERFORM SATISFACTORY MILITARY SERVICE
DATE 25 NOV 68 SIGNED _____

STATEMENT NO. 2 (Upon release from active duty or ACDUTRA) DURING MY TOUR OF DUTY FROM _____ TO _____ THERE HAS BEEN NO CHANGE IN MY PHYSICAL CONDITION, AND TO THE BEST OF MY KNOWLEDGE, I AM NOT SUFFERING ANY DISABILITY, DEFECT OR ILLNESS, WHICH WAS NOT PRESENT UPON ENTRY OR ACQUIRED DURING THIS TOUR OF DUTY.

DATE _____ SIGNED _____

19. INCLS (Check when inclosed)
☒ COPY OR EXTRACT OF PERTINENT ORDERS AND ANY AMENDMENTS THERETO ☐ REPORT OF MEDICAL EXAMINATION

DD FORM 1 MAR 66 **220** REPLACES EDITION OF 1 OCT 57, EXISTING SUPPLIES OF WHICH WILL BE USED.

ACTIVE DUTY REPORT

DEPARTMENTS OF THE ARMY AND THE AIR FORCE
NATIONAL GUARD BUREAU
WASHINGTON, D.C. 20310

SPECIAL ORDERS
NUMBER 196M

27 September 1968

1. By dir of the SAF announcement is made of the ext of Fed recog to the fol ANG offs in grade, State and on date indc, such offs having qual under the provisions of 32 USC 305 and 307:

GRADE	NAME	SN	UNIT	STATE	DATE OF FED RECOG
CAPT ROBERT L WILLIAMS		FG2098980	163 Tac Ftr Sq	IN	28 Aug 68
2DLT RICHARD A KEEHFUS		FG3235243	108 Tac Ftr Sq	NY	7 Jun 68
CAPT JOHN H OCONNOR JR		FG3069761	137 Mil Alft Sq	NY	7 Aug 68
2DLT BARRY C FAWCETT		FG3244757	269-1 Mbl Comm Sq	OH	8 Sep 68
2DLT EDWARD B BOWERS JR		FG3244740	157 Ftr Intcp Sq	SC	20 Sep 68
2DLT GEORGE W BUSH		FG3244754	111 Ftr Intcp Sq	TX	4 Sep 68
2DLT MICHAEL H EDEN		FG3244755	182 Ftr Intcp Sq	TX	13 Sep 68

2. By dir of the SAF announcement is made of the ext of Fed recog of the prom of the fol ANG offs in grade, State and on date indc, offs having qual for prom under the provisions of 10 USC, 8374, 8379 and ANGR 36-04:

GRADE	NAME	SN	UNIT	STATE	EFF DATE
MAJ LAWRENCE C CABRINHA		FG3059130	199 Ftr Intcp Sq	HI	5 Sep 68
LTCOL(DC) ARNOLD J GIVEN JR		FG999329	Hq WV ANG	WV	21 Aug 68

BY ORDER OF THE SECRETARY OF THE ARMY AND THE AIR FORCE:

OFFICIAL

C. BOATWRIGHT
Colonel, NGB
Executive, National Guard Bureau

WINSTON P. WILSON
Major General
Chief, National Guard Bureau

DISTR

15 ea State for ea Off
2 ea Off listed in Para 1 to HQ ARPC (RPCA-3) plus 4 cys
1 USAFMPC (AFPMHDS) Randolph AFB TX
1 USAFMPC (AFPMAJB1) Randolph AFB TX
1 NGPA
1 NGB MSS
100 NG-AFFHO

DEPARTMENT OF THE AIR FORCE
HEADQUARTERS 3550TH PILOT TRAINING WING (ATC)
MOODY AIR FORCE BASE, GEORGIA 31601

AERONAUTICAL ORDER   2 December 1968
119

The following officers, 3550th Stu Sq, ATC, Moody AFB, GA 31601, Class
70-04, who are assigned to a course of instruction for qualification as
Pilot, are required to participate frequently and regularly in aerial
flights as crew members per sec 102, EO 11157, 22 Jun 64, and para 4-4a,
AFM 35-13. This order is effective for the period 3 December 1968 through
2 December 1969, unless sooner relieved or suspended therefrom by competent
authority. FSC 7Y. Officers will comply with paragraph 2-10, AFM 35-13.
Authority: Para 4-8a, AFM 35-13.

GRADE, NAME & AFSN

CAPT RALPH A HINE, FV3175063, SSAN
2D LT RALPH P ANDERSON, FV3233984, SSAN
2D LT DANIEL C BEAUDETTE, FV3232836, SSAN
2D LT DAVID C BENTLEY, FV3227651, SSAN
2D LT CHARLES M BIDDULPH, FV3215853, SSAN
2D LT WILLIAM B BIRDWELL, FV3227414, SSAN
2D LT MILTON D BLAND, FV3227011, SSAN
2D LT JAMES J BONIN JR, FV3227724, SSAN
2D LT GEORGE W BUSH, FG3244754, SSAN   ANG
2D LT STEVEN A BRANER, FV3227013, SSAN
2D LT JOHN H BRUNSON, FV3227630, SSAN
2D LT CHARLES W BURTON, FV3194475, SSAN
2D LT MICHAEL J BONVISSUTO, FV3231010, SSAN
2D LT LAWRENCE R CHALMER, FV3233435, SSAN
2D LT JOSEPH A CHANEY, FV3227423, SSAN
2D LT LUIS R COLON, FV3227717, SSAN
2D LT WAYNE L COURTNEY, O105578, SSAN   USMC
2D LT LARRY L CUNNINGHAM, FV3227579, SSAN
2D LT ROGER C DAHLBERG, FV3227591, SSAN
2D LT HARVEY D DAHLJELM, FV3232404, SSAN
2D LT ARTHUR DEAN, FV3226900, SSAN
2D LT NORMAN R DOTTI, FV3233079, SSAN
2D LT HARRY T DRURY III, FV3227381, SSAN
2D LT THOMAS A DUCKETT, FV3227629, SSAN
2D LT MALCOLM E EMERSON, FV3194038, SSAN
2D LT ALLEN M ERLE, FV3226438, SSAN
2D LT RUFUS J FRAZIER JR, FV3231130, SSAN
2D LT SALVATORE A GIRIFALCO, FV3233060, SSAN
2D LT THOMAS J GOETZ, FV3232451, SSAN
2D LT BRUCE R GOULD, FV3227505, SSAN
2D LT ROSS L GRIGGS, FV3226461, SSAN
2D LT PAUL V GUNVILLE, FV3227650, SSAN
2D LT DAVID E HANIFL, FV3227366, SSAN
2D LT JEROME D HATCH, FV3226520, SSAN
2D LT LARRY R HIGGS, FV3234424, SSAN

Receipt Acknowledged 0750
Date/ ____ ruff Time ____
Signature ____

AO-119

AO-119, HQ 3550th Plt Tng Wg, (ATC), Moody AFB, Ga 31601, 2 Dec 1968

2D LT BRUCE E HENRY, FV3226947, SSAN
2D LT JAMES W HILL JR, FV3211150, SSAN
2D LT ALEX J HOUSE, FV3231135, SSAN
2D LT OMAR L HUMPHREY, O108654, SSAN   USMCR
2D LT RICHARD M JOBBINS, FV3211688, SSAN
2D LT ROBERT G JONES, FV3227447, SSAN
2D LT RONALD K KELSEY, FV3226597, SSAN
2D LT JEFFREY S KENYON, FV3233455, SSAN
2D LT JAMES F KOLONOSKI, FV3227722, SSAN
2D LT KENNETH W KOWALSKI, FV3194784, SSAN
2D LT PETER J LANDRY, FV3239413, SSAN
2D LT LARRY R LEROY, FV3210021, SSAN
2D LT TERRANCE J MCCOLLUM, FV3234077, SSAN
2D LT ALTON A MCKNIGHT JR, FV3227525, SSAN
2D LT JIMMY L MCLEAN, FV3239418, SSAN
2D LT ROBERT S HAGER, FV3233239, SSAN
2D LT RICHARD E NOREN JR, FV3227592, SSAN
2D LT MICHAEL J PAVLICK, FV3227001, SSAN
2D LT EMILE C PEROYEA III, FV3227462, SSAN
2D LT THOMAS J RENKEY, FV3234436, SSAN
2D LT PAUL F REPP, FV3231152, SSAN
2D LT BERNARD S REYNOLDS, FV3226617, SSAN
2D LT IRVING F ROMER, FV3227593, SSAN
2D LT ARDEN W SCHOENI, FV3227534, SSAN
2D LT JOHN W SCHWAB JR, O107535, SSAN   USMCR
2D LT JOSEPH F SMART, FV3226531, SSAN
2D LT MICHAEL S STRAWN, FV3227703, SSAN
2D LT JAMES A THOMPSON, FV3227760, SSAN
2D LT ROBERT B TREVATHAN JR, FV3227747, SSAN
2D LT RUSSELL G WENDT, FV3227561, SSAN
2D LT WALTER F WERNER JR, FV3212075, SSAN
2D LT BENNY E WHITE, O107570, SSAN   USMCR
2D LT LARRY L WILLIAMS, FV3227498, SSAN
2D LT HENRY J YEACKLY, III, FV3227691, SSAN
2D LT ROGER J BESTLAND, FV3227582, SSAN

                              CLARENCE S PARKER, Colonel, USAF
                              Commander

JOEL W ..... aptain, USAF
Chief, Administrative Services

DISTRIBUTION
"AO" Plus
 1 - ATC (ATPPR-CF)
70 - USAFMPC (AFPMDR)
        Randolph AFB, TX 78148

AO-119

RECORD OF MILITARY STATUS OF REGISTRANT	submitted initially and immediately upon chang...us. ....rences preceding each item refer to the Universa. ....of Training and Service Act, as amended, and Armed Forces Reserve Act of 1952, as amended.	DATE 9 Dec 68

TO: (Number and address of Local Board of jurisdiction)
Local Board No 294
201 Fannin St.
Houston, Texas 77002

FROM: (To include mailing address)
Commander: 147th Ftr Gp (TEXANG)
P.O. Box 34567
Houston, Texas 77034

1. LAST NAME - FIRST NAME - MIDDLE INITIAL	2. GRADE, RATE OR RANK	3. SERVICE NUMBER	4. SELECTIVE SVC NO.
BUSH, GEORGE W.	Amn	AF26230638	1-1 62 46 1-80

5. DATE OF BIRTH	6. HOME ADDRESS	7. ARMED FORCE
6 Jul 46	5000 Longmont Apt #8 Houston, Texas 77027	AF TEXANG

8. ORGANIZATION	9. LOCATION	10. PERIOD OF 3 TO 6 MOS ACTIVE DY FOR TNG¹	
147th Cmbt Spt Sq	Ellington AFB, Texas	FROM	TO

11. THE RECORDS OF THIS OFFICE PERTAINING TO THE ABOVE-NAMED INDIVIDUAL EVIDENCE THE FOLLOWING: (Check applicable subitem(s))

a. SEC 6(c)(2)(A) UMT&SA - WAS ENLISTED OR APPOINTED IN AN "ORGANIZED UNIT" OF THE NATIONAL GUARD OF THE STATE OF ___ ON ___

b. SEC 6(d)(1) UMT&SA - WAS SELECTED FOR ENROLLMENT OR CONTINUANCE IN ONE OF THE FOLLOWING AND HAS EXECUTED A DEFERMENT AGREEMENT:
- [ ] SENIOR DIVISION OF THE RESERVE OFFICERS' TRAINING CORPS.
- [ ] PLATOON LEADERS' CLASS OF THE MARINE CORPS.
- [ ] NAVAL AND MARINE CORPS OFFICER CANDIDATE TRAINING PROGRAM.
- [ ] RESERVE OFFICERS CANDIDATE PROGRAM OF THE NAVY.
- [ ] OFFICER PROCUREMENT PROGRAMS OF THE COAST GUARD AND COAST GUARD RESERVE.
- [ ] APPOINTED ENSIGN, NAVAL RESERVE, WHILE UNDERGOING PROFESSIONAL TRAINING.
- [ ] COURSE OF INSTRUCTION WAS [ ] COMPLETED [ ] TERMINATED ON ___
REGISTRANT WAS COMMISSIONED ON ___ AND CONTINUES IN A RESERVE COMMISSIONED STATUS.

c. SEC 6(d)(3) UMT&SA - WAS COMMISSIONED ON ___ IN A RESERVE COMPONENT OF THE ARMED FORCE ON ___ AFTER COMPLETION OF OFFICERS' CANDIDATE SCHOOL & CONTINUES IN A RESERVE COMMISSIONED STATUS

d. SEC 262 UMT&SA - IS A FULLY QUALIFIED AND SELECTED AVIATION CADET APPLICANT WHO SIGNED AN AGREEMENT OF SERVICE ON ___

e. SEC 262, AFRA - WAS ENLISTED ON ___ FOR 2 YEARS.

f. WAS ENLISTED ON ___ FOR 8 YEARS AND HAS AGREED TO ENTER ON 2 YEARS ACTIVE DUTY.

TO BE USED ONLY WHEN ABOVE SUBITEMS ARE NOT APPLICABLE

g. WAS ENLISTED, APPOINTED, OR COMMISSIONED IN A RESERVE COMPONENT OF THE ARMED FORCE ON ___ .

[X] h. HAVING BEEN [X] ENLISTED [ ] APPOINTED A COMMISSIONED OR WARRANT OFFICER AS CHECKED ABOVE:
- [ ] HAS CONTINUED TO SERVE SATISFACTORILY IN OTHER THAN READY RESERVE UNIT.
- [ ] IS SERVING SATISFACTORILY IN A UNIT OF THE READY RESERVE.
- [ ] HAS COMPLETED ON ___ 8 YEARS OF SATISFACTORY SERVICE, INCLUDING NOT LESS THAN 3 CONSECUTIVE MONTHS OF ACTIVE DUTY TRAINING, AS A MEMBER OF A UNIT OF THE READY RESERVE.
- [ ] CEASED TO SERVE SATISFACTORILY.
- [ ] TRANSFERRED TO THE [ ] STANDBY RESERVE [ ] RETIRED RESERVE.
- [ ] WAS DISCHARGED ON ___ AS A MEMBER OF THE ___ NATIONAL GUARD OF THE STATE OF ___ AND BECAME A MEMBER OF THE ___ RESERVE.
- [X] WAS DISCHARGED ON 3 Sep 68 AS A RESERVE OF THE Air Force BY REASON OF Accepted a Commission as an Officer in the TEXANG.

12. REMARKS

None

13. TYPED NAME, GRADE AND TITLE OF AUTHENTICATING OFFICER	14. SIGNATURE OF AUTHENTICATING OFFICER
DON H. BREWER, MSGT, Personnel Supv.	Don H Brewer

¹ Complete as required by Armed Force concerned.

DD FORM 44 (1 NOV 55)   PREVIOUS EDITIONS OF THIS FORM ARE OBSOLETE.   GPO 924-183

1969

Bush's first full year as a Guardsman was uneventful. He applied for pilot training on the T-33A and F-102A on March 20, and completed his training on the T-31/T-37/T-38 on December 2 (177–8). His September 9 Personnel Record Card (179–80) indicates that he earned 253 points from May 1968 to April 1969—a number that puts his disputed, but certainly far smaller, 1972–3 totals in perspective. Bush was awarded the rating of pilot on November 5 (183) and released from active duty training back into the reserve at the end of that month (185). On December 1 he pledged once again to "be a member of the Ready Reserve until 26 May 1974" (186), and an annual status report from the same day (188) confirms that he "continues to participate satisfactorily."

DEPARTMENTS OF THE ARMY AND THE AIR FORCE
NATIONAL GUARD BUREAU

APPLICATION FOR TRAINING

PART I
GENERAL INFORMATION
(To be completed by applicant)

1. LAST NAME	FIRST NAME	MIDDLE NAME	2. GRADE	3. AFSN	DATE OF BIRTH
BUSH	GEORGE	WALKER	2D LT	FG 3244754	6 July 1946

5. MAILING ADDRESS	6. UNIT OF ASSIGNMENT AND ADDRESS
5000 Longmont, #8 Houston, Texas 77027	147th Fighter group P. O. Box 34567 Houston, Texas 77034

7. TRAINING REQUESTED - COURSE NUMBER - TITLE

112501Z - Pre Interceptor Training (T-33A)
112500D - Interceptor Pilot Training (F-102A Long Course)

8. COURSE LOCATION	9. COURSE DURATION
Perrin AFB	112501Z - Appx 5 Wk. 112500D - Appx 16 Wks.

10. DESIRE TO ENTER TRAINING (Date)	11. WILL ACCEPT ANY DATE UNTIL (Date)
8 Dec 1968 (See Item 46)	See Item 46

12. AIRMEN ONLY
THE ABOVE REQUESTED COURSE IS PART OF PREVIOUSLY ALLOCATED NON PRIOR SERVICE QUOTA   N/A | 13. YES | 14. NO |

15. SIGNATURE OF APPLICANT	16. DATE
George W. Bush	20 March 1969

PART II
(To be completed by custodian of Field Personnel Records)

17. CIVILIAN OCCUPATION	18. AIR TECHNICIAN	19. EDUCATIONAL LEVEL
Student	☐ YES ☑ NO	BA

20. AIRMAN QUALIFYING EXAMINATION (AQE)	21. PRIMARY AFSC	DATE AWARDED	22. ADDITIONAL AFSC'S
N/A	0006	4 Sept 1968	None

23. DUTY AFSC	24. TMSD	TFCSD	25. PAY DATE
0006	27 May 1968	4 Sept 1968	27 May 1968

26. SECURITY CLEARANCE (Specify Interim or Final)	27. MARITAL STATUS	28. NUMBER DEPENDENTS (E-1 thru E-4)
Secret	Single	None

29. OVER 4 YEARS ENLISTED SERVICE (0-1 thru 0-3) ☐ YES ☑ NO	30. FLYING STATUS ☐ YES ☑ NO	31. AERO RATING N/A

32. FLYING HOURS

JET	-0-
CONV	-0-
FIRST PILOT	-0-

33. PHYSICAL PROFILE SERIAL (Airman) - DIAGNOSIS OF DEFECTS (If a digit other than "1" is recorded. Use block "46" if more space is needed)

P	U	L	H	E	S	SUFFIX
-						

N/A

34. SERVICE SCHOOLS ATTENDED.   COURSE NUMBER   TITLE   DATE COMPLETED

P-V4A - A (111103) - Undergraduate Pilot Training   2 Dec 1969
(T-31/T-37/T-38)

I certify to the accuracy of the above information and that all applicable provisions of AFM 50-5 and ANGR 53-05 have been complied with.

21 March 1969	RUFUS G. MARTIN, Capt, TexANG	
DATE	Personnel Staff Officer	SIGNATURE
	NAME, GRADE AND TITLE, TYPED	

NGB FORM 85
31 OCT 66   (This Form replaces NGB Form 65, dated 22 Mar 64, which is obsolete and will not be used)

PART III
(To be completed by Comptroller)

	CURRENT FISCAL YEAR	CARRY-OVER
35. PAY AND ALLOWANCES	2529.87	
36. FICA (Employers)	84.55	
37. STUDENTS TRAVEL A. MODE OF TRAVEL TP B. NR DAYS ROUND TRIPS 1	54.90	
38. HOUSEHOLD GOODS OR EXCESS BAGGAGE		
39. DEPENDENTS TRAVEL		
40. CLOTHING		
41. OTHER (Identify)		
42. ESTIMATED NUMBER OF DAYS ACCRUED 13	169.47	
43. TOTAL COST	2839.00	
44. PAY AND ALLOWANCES PER MONTH (Including FICA)	587.85 (Per day if less than one month)	

45. VERIFICATION BY COMPTROLLER

(signature)

(SIGNATURE)

RUFUS E MARTIN, Capt TexANG
Personnel Staff Officer

(NAME AND RANK-TYPED)

46. REMARKS

Officer is presently attending Undergraduate Pilot Training with the
3550th Student Squadron, Moody AFB, Georgia. Request class assignment for
course 11250IZ and course 11250OD be as close to release date of 2 Dec 1969
from Undergraduate Pilot Training as possible. This officer is medically
certified for military duty and possesses an approved valid physical.

FOR USE BY NGB

DOCUMENT NUMBER	DATE
AMOUNT-CURRENT FY $	

NGB FORM 65
31 OCT 66

(This Form replaces NGB Form 65, dated 22 Mar 54, which is obsolete and will not be used)

TRANSFER ACTIONS

FROM (UNIT)	TO (UNIT)	EDCSA	ORDER NO.	PAR	HQ	DT. OF ORDER
147 Cmbt Spt Sq	111 FIS TEXANG	4 Sep 68	ANG-A 146	1	AGTEX	28 Aug 68
			ORDER NO.	PAR	HQ	DT. OF ORDER

ANNUAL STATEMENT OF CREDITS AT AF FORM 1288A MAR 67 PREVIOUS EDITION OF THIS FORM WILL BE USED UNTIL STOCK IS EXHAUSTED.

PREPARING UNIT:

147 Ftr Gp TEXANG Ellington AFB Tex

CSS

A review of your record indicates that during the anniversary year ending _26 May 69_ you have been credited with these points and federal services.

TO:

BUSH, GEORGE W. 2LT

PART 1 MPERR COPY

DATE	9 Sep 69

ANNUAL REPORT OF TOTAL ALLOWABLE POINTS AND FEDERAL SERVICE

ACTIVE DUTY	226
INACTIVE DUTY	12
CORRESPONDENCE COURSES	0
GRATUITOUS CREDIT	15
TOTAL POINTS	253

YEAR OF SATISFACTORY SERVICE FOR RETIREMENT

[X] Yes [ ] No

FORWARD ANY CLAIM FOR POINTS, IN ADDITION TO THOSE LISTED ABOVE, TOGETHER WITH SUBSTANTIATION OF CLAIM, TO THE ABOVE PREPARING UNIT.

147 CSS

USAF RESERVE PERSONNEL RECORD CARD -- FOR RETENTION, PROMOTION, AND RETIREMENT

NAME (LAST, FIRST, MIDDLE INITIAL)	GRADE	SERVICE NUMBER	PERIOD COVERED	CARD NR
BUSH, GEORGE W.	2LT	AF26230638	27 May 68 - 26 May 69	1
			YEAR FOR RETIREMENT BEGINS / YEAR FOR RETENTION BEGINS	
			27 May 68 / 27 May 68	

6 Jul 46	NA	CODES FOR COLUMN HEADINGS
DATE OF BIRTH	AERO RATING	UTA - UNIT TRAINING ASSEMBLY APDY - APPROPRIATE DUTY EQT - EQUIVALENT TRAINING YP - TRAINING PERIOD

COMPUTATION OF SERVICE AND TRAINING POINTS

DATE	ACTIVE DUTY				INACTIVE DUTY TRAINING											TOTAL POINTS (ACROSS)	TOTAL POINTS (CUMULATIVE)
	FROM	TO	NR OF	UTA	APDY	EQT	YP	EXT COURSE	FLYING		INST		PREP INST				
	DAY MO	DAY MO	POINTS	PTS	PTS	PTS	PTS	CRS	HRS PTS	HRS	PTS	HRS	PTS	HRS	PTS		
27 May 68				2	2											2	2
29 May 68					2											2	4
25 Aug 68	14 Jul 25 Aug	43														43	47
7 Sep 68				2												2	49
9 Sep 68				2												2	51
2 Nov 68				2												2	53
3 Nov 68				2												2	55
26 May 69	25 Dec 31 Mar	183														183	238
26 May 69	FOR RESERVE MEMBERSHIP FROM 27 May 68 thru 26 May 69															15	253
	PERMANENTLY CLOSED																

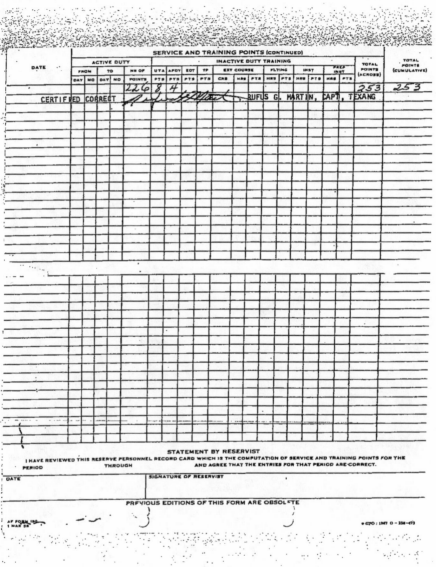

SERVICE AND TRAINING POINTS (CONTINUED)

DATE	ACTIVE DUTY																		TOTAL POINTS (ACROSS)	TOTAL POINTS (CUMULATIVE)
	FROM		TO		NR OF POINTS	INACTIVE DUTY TRAINING														
						UTA PTS	APDY PTS	EOT PTS	TP PTS	EXT COURSE CRS	FLYING HRS PTS		INST HRS PTS		PREP INST HRS PTS					
	DAY	MO	DAY	NO																
					226	8	4												253	253
CERTIFIED CORRECT									RUFUS G. MARTIN, CAPT, TEXANG										

STATEMENT BY RESERVIST

I HAVE REVIEWED THIS RESERVE PERSONNEL RECORD CARD WHICH IS THE COMPUTATION OF SERVICE AND TRAINING POINTS FOR THE
PERIOD   THROUGH   AND AGREE THAT THE ENTRIES FOR THAT PERIOD ARE CORRECT.

DATE	SIGNATURE OF RESERVIST

PREVIOUS EDITIONS OF THIS FORM ARE OBSOLETE

AF FORM 180
1 MAR 38

☆ GPO : 1947 O - 256-473

DEPARTMENTS OF THE ARMY AND THE AIR FORCE
NATIONAL GUARD BUREAU
WASHINGTON, D.C.   20310

SPECIAL ORDERS   6 October 1969

NUMBER   223M   E X T R A C T

2. Announcement is made of the verified pay date (TMSD) for the following
Air National Guard officers Federally recognized in the State indication. Any
previous orders in conflict with this paragraph are rescinded.

GRADE	NAME	SSAN	STATE	PAY DATE
2DLT	RALPH T MARAMAN	FG	AL	14 Jul 55
2DLT	GARY L STARLING	FG	AR	11 Feb 67
2DLT	CALDWELL LENT	FG	CA	8 Jul 65
CAPT(NC)	LORNA J MATSON	FG	CA	1 Nov 68
2DLT(NC)	SUE E MICHALAK	FG	CA	4 Dec 68
1STLT	RALPH G SANTOLUCITO	FG	CA	8 Oct 56
2DLT	MICHAEL A CUSHMAN	FG	DC	18 Dec 66
2DLT	MICHAEL Y M CHOW	FG	HI	17 Jan 67
2DLT	ROBERT B SLACK	FG	IL	17 Feb 68
2DLT	LARRY G MEEKER	FG	KS	1 Oct 68
2DLT	THOMAS G MOONEY	FG	KY	29 Jun 64
2DLT(MSC)	GERALD G LANDRY	FG	LA	15 Aug 67
2DLT	ROBERT F LEMOINE	FG	LA	24 Jun 68
1STLT	JOSEPH J SCALABRIN JR	FG	MD	9 Oct 64
1STLT	WILBUR K SMITH	FG	MD	20 Jan 64
2DLT	WALTER T SANTUCCI	FG	MA	20 Jun 62
2DLT	JEROME R SATKUS	FG	MA	23 Nov 65
1STLT(NG)	KATHLEEN D BARNEY	FG	MI	19 Dec 68
2DLT	CHARLES A BRETHEN III	FG	MI	6 Sep 68
2DLT	WILLIAM T LINCOLN	FG	MI	11 Jan 66
1STLT	O LARRY SECREST	FG	MI	10 Jan 66
2DLT	SAM R SMITH	FG	MI	12 Mar 55
2DLT	JAMES R STODDARD	FG	MI	21 Oct 55
2DLT	JOHN P SILLIMAN JR	FG	MN	14 Mar 66
2DLT	GAINES E MILES	FG	MS	20 May 68
2DLT	JAMES L SPIRES	FG	MS	20 Feb 68
2DLT	THOMAS W SCHLATTER	FG	MO	29 Jul 67
2DLT	ERROL L SMITH	FG	MO	16 Apr 66
2DLT	HOWARD H SHRIER	FG	NB	24 Aug 65
2DLT	PETER P BOUCHER	FG	NH	2 May 64
2DLT	EVERETT L BRAMHALL JR	FG	NH	15 Jan 66
2DLT	KENNETH R CLARK	FG	NH	24 May 68
2DLT	THOMAS F COCKS	FG	NJ	7 Jun 65
2DLT	DAVID A DEMONT	FG	NY	11 Jul 66

PAAF-NGB SO #223M, DATED 6 Oct 1969

1STLT	ROY R SPELLS		FG	NY	1 Jul 55
2DLT	JOHN D BROWNLEE		FG	OH	5 Oct 55
2DLT	CHRISTOPHER A MEALY		FG	OH	3 Jun 66
2DLT	BEIRN STAPLES		FG	OH	30 Apr 63
1STLT	JOHN F BLADY		FG	PA	21 Nov 64
2DLT	JOHN E CSAKLOS		FG	PA	21 May 68
2DLT	WALLACE G MURFIT		FG	PA	2 Jul 68
CAPT	DONALD J SEAMAN		FG	PA	5 Dec 49
2DLT	JAMES A STUART		FG	PR	6 Jul 65
2DLT	FRANCIS E FAUBERT		FG	RI	19 May 66
2DLT	JAMES C BAILEY		FG	TN	7 Aug 68
2DLT	CHARLES G CORNELIUS		FG	TN	8 Jun 68
1STLT	ROBERT H SIMMONS		FG	TN	12 Jul 64
2DLT	GEORGE W BUSH		FG	TX	27 May 68
1STLT(NC)	NAOMI B LOFTUS		FG	UT	16 Nov 68
2DLT(NC)	SONNET S MARLER		FG	UT	16 Nov 68
2DLT(NC)	SHARON K MARTZ		FG	WY	10 Jun 68

BY ORDER OF THE SECRETARIES OF THE ARMY AND THE AIR FORCE:

WINSTON P. WILSON
Major General
Chief, National Guard Bureau

OFFICIAL

JOSEPH K JELINEK
Colonel, NGB
Executive, National Guard Bureau

DISTRIBUTION:

1 ea. off file, NG-ANGPM
4 ea. State, (1) for ea off (2) to be mailed by State to off Unit of Asgmt
& CBPO
25 Air Pers Div (NG-ANGPM)

MASTER FILE

AUG

DEPARTMENT OF THE AIR FORCE
HEADQUARTERS 3550TH PILOT TRAINING WING (ATC)
MOODY AIR FORCE BASE, GEORGIA 31601

AERONAUTICAL ORDER   5 NOVEMBER 1969
135

THE FOLLOWING OFFICERS, 3550 STU SQ, ATC, THIS STN, HAVING SUCCESSFULLY
COMPLETED COURSE P-V4A-A, UNDERGRADUATE PILOT TRAINING, CLASS 70-04,
GRADUATING 26 NOVEMBER 1969, ARE AWARDED THE AERONAUTICAL RATING OF PILOT
EFFECTIVE 26 NOVEMBER 1969, PER PARA 1-14C, AFM 35-13, AND ARE REQUIRED TO
PARTICIPATE FREQUENTLY AND REGULARLY IN AERIAL FLIGHTS IN SUCH RATING PER
SEC .102, EO 11157, 22 JUN 64, AND PARA 2-5A, AFM 35-13. FSC CHANGED FROM
7Y TO 1Y. OFFICERS WILL COMPLY WITH PARA 2-10, AFM 35-13. AUTHORITY:
PARA 1-7B(1), AFM 35-13.

GRADE, NAME, & SSAN

CAPT MICHAEL J DEPAUL,
CAPT RALPH A HINE,
2D LT RALPH P ANDERSON,
2D LT GEORGE R BARNES,
2D LT DAVID C BENTLEY,
2D LT ROGER J BESTLAND,
2D LT CHARLES M BIDDULPH,
2D LT WILLIAM B BIRDWELL,
2D LT JOHN H BRUNSON,
2D LT CHARLES W. BURTON,
2D LT GEORGE W. BUSH, [NANG]
2D LT JOSEPH A. CHANEY,
2D LT ROGER C DAHLBERG,
2D LT NORMAN R DOTTI,
2D LT THOMAS A DUCKETT,
2D LT MALCOLM E. EMERSON,
2D LT RUFUS J FRAZIER, JR.,
2D LT SALVATORE A GIRIFALCO,
2D LT THOMAS J GOETZ,
2D LT ROSS L GRIGGS,
2D LT PAUL V GUNVILLE,
2D LT DAVID E HANIFL,
2D LT BRUCE E HENRY,
2D LT LARRY R HIGGS,
2D LT JAMES W HILL, JR.,
2D LT RICHARD M JOBBINS,
2D LT RONALD K KELSEY,
2D LT JEFFERY S KENYON,
2D LT JAMES F KOLONOSKI,
2D LT LARRY R LEROY,
2D LT TERRANCE J MCCOLLUM,

AO-135

AO-135; HQ 3550 PLT TNG WG, ATC, MOODY AFB, GA 31601, 5 NOVEMBER 1969

2D LT ALTON A MCKNIGHT JR.,
2D LT JIMMY L MCLEAN,
2D LT ROBERT S NAGER,
2D LT RICHARD E NOREN JR.,
2D LT EMILE C PEROYEA III,
2D LT THOMAS J RENKEY,
2D LT PAUL F REPP,
2D LT BERNARD S REYNOLDS,
2D LT IRVING F ROMER,
2D LT ARDEN W SCHOENI,
2D LT JOSEPH F SMART,
2D LT ROBERT B TREVATHAN JR.,

CLARENCE S. PARKER, COLONEL, USAF
COMMANDER

MARY M ABBOTT, CAPTAIN, USAF
CHIEF OF ADMINISTRATION

DISTRIBUTION
"AO" PLUS
1 - ATC (ATPPR-CF)
43 - USAFMPC (AFPMDR)
   RANDOLPH AFB, TX 78148

2

AO-135

THIS IS AN IMPORTANT RECORD
SAFEGUARD IT

1. LAST NAME-FIRST NAME-MIDDLE NAME	2. SERVICE NUMBER	3. SOCIAL SECURITY NUMBER
BUSH GEORGE WALKER	▮▮▮▮ FG	▮▮▮ ▮▮ ▮▮▮▮

PERSONAL DATA

4. DEPARTMENT, COMPONENT AND BRANCH OR CLASS	9a. GRADE, RATE OR RANK	9b. PAY GRADE	c. DATE OF RANK	DAY	MONTH	YEAR
AIR FORCE, ANGUS	2d Lt (P) 4 Sep 68	0-1		4	Sep	1968

7. U. S. CITIZEN		8. PLACE OF BIRTH (City and State or Country)		c. DATE OF BIRTH	DAY	MONTH	YEAR
☐ YES	☐ NO NA	NA			NA		

SELECTIVE SERVICE DATA

10a. SELECTIVE SERVICE NUMBER	b. SELECTIVE SERVICE LOCAL BOARD NUMBER, CITY, COUNTY, STATE AND ZIP CODE		c. DATE INDUCTED
41 62 46 1480	#294, Selective Service System, Room 907, 201 Fannin St, Houston TX 77002		DAY	MONTH	YEAR
			NA		

TRANSFERS OR DISCHARGE DATA

11a. TYPE OF TRANSFER OR DISCHARGE	b. STATION OR INSTALLATION AT WHICH EFFECTED
Release from active duty	Moody AFB GA 31601

c. REASON AND AUTHORITY		d. EFFECTIVE DATE	DAY	MONTH	YEAR
NA			29	Nov	69

12. LAST DUTY ASSIGNMENT AND MAJOR COMMAND	13a. CHARACTER OF SERVICE	b. TYPE OF CERTIFICATE ISSUED
NA	HONORABLE	NA

14. DISTRICT, AREA COMMAND OR CORPS TO WHICH RESERVIST TRANSFERRED	15. REENLISTMENT CODE
ANG, State of Texas	NA

SERVICE DATA

16. TERMINAL DATE OF RESERVE/UNTSR OBLIGATION	17. CURRENT ACTIVE SERVICE OTHER THAN BY INDUCTION	a. TERM OF SERVICE (Years)	c. DATE OF ENTRY
DAY	MONTH	YEAR	a. SOURCE OF ENTRY: ☐ ENLISTED (First Enlistment) ☐ ENLISTED (Prior Service) ☐ REENLISTED ☒ OTHER ACDUTRA Sec 505, USC 32	Indef	DAY	MONTH	YEAR
26	May	1974			22	Nov	1968

18. PRIOR REGULAR ENLISTMENTS	19. GRADE, RATE OR RANK AT TIME OF ENTRY INTO CURRENT ACTIVE SVC	20. PLACE OF ENTRY INTO CURRENT ACTIVE SERVICE (City and State)
NA	NA	NA

21. HOME OF RECORD AT TIME OF ENTRY INTO ACTIVE SERVICE (Street, RFD, City, County, State and ZIP Code)	22.	STATEMENT OF SERVICE	YEARS	MONTHS	DAYS
NA	CREDITABLE FOR BASIC PAY PURPOSES	(1) NET SERVICE THIS PERIOD	NA		
		(2) OTHER SERVICE	NA		
23a. SPECIALTY NUMBER & TITLE	b. RELATED CIVILIAN OCCUPATION AND D.O.T. NUMBER	(3) TOTAL (Line (1) plus Line (2))	NA		
NA	NA	b. TOTAL ACTIVE SERVICE	NA		
		c. FOREIGN AND/OR SEA SERVICE	NA		

24. DECORATIONS, MEDALS, BADGES, COMMENDATIONS, CITATIONS AND CAMPAIGN RIBBONS AWARDED OR AUTHORIZED
NA

25. EDUCATION AND TRAINING COMPLETED
UPT Crse #P-V4A-A Nov 69

VA AND IMP. SERVICE DATA

26a. NON-PAY PERIODS/TIME LOST (Preceding Two Years)	b. DAYS ACCRUED LEAVE PAID	27a. INSURANCE IN FORCE (NSLI or USGLI)	b. AMOUNT OF ALLOTMENT	c. MONTH ALLOTMENT DISCONTINUED
None	19	☐ YES ☐ NO NA	$ NA	NA
	28. VA CLAIM NUMBER	29. SERVICEMEN'S GROUP LIFE INSURANCE COVERAGE		
	C- NA	☒ $10,000 ☐ $5,000 ☐ NONE		

REMARKS

30. REMARKS
Blood Group: O(P) College - BA Degree (History)

AUTHENTICATION

31. PERMANENT ADDRESS FOR MAILING PURPOSES AFTER TRANSFER OR DISCHARGE (Street, RFD, City, County, State and ZIP Code)	32. SIGNATURE OF PERSON BEING TRANSFERRED OR DISCHARGED
NA	*George W Bush* 2/Lt

33. TYPED NAME, GRADE AND TITLE OF AUTHORIZING OFFICER	34. SIGNATURE OF OFFICER AUTHORIZED TO SIGN
NORAN W CLATANOFF, 1st Lt, USAF Chief, Career Control	*Noran W Clatanoff*

DD FORM 214   PREVIOUS EDITIONS OF THIS FORM ARE OBSOLETE.

ARMED FORCES OF THE UNITED STATES
REPORT OF TRANSFER OR DISCHARGE

2

READY RESERVE SERVICE AGREEMENT

NAME (Last - first - middle)	RESIDENCE ADDRESS (Street No., Street, City, State)
BUSH, GEORGE W.	5000 Longmont #8 Houston, Tx 77027

RESERVE COMPONENT	MILITARY GRADE	SERVICE NUMBER
ANGUS	2d Lt	████FG

ZIP CODE	SOCIAL SECURITY NUMBER
77034	

I agree to be a member of the Ready Reserve until ___26 May 74___
DATE -- SEE NOTE BELOW *

I certify that as a member of the Ready Reserve until that date I am and will remain immediately available for any active duty, including active duty for training, to which I may be ordered in accordance with law.

I further certify that I understand that I will not be released from this agreement upon my own application unless all of the three following conditions have been met:

    1. there has been a substantial change in my status or circumstances;

    2. I have requested, prior to the date of an alert or notice of mobilization or the date of orders to active duty, either

        a. transfer to the Standby Reserve, or

        b. transfer to the Retired Reserve, or

        c. discharge from the armed force of which I am a member; and

    3. that request has been approved.

THIS AGREEMENT BECOMES EFFECTIVE UPON MY SIGNING IT, BELOW.

SIGNATURE OF MILITARY DEPT REPRESENTATIVE	SIGNATURE OF MEMBER	DATE SIGNED
[signature]	*George W Bush*	1 Dec 69

* NOTE: The date inserted in the first sentence of this agreement (above) must be one of the following, whichever is appropriate.

    For officers (including warrant officers) either:

        a) 3 or more years from the date the agreement is signed; or

        b) the date of the signer's eligibility for transfer to the Retired Reserve

    For enlisted men the date must be one or more years from the date the agreement is signed.

DD FORM 1644
JAN 68

STATEMENT OF UNDERSTANDING

FOR READY RESERVE AIR FORCE RESERVE MEMBER

_____

I understand that, until discharged or transferred by proper authority, I will remain a member of the Ready Reserve after my Ready Reserve Service Agreement expires. Release from the Ready Reserve is a separate action, and I understand that, upon termination of this agreement, my eligibility for transfer from the Ready Reserve will be determined under current laws and regulations. I further understand that I may voluntarily request transfer from the Ready Reserve at any time subsequent to the termination of my Ready Reserve Service Agreement except in time of war or national emergency declared by Congress.

Additionally, I understand that as long as I remain assigned to the Ready Reserve I am subject to involuntary order to active duty in time of war or national emergency declared by the Congress, national emergency declared by the President, or when otherwise authorized by law.

_____
(TYPED NAME OF MEMBER)

RECORD OF MILITARY STATUS OF REGISTRANT	● submitted initially and immediately upon change status. erences preceding each item refer to the Universal Military Training and Service Act, as amended, and Armed Forces Reserve Act of 1952, as amended.	DATE 1 Dec 69

TO: (Number and address of Local Board of Jurisdiction)
Local Board #62
Houston, Tx 77002

FROM (To include mailing address)
Commander, 147th Ftr Gp (TEXANG)
P. O. Box 34567, Houston, Tx 77034

1. LAST NAME - FIRST NAME - MIDDLE INITIAL	2. GRADE, RATE OR RANK	3. SERVICE NUMBER	4. SELECTIVE SVC NO.
BUSH, GEORGE W.	2d Lt	███████FG	41 62 46 148C

5. DATE OF BIRTH	6. HOME ADDRESS		7. ARMED FORCE
N/A	5000 Longmont #8 Houston, Tx 77027		AF TEXANG

8. ORGANIZATION	9. LOCATION	10. PERIOD OF 3 TO 6 MOS. ACTIVE DY FOR TNG
147th Ftr Gp	Ellington AFB, Texas	FROM / TO

11. THE RECORDS OF THIS OFFICE PERTAINING TO THE ABOVE-NAMED INDIVIDUAL EVIDENCE THE FOLLOWING:
(Check applicable subitem(s))

a. SEC 6(c)(2)(A) UMT&SA - WAS ENLISTED OR APPOINTED IN AN "ORGANIZED UNIT" OF THE NATIONAL GUARD OF THE STATE OF _____ ON _____

b. SEC 6(d)(1) UMT&SA - WAS SELECTED FOR ENROLLMENT OR CONTINUANCE IN ONE OF THE FOLLOWING AND HAS EXECUTED A DEFERMENT AGREEMENT:
☐ SENIOR DIVISION OF THE RESERVE OFFICERS' TRAINING CORPS.
☐ PLATOON LEADERS' CLASS OF THE MARINE CORPS.
☐ NAVAL AND MARINE CORPS OFFICER CANDIDATE TRAINING PROGRAM.
☐ RESERVE OFFICERS CANDIDATE PROGRAM OF THE NAVY.
☐ OFFICER PROCUREMENT PROGRAM OF THE COAST GUARD AND COAST GUARD RESERVE.
☐ APPOINTED ENSIGN, NAVAL RESERVE, WHILE UNDERGOING PROFESSIONAL TRAINING.
☐ COURSE OF INSTRUCTION WAS ☐ COMPLETED ☐ TERMINATED ON _____
REGISTRANT WAS COMMISSIONED ON _____ AND CONTINUES IN A RESERVE COMMISSIONED STATUS.

c. SEC 6(d)(2) UMT&SA - WAS COMMISSIONED ON _____ IN A RESERVE COMPONENT OF THE ARMED FORCE ON _____ AFTER COMPLETION OF OFFICERS' CANDIDATE SCHOOL & CONTINUES IN A RESERVE COMMISSIONED STATUS

d. SEC 6(a) UMT&SA - IS A FULLY QUALIFIED AND SELECTED AVIATION CADET APPLICANT WHO SIGNED AN AGREEMENT OF SERVICE ON _____ FOR 8 YEARS.

e. SEC 262(c), AFRA - WAS ENLISTED ON _____ FOR 8 YEARS AND HAS AGREED TO ENTER ON 2 YEARS ACTIVE DUTY.

f. WAS ENLISTED ON _____

TO BE USED ONLY WHEN ABOVE SUBITEMS ARE NOT APPLICABLE

g. WAS ENLISTED, APPOINTED, OR COMMISSIONED IN A RESERVE COMPONENT OF THE ARMED FORCE ON _____

h. HAVING BEEN ☐ ENLISTED ☐ APPOINTED A COMMISSIONED OR WARRANT OFFICER AS CHECKED ABOVE:
☐ HAS CONTINUED TO SERVE SATISFACTORILY IN OTHER THAN READY RESERVE UNIT.
☐ IS SERVING SATISFACTORILY IN A UNIT OF THE READY RESERVE.
☐ HAS COMPLETED ON _____ 8 YEARS OF SATISFACTORY SERVICE, INCLUDING NOT LESS THAN 3 CONSECUTIVE MONTHS OF ACTIVE DUTY TRAINING, AS A MEMBER OF A UNIT OF THE READY RESERVE.
☐ CEASED TO SERVE SATISFACTORILY.
☐ TRANSFERRED TO THE ☐ STANDBY RESERVE ☐ RETIRED RESERVE.
☐ WAS DISCHARGED ON _____ AS A MEMBER OF THE _____ NATIONAL GUARD OF THE STATE OF _____ AND BECAME A MEMBER OF THE _____ RESERVE.
☐ WAS DISCHARGED ON _____ AS A RESERVE OF THE _____ BY REASON OF _____

12. REMARKS
Annual report - continues to participate satisfactorily.

13. TYPED NAME, GRADE AND TITLE OF AUTHENTICATING OFFICER	14. SIGNATURE OF AUTHENTICATING OFFICER
RUFUS G. MARTIN, Capt, TexANG Personnel Staff Officer	*[signature]*

¹ Complete as required by Armed Force concerned.

DD FORM 44 (1 NOV 55)   PREVIOUS EDITIONS OF THIS FORM ARE OBSOLETE.   GPO 924-162

1970

1970 was a banner year for Bush, as he racked up 340 service points (199–200), completed his twenty-one-week training course on the F-102 (he is noted as "certified combat ready" on 202), and was recommended successfully for promotion to 1st Lieutenant (209–10, 212–19). His performance apparently excited the Guard enough that it saw fit to issue a press release celebrating his first solo flight (196). The initial releases of Bush's military records only included the first page of this release. As this book was going to press the complete document, along with others, were made available, and they are included in the final chapter.

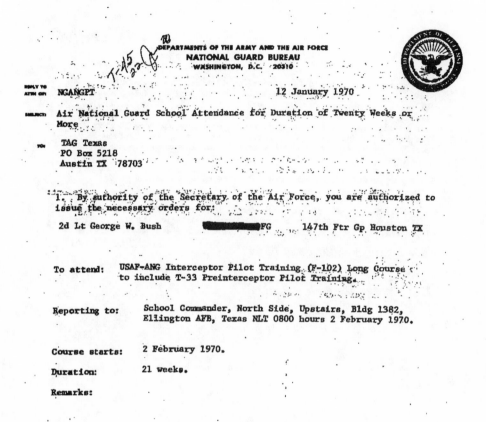

DEPARTMENTS OF THE ARMY AND THE AIR FORCE
NATIONAL GUARD BUREAU
WASHINGTON, D.C. 20310

REPLY TO
ATTN OF: NGANGPT

12 January 1970

SUBJECT: Air National Guard School Attendance for Duration of Twenty Weeks or More

TO: TAG Texas
PO Box 5218
Austin TX 78703

1. By authority of the Secretary of the Air Force, you are authorized to issue the necessary orders for:

2d Lt George W. Bush   FG   147th Ftr Gp Houston TX

To attend: USAF-ANG Interceptor Pilot Training (F-102) Long Course to include T-33 Preinterceptor Pilot Training.

Reporting to: School Commander, North Side, Upstairs, Bldg 1382, Ellington AFB, Texas NLT 0800 hours 2 February 1970.

Course starts: 2 February 1970.

Duration: 21 weeks.

Remarks:

2. Fund citations will be in accordance with the provisions of Volume X, AFM 300-4.

3. Orders assigning members to attend school, will indicate clearance for access to classified material and equipment up to and including secret under the provisions of AFR 205-6. The series number shown below will be included in orders.

ET 45-70-55

Series No. _____

4. Orders issued should contain information required by AFM 10-3 and Volume III, AFM 177-105, and will include the applicable law under which the member is ordered to active duty for training. Unless otherwise specified, the reference law is Section 505, Title 32, U. S. C. Compliance with applicable administrative procedures outlined in Part I, USAF Formal Schools Catalog is required. Reporting instructions to include hour of reporting which must be shown in orders are contained in AFM 50-5.

5. Transportation of dependents and shipment of household goods is authorized in accordance with current JTRs.

6. If student is an airman, orders will include the following statement: "AFAFC (Attn: CPF), 3800 York Street, Denver, Colorado, 80205, will be billed directly on a monthly basis for subsistence charges incurred.

FOR THE CHIEF, NATIONAL GUARD BUREAU:

RAYMOND J. HIGGINS
Chief, Air Personnel Division

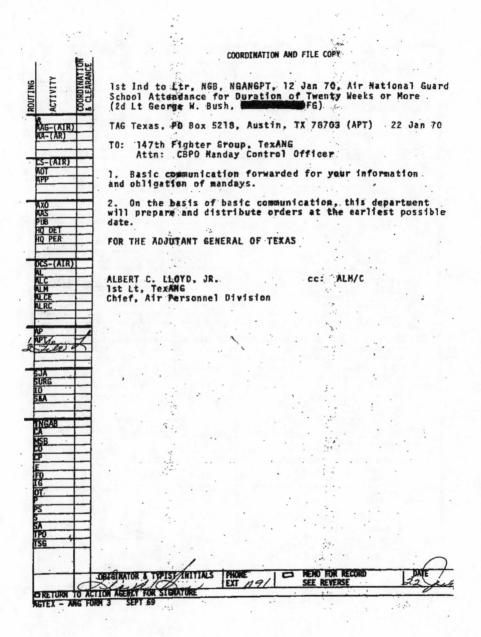

COORDINATION AND FILE COPY

1st Ind to Ltr, NGB, NGANGPT, 12 Jan 70, Air National Guard
School Attendance for Duration of Twenty Weeks or More.
(2d Lt George W. Bush, ▉▉▉▉▉▉FG).

TAG Texas, PO Box 5218, Austin, TX 78703 (APT)   22 Jan 70

TO: 147th Fighter Group, TexANG
     Attn: CBPO Manday Control Officer

1. Basic communication forwarded for your information
and obligation of mandays.

2. On the basis of basic communication, this department
will prepare and distribute orders at the earliest possible
date.

FOR THE ADJUTANT GENERAL OF TEXAS

ALBERT C. LLOYD, JR.   cc: ALM/C
1st Lt, TexANG
Chief, Air Personnel Division

04-201

REQUEST AND AUTHORIZATION FOR ACTIVE DUTY TRAINING/ACTIVE DUTY TOUR

TO: AGTEX-XO	FROM: AGTEX-AT

[X] BY ORDER OF THE SAF (VOLUNTARILY & WITH CONSENT OF THE GOVERNOR)

2. GRADE, LAST NAME, FIRST, MIDDLE INITIAL, AFSN	3. PAFSC
2D LT BUSH, GEORGE W. ████████ FG	0006

4. PRESENT ADDRESS	5. ON FLYING STATUS	6. AERO RATING
5000 Longmont #8 Houston, TX 77027	[X] YES ☐ NO	Rated

7. IS ORDERED TO ACTIVE DUTY FOR **143** DAYS PLUS REQUIRED TRAVEL TIME **and accrued leave**

8. PURPOSE (Type) ☐ ANNUAL TOUR [X] SCHOOL TOUR ☐ SPECIAL TOUR OF ACDUTRA ☐ SPECIAL TOUR OF AD
TITLE (Indicate specific school course or special tour title), Sec 505, USC 32

9. ANG ASSIGNMENT	10. UNIT OF ATTACHMENT
147th Fighter Group, PO Box 34567 TexANG, Houston, TX	NOT APPLICABLE

11. INDIVIDUAL WILL REPORT TO	HOUR	DAY	MONTH	YEAR
School Commander, North Side, Upstairs, Bldg 1382, Ellington AFB, Texas	NLT 0800	2	Feb	70
12. INDIVIDUAL WILL BE RELEASED FROM ORGANIZATION ATTACHED/ASSIGNED FOR ACTIVE DUTY TRAINING ON		27	Jun	70

13. INDIVIDUAL [X] IS ☐ IS NOT AUTHORIZED TO PARTICIPATE IN FLYING ACTIVITIES DURING THE PERIOD OF ACTIVE DUTY COVERED BY THIS ORDER.
14. AUTHORITY See Item 18 (Remarks)

15. INDIVIDUAL WILL PROCEED FROM PRESENT ADDRESS IN SUFFICIENT TIME TO COMPLY WITH REPORTING TIME AND DATE.

16. MODES OF TRANSPORTATION [X] AUTHORIZED ☐ DIRECTED ☐ TPC

MILITARY [X] AIRCRAFT	COMMERCIAL
	[X] AIRCRAFT ☐ RAIL [X] BUS

17. TON, PAY, ALLOWANCES, AND TRAVEL CHARGEABLE TO: FY70 5703850 560 4156. P523.02 (P&A) P523.05 (UG) P523.09 (Tvl) S594700 TDY. FY70 5703850 560 4145 P523.09 AOR AOR S41450C

18. REMARKS Security Clearance SECRET Series No ET-45-70-55. To Attend USAF ANG Intcp Plt Tng (F-102) Long Crse to include T-33 Pre Intcp Plt Tng Copy of paid vouchers will be furnished BAO, TexANG, Ellington AFB, TX NGB (NG-AFPS) Ltr, School Attendance of ANG Off for Duration of Less Than Twenty Weeks dated 12 Jan 70. Crse Duration: 21 weeks. Transportation of (OVER

19. DATE 22Jan70	21. APPROVING OFFICIAL (Typed Name and Grade) ALBERT C. LLOYD, JR. 1st Lt, TexANG Chief, Air Pers Division	22. SIGNATURE *Albert C. Lloyd Jr.*
20. PHONE NO. Ext 74		

23. DESIGNATION AND LOCATION OF HEADQUARTERS DEPARTMENT OF THE AIR FORCE STATE OF TEXAS ADJUTANT GENERAL'S DEPARTMENT Post Office Box 5218 Austin, Texas 78703	24. ANG ORDER NO. ANG-T 45 26. FOR THE GOVERNOR	25. DATE 22 Jan 70

27. DISTRIBUTION	28. SIGNATURE ELEMENT OF ORDERS AUTHENTICATING OFFICIAL
1 — Master 201 2 — AGTEX-AT 1 — ANG Liaison Off, LMTC, OPA 1 — NGB (NG-AFCB) 50 — Unit of Assignment, 147 FG 5 — BAO, TexANG, Ellington AFB, TX 5 — Sch Comdr, N Side Upstairs 65 — Total Bldg 1382, Ellington AFB, TX	E. G. HERBER Major, TexANG Air Administrative Officer

AF FORM 938 FEB 67

DIRECT ENTRY TECH TNG – OFFICER – LESS THAN 20 WEEKS

Item 18 Cont'd — dependents and shipment of household goods is authorized in accordance with current JTRs.

Office of Information   FOR IMMEDIATE RELEASE
147th Combat Crew Training Group   spl to The Houston Post
Texas Air National Guard   and The Houston Chronicle
Houston, Texas 77034   w/art

    ELLINGTON AFB, Tex., March 24, 1970---George Walker Bush is one
member of the younger generation who doesn't get his kicks from pot
or hashish or speed. Oh, he gets high, all right, but not from
narcotics.

    Bush is a second lieutenant attached to the 111th Combat Crew
Training Squadron, 147th Combat Crew Training Group, Texas Air National
Guard at Houston.

    Lt Bush recently became the first Houston pilot to be trained by
the 147th and to solo in the F-102 Fighter Interceptor, a supersonic,
all-weather aircraft.

    In January, the 147th's mission was changed from active air defense
of the Texas Gulf Coast to a new mission--to train and make combat-ready
all Air National Guard F-102 fighter pilots in the United States.

    Lt Bush was the first member of the 147th to be trained by people
he will be working with in the future.

    After his solo, a milestone in the career of any fighter pilot,
Lt Bush couldn't find enough words to adequately express the feeling of
solo flight.

    "It was really neat. It was fun, and very exciting", he said.
"I felt really serene up there. It's exciting to be alone in such a big
aircraft and it's a real challenge to fly such a powerful airplane by

MORE

| STATE (ANG) TEXAS | | | AIR RESERVE FORCES RETIREMENT CREDIT SUMMARY | | | | | | | | |

BREAKS IN SERVICE (Include complete breaks and assignment to Inactive Reserve Status)
none

DATE OF INITIAL ENTRY INTO SERVICE
27 May 68

BUSH, GEORGE W.
70

ACTIVE DUTY PRIOR TO 1 JUL 49
none

☐ WORLD WAR II
☐ KOREAN CONFLICT

DATE SERVICE FOR RETIREMENT BEGINS
27 May 68

ANNIVERSARY RETIREMENT DATE
27 May 68

ALLOWABLE FEDERAL SERVICE		STATUS	ACTIVE DUTY POINTS A	IN-ACTIVE DUTY POINTS B	ECI POINTS C	GRATU-ITOUS POINTS D	TOTAL POINTS E	RETIRE-MENT POINTS F	SATISFACTORY FEDERAL SERVICE			SOURCE DOCUMENT OR POSTING AUTHORITY J
									YEARS G	MONTHS H	DAYS I	
PRIOR TO 1 JULY 1949												
DATES					ON OR AFTER 1 JULY 1949							
FROM	TO											
27 May 68	26 May 69	AUG	226	12	0	15	253	253	1	0	0	AF FM 190
CERTIFIED CORRECT						ROGER W. BIVENS, 1st Lt, NGAUSPM, 21 May 70						

AF FORM 712
AUG 67
PREVIOUS EDITION OF THIS FORM WILL BE USED UNTIL STOCK IS EXHAUSTED

COPY: 2—FIELD PERSONNEL RECORD

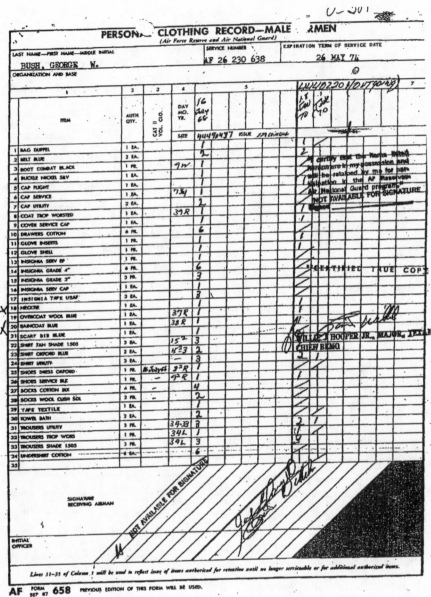

PERSONAL CLOTHING RECORD—MALE AIRMEN
(Air Force Reserve and Air National Guard)

LAST NAME—FIRST NAME—MIDDLE INITIAL	SERVICE NUMBER	EXPIRATION TERM OF SERVICE DATE
BUSH, GEORGE W.	AF 26 230 638	26 MAY 74

ORGANIZATION AND BASE

	ITEM	AUTH. QTY.	CAT II VOL. CLO.	SIZE				
1	BAG DUFFEL	1 EA.			2			
2	BELT BLUE	2 EA.						
3	BOOT COMBAT BLACK	1 PR.		9W	1			
4	BUCKLE NICKEL SILV	1 EA.			1			
5	CAP FLIGHT	1 EA.			1			
6	CAP SERVICE	1 EA.		7¾	1			
7	CAP UTILITY	2 EA.			2			
8	COAT TROP WORSTED	1 EA.		39R	1			
9	COVER SERVICE CAP	1 EA.			1			
10	DRAWERS COTTON	6 PR.			6			
11	GLOVE INSERTS	1 PR.			1			
12	GLOVE SHELL	1 PR.			1			
13	INSIGNIA SERV BP	1 PR.			1			
14	INSIGNIA GRADE 4"	6 PR.			6			
15	INSIGNIA GRADE 3"	3 PR.			3			
16	INSIGNIA SERV CAP	1 EA.			1			
17	INSIGNIA TAPE USAF	3 EA.			3			
18	NECKTIE	1 EA.			1			
19	OVERCOAT WOOL BLUE	1 EA.		37R	1			
20	RAINCOAT BLUE	1 EA.		38R	1			
21	SCARF BIB BLUE	1 EA.			1			
22	SHIRT TAN SHADE 1505	3 EA.		15²	3			
23	SHIRT OXFORD BLUE	2 EA.		15²3	2			
24	SHIRT UTILITY	3 EA.			3			
25	SHOES DRESS OXFORD	1 PR.		9³R	1			
26	SHOES SERVICE BLK	1 PR.		9³R	1			
27	SOCKS COTTON BLK	6 PR.			4			
28	SOCKS WOOL CUSH SOL	2 PR.			2			
29	TAPE TEXTILE	1 EA.			2			
30	TOWEL BATH	2 EA.			2			
31	TROUSERS UTILITY	3 PR.		34-33	3			
32	TROUSERS TROP WORS	1 PR.		34L	1			
33	TROUSERS SHADE 1505	3 PR.		34L	3			
34	UNDERSHIRT COTTON	6 EA.			6			
35								

CERTIFIED TRUE COPY

WILLIE J HOOPER JR., MAJOR, TEXAS
CHIEF BMSQ

SIGNATURE RECEIVING AIRMAN

NOT AVAILABLE FOR SIGNATURE

INITIAL OFFICER

Lines 31-35 of Column 1 will be used to reflect issue of items authorized for retention until no longer serviceable or for additional authorized items.

AF FORM 658   SEP 47   PREVIOUS EDITION OF THIS FORM WILL BE USED.

PREPARING UNIT:
117th FG TexANG Ellington AFB, TX

FIS

A review of your record indicates that
during the anniversary year ending
26 May 70 you have been cred-
ited with these points and federal services.

TO:
2nd Lt GEORGE W BUSH

⬛⬛⬛ FG

PART 1 MPERS COPY

DATE: 7 Jun 70	
ANNUAL REPORT OF TOTAL ALLOW-ABLE POINTS AND FEDERAL SERVICE	
ACTIVE DUTY	313
INACTIVE DUTY	12
CORRESPONDENCE COURSES	00
GRATUITOUS CREDIT	15
TOTAL POINTS	340

YEAR OF SATISFACTORY
SERVICE FOR RETIREMENT
☒ Yes ☐ No.
FORWARD ANY CLAIM FOR POINTS, IN
DITION TO THOSE LISTED ABOVE, TOGET
WITH SUBSTANTIATION OF CLAIM, TO
THE ABOVE PREPARING UNIT

FIS

USAF RESERVE PERSONNEL RECORD CARD - FOR RETENTION, PROMOTION, AND RETIREMENT

NAME (LAST, FIRST, MIDDLE INITIAL)	GRADE	SERVICE NUMBER	PERIOD COVERED	CARD NR
BUSH, GEORGE W	2d Lt	FG3244754	27 May 69 - 26 May 70	2
		SSAN ⬛⬛⬛	YEAR FOR RETIREMENT BEGINS 27 May 68	YEAR FOR RETENTION BEGINS 27 May (253)
DATE OF BIRTH 6 Jul 46		AERO RATING NR		

CODES FOR COLUMN HEADINGS
UTA - UNIT TRAINING ASSEMBLY   APY - APPROPRIATE DUTY
EQT - EQUIVALENT TRAINING   TP - TRAINING PERIOD.

COMPUTATION OF SERVICE AND TRAINING POINTS

DATE	ACTIVE DUTY				INACTIVE DUTY TRAINING																TOTAL POINTS (ACROSS)	TOTAL POINTS (CUMULATIVE)
	FROM		TO		NR OF	UTA	APPV	EQT	TP	RET COURSE		FLYING		INST		PREV MBT						
	DAY	MO	DAY	MO	POINTS	PTS	PTS	PTS	PTS	CRD	HRS	PTS	HRS	PTS	HRS	PTS	HRS	PTS				
28 Nov 69		27 Mar	28		186																186	186
1 Dec 69		1 Dec	1	Dec	1																1	187
2 Dec 69								1													1	188
3 Dec 69								1													1	189
4 Dec 69								1													1	190
6 Dec 69						1															2	192
7 Dec 69						2															2	194
12 Dec 69		8 Dec	12	Nov	5																5	199
18 Dec 69		15 Dec	18	Dec	4																4	203
5 Jan 70		5 Jan	5	Jan	1																1	204

DATE	ACTIVE DUTY					INACTIVE DUTY TRAINING													TOTAL POINTS (ACROSS)	TOTAL POINTS (CUMULA)
	FROM		TO		M	UTA	APDT	ECT	TP	RET COURSE			FLTI			INST		PREP INST		
	DAY	MO	DAY	MO	PL	PTS	PTS	PTS	PTS	CRS	HRS	PTS	HRS	P	HRS	PTS	HRS	PTS		206
8 Jan 70	7	Jan	8	Jan	pa	2													2	206
11 Jan 70						2													2	208
11 Jan 70						2													2	210
30 Jan 70								1											1	211
2 May 70	2	Feb	26	May	114														114	325
26 May 70		FOR RESERVE MEMBERSHIP FROM 27 MAY 69 THROUGH 26 MAY 70																	15	340
		PERMANENTLY CLOSED																		
					3/3	8		4											340	340
	CERTIFIED CORRECT							RUFUS G. MARTIN, Capt. TexANG												

LAST NAME	FIRST NAME	MI	AFSN	GRADE	PLACE OF BIRTH		DATE OF LAST OER
BUSH, GEORGE. W.			FG32447754	1st Lt	72 APR 30	New Haven, Conn.	72 APR 30	2

CHRONOLOGICAL LISTING OF SERVICE

EODA	DAFSC	BRIEF DESCRIPTION OF DUTY—ORGANIZATION AND STATION
27May68 to 3Sep68		En1, NG Amn, Prin Dy Apr Adm Spec, RES (TexANG)
4Sep68	0006	Pilot Trainee, 111b Fighter Interceptor Squadron, Ellington AFB, Texas (TexANG)
26Nov68	0006	Stu Plt Tng, P-VA-A, 3550 Stu Sq, Moody AFB, Ga. (ATC)
		Total AD/ACDUTRA as of 26 May 69: 2d Lt, 226 days
69Dec29	0006	Pilot Trainee, 111th Fighter Interceptor Squadron, Ellington AFB, Texas (TexANG)
70 Jun 20	1125D	Pilot, Ftr Intcp, 111th Ftr Intcp Sq, Ellington AFB, Tx (TexANG)
		Total AD/ACDUTRA as of 70 May 26: 2d Lt 313 days
		Total AD/ACDUTRA as of 71 May 26: 2d Lt - 43 days, 1st Lt - 3 days
		Unit redesignated 111th Ftr Intcp Sq (Trng)

COMBAT REPORT

10. REMARKS Previous Service Numbers: AF26230538
Selective Service Number: 41-62-46-1480
Reserve Status Expires: 26 May 74   Code: AA
Clv Occupation: Aviatorics   Since:
Appointed: T L ... C ANG: ... ...
Unif. Maint. Alwo. Entitlement: ... ... Last Paid: ... ...
Next Payment Due: ...
Last Physical: ... ...   Class: ...
TAFCS: ...
TAFCS: ...

PERSONNEL ACTION REQUEST

DATE	NIZATION AND LOCATION
70 Jul 9	111th CCTS Ellington AFB, Tx

GRADE	SSAN	PERSONNEL ACTION NR
2d Lt		303

LAST NAME-FIRST NAME-MIDDLE INITIAL

BUSH, GEORGE W.

FROM:

147th CSS (CBPO—OR)

TO:

147th CCTS (SOCR)

REQUESTED ACTION

SECTION I

- [X] AWARD AFSC 1125D AS Primary • AFSC
- [ ] CHANGE PAFSC FROM_____ TO_____
- [ ] CHANGE CAFSC FROM_____ TO_____
- [ ] CHANGE FLYING STATUS CODE TO_____
- [ ] CHANGE FUNCTIONAL CATEGORY TO_____
- [ ] CHANGE/ANNOUNCE (ODSD) (DEROS) TO_____
- [ ] CHANGE AD SVC COMMITMENT TO_____
- [ ] ASSIGN RATED POSITION IDENTIFIER_____
- [X] ASSIGN FUNCTIONAL ACCOUNT CODE 3110 •
- [ ] ASSIGN PRO PAY RATING ___ AFSC
- EFFECTIVE_____
- [X] ASSIGN DAFSC 1125D • DUTY TITLE Pilot, Ftr Intcpt
- [X] RPTG OFFL IS Major William D. Harris, Jr. AND FOR_____
- [X] OTHER "See Remarks"
- [X] AUTHORITY AFM 35-1, AFM 36-1 & AFM 36-10.

- [X] WITHDRAW AFSC 0006
- [ ] WITHDRAW PRO PAY RATING_____ AFSC
- EFFECTIVE_____
- [ ] OJT: EFFECTIVE_____
  - [ ] ENTER AFSC_____ CODE_____
  - [ ] CONTINUE AFSC_____ CODE_____
  - [ ] WITHDRAW AFSC_____ CODE_____
  - [ ] COMPLETED AFSC_____ CODE_____
- [X] ASSIGN PROGRAM ELEMENT CODE 5AH •
- [ ] ADJUST DOS TO_____
- [ ] ADJUST (TAFMSD) (PAY DATE) TO_____ EFFECTIVE 70 Jun 20

TYPED NAME, GRADE AND POSITION TITLE

DON H. BREWER, MSGT, PERS SUPV

SIGNATURE OF SUPERVISOR/REQUESTING OFFICIAL

SECTION II

- [ ] I DO
- [ ] DO NOT CONCUR

CONCURRENCE

SIGNATURE OF INDIVIDUAL CONCERNED

SECTION III DUTY STATUS CHANGE

CHANGE DUTY STATUS FROM_____ TO_____

EFFECTIVE_____ HOURS, 19___ LOCATION:_____

SECTION IV ASSIGNMENT ACTION

ASSIGNMENT ACTION NUMBER_____ REPT NLT_____

EDCSA_____

ASSIGN FROM_____

SECTION V APPROVAL BY COMMANDER OR AUTHORIZED REPRESENTATIVE

	TYPED NAME, GRADE AND POSITION TITLE	SIGNATURE	DATE
FOR THE COMMANDER	JERRY B. KILLIAN, LT COL, COMMANDER		70 JUL 10

SECTION VI ACTION BY CBPO OFFICER

- [X] APPROVED
- [ ] DISAPPROVED
- [ ] BOARD ACTION REQUIRED

HEADQUARTERS 147th Cmbt Spt Sq
Ellington AFB, Tx

	TYPED NAME, GRADE AND POSITION TITLE	SIGNATURE	DATE
FOR THE COMMANDER	RUFUS G. MARTIN, CAPT, PERS STAFF OFF		70 JUL 11

THIS AUTHORIZATION REMAINS IN EFFECT AFTER AIRMAN'S DISCHARGE AND IMMEDIATE REENLISTMENT AT THE SAME STATION, PROVIDED THAT HE HAS NO BREAK IN MILITARY SERVICE.

SECTION VII REMARKS

Officer certified combat ready in F-102.

SECTION VIII CBPO COORDINATION RECORD

ADM	ASGMTS	C & T	OJT	FT	R & S	SA	ER/PR	RP
	AR	I & OP	MA	MR	MP	CM	PA	

OR 3

AF FORM 1098
DEC. 69

PREVIOUS EDITION WILL BE USED

U. S. GOVERNMENT PRINTING OFFICE: 1970 O—370-259

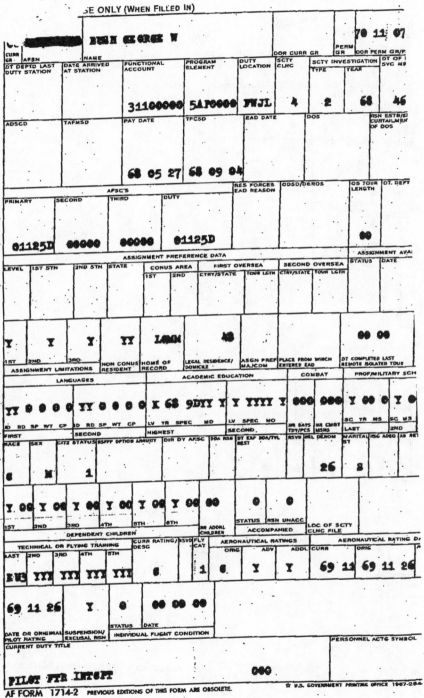

SE ONLY (WHEN FILLED IN)

BUSH GEORGE W

70 11 07

| CURR GR AFSN | NAME | | | | | DOR CURR GR | PERM GR | DOR PERM GR/P | DT OF SVC MO |
| DT DEPTD LAST DUTY STATION | DATE ARRIVED AT STATION | FUNCTIONAL ACCOUNT | PROGRAM ELEMENT | DUTY LOCATION | SCTY CLNC | SCTY INVESTIGATION TYPE YEAR | | | |

31160000 5AP0000 FWJL 4 2 68 46

| ADSCD | TAFMSD | PAY DATE | TFCSD | EAD DATE | DOS | RSN ESTB/C CURTAILMEN OF DOS |

68 05 27 68 09 04

| AFSC'S | | | | RES FORCES EAD REASON | ODSD/DEROS | OS TOUR LENGTH | DT. DEPT |
| PRIMARY | SECOND | THIRD | DUTY | | | | |

01125D 00000 00000 01125D 00

ASSIGNMENT PREFERENCE DATA   ASSIGNMENT AVA

| LEVEL | 1ST STN | 2ND STN | STATE | CONUS AREA | | FIRST OVERSEA | | SECOND OVERSEA | | STATUS | DATE |
| | | | | 1ST | 2ND | CTRY/STATE | TOUR LGTH | CTRY/STATE | TOUR LGTH | | |

Y Y Y YY LMMM 48 00 00

1ST	2ND	3RD	NON CONUS RESIDENT	HOME OF RECORD	LEGAL RESIDENCE/ DOMICILE	ASGN PREF/ MAJCOM	PLACE FROM WHICH ENTERED EAD	DT COMPLETED LAST REMOTE ISOLATED TOUR
ASSIGNMENT LIMITATIONS								
LANGUAGES			ACADEMIC EDUCATION			COMBAT		PROF/MILITARY SCH

YY 0 0 0 0 YY 0 0 0 0 X 68 9DYY Y Y YYYY Y 000 000 Y 00 0 Y 0

1D RD SP WT CP	1D RD SP WT CP	LV TR SPEC	MO	LV SPEC	MO	NR DAYS TDY/PCS	NR CMBT MSNS	SC TR MS LAST	SC MS 2ND
FIRST	SECOND	HIGHEST		SECOND					
RACE	SEX	CITZ STATUS	RSFPP OPTION ANNUITY	DIR DY AFSC	DDA RSN	DT EXP NON/TVL REST	RSVD REL DEROM	MARITAL ST	HSG ADEQ	AS RET

6 M 1 26 S

Y 00 Y 00 Y 00 Y 00 Y 00 Y 00 00 0 0

1ST	2ND	3RD	4TH	5TH	6TH	NR ADDNL CHILDREN	STATUS	RSN UNACC	LOC OF SCTY CLNC FILE
DEPENDENT CHILDREN							ACCOMPANIED		
TECHNICAL OR FLYING TRAINING					CURR RATING/ DESG	RSVD	FLY CAT	AERONAUTICAL RATINGS				AERONAUTICAL RATING D
LAST	2ND	3RD	4TH	5TH				ORIG	ADV	ADDL	CURR	ORIG

EU3 YYY YYY YYY YYY 6 1 6 Y Y 69 11 69 11 26

69 11 26 Y 0 00 00 00

	SUSPENSION/ EXCUSAL RSN	STATUS	DATE					PERSONNEL ACTG SYMBOL
DATE OR ORIGINAL PILOT RATING		INDIVIDUAL FLIGHT CONDITION						
CURRENT DUTY TITLE								

PILOT FTR INTCPT 000

AF FORM 1714-2 PREVIOUS EDITIONS OF THIS FORM ARE OBSOLETE.   ☆ U.S. GOVERNMENT PRINTING OFFICE 1967-284

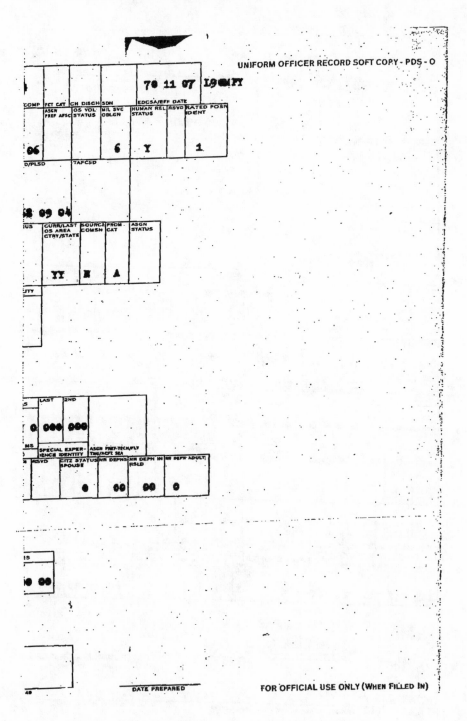

UNIFORM OFFICER RECORD SOFT COPY - PDS - O

70 11 07 19   FY

| COMP | FCT CAT | CH DISCH | SDN | EDCSA/EFF DATE | | |
| | ASGN PREF AFSC | OS VOL STATUS | MIL SVC OBLGN | HUMAN REL STATUS | RSVD | RATED POSN IDENT |

| 06 | | | 6 | Y | | 1 |
| D/PLSD | | TAFCSD | | | | |

8 09 04

| IUS | CURR/LAST OS AREA CTRY/STATE | SOURCE COMSN | PROM CAT | ASGN STATUS |
| | YY | N | A | |

UTY

S	LAST	2ND		
0	000	000		
MS	SPECIAL EXPER- IENCE IDENTITY	ASGN PREF-TECH/FLY TNG/ACFT SEA		
RSVD	CITZ STATUS SPOUSE	NR DEPNS	NR DEPN IN HSLD	NR DEPN ADULT
	8	00	00	0

| 15 |
| 00 00 |

| 48 | | DATE PREPARED | FOR OFFICIAL USE ONLY (WHEN FILLED IN) |

DEPARTMENT OF THE AIR FORCE
HEADQUARTERS 147TH COMBAT CREW TRAINING GROUP (ANG)
ELLINGTON AIR FORCE BASE, TEXAS 77030

SPECIAL ORDER
M - 27

5 August 1970

1. The following named officers/crewmembers are Flying Status Code (FSC) 1-Y (effective date indicated), meet ADC skill qualification indicated IAW AFM 51-102/ADC Sup 1, are authorized Passenger Carrying Pilots (PCP) IAW ADCR 55-18 (where indicated) and are Operational/Ready (O/R) or qualified in type aircraft indicated (*indicates Co-Pilot only qualified) Auth: AFM 60-1, ADCR 55-18, and AFM 51-102/ADC Sup 1.

NAME/GRADE/SSN/UNIT	PCP FTF	T33	C54	FSC 1-Y DATE	ADC SKILL RATING	O/R QUALIFIED FTF	T33	C54
ATTACHED								
B/GEN WALTER B STAUDT ⬛⬛⬛ FG	X	X	X	1 Jan 61	Expert	X	X	X
MAJ JOHN E STREIT ⬛⬛⬛ FV		X		1 Jan 61	N/A		X	
CAPT KENNETH J GURRY ⬛⬛⬛ FV		X		13 May 64	N/A		X	
147TH CCTG								
LTC BOBBY W HODGES ⬛⬛⬛ FG	X	X	X	1 Jan 61	Expert	X	X	X
LTC ROBERT J BLISSARD ⬛⬛⬛ FG	X	X		1 Jan 61	Expert	X	X	
MAJ EDGAR J HOLT ⬛⬛⬛ FG	X	X	X	1 Jan 61	Expert	X	X	X
MAJ DAVID H OWEN ⬛⬛⬛ FG	—			1 Jan 61	Skilled	X		
MAJ JAMES R BATH ⬛⬛⬛ FG		X		4 Aug 61	N/A		X	
MAJ HERBERT E ADAMS ⬛⬛⬛ FG	X	X		1 Jan 61	Expert	X	X	
CAPT GARY R WALSTON ⬛⬛⬛ FG		X		22 Oct 65	N/A		X	

M - 27

SO M-27 147th CCTG, TexANG, Ellington AFB, TX 5 Aug 70

NAME/GRADE/SSN/UNIT	PCP FTF	T33	C54	FSC 1-Y DATE	ADC SKILL RATING	O/R QUALIFIED FTF	T33	C54
111TH CCTS								
LTC JERRY B KILLIAN ████████ FG	X	X		1 Jan 61	Expert	X	X	X
LTC RICHARD D VIA ████████ FG	X	X	X	1 Jan 61	Expert	X	X	X
MAJ HARRY L SHACKELFORD ████████ FG				1 Jan 61	Skilled	X		
MAJ RICHARD A LAIDLEY ████████ FG	X			1 Jan 61	Expert	X		
MAJ STUART M PRESENT ████████ FG	X			1 Jan 61	Expert	X		
MAJ ARDA J ROY ████████ FG	X			1 Jan 61	Expert	X		
MAJ WILLIAM D HARRIS ████████ FG	X	X		1 Jan 61	Expert	X	X	X*
MAJ MAURICE H UDELL ████████ FG	X			1 Jan 61	Skilled	X		
MAJ VINCENT P CERISANO ████████ FG	X	X		1 Jan 61	Expert	X	X	X*
MAJ THOMAS E HUBELI ████████ FG	X			1 Jan 61	Expert	X		
MAJ ALOYSIUS M STEPCHINSKI ████████ FG		X		1 Jan 61	N/A		X	X*
CAPT CHARLES J WHITSETT ████████ FG	X			1 Jan 61	Skilled	X		
CAPT DAVID R BLUE ████████ FG	X			7 Dec 62	Expert	X		
CAPT DON R HAZELTINE ████████ FG				1 Jan 61	Qualified	X		

2

SO M-27 147TH CCTG, TexANG, Ellington AFB, TX 5 Aug 70

NAME/GRADE/SSN/UNIT	PCP			FSC 1-Y	ADC SKILL	O/R QUALIFIED		
	FTF	T33	C54	DATE	RATING	FTF	T33	C54
CAPT ARTHUR E WUNDER ▮▮▮▮▮ FG	X	X		27 Mar 64	Expert	X	X	
CAPT RICHARD L JACOBS ▮▮▮▮▮ FG	X	.		12 May 61	Expert	X		
CAPT JAMES B PASCAL ▮▮▮▮▮ FG		X		4 Aug 66	Skilled	X		
CAPT KENNETH L FARRIS ▮▮▮▮▮ FG				1 Jan 61	Expert	X		
CAPT EDWARD D MENDENHALL ▮▮▮▮▮ FG	X			1 Jan 61	Expert	X		
CAPT JAMES R MAYO ▮▮▮▮▮ FG	X			12 Sep 62	Expert	X		
CAPT BARRON D GRAY ▮▮▮▮▮				1 May 69	Qualified	X	X	
CAPT CHARLES MASLONKA JR ▮▮▮▮▮ FG	X	X		1 Jan 61	Expert	X	X	
CAPT OTIS L FINKELMAN ▮▮▮▮▮ FG				1 Jan 61	Skilled	X		
CAPT KENNETH D KNIGHT ▮▮▮▮▮ FG	X			1 Jan 61	Expert	X		
CAPT DON S CORWALL ▮▮▮▮▮ FG				30 Mar 62	Skilled	X		
ILT DEAN A ROOME ▮▮▮▮▮ FG				6 Jun 69	Qualified	X		*X
2LT FRED E BRADLEY ▮▮▮▮▮ FG				23 Aug 69	Qualified	X		*X
2LT LEE M HONEYCUTT ▮▮▮▮▮				19 Jul 69	Qualified	X		
2LT GEORGE W. BUSH ▮▮▮▮▮ FG				26 Nov 69	Qualified	X		

3

SO M-27 147TH CCTG, TexANG, Ellington AFB, TX 5 Aug 70

NAME/GRADE/SSN/UNIT	PCP FTF T-33 C54			FSC 1-Y DATE	ADC SKILL RATING	O/R QUALIFIED FTF T33 C54		
147TH GROUP AIR FORCE ADVISOR								
LTC PHILLIP R HANNEMAN ▓▓▓▓ FR	X	X		1 Jan 61	Expert	X	X	
147TH CAMRON								
LTC DAVID K BARNELL ▓▓▓▓ FG	X	X	X	1 Jan 61	Skilled	X	X	X
MAJ DEAN T LANDON ▓▓▓▓ FG	X	X		30 Mar 62	Skilled	X	X	X*
MSGT GALE D NOWLIN FG ▓▓▓▓			X	N/A	N/A			X
TSGT LOUIS E GUIDRY FG ▓▓▓▓			X	N/A	N/A			X
147TH CSS								
MAJ WILLIAM M CALHOUN ▓▓▓▓ FG			X	1 Jan 61	N/A			X

FOR THE COMMANDER

[signature]

DON B. BREWER, MSGT, TEXANG
Asst Admin Officer

DISTRIBUTION
M

DEPARTMENTS OF THE ARMY AND THE AIR FORCE
NATIONAL GUARD BUREAU

PROCEEDINGS OF A FEDERAL RECOGNITION EXAMINING BOARD

| CONVENED PURSUANT TO PARAGRAPH | SPECIAL ORDERS NO. | HEADQUARTERS Air Def Wpns | DATED |
| 1 | A-2532 | Ctr, Tyndall AFB, Fl ARMY | 24 August 1970 |

| PLACE | | DATE | HOUR |
| Ellington AFB, Texas | | 7 November 1970 | 0900 |

PRESENT: (All the members)

LT COL JERRY B. KILLIAN, ▮▮▮▮▮▮ FG, President
LT COL PHILIP R. HANNEMAN, ▮▮▮ FR, Member
CAPT RUFUS G. MARTIN, ▮▮▮▮▮ FG, Recorder

The order directing the applicant _____ GEORGE WALKER BUSH ▮▮▮▮▮ FG

111th FIS _____ Air National Guard _____ Texas
(UNIT) (NAME IN FULL) (BRANCH) 1st Lt (SERVICE NUMBER)
(GRADE)

To report for examination to determine his qualifications for Federal recognition as _____
Air National Guard
(BRANCH) _____ and the orders convening the Board were read.

The applicant was asked if he objected to examination by any member of the Board, to which he replied in the negative.
The members of the Board and the Recorder were duly sworn.
The Board proceeded with the examination and finds that—

| HIS PHYSICAL QUALIFICATIONS ARE SATISFACTORY | HIS MORAL CHARACTER IS SATISFACTORY | HIS GENERAL QUALIFICATIONS ARE SATISFACTORY |
| ☐ YES ☐ NO | ☐ YES ☐ NO | ☐ YES ☐ NO |

PROFESSIONAL QUALIFICATIONS

The Board then proceeded with the examination of the professional qualifications of the applicant and finds that—

The board was conducted in accordance with ANGR 36-03.

The board finds the candidate qualified for promotion to the grade and position for which recommended.

NGB FORM 89
1 OCT 57

PROFESSIONAL QUALIFICATIONS—Continued

MILITARY KNOWLEDGE QUALIFICATIONS ARE SATISFACTORY
☐ YES ☐ NO   GENERAL AVERAGE

ABILITY QUALIFICATIONS ARE SATISFACTORY
☐ YES ☐ NO

NON-MILITARY EDUCATIONAL QUALIFICATIONS ARE SATISFACTORY
☐ YES ☐ NO

CIVILIAN EXPERIENCE QUALIFICATIONS ARE SATISFACTORY
☐ YES ☐ NO

FINDINGS OF THE BOARD

THE BOARD FINDS THAT THE APPLICANT IS

PHYSICALLY— ☐ QUALIFIED ☐ NOT QUALIFIED   GENERALLY— ☐ QUALIFIED ☐ NOT QUALIFIED
MORALLY— ☒ QUALIFIED ☐ NOT QUALIFIED   PROFESSIONALLY— ☐ QUALIFIED ☐ NOT QUALIFIED

FOR THE APPOINTMENT SOUGHT, AND RECOMMENDS THAT HE BE (NOT) GRANTED FEDERAL RECOGNITION

DATE, EXAMINATION COMPLETED

7 November 1970

(RECORDER, GENERAL OFFICERS BOARD)

(MEDICAL OFFICER, GENERAL OFFICERS BOARD)

INCLOSURES

JERRY B. KILLIAN, Lt Col, TexANG

PHILLIP W. HANNEMAN, Lt Col, TexANG

RUFUS G. MARTIN, Capt, TexANG

DEPARTMENT OF THE AIR FORCE
HEADQUARTERS 147TH FIGHTER GROUP (TNG)
ELLINGTON AIR FORCE BASE, TEXAS 77030

SPECIAL ORDER
M - 38

30 October 1970

1. The following named officers are Flying Status Code (FSC) 1-Y (effective
date indicated); meet ADC skill qualification indicated IAW AFM 51-102/ADC
Sup 1; are authorized Passenger Carrying Pilots (PCP) IAW ADCR 55-18 (where
indicated) and are Operational Ready (O/R) or qualified in type aircraft
indicated (*indicated copilot only qualified).

NAME/GRADE/SSN/UNIT 111TH FIS	PCP FTF T33 C54	FSC 1-Y DATE	ADC SKILL RATING	O/R QUALIFIED FTF T33 C54
CAPT KENNETH D KNIGHT	X	1 Jan 61	Expert	X
1LT DEAN A ROOME		6 Jun 69	Qualified	X *X
2LT FRED E BRADLEY		23 Aug 69	Qualified	X
2LT LEE M HONEYCUTT		19 Jul 69	Qualified	X
2LT GEORGE W BUSH		26 Nov 69	Qualified	X
2LT HARRY J GLAUSER		16 Oct 69	Qualified	X

FOR THE COMMANDER

Don H. Brewer (signature)

DON H. BREWER, MSGT, TEXANG
Asst Admin Officer

DISTRIBUTION
M

M - 38

FROM: 111th Fighter Interceptor Squadron   3 NOV 1970

SUBJECT: Promotion of Officer

TO: 147th Fighter Group (GPCR)

1. Recommend the following officer be promoted to the grade and position indicated:

    a. GEORGE W. BUSH, 2d Lt, ███████████

    b. Recommended grade, position and applicable unit manning document: 1st Lt, Pilot, Fighter Interceptor, 111th Fighter Interceptor Squadron (R1637EV).

2. This officer completed the prescribed minimum creditable promotion service on 4 March 1970, and meets the other requirements prescribed in paragraph 4, ANGR 36-04. Request Lt Bush be examined by a Federal Recognition Board for the purpose of being promoted to 1st Lt on 7 November 1970.

3. Lt Bush is a dynamic outstanding young officer. He clearly stands out as a top notch fighter interceptor pilot. Lt Bush is possessed of sound judgement, yet is a tenacious competitor and an aggressive pilot. He is mature beyond his age and experience level as evidenced by his recent participation in the unit firing deployment. During this deployment, Lt Bush delivered both primary and secondary weapons from the F-102. The tactics and procedures conformed to a test project and were, therefore, more difficult to perform. Lt Bush performed in an outstanding manner, bringing credit to himself and the unit. He also participated in a practice element deployment and practiced simulated weapons delivery on varying geometries and tactics solutions. Lt Bush's skills far exceed his contemporaries. He is a natural leader whom his contemporaries look to for leadership. Lt Bush is also a good follower with outstanding disciplinary traits and an impeccable military bearing. He reflects credit upon himself and the Air National Guard. Lt Bush possesses vast potential and should be promoted well ahead of his contemporaries.

4. This promotion will result in the following authorized versus assigned grades within the unit:

	AUTHORIZED	ASSIGNED
Lt Colonel	5	3
Major	4	7
Captain	8	13
Lieutenants	13	7

JERRY B. KILLIAN, Lt Colonel, TexANG
Commander

3rd Ind to Ltr, 111th Fighter Interceptor Squadron, 3 Nov 70,
Promotion of Officer (2Lt George W. Bush, ████████ FG)

President, Federal Recognition Examining Board   **10 NOV 1970**

TO: TAG Texas

1. Subject officer examined on 7 November 1970.

2. Report of board proceedings, NGB Form 89, attached.

      SIGNED

JERRY B. KILLIAN, Lt Colonel, TexANG   4 Atch
President of the Board   n/c

1st Ind to 147th Cmbt Spt Sq (SQCR) Ltr, 3 Nov 70 , Promotion of
Officer (George W. Bush, 2d Lt)

3 NOV 1970

147th Fighter Group (GPCR)

TO: AGTEX-AP-O

Recommend approval. Lieutenant Bush is an outstanding officer who
performs all assigned tasks in a superior manner.

    SIGNED

BOBBY W. HODGES, Lt Colonel, TexANG
Commander

DISPOSITION FORM

(AR 340-15)

REFERENCE OR OFFICE SYMBOL	SUBJECT
AP-O	Promotion of Officer (2nd Lt George W Bush)

TO Gen Staudt
Gen Rose

FROM Captain Currie

DATE 5 Nov 70   CMT

IN TURN

The attached recommendation for promotion of 2LT GEORGE W BUSH, ▆▆▆▆▆ is forwarded for your review and/or comment.

R.E. CURRIE
Captain, TexANG
Chief, Officer Personnel Branch

1 Atch
a/s

Personnel
approval.

6 Nov 70

DA FORM 2496
1 FEB 62

REPLACES DD FORM 96, EXISTING SUPPLIES OF WHICH WILL BE
ISSUED AND USED UNTIL 1 FEB 63 UNLESS SOONER EXHAUSTED.

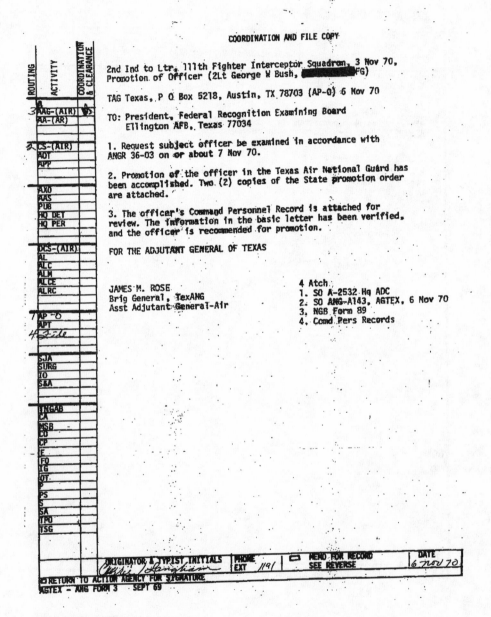

COORDINATION AND FILE COPY

2nd Ind to Ltr, 111th Fighter Interceptor Squadron, 3 Nov 70, Promotion of Officer (2Lt George W Bush, ████████FG)

TAG Texas, P O Box 5218, Austin, TX 78703 (AP-O) 6 Nov 70

TO: President, Federal Recognition Examining Board
      Ellington AFB, Texas 77034

1. Request subject officer be examined in accordance with ANGR 36-03 on or about 7 Nov 70.

2. Promotion of the officer in the Texas Air National Guard has been accomplished. Two (2) copies of the State promotion order are attached.

3. The officer's Command Personnel Record is attached for review. The information in the basic letter has been verified, and the officer is recommended for promotion.

FOR THE ADJUTANT GENERAL OF TEXAS

JAMES M. ROSE
Brig General, TexANG
Asst Adjutant General-Air

4 Atch
1. SO A-2532 Hq ADC
2. SO ANG-A143, AGTEX, 6 Nov 70
3. NGB Form 89
4. Comd Pers Records

ROUTING | ACTIVITY | COORDINATION & CLEARANCE

3 AAG-(AIR)
AA-(AR)

2 CS-(AIR)
AOT
APP

AXO
AAS
PUB
HQ DET
HQ PER

DCS-(AIR)
AL
ALC
ALM
ALCE
ALRC

7 AP-O
APT
4 File

SJA
SURG
IO
S&A

INGAB
CA
NSB
CO
CP
IE
FO
IG
OT
PS
S
SA
TPO
TSG

ORIGINATOR & TYPIST INITIALS | PHONE EXT 1191 | MEMO FOR RECORD SEE REVERSE | DATE 6 nov 70

RETURN TO ACTION AGENCY FOR SIGNATURE
AGTEX — ANG FORM 3   SEPT 69

STATE OF TEXAS
ADJUTANT GENERAL'S DEPARTMENT
Post Office Box 5218
Austin, Texas 78703

SPECIAL ORDER   6 November 1970
ANG-A *143*

1. SECOND LIEUTENANT LLOYD M BENTSEN III, ████████, 147th
Combat Support Squadron, Ellington AFB, TX 77034 is promoted
to the grade of FIRST LIEUTENANT in the TexANG. Officer will
report at time and place designated by President of the Federal
Recognition Examining Board, Ellington AFB, TX 77034, for
purpose of examination for Federal Recognition in the grade to
which promoted. Authority: ANGR 36-04.

2. SECOND LIEUTENANT FRED E BRADLEY, ████████, 111th Fighter
Interceptor Squadron, Ellington AFB, TX 77034 is promoted to
the grade of FIRST LIEUTENANT in the TexANG. Officer will
report at time and place designated by President of the Federal
Recognition Examining Board, Ellington AFB, TX 77034, for
purpose of examination for Federal Recognition in the grade to
which promoted. Authority: ANGR 36-04.

3. SECOND LIEUTENANT GEORGE W BUSH, ████████, 111th Fighter
Interceptor Squadron, Ellington AFB, TX 77034 is promoted to
the grade of FIRST LIEUTENANT in the TexANG. Officer will
report at time and place designated by President of the Federal
Recognition Examining Board, Ellington AFB, TX 77034, for
purpose of examination for Federal Recognition in the grade to
which promoted. Authority: ANGR 36-04.

4. MAJOR DANIEL D. CLINTON, JR, ████████, 147th Civil
Engineering Flight, Ellington AFB, TX 77034 is promoted to
the grade of LIEUTENANT COLONEL in the TexANG. Officer will
report at time and place designated by President of the Federal
Recognition Examining Board, Ellington AFB, TX 77034, for
purpose of examination for Federal Recognition in the grade to
which promoted. Authority: ANGR 36-04.

FOR THE GOVERNOR

E. C. HERBER   DISTRIBUTION
Lt Colonel, TexANG   45 - AGTEX-AP-O
Air Administrative Officer   1 - AGTEX-A
                                     46 - Total

DEPARTMENTS OF THE ARMY AND THE AIR FORCE
NATIONAL GUARD BUREAU
WASHINGTON, D.C. 20310

SPECIAL ORDER
NUMBER   287M   7 December 1970

By order of the Secretary of the Air Force and Direction of the President, each
of the following officers (ANGUS) is extended Fed recognition and promoted ResAF
to the grade indicated, per 10 USC 8365(c), 8366(c), 8374, 8376 and 8379,
effective date shown. Authority: Chapter 21 and 24, AFM 35-3.

NAME	SSAN	UNIT	EFFECTIVE DATE	STATE
LIEUTENANT COLONEL TO COLONEL				
DONALD L HARMON	FG	On EAD	21 Dec 70	KY
MAJOR TO LIEUTENANT COLONEL				
PIERRE HAVRE	FG	Hq 146 Tac Alft Wg	29 Nov 70	CA
ROBERT J MITTON	FG	163 Civ Engrg Flt	24 Nov 70	CA
ALEX P RICKMAN	FG	158 MASq	7 Dec 70	GA
MILTON MATTER JR	FG	113 Tac Ftr Sq	19 Oct 70	IN
LESTER A ROBERTS	FG	113 Tac Ftr Sq	19 Oct 70	IN
RALPH B CAMPBELL JR	FG	110 CAM Sq	13 Nov 70	MI
L ROBERT KREIZINGER	FG	155 Civ Engrg Flt	7 Dec 70	NE
JAMES T FLYNN	FG	105 Cmbt Spt Sq	30 Dec 70	NY
ROY C DESHA	FG	Hq 118 MAWg	2 Nov 70	TN
ALBERT C GROSS JR	FG	Hq 118 MAGp	2 Nov 70	TN
CLARENCE SUITER JR	FG	118 Spt Sq	2 Nov 70	TN
MELVIN D. BROWN	FG	167 Sup Sq	17 Dec 70	WV
PHILIP J CONLON	FG	Hq 128 ADWg	12 Dec 70	WI
CAPTAIN TO MAJOR				
ROBERT H RUHLE	FG	144 Tac Alft Sq	20 Nov 70	AK
JOHN C WITHERS	FG	113 Cmbt Spt Sq	25 Nov 70	DC
HARRY G NICHOL JR	FG	118 Aeromed Evac Sq	19 Oct 70	TN
BRUCE H LAUDERDALE	FG	116 FISq	4 Dec 70	WA
ROBERT A STELTER	FG	128 Sup Sq	20 Aug 70	WI
FRANKLIN J SMITH	FG	153 Spt Sq	23 Oct 70	WY
FIRST LIEUTENANT TO CAPTAIN				
CATHERINE M AVIANANTOS	FG	197 Aeromed Evac Flt	4 Oct 70	AZ
CLAYTON J ARNOLD JR	FG	161 USAF Disp	12 Jul 70	AZ
ROBERT S LAKE	FG	195 Tac Alft Sq	20 Nov 70	CA
WILLIAM S LUCIDO	FG	194 FISq	15 Oct 70	CA
JOHN R NELSON	FG	195 Tac Alft Sq	20 Nov 70	CA
MARY S HUBER	FG	109 Aeromed Evac Flt	23 Oct 70	MN
EDWARD J PASQUARELLA	FG	109 USAF Disp	25 Nov 70	NY
HARRY W ROBERTS JR	FG	136 Tac Ftr Sq	22 Oct 70	NY
ALBERT J SHULUSKY III	FG	137 Air Spt Sq	7 Dec 70	NY

SO 287M, DAAF-NGB, DATED 7 DECEMBER 1970

FIRST LIEUTENANT TO CAPTAIN

NAME	SSAN	UNIT	EFF DATE	STATE
RUTH E STOTZ	FG	139 Aeromed Evac Flt	6 Dec 70	NY
ROBERT S IVY	FG	185 MASq	28 Oct 70	OK
FRANK E HOCH	FG	142 Mbl Comm Sq	6 Aug 70	OR
MAUREEN T EWEN	FG	103 Aeromed Evac Flt	9 Oct 70	PA
EUGENE V FALSETTI	FG	112 CAM Sq	13 Aug 70	PA
KAREN L WEIGLE	FG	147 Aeromed Alft Sq	5 Dec 70	PA
FRANCIS W OWENS	FG	114 Cmbt Spt Sq	14 Oct 70	SD
ROBERT A BUNN	FG	Hq 118 MAWg	10 Nov 70	TN
ROBERT H SIMMONS	FG	118 Civ Engrg Flt	10 Nov 70	TN
SPENCE L WILSON	FG	155 MASq	23 Nov 70	TN
CAROL R BLOCKER	FG	187 Aeromed Alft Sq	5 Dec 70	WY

SECOND LIEUTENANT TO FIRST LIEUTENANT

NAME	SSAN	UNIT	EFF DATE	STATE
BERTHA E CASSARO	FG	162 USAF Disp	23 Sep 70	AZ
GARY J BIEN	FG	189 Sup Sq	21 Nov 70	AR
CHARLES R MONTEITH JR	FG	101 CAM Sq	19 Nov 70	ME
WALTON W ROGERS	FG	135 Civ Engrg Flt	9 Dec 70	MD
WILLIAM M HAWKINS	FG	172 Sup Sq	14 Dec 70	MS
MELVIN L WATSON	FG	Hq NV ANG	19 Nov 70	NV
HUGH H WILLIAMS	FG	188 Tac Ftr Sq	10 Dec 70	NM
JOHN C THOMAS	FG	193 TEW Sq	11 Jul 70	PA
LAWRENCE A SITTIG	FG	175 Tac Ftr Sq	23 Oct 70	SD
JAMES E PERKINS	FG	155 MASq	19 Nov 70	TN
JAMES C PERKINSON	FG	105 MASq	6 Dec 70	TN
FRED E BRADLEY	FG	111 FISq	7 Nov 70	TX
GEORGE W BUSH	FG	111 FISq	7 Nov 70	TX

BY ORDER OF THE SECRETARIES OF THE ARMY AND THE AIR FORCE:

OFFICIAL

JOSEPH R. JELINEK, Colonel, NGB
Executive, National Guard Bureau

WINSTON P. WILSON, Major General
Chief, National Guard Bureau

DISTRIBUTION:

10 ea State for ea Off
2 USAFMPC (DPMAJB1A)
2 USAFMPC (SGPSS)
2 USAFMPC (SGPSSM)
1 NGI
100 NGFPMO

MASTER FILE

1. LAST NAME FIRST NAME MI AFSN GRADE 131... APR 7 16

BUSH, GEORGE W. FG3244754

2. GRADE DATA

TEMPORARY	PERMANENT	EFF. DATE	DATE OF RANK
	2D Lt	4 Sep 1968	
	1st Lt	70 Nov 7	

4. FORMAL EDUCATION

SCHOOL—COLLEGE—UNIVERSITY	DEGREE	YEAR
Yale University	BA(Hist)	1968

SPECIAL EDUCATION/QUALIFICATIONS

3. SERVICE SCHOOLS
TECHNICAL—FLYING TRAINING

SCHOOL, COURSE AND NUMBER	LENGTH	YEAR
UPT Cls#P-V43-A Moody AFB, Ga, ANC112581	53 Wks	69Nov
F-33 Preintop Plt Tng, ANC112581	5 Wks	70Feb
F102 Intop Plt Tng, ANG 112500D	16 Wks	70Jun

AWARDS
SAEMR (P)

OTHER GRADE DATA

3. FOREIGN SERVICE

DATE DEPARTED	LOCATION	DATE RETURNED

PROFESSIONAL

COURSE

FOREIGN SERVICE SUMMARY

OSSD

6. DECORATIONS AND AWARDS

DECORATIONS AND AUTHORITY

7. SECURITY DATA

TYPE	DATE	REPORT FILED
BI	20Aug61	Hq USAF IOD51-1793

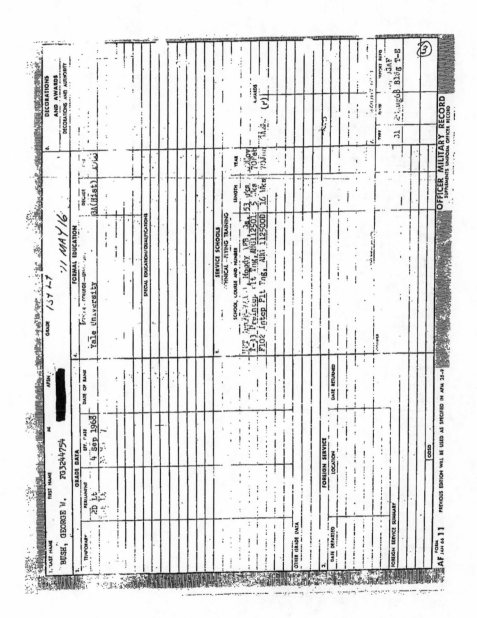

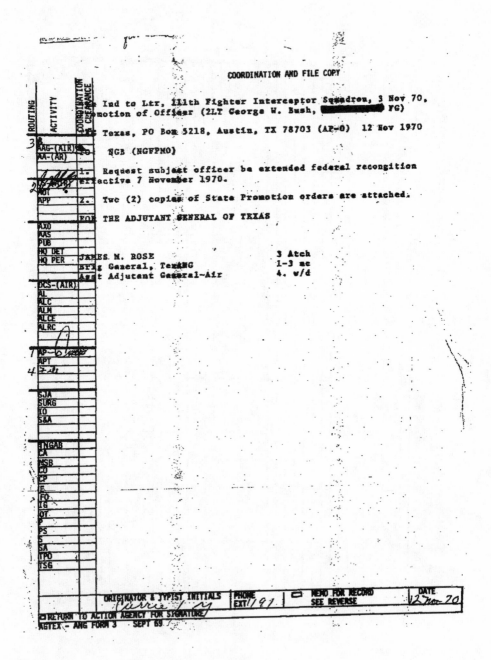

COORDINATION AND FILE COPY

Ind to Ltr, 111th Fighter Interceptor Squadron, 3 Nov 70, promotion of Officer (2LT George W. Bush, ████████ FG)

Texas, PO Box 5218, Austin, TX 78703 (AP-0)   12 Nov 1970

NGB (NGFPMO)

1. Request subject officer be extended federal recognition effective 7 November 1970.

2. Two (2) copies of State Promotion orders are attached.

FOR THE ADJUTANT GENERAL OF TEXAS

JAMES M. ROSE	3 Atch
Brig General, TexANG	1-3 ac
Asst Adjutant General-Air	4. w/d

ROUTING ACTIVITY COORDINATION CLEARANCE

3 AAG-(AIR)
   AA-(AR)
2 MOI
   APP

   AXO
   AAS
   PUB
   HQ DET
   HQ PER

   DCS-(AIR)
   AL
   ALC
   ALM
   ALCE
   ALRC

7 AP-0
   APT
4

   SJA
   SURG
   IO
   S&A

   SNGAB
   CA
   MSB
   CO
   CP
   E
   FO
   IG
   OT
   P
   PS
   S
   SA
   TPO
   TSG

ORIGINATOR & TYPIST INITIALS PHONE EXT/191 ☐ MEMO FOR RECORD SEE REVERSE DATE 12 nov 70

☐ RETURN TO ACTION AGENCY FOR SIGNATURE

AGTEX - ANG FORM 3   SEPT 69

1971

Bush's military records for 1971 are relatively slender; he appears to remain committed to the Guard. In his Officer Effectiveness Report for November 1969 through April 1972 (228–9), the first such form we have, he is given the highest possible ratings for the performance of his duties, effectiveness at working with others, leadership, and military qualities, though rated slightly lower on knowledge of his duties and his judgment. Accompanying statements (229, 230) characterize Bush as a disciplined officer whose main strengths are "eagerness to participate in the unit's activities and his ability to work harmoniously with others," while improving his proficiency as a pilot. He is credited with 137 service points for the year (231–4)—somewhat less than in previous years, but still satisfactory.

DEPARTMENT OF THE AIR FORCE
HEADQUARTERS 147TH FIGHTER GROUP (TNG)
ELLINGTON AIR FORCE BASE, TEXAS 77030

SPECIAL ORDER
F - 10

11 January 1971

1. Fol named off and/or amn, orgns indicated this station, are ordered
to attend Annual Active Duty Training at the Air National Guard training
site Ellington AFB, Texas for the period indicated. (Aero rating and fly
status as indicated). Personnel will report to their unit commander for
duty on effective date of training. Movement of dependents and household
effects at government expense not authorized. Per diem and TPC authorized in accordance with JD 25-69 dated effective 9 July 1969. Rated personnel on flying status are authorized to participate in flying activities
during the period covered by this order. Airmen within commuting distance
(50mi) are authorized basic allowances for subsistence at the rate of
$2.57 per day (Per diem not payable) when rations in kind not available
per paragraph 30102c DODPM. The bearer being the agent of an Air Force
Reserve member on active duty in excess of 72 hours is authorized commissary privileges only for the period covered by these orders. Individuals
not on active duty in excess of 72 hours are not authorized commissary
privileges. P/A (Off)5713850-561-4156-P521.01-S380000 (Amn) 5713850-561-
4156-P521.07-S380000. Trans: (Off) 5713850-561-4145-P521.14-408-S414502
(Amn) 5713850-561-4145-P521.18-408-S414502. PD: (Off) 5713850-561-4145-
P521.20-409-S414502 (Amn) 5713850-561-4145-P521.24-409-S414502. Auth:
ANGM 50-01. Title 32, USC, Sec 503 (Formerly Sec 94, National Defense Act).

111TH FIGHTER INTERCEPTOR SQUADRON	NO DAYS	PERIOD
CAPT WAYNE E WARE ████████	1	18Jan71 thru 18Jan71
PAFSC: 1125D Plt On-fly Scty Clnc: Secret		
25411 Stone Mill Lane, Spring TX 77373		
1ST LT GEORGE W BUSH JR ████████	1	12Jan71 thru 12Jan71
PAFSC: 1125D Plt On-fly Scty Clnc: Secret		
5320 Beverly Hill Lane, Hou TX 77027		

2. SMOP 1 SO F-566, this hqs, dtd 11Dec70, pertaining to CAPT OTIS L. FINKLEMAN,
████████ 111th FIS only as reads "NO DAYS": 1, PERIOD: 15Dec70 thru 15Dec70,
is amended to read "NO DAYS": 1, PERIOD: 14Dec70 thru 14Dec70.

3. SMOP 2 SO F-566, this hqs, dtd 11Dec70, pertaining to CAPT OTIS L. FINKLEMAN,
████████ 111th FIS only as reads o/a 15Dec70 is amended to read o/a 14Dec70.

FOR THE COMMANDER

DON H. BREWER, MSGT, TEXANG
Asst Admin Officer

F - 10

DISTRIBUTION
F

RECEIVED
JAN 22 1971
TexANG
ADMINISTRATIVE
SERVICES

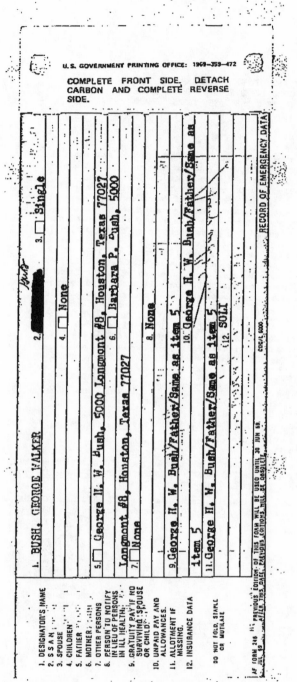

U.S. GOVERNMENT PRINTING OFFICE: 1969–359–472

COMPLETE FRONT SIDE. DETACH CARBON AND COMPLETE REVERSE SIDE.

RECORD OF EMERGENCY DATA

1. DESIGNATOR'S NAME — BUSH, GEORGE WALKER

2. S S A N.

3. SPOUSE — 3. ☐ Single

4. CHILDREN — 4. ☐ None

5. FATHER — 5. ☐ George H. W. Bush, 5000 Longmont #8, Houston, Texas 77027

6. MOTHER — 6. ☐ Barbara P. Bush, 5000 Longmont #8, Houston, Texas 77027

7. OTHER PERSONS — 7. ☐ None

8. PERSON TO NOTIFY IN LIEU OF PERSONS IN ILL HEALTH — 8. None

9. GRATUITY PAY IF NO SURVIVING SPOUSE OR CHILD — 9. George H. W. Bush/Father/Same as item 5

10. UNPAID PAY AND ALLOWANCES — 10. George H. W. Bush/Father/Same as item 5

11. ALLOTMENT IF MISSING — 11. George H. W. Bush/Father/Same as item 5

12. INSURANCE DATA — 12. SGLI $5000

DO NOT FOLD, STAPLE OR MUTILATE

AF FORM 246 PREVIOUS EDITION OF THIS FORM WILL BE USED UNTIL 30 JUN 69.
JUL 68 AFTER THIS DATE, PREVIOUS EDITIONS WILL BE OBSOLETE.

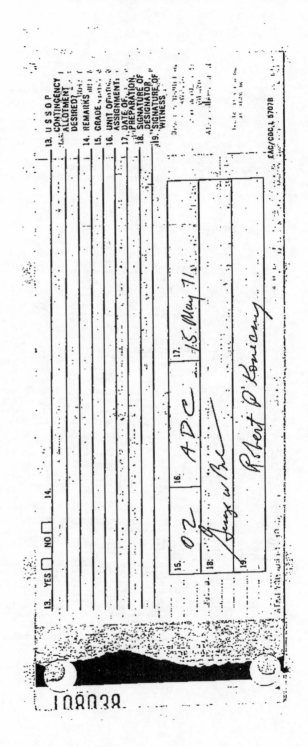

MASTER FILE ⑥

IDENTIFICATION DATA (Read AFM 36–10 carefully before filling out any item.)

1. LAST NAME—FIRST NAME—MIDDLE INITIAL	2. AFSN·SSAN	3. ACTIVE DUTY GRADE	4. PERMANENT GRADE
BUSH, GEORGE W	▓▓▓▓ FG	NONEAD	1st Lt

5. ORGANIZATION, COMMAND AND LOCATION	6. AERO RATING	CODE	7. PERIOD OF REPORT
111th Ftr Intcp Sq	C	1	FROM: 27 Nov 69 THRU: 30 Apr 71
Ellington AFB, Texas	8. PERIOD OF SUPERVISION		9. REASON FOR REPORT
Texas ANG (ADC)			Annual Report

II. DUTIES—PAFSC 1125D. DAFSC 1125D. Pilot, Fighter Interceptor, Squadron level. Pilots F102 type aircraft and performs airborne intercepts as required by assigned missions.

166 Active Duty Days/78 Training Periods

III. RATING FACTORS (Consider how this officer is performing on his job.)

1. KNOWLEDGE OF DUTIES

NOT OBSERVED	SERIOUS GAPS IN HIS KNOWLEDGE OF FUNDAMENTALS OF HIS JOB.	SATISFACTORY KNOWLEDGE OF ROUTINE PHASES OF HIS JOB.	WELL INFORMED ON MOST PHASES OF HIS JOB.	EXCELLENT KNOWLEDGE OF ALL PHASES OF HIS JOB.	EXCEPTIONAL UNDERSTANDING OF HIS JOB. EXTREMELY WELL INFORMED ON ALL PHASES.
				X	

2. PERFORMANCE OF DUTIES

NOT OBSERVED	QUALITY OR QUANTITY OF WORK OFTEN FAILS TO MEET JOB REQUIREMENTS.	PERFORMANCE MEETS ONLY MINIMUM JOB REQUIREMENTS.	QUANTITY AND QUALITY OF WORK ARE VERY SATISFACTORY.	PRODUCES VERY HIGH QUANTITY AND QUALITY OF WORK MEETS ALL SUSPENSES.	QUALITY AND QUANTITY OF WORK ARE CLEARLY SUPERIOR AND TIMELY.
					X

3. EFFECTIVENESS IN WORKING WITH OTHERS

NOT OBSERVED	INEFFECTIVE IN WORKING WITH OTHERS. DOES NOT COOPERATE.	SOMETIMES HAS DIFFICULTY IN GETTING ALONG WITH OTHERS.	GETS ALONG WELL WITH PEOPLE UNDER NORMAL CIRCUMSTANCES.	WORKS IN HARMONY WITH OTHERS. A VERY GOOD TEAM WORKER.	EXTREMELY SUCCESSFUL IN WORKING WITH OTHERS. ACTIVELY PROMOTES HARMONY.
					X

4. LEADERSHIP CHARACTERISTICS

NOT OBSERVED	OFTEN WEAK. FAILS TO SHOW INITIATIVE AND ACCEPT RESPONSIBILITY.	INITIATIVE AND ACCEPTANCE OF RESPONSIBILITY ADEQUATE IN MOST SITUATIONS.	SATISFACTORILY DEMONSTRATES INITIATIVE AND ACCEPTS RESPONSIBILITY.	DEMONSTRATES A HIGH DEGREE OF INITIATIVE AND ACCEPTANCE OF RESPONSIBILITY.	ALWAYS DEMONSTRATES OUTSTANDING INITIATIVE AND ACCEPTANCE OF RESPONSIBILITY.
					X

5. JUDGEMENT

NOT OBSERVED	DECISIONS AND RECOMMENDATIONS OFTEN WRONG OR INEFFECTIVE.	JUDGEMENT IS USUALLY SOUND BUT MAKES OCCASIONAL ERRORS.	SHOWS GOOD JUDGEMENT RESULTING FROM SOUND EVALUATION OF FACTORS.	SOUND, LOGICAL THINKER. CONSIDERS ALL FACTORS TO REACH ACCURATE DECISIONS.	CONSISTENTLY ARRIVES AT RIGHT DECISION EVEN ON HIGHLY COMPLEX MATTERS.
				X	

6. ADAPTABILITY

NOT OBSERVED	UNABLE TO PERFORM ADEQUATELY IN OTHER THAN ROUTINE SITUATIONS.	PERFORMANCE DECLINES UNDER STRESS OR IN OTHER THAN ROUTINE SITUATIONS.	PERFORMS WELL UNDER STRESS OR IN UNUSUAL SITUATIONS.	PERFORMANCE EXCELLENT EVEN UNDER PRESSURE OR IN DIFFICULT SITUATIONS.	OUTSTANDING PERFORMANCE UNDER EXTREME STRESS. MEETS THE CHALLENGE OF DIFFICULT SITUATIONS.
					X

7. USE OF RESOURCES

NOT OBSERVED (M ?)	INEFFECTIVE IN CONSERVATION OF RESOURCES.	USES RESOURCES IN A BARELY SATISFACTORY MANNER.	CONSERVES BY USING ROUTINE PROCEDURES.	EFFECTIVELY ACCOMPLISHES SAVINGS BY DEVELOPING IMPROVED PROCEDURES.	EXCEPTIONALLY EFFECTIVE IN USING RESOURCES.
	MATERIEL PERSONNEL	MATERIEL PERSONNEL	MATERIEL PERSONNEL	MATERIEL PERSONNEL	MATERIEL PERSONNEL

8. WRITING ABILITY AND ORAL EXPRESSION

NOT OBSERVED (W S)	UNABLE TO EXPRESS THOUGHTS CLEARLY. LACKS ORGANIZATION.	EXPRESSES THOUGHTS SATISFACTORILY ON ROUTINE MATTERS.	USUALLY ORGANIZES AND EXPRESSES THOUGHTS CLEARLY AND CONCISELY.	CONSISTENTLY ABLE TO EXPRESS IDEAS CLEARLY.	OUTSTANDING ABILITY TO COMMUNICATE IDEAS TO OTHERS.
	WRITE SPEAK	WRITE SPEAK	WRITE SPEAK	WRITE SPEAK	WRITE X SPEAK X

IV. MILITARY QUALITIES (Consider how this officer meets Air Force standards.)

NOT OBSERVED	BEARING OR BEHAVIOR INTERFERE SERIOUSLY WITH HIS EFFECTIVENESS.	CARELESS BEARING AND BEHAVIOR DETRACT FROM HIS EFFECTIVENESS.	BEARING AND BEHAVIOR CREATE A GOOD IMPRESSION.	ESPECIALLY GOOD BEHAVIOR AND BEARING. CREATES A VERY FAVORABLE IMPRESSION.	BEARING AND BEHAVIOR ARE OUTSTANDING. HE EXEMPLIFIES TOP MILITARY STANDARDS.
					X

AF FORM 77 JAN 66 PREVIOUS EDITION OF THIS FORM WILL BE USED UNTIL 30 JUN 69. AFTER THIS DATE, PREVIOUS EDITIONS WILL BE OBSOLETE.

COMPANY GRADE OFFICER EFFECTIVENESS REPORT

V. OVER-ALL EVALUATION (Compare this officer ONLY with officers of the same grade.)

SPECIFIC JUSTIFICATION REQUIRED FOR THESE SECTIONS							SPECIFIC JUSTIFICATION REQUIRED FOR THESE SECTIONS
☐	☐	☐	☐ ☐ ☐			☐ ☐	☒	☐
UNSATIS-FACTORY	MARGINAL	BELOW AVERAGE	EFFECTIVE AND COMPETENT			VERY FINE	EXCEPTIONALLY FINE	OUTSTANDING

VI. PROMOTION POTENTIAL

1. DOES NOT DEMONSTRATE A CAPABILITY FOR PROMOTION AT THIS TIME.	☐	2. PERFORMING WELL IN PRESENT GRADE. SHOULD BE CONSIDERED FOR PROMOTION ALONG WITH CONTEMPORARIES.	☐
3. DEMONSTRATES CAPABILITIES FOR INCREASED RESPONSIBILITY. CONSIDER FOR ADVANCEMENT AHEAD OF CONTEMPORARIES.	☐	4. OUTSTANDING GROWTH POTENTIAL BASED ON DEMONSTRATED PERFORMANCE. PROMOTE WELL AHEAD OF CONTEMPORARIES.	☒

VII. COMMENTS

FACTS AND SPECIFIC ACHIEVEMENTS: Lt Bush is an exceptionally fine young officer and pilot. After completing the F102 all weather interceptor school in November 1969, he came to this unit as a highly qualified fighter interceptor pilot. Lt Bush possesses sound judgment and is mature beyond his age and experience level. During the last weapons firing deployment, he delivered both primary and secondary weapons from the F102. Lt Bush performed in an outstanding manner, following the test project requirements set forth. He also participated in a practice element deployment during annual field training. He was easily able to handle intercepts with varying geometries and tactics selections. He continually flies intercept missions with the unit to increase his proficiency even further. Lt Bush is a natural leader but he is also a good follower of military discipline. Lt Bush has outstanding growth potential and should be promoted well ahead of his contemporaries. STRENGTHS: Lt Bush's main strengths are his eagerness to participate in the unit's activities and his ability to work harmoniously with others. SUGGESTED ASSIGNMENTS: At the present time Lt Bush should continue to serve as a squadron pilot. This will enable him to gain valuable knowledge of the Air National Guard's role in the defense of this country and experience as a pilot. SELF IMPROVEMENT EFFORTS: Lt Bush makes an effort to learn more about the all weather interceptor's mission and capability by attending squadron briefings and studying available material in his spare time. OTHER COMMENTS: Lt Bush is employed by Statford of Texas. He is on the managerial staff of this diversified company and tells the story of the Air National Guard and the USAF to the public at every opportunity. Since completing pilot training in November 1969 and F102 all weather interceptor school in June 1970, he has made a concentrated effort to improve his proficiency as a pilot. He is a member of the National Guard Association of the United States and Texas.

VIII. REPORTING OFFICIAL

NAME, GRADE, AFSN/SSAN, AND ORGANIZATION	DUTY TITLE		SIGNATURE	
WILLIAM D. HARRIS JR, Major	Pilot, Ftr Intcp			
FG, 111th FIS	AERO RATING	CODE	DATE	
Texas ANG (ADC)	B	1	26 May 1971	

IX. REVIEW BY INDORSING OFFICIAL

I concur with the comments and ratings of the reporting and indorsing officials.

NAME, GRADE, AFSN/SSAN, AND ORGANIZATION	DUTY TITLE		SIGNATURE	
JERRY B. KILLIAN, Lt Colonel	Squadron Commander			
FG, 111th FIS	AERO RATING	CODE	DATE	
Texas ANG (ADC)	A	1	27 May 1971	

● GPO : 1969 O – 328-191

LAST NAME-FIRST NAME-MIDDLE INITIAL	SSAN	ACTIVE DUTY GRADE
BUSH, GEORGE W	▓▓▓▓▓▓▓	NONEAD

(CHECK APPROPRIATE BLOCK AND COMPLETE AS APPLICABLE)

☒ SUPPLEMENTAL SHEET TO RATING FORM WHICH COVERS THE FOLLOWING PERIOD OF REPORT	☐ LETTER OF EVALUATION COVERING THE FOLLOWING PERIOD OF OBSERVATION

FROM	THRU	FROM	THRU
27 Nov 69	30 Apr 71		

Precede comments by appropriate data, i.e. section continuation, indorsement continuation, additional indorsement, etc. Follow comments by the authentication to include: name, grade, AFSN, organization, duty title, date and signature.

ADDITIONAL INDORSEMENT

I concur with the ratings of the reporting and indorsing officials. Lieutenant Bush is an outstanding young pilot and officer and is a credit to this unit. I have personally observed his participation, and without exception, his performance has been noteworthy. This officer is rated in the upper 10% of his contemporaries.

[signature]

BOBBY W. HODGES, Lt Colonel, ▓▓▓▓▓▓ FG, 147th Ftr Gp, Commander, 27 May 1971

TRANSFER ACTIONS

OM (UNIT)	TO (UNIT)	EDCSA	ORDER NO.	PAR	HQ	DT OF ORDER

PREPARING UNIT:
147th Ftr Gp, TexANG, Ellington AFB, TX

FIS

A review of your record indicates that during the anniversary year ending __26 May 71__ you have been credited with these points and federal services.

TO:

1ST LT GEORGE W. BUSH

DATE	21 Jun 71
ANNUAL REPORT OF TOTAL ALLOWABLE POINTS AND FEDERAL SERVICE	
ACTIVE DUTY	46
INACTIVE DUTY	76
CORRESPONDENCE COURSES	00
GRATUITOUS CREDIT	15
TOTAL POINTS	137

YEAR OF SATISFACTORY SERVICE FOR RETIREMENT

[X] Yes [ ] No

FORWARD ANY CLAIM FOR POINTS, IN ADDITION TO THOSE LISTED ABOVE, TOGETHER WITH SUBSTANTIATION OF CLAIM, TO THE ABOVE PREPARING UNIT.

PART 1 MPERR COPY

FIS

USAF RESERVE PERSONNEL RECORD CARD -- FOR RETENTION, PROMOTION, AND RETIREMENT

NAME (LAST, FIRST, MIDDLE INITIAL)	GRADE	SERVICE NUMBER	PERIOD COVERED	CARD NR
BUSH, GEORGE W.	LT 1ST SSAN FG		27 May 70 - 26 May 71	3

YEAR FOR RETIREMENT BEGINS 27 May 68   YEAR FOR RETENTION BEGINS 27 May 70 (340)

CODES FOR COLUMN HEADINGS
UTA - UNIT TRAINING ASSEMBLY   APDY - APPROPRIATE DUTY
EQT - EQUIVALENT TRAINING   TP - TRAINING PERIOD

DATE OF BIRTH 6 Jul 46   AERO RATING PLT ON-FLY NR

COMPUTATION OF SERVICE AND TRAINING POINTS

DATE	ACTIVE DUTY					INACTIVE DUTY TRAINING												TOTAL POINTS (ACROSS)	TOTAL POINTS (CUMULATIVE)
	FROM		TO		NR OF	UTA	APDY	EQT	TP	EXT COURSE		FLYING		INST		PREP INST			
	DAY	MO	DAY	MO	POINTS	PTS	PTS	PTS	PTS	CRS	HRS	PTS	HRS	PTS	HRS	PTS	HRS	PTS		
27 Jun 70	27 May	27 Jun			32														32	32
10 Jul 70									1										1	33
11 Jul 70						2													2	35
12 Jul 70						2													2	37
13 Jul 70									1										1	38
16 Jul 70									1										1	39
24 Jul 70	19 Jul	24 Jul			6														6	45
29 Jul 70									1										1	46
31 Jul 70									1										1	47
4 Aug 70									1										1	48

SERVICE AND TRAINING POINTS (CONTINUED)

DATE	ACTIVE DUTY FROM DAY MO	ACTIVE DUTY TO DAY MO	NR OF POINTS	UTA PTS	APDY PTS	EOT PTS	TP PTS	EXT COURSE CRS	FLYING HRS	FLYING PTS	INST HRS	INST PTS	PREP INST HRS	PREP INST PTS	TOTAL POINTS (ACROSS)	TOTAL POINTS (CUMULATIVE)
																48
8 Aug 70				2											2	50
9 Aug 70				2											2	52
14 Aug 70	10 Aug	14 Aug	5												5	57
18 Aug 70							1								1	58
24 Aug 70				2W			1								1	59
25 Aug 70				2W			1								1	60
12 Sep 70				2											2	62
13 Sep 70				2											2	64
15 Sep 70							1								1	65
18 Sep 70							1								1	66
3 Oct 70				2											2	68
4 Oct 70				2											2	70
17 Oct 70							1								1	71
22 Oct 70							1								1	72
5 Nov 70							1								1	73
7 Nov 70				2											2	75
9 Nov 70				2											2	77
23 Nov 70							1								1	78
24 Nov 70							1								1	79
25 Nov 70							1								1	80
5 Dec 70				2											2	82
6 Dec 70				2											2	84
17 Dec 70	16 Dec	17 Dec	2												2	86
3 Jan 71							1								1	87
9 Jan 71				2											2	89
10 Jan 71				2											2	91
12 Jan 71	12 Jan	12 Jan	1												1	92
14 Jan 71							1								1	93
19 Jan 71							1								1	94
26 Jan 71							1								1	95
6 Feb 71				2											2	97
7 Feb 71				2											2	99
4 Mar 71							1								1	100
4 Mar 71							1								1	101
11 Mar 71						2									2	103
23 Mar 71						1									1	104
26 Mar 71						1	1								2	106
2 Apr 71							1								1	107
3 Apr 71							1								1	108
4 Apr 71							1								1	109
8 Apr 71							1								1	110
9 Apr 71							1								1	111
17 Apr 71				2											2	113
18 Apr 71				2											2	115
29 Apr 71							1								1	116

AF FORM 190
FEB 69

PREVIOUS EDITION OF THIS FORM WILL
BE USED UNTIL STOCK IS EXHAUSTED.

* GPO : 1969 O—332-942

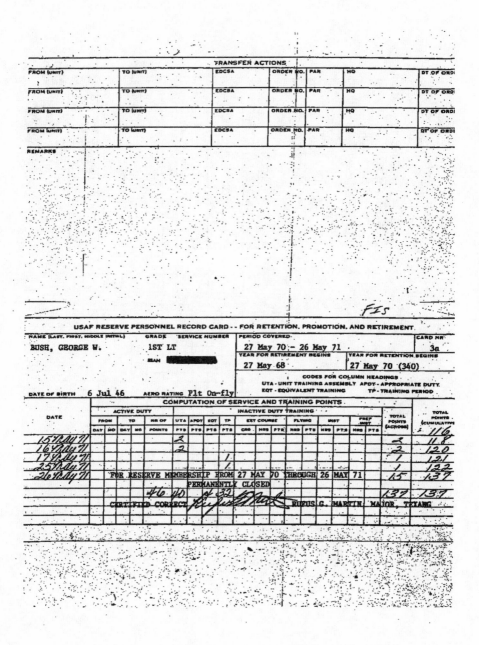

FIS

USAF RESERVE PERSONNEL RECORD CARD -- FOR RETENTION, PROMOTION, AND RETIREMENT

NAME (LAST, FIRST, MIDDLE INITIAL)	GRADE	SERVICE NUMBER	PERIOD COVERED	CARD NR
BUSH, GEORGE W.	1ST LT		27 May 70 – 26 May 71	3a
			YEAR FOR RETIREMENT BEGINS 27 May 68	YEAR FOR RETENTION BEGINS 27 May 70 (340)

DATE OF BIRTH 6 Jul 46   AERO RATING Plt On-fly

CODES FOR COLUMN HEADINGS
UTA - UNIT TRAINING ASSEMBLY APDY - APPROPRIATE DUTY
EQT - EQUIVALENT TRAINING TP - TRAINING PERIOD

COMPUTATION OF SERVICE AND TRAINING POINTS

DATE	ACTIVE DUTY					INACTIVE DUTY TRAINING													TOTAL POINTS (ACROSS)	TOTAL POINTS (CUMULATIVE)
	FROM		TO		NR OF POINTS	UTA PTS	APDY PTS	EQT PTS	TP PTS	EST COURSE		FLYING		INST		PREP INST				
	DAY	MO	DAY	MO						CRS	HRS	PTS	HRS	PTS	HRS	PTS	HRS	PTS		
15 May 71						2													2	116
16 May 71						2													2	118
17 May 71									1										1	120
25 May 71									1										1	121
26 May 71																			15	122

FOR RESERVE MEMBERSHIP FROM 27 MAY 70 THROUGH 26 MAY 71
PERMANENTLY CLOSED

137   137

CERTIFIED CORRECT   RUFUS G. MARTIN MAJOR, TEXANG

SERVICE AND TRAINING POINTS (CONTINUED)

DATE	ACTIVE DUTY				INACTIVE DUTY TRAINING													TOTAL POINTS (CREDIT)	TOTAL POINTS (CUMULATIVE)
	FROM	TO	NO OF		UTA	APDY	EQT	TP	RET COURSE		FLYING		INST		PRI INST				
	DAY	NO	DAY	NO	POINTS	PTS	PTS	PTS	PTS	CRS	HRS	PTS	HRS	PTS	HRS	PTS	HRS	PTS		

AF FORM 190
FEB 69   PREVIOUS EDITION OF THIS FORM WILL BE USED UNTIL STOCK IS EXHAUSTED.

DEPARTMENT OF THE AIR FORCE
HEADQUARTERS 147TH FIGHTER GROUP (TNG)
ELLINGTON AIR FORCE BASE, TEXAS 77030

SPECIAL ORDER   16 August 1971
P - 11

The program element code for all personnel assigned to Hq 147th Ftr Gp
(Trng), 111th Ftr Intcp Sq (Trng), 147th Supply Sq, 147th Consol Acft
Maint Sq, 147th Cmbt Spt Sq, 147th USAF Disp and 147th Civ Engrg Flt is
changed from 5AH to 5AP effective 1 Jul 1971.

FOR THE COMMANDER

[signature]

DON H. BREWER, MSGT, TEXANG   DISTRIBUTION
Asst Admin Officer   P

15 SEP 1971

1LT   BUSH GEORGE W
2039 ONE HALF SOUTH BLVD
HOUSTON,TX
77006

SSN 410062461480

RESERVE COMPONENT: TEX   ANG

ORGANIZATION: 0111 FIGHTER INTERCEPT SQ

DD FORM 44 (MILITARY STATUS OF REGISTRANT)
ANNUAL REPORT - CONTINUES TO PARTICIPATE SATISFACTORILY

PAS: L9CMPY48

RUFUS G MARTIN, MAJOR, TEXANG
PERSONNEL STAFF OFFICER

(PLEASE READ INSTRUCTIONS ON THE REVERSE SIDE BEFORE COMPLETING / SUBMITTING THIS FORM)

SERVICEMEN'S GROUP LIFE INSURANCE ELECTION

IMPORTANT — This form does not apply to and cannot be used for any other Government Life Insurance. It is to be used only for Servicemen's Group Life Insurance.

USE THIS FORM FOR ▶	1. REDUCING OR REFUSING INSURANCE	2. STATING TO WHOM AND HOW INSURANCE SHOULD BE PAID

(Do not make erasures, corrections or changes. Complete a new form)

LAST NAME - FIRST NAME - MIDDLE NAME	RANK, TITLE OR GRADE	SERVICE OR SOCIAL SECURITY NO.
BUSH, GEORGE WALKER	1st Lt	██████████ G

BRANCH OF SERVICE (Do not abbreviate)	CURRENT DUTY LOCATION
Texas Air National Guard	111th Ftr Intcp Sq, Ellington AFB, Texas 77030

1. REDUCING OR REFUSING INSURANCE

By law you are automatically insured for $15,000. If you do not want $15,000 insurance write below in your own handwriting "I want only $10,000 insurance" or "I want only $5,000 insurance" or "I want no insurance" as you prefer. Reduced or refused insurance can be restored only by written request with proof of good health and compliance with other requirements.

▶ _____ **BE SURE TO COMPLETE PART 2** ⬇

2. BENEFICIARY(IES) AND PAYMENT TO BENEFICIARY(IES) (Read instructions C and D on reverse)

IMPORTANT — You must write in the spaces below
(1) "By Law" in your own handwriting if you wish the law to apply (as explained on reverse) or,
(2) The names and other information for persons you want to receive your insurance. If you insert "36" under "Payments to Beneficiary," payment will be made only in 36 equal monthly installments.

I DESIGNATE THE FOLLOWING BENEFICIARIES TO RECEIVE PAYMENT OF MY INSURANCE PROCEEDS AS SHOWN BELOW:

COMPLETE NAME AND ADDRESS OF EACH BENEFICIARY (If married woman, give her own first and middle names and husband's last name)	RELATION-SHIP TO INSURED	SHARES TO BE PAID TO EACH BENEFICIARY (Use fractions such as 1/2, 2/3 or 3/4)	PAYMENTS TO BENEFICIARY (Insert "36" if only monthly payments desired. See D on reverse)
PRINCIPAL (First) By LAW			Lump Sum
CONTINGENT (Second - If principal beneficiary dies before me or before completion of installment payments to the principal beneficiary)			

NOTE: If more than one principal beneficiary is named, the share of any such beneficiary who dies before me shall be distributed equally among the surviving principal beneficiaries. If there is no surviving principal beneficiary the proceeds shall be distributed equally to the surviving contingent beneficiaries. This Designation of Beneficiary shall be void if none of the designated beneficiaries is living at my death. If after completion of this form my insurance is increased, this beneficiary designation shall apply to the full amount in force unless a new designation is made.

I UNDERSTAND that this form cancels any prior beneficiary or payment instructions and that unless I have named the beneficiary(ies) above, my insurance will be paid under the "Provisions of the Law" as explained on the reverse of this form.

SIGN HERE IN INK ▶ *(signature)*	DATE COMPLETED 7 Oct 71
(Signature of member) (Do not print)	

WITNESSED AND RECEIVED BY: *(signature)*	RANK, TITLE OR GRADE MSgt	ORGANIZATION 147th Cmbt Spt Sq	DATE RECEIVED 2 Oct 71

VA FORM SEP 1970 **29-8286**   SUPERSEDES VA FORM 29-8286, NOV 1965, WHICH WILL NOT BE USED.   FOR THE UNIFORMED SERVICES USE 3

IMPORTANT - READ CAREFULLY

PROVISIONS OF THE LAW FOR PAYMENT OF INSURANCE

If you do not name a beneficiary to receive the proceeds of your insurance, it will be paid under the provisions of the law, to your survivor(s) in the following order:

1. Widow or widower; if none, it is payable to
2. Child or children in equal shares with the share of any deceased child distributed among the descendants of that child; if none, it is payable to
3. Parent(s) in equal shares; if none, it is payable to
4. A duly appointed executor or administrator of the insured's estate, and if none to
5. Other next of kin.

NOTE: If you do not want your insurance paid as provided above, you must name the beneficiary(ies) in Part 2.

INSTRUCTIONS TO MEMBER

GENERAL

A. Make certain you complete all the appropriate item(s).

B. All entries, except the signature and those requested to be in your handwriting, should be typed or printed in ink.

C. DESIGNATION OF BENEFICIARY

- Completing this form will cancel any prior beneficiary or payment instructions. You should write "By Law" or name a beneficiary(ies) in Part 2. (See "IMPORTANT" on front)

There are no restrictions on the beneficiaries you may name. In some family situations such as if you are a step-child or step-parent or were abandoned by a parent or are separated from your wife, etc., you may by naming beneficiaries specifically include or exclude certain persons as you desire.

1. A change of beneficiary may be made by the insured at any time without the knowledge or consent of the beneficiary, and this right cannot be waived or restricted.

2. A Designation of Beneficiary may not be changed by correcting entries on earlier designations. If a change of a prior designation of beneficiary is desired, a new VA Form 29-8286 should be completed to show the name(s) of the new beneficiary(ies) in Part 2.

3. No designation or change of beneficiary will be valid unless it is received in writing over your signature, by your Uniformed Service, before your death.

D. PAYMENTS TO BENEFICIARY

In case of your death the beneficiary can elect to receive the insurance in a single payment of the face value or in 36 equal monthly installments. If you so desire you can limit a beneficiary to receiving the insurance in 36 equal monthly installments by inserting "36" in the space provided on the front of the form.

E. Make certain all three copies of this form are completed and signed.

DIRECTIONS TO UNIFORMED SERVICES

- Make sure "By Law" or beneficiary identification appears in Part 2.

- The personnel or other responsible activity should explain to the member the need for naming beneficiaries in family situations such as those referred to under C above. Also if a member is designating a beneficiary other than would be normal under his family circumstances, see "Unusual Beneficiary Designations" Servicemen's Group Life Insurance Handbook, VA Handbook 29-66-1.

- This form must be signed and dated, below the signature of the member, by an authorized representative of the Uniformed Service.

- This form, properly executed, is authority to a payroll office to reduce the deductions for insurance purposes or not to make such deductions, if the amount of insurance is changed or canceled.

- Disposition of copies:

Original - Must be promptly filed in the official personnel file of the member.

1st copy - To member. This copy for informational purposes only.

2nd copy - For the Uniformed Service use. This 2nd copy should not be sent to the Office of Servicemen's Group Life Insurance or to the Veterans Administration.

1972

This is the year when things began to go wrong for 1st Lieutenant George W. Bush. As confirmed in payroll records released in 2004 (241–3), Bush served regularly through April; thereafter he seems to have dropped off the radar screen.[1]

Bush's annual Officer Effectiveness Report for the 1971–72 period (244–5) continued to give him high marks, though his ratings on performance of duties and leadership dropped a notch from the previous year. As in 1971, reporting official William Harris calls Bush an "exceptional" pilot. But there is also a hint that Bush is being pulled in other directions: Along with "progressing satisfactorily" in a Squadron Officer's correspondence course, Bush is "very active in civic affairs" and "has recently accepted the position as campaign manager for a candidate for the United States Senate." What Harris fails to mention is that the Senate seat in question is far away in Alabama.

[1] As the first-quarter record from 1973 (277, in the next section) notes, Bush was credited for only four days of service from May 1972 through the end of the year: November 11–14, 1972.

Bush's retirement (247) and personnel credit records (248–50) show that his number of points has continued to drop, down to a total of 112 for 1971–72.

Bush completed his aborted Application for Reserve Assignment at the 9921st Air Reserve Squadron in Montgomery, Alabama, on May 24 (251); Reese Bricken's peculiar response was typed on the back of the form (252). Rufus Martin and Charles Shoemake of the Texas ANG recommended approval (253), but they were overruled by Gwen Dallin's memo (254), undated but stamped as received on July 21.

Back in May, Bush had skipped his annual physical. Finally, after he apparently failed to appear at the base for several months, Bush was "suspended from flying status" effective August 1; the suspension was ordered in a September 5 memo from Colonel Bobby Hodges, forwarded by Major Rufus Martin on September 19 (256), and recorded in a memo labeled "Aeronautical Orders Number 87" signed by Army Major General Frances Greenlief, and Air Force Colonel Waldo Timm, both of the National Guard Bureau (258–9). In both cases the reason for Bush's suspension is given as "Failure to accomplish annual medical examination."

Even as all this was going on, Bush was still pursuing his transfer to a unit in Alabama. On September 5, the same day Hodges wrote his memo on the suspension of Bush's flight status, Bush wrote to Killian requesting "permission to perform equivalent duty" with the 187th Tactical Reconnaissance Group in Montgomery, Alabama. "This duty would be for September, October, and November," he noted (260). Killian, Hodges, and Shoemake approved the request (261, 262). And finally Bush's request was approved by Captain Kenneth Lott of the 187th—but Lott's memo (263) made clear that he took Bush at his word, giving the Unit Training Assembly dates for October and November only, and noting that Bush had missed the UTA for September. He also noted that "Lieutenant Bush will not be able to satisfy his flight requirements with our group."

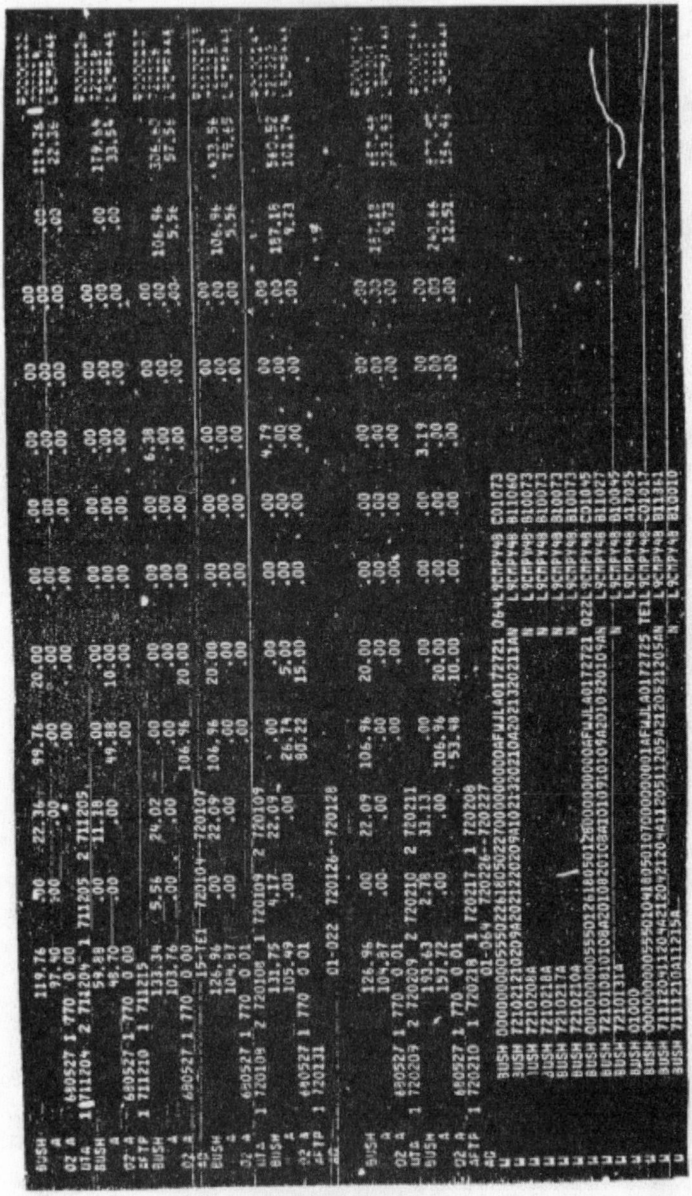

```
BUSH          119.76   .00   22.36   99.76   20.00   .00   .00   .00   .00   .00           119.26
 A             97.40   .00     .00     .00     .00   .00   .00   .00   .00   .00    .00     22.36
02 A   680527 1 770   0 00             .00     .00   .00   .00   .00   .00   .00
UTA  1 711204  2 711204  1 711205  2 711205
BUSH           59.88   .00   11.18     .00     .00   .00   .00   .00   .00   .00           179.64
 A             48.70   .00     .00   49.88   10.00   .00   .00   .00   .00   .00    .00     33.54
02 A   680527 1 770   0 00             .00     .00   .00   .00   .00   .00   .00
AFTP 1 711210  1 711215
BUSH          133.34  5.56   24.02     .00     .00   .00   .00  6.38   .00   .00           306.60
 A            103.76   .00     .00     .00     .00   .00   .00   .00   .00   .00  106.96    97.56
02 A   680527 1 770   0 00          106.96   20.00   .00   .00   .00   .00   .00    5.56
AD               15-TE1  720104--720107
BUSH          126.96   .00   22.09  106.96   20.00   .00   .00   .00   .00   .00           433.56
 A            104.87   .00     .00     .00     .00   .00   .00   .00   .00   .00  106.96    79.65
02 A   680527 1 770   0 01             .00     .00   .00   .00   .00   .00   .00    5.56
UTA  1 720108  2 720108  1 720109  2 720109
BUSH          131.75  4.17   22.09     .00     .00   .00   .00  4.79   .00   .00           560.52
 A            105.49   .00     .00   26.74    5.00   .00   .00   .00   .00   .00  187.16   101.74
02 A   680527 1 770   0 01           80.22   15.00   .00   .00   .00   .00   .00    9.73
AFTP 1 720131
AD               01-022  720126--720128

BUSH          126.96   .00   22.09  106.96   20.00   .00   .00   .00   .00   .00
 A            104.87   .00     .00     .00     .00   .00   .00   .00   .00   .00  187.16
02 A   680527 1 770   0 01             .00     .00   .00   .00   .00   .00   .00    9.73
UTA  1 720209  2 720209  2 720210  2 720211
BUSH          193.63  2.78   33.13     .00     .00   .00   .00  3.19   .00   .00
 A            157.72   .00     .00  106.96   20.00   .00   .00   .00   .00   .00  243.66
02 A   680527 1 770   0 01           53.48   10.00   .00   .00   .00   .00   .00   12.51
AFTP 1 720210  1 720218  1 720217  1 720206
AD               01-064  720226--720227
     BUSH 000000000555022618050227000000000AFWJLA0172721  064L9CMPY48  C01073
     BUSH 72102121020 9A2021220209A1021320210A2021320211AN    L9CMPY48  B11060
     BUSH 7210208A                                        N   L9CMPY48  B10073
     BUSH 7210218A                                        N   L9CMPY48  B10073
     BUSH 7210217A                                        N   L9CMPY48  B10073
     BUSH 7210210A                                        N   L9CMPY48  B10073
     BUSH 000000000555012618050128000000000AFWJLA0172721  022L9CMPY48  C01045
     BUSH 721010810108A2010820108A1010910109A2010920109AN     L9CMPY48  B11027
     BUSH 7210131A                                        N   L9CMPY48  B10045
     BUSH 01000                                               L9CMPY48  A17025
     BUSH 000000000555010418050107000000001AFWJLA0172725  TE1L9CMPY48  C01017
     BUSH 711120411204A2120421204A11120511205A21205212O5AN    L9CMPY48  B11361
     BUSH 7111210A11215A                                  N   L9CMPY48  B10010
```

Pag1 — 1972
1ST QTR

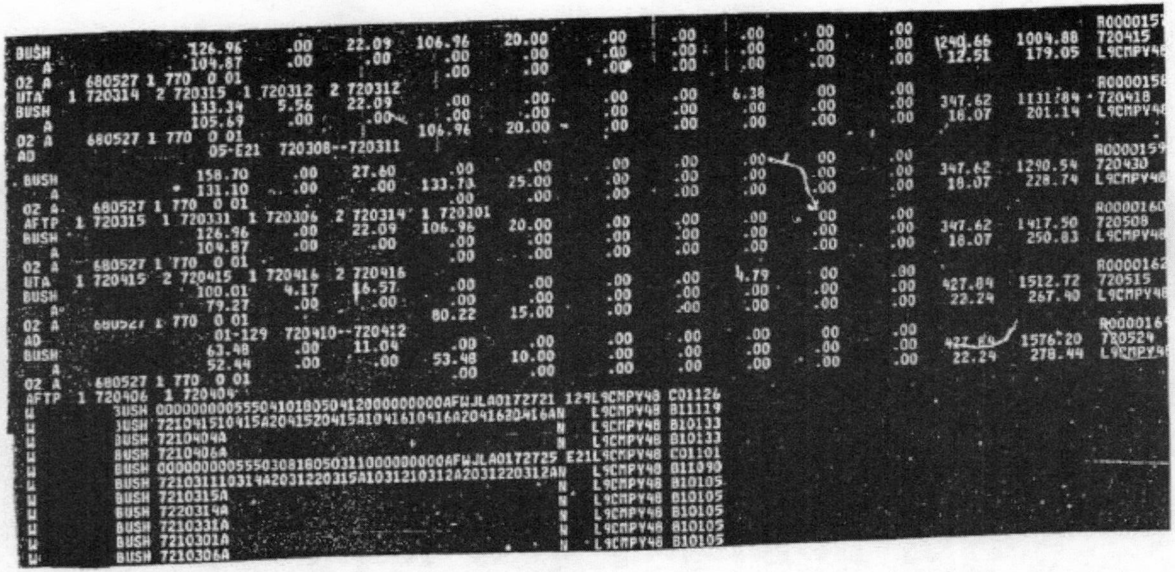

SSAN: NAME   FV SSAN   RS PG PC GR DT RNK PGR LC PAY DT CUR PAS NEW PAS PREV PAS ASGN DT GAIN DT DAILY PAY
         BUSH GEORGE W   A--0 02 701107 01 N 690527 L%CMPV%8   660504   2763
CHECK ADDRESS   STREET NUMBER   CITY   ST ZI CC PD TO DT PF PS PAY ST END RAF TYPE INC PAY
2910 WESTHEIMER   HOUSTON   TX 770   700427   2 A   -999999   -999999
                                                                                                      MOV DATE JUMA DT SGLI
BAQ START END   BAS START   END   HFP ST END   FDP ST END   FSA I ST END   FSA II ST END BAQ DEP   720628 31337F006
[N-   E-   RE-IN
U-4 DATA   FITW CUR QTR FITW YR TO DT 'FICA CUR QTR' FICA YR TO DT DEBT ANT-APPRO-TYPE-OBD CD-COLL RT LWR CFW LWR FFY   IUCI
99-01-00-0-   0000000-0000000 027844-0157620 000000-0000000 002224-00+2784 VALID TRANSACTION PROCESSING DATES THIS QUARTER.   0

UTAS CUR FY UTAS PR FY AFTP CUR FY AFTP PR FY DAYS PD LEAVE PD
00-00-00-00 12-12-12-04 00-00-00-00 07-09-10-02 000-03I 00-00-00 01-

%607%0610 BUSH L%CMPV%8

MON YR 01 02 03 04 05 06 07 08 09 10 11 12 13 14 15 16 17 18 19 20 21 22 23 24 25 26 27 28 29 30 31SGLI AGN UTAS MASTER REVIEW MSGS
JAN 72   50 50 50 50 22 32 32 02   30 30   50 50 50   30 0   0   04
FEB 72   30 50 50 50 22   23 32   50 50   99 0   0   04
MAR 72 30   50 50 50   22 22   30 0   0   04
APR 72   30 30   99 40   0   04 PROBLEM MR CODES
MAY 72   00
JUN 72   00
JUL 72   99 0   0   00 MF G-C COUNTERS
AUG 72   00 1111111PP
SEP 72   00
OCT 72   99 0   0   00
NOV 72   00
DEC 72   00

PROCESSED BY DPABPE   13 JUN 19

IDENTIFICATION DATA (Read AFM 36-10 carefully before filling out this form)			
1. LAST NAME—FIRST NAME—MIDDLE INITIAL BUSH, GEORGE W.	2. AFSN/SSAN ▓▓▓▓ FG	3. ACTIVE DUTY GRADE NONEAD	4. PERMANENT GRADE 1st Lt
3. ORGANIZATION, COMMAND AND LOCATION 111th Ftr Intcp Sq (Tng) Ellington AFB, Texas Texas ANG (ADC)	6. AERO RATING: C CODE: 1	7. PERIOD OF REPORT FROM: 1 May 71 THRU: 30 Apr 72	
	8. PERIOD OF SUPERVISION	9. REASON FOR REPORT Annual Report	

II. DUTIES—PAFSC 1125D DAFSC 1125D Pilot, Fighter Interceptor, Squadron level. Pilots F102 type aircraft and performs airborne intercepts as required by assigned missions.

22 Active Duty Days/82 Training Periods

III. RATING FACTORS (Consider how this officer is performing on his job.)

1. KNOWLEDGE OF DUTIES

NOT OBSERVED	SERIOUS GAPS IN HIS KNOWLEDGE OF FUNDAMENTALS OF HIS JOB.	SATISFACTORY KNOWLEDGE OF ROUTINE PHASES OF HIS JOB.	WELL INFORMED ON MOST PHASES OF HIS JOB.	EXCELLENT KNOWLEDGE OF ALL PHASES OF HIS JOB.	EXCEPTIONAL UNDERSTANDING OF HIS JOB. EXTREMELY WELL INFORMED ON ALL PHASES.
○				X	

2. PERFORMANCE OF DUTIES

NOT OBSERVED	QUALITY OR QUANTITY OF WORK OFTEN FAILS TO MEET JOB REQUIREMENTS.	PERFORMANCE MEETS ONLY MINIMUM JOB REQUIREMENTS.	QUANTITY AND QUALITY OF WORK ARE VERY SATISFACTORY.	PRODUCES VERY HIGH QUANTITY AND QUALITY OF WORK. MEETS ALL SUSPENSES.	QUALITY AND QUANTITY OF WORK ARE CLEARLY SUPERIOR AND TIMELY.
○				X	

3. EFFECTIVENESS IN WORKING WITH OTHERS

NOT OBSERVED	INEFFECTIVE IN WORKING WITH OTHERS. DOES NOT COOPERATE.	SOMETIMES HAS DIFFICULTY IN GETTING ALONG WITH OTHERS.	GETS ALONG WELL WITH PEOPLE UNDER NORMAL CIRCUMSTANCES.	WORKS IN HARMONY WITH OTHERS. A VERY GOOD TEAM WORKER.	EXTREMELY SUCCESSFUL IN WORKING WITH OTHERS. ACTIVELY PROMOTES HARMONY.
○					X

4. LEADERSHIP CHARACTERISTICS

NOT OBSERVED	OFTEN WEAK. FAILS TO SHOW INITIATIVE AND ACCEPT RESPONSIBILITY.	INITIATIVE AND ACCEPTANCE OF RESPONSIBILITY ADEQUATE IN MOST SITUATIONS.	SATISFACTORILY DEMONSTRATES INITIATIVE AND ACCEPTS RESPONSIBILITY.	DEMONSTRATES A HIGH DEGREE OF INITIATIVE AND ACCEPTANCE OF RESPONSIBILITY.	ALWAYS DEMONSTRATES OUTSTANDING INITIATIVE AND ACCEPTANCE OF RESPONSIBILITY.
○				X	

5. JUDGEMENT

NOT OBSERVED	DECISIONS AND RECOMMENDATIONS OFTEN WRONG OR INEFFECTIVE.	JUDGEMENT IS USUALLY SOUND BUT MAKES OCCASIONAL ERRORS.	SHOWS GOOD JUDGEMENT RESULTING FROM SOUND EVALUATION OF FACTORS.	SOUND, LOGICAL THINKER. CONSIDERS ALL FACTORS TO REACH ACCURATE DECISIONS.	CONSISTENTLY ARRIVES AT RIGHT DECISION EVEN ON HIGHLY COMPLEX MATTERS.
⊙					X

6. ADAPTABILITY

NOT OBSERVED	UNABLE TO PERFORM ADEQUATELY IN OTHER THAN ROUTINE SITUATIONS.	PERFORMANCE DECLINES UNDER STRESS OR IN OTHER THAN ROUTINE SITUATIONS.	PERFORMS WELL UNDER STRESS OR IN UNUSUAL SITUATIONS.	PERFORMANCE EXCELLENT EVEN UNDER PRESSURE OR IN DIFFICULT SITUATIONS.	OUTSTANDING PERFORMANCE UNDER EXTREME STRESS. MEETS THE CHALLENGE OF DIFFICULT SITUATIONS.
⊙					X

7. USE OF RESOURCES

NOT OBSERVED	INEFFECTIVE IN CONSERVATION OF RESOURCES.	USES RESOURCES IN A BARELY SATISFACTORY MANNER.	CONSERVES BY USING ROUTINE PROCEDURES.	EFFECTIVELY ACCOMPLISHES SAVINGS BY DEVELOPING IMPROVED PROCEDURES.	EXCEPTIONALLY EFFECTIVE IN USING RESOURCES.
Ⓜ Ⓟ	MATERIEL PERSONNEL	MATERIEL PERSONNEL	MATERIEL PERSONNEL	MATERIEL PERSONNEL	☒MATERIEL ☒PERSONNEL

8. WRITING ABILITY AND ORAL EXPRESSION

NOT OBSERVED	UNABLE TO EXPRESS THOUGHTS CLEARLY. LACKS ORGANIZATION.	EXPRESSES THOUGHTS SATISFACTORILY ON ROUTINE MATTERS.	USUALLY ORGANIZES AND EXPRESSES THOUGHTS CLEARLY AND CONCISELY.	CONSISTENTLY ABLE TO EXPRESS IDEAS CLEARLY.	OUTSTANDING ABILITY TO COMMUNICATE IDEAS TO OTHERS.
Ⓦ Ⓢ	WRITE SPEAK	WRITE SPEAK	WRITE SPEAK	WRITE SPEAK	☒WRITE ☒SPEAK

IV. MILITARY QUALITIES (Consider how this officer meets Air Force standards.)

NOT OBSERVED	BEARING OR BEHAVIOR INTERFERE SERIOUSLY WITH HIS EFFECTIVENESS.	CARELESS BEARING AND BEHAVIOR DETRACT FROM HIS EFFECTIVENESS.	BEARING AND BEHAVIOR CREATE A GOOD IMPRESSION.	ESPECIALLY GOOD BEHAVIOR AND BEARING. CREATES A VERY FAVORABLE IMPRESSION.	BEARING AND BEHAVIOR ARE OUTSTANDING. HE EXEMPLIFIES TOP MILITARY STANDARDS.
○					X

AF FORM 77 JAN 59 PREVIOUS EDITION OF THIS FORM WILL BE USED UNTIL 30 JUN 69. AFTER THIS DATE, PREVIOUS EDITIONS WILL BE USED   MICROFILMED 07 JUL 72   COMPANY GRADE OFFICER EFFECTIVENESS REPORT

V. OVER-ALL EVALUATION (Compare this officer ONLY with officers of the same grade.)

SPECIFIC JUSTIFICATION REQUIRED FOR THESE SECTIONS						SPECIFIC JUSTIFICATION REQUIRED FOR THESE SECTIONS
□	□	□	□ □ □	□ □	X □	
UNSATIS-FACTORY	MARGINAL	BELOW AVERAGE	EFFECTIVE AND COMPETENT	VERY FINE	EXCEPTIONALLY FINE	OUTSTANDING

VI. PROMOTION POTENTIAL

1. DOES NOT DEMONSTRATE A CAPABILITY FOR PROMOTION AT THIS TIME.	□	2. PERFORMING WELL IN PRESENT GRADE. SHOULD BE CONSIDERED FOR PROMOTION ALONG WITH CONTEMPORARIES. □
3. DEMONSTRATES CAPABILITIES FOR INCREASED RESPONSIBILITY. CONSIDER FOR ADVANCEMENT AHEAD OF CONTEMPORARIES.	X	4. OUTSTANDING GROWTH POTENTIAL BASED ON DEMONSTRATED PERFORMANCE. PROMOTE WELL AHEAD OF CONTEMPORARIES. □

VII. COMMENTS FACTS AND SPECIFIC ACHIEVEMENTS: Lt Bush is an exceptional fighter inter-ceptor pilot and officer. He eagerly participates in scheduled unit activities. During the past year he participated in several target force deployments and an F-102 aircraft element deployment to Canada. His conduct and professional approach to the mission were certainly exemplary and apparent to observers. His skills as an interceptor pilot enabled him to complete all his ADC intercept missions during the Canadian deployment with ease. STRENGTHS: Lt Bush's major strength is his ability to work with others. He makes a welcome addition to any group or team effort. SUGGESTED ASSIGNMENTS: Lt Bush should be retained in his present assignment. He has gained valuable experience in the operations area and would be a welcome addition to any fighter squadron. SELF IMPROVE-MENT EFFORTS: Lt Bush is presently enrolled in the Squadron Officer's School by correspondence and progressing satisfactorily. He also participates in unit ground schools and briefings to stay abreast of the F-102 weapons employment and the ADC mission. OTHER COMMENTS: Lt Bush is very active in civic affairs in the community and manifests a deep interest in the operation of our government. He has recently accepted the position as campaign manager for a candidate for United States Senate. He is a good representative of the military and Air National Guard in the business world. His abilities and anticipated future assignments make him a valuable asset. He is a member of the National Guard Association of the United States and Texas.

VIII. REPORTING OFFICIAL

NAME, GRADE, AFSN/SSAN, AND ORGANIZATION	DUTY TITLE	SIGNATURE
WILLIAM D. HARRIS, JR., Major	Pilot, Ftr Intcp	
FG, 111th FIS (Tng)	AERO RATING CODE	DATE
Texas ANG (ADC)	Command Pilot 1	26 MAY 1972

IX. REVIEW BY INDORSING OFFICIAL

I concur with the comments and ratings of the reporting official.

NAME, GRADE, AFSN/SSAN, AND ORGANIZATION	DUTY TITLE	SIGNATURE
JERRY B. KILLIAN, Lt Colonel	Squadron Commander	
FG, 111th FIS (Tng)	AERO RATING CODE	DATE
Texas ANG (ADC)	Command Pilot 1	26 MAY 1972

* GPO : 1949 O - 328-191

1 3 JUN 1972

LAST NAME-FIRST NAME, INITIAL	SSAN	FG	ACTIVE DUTY GRADE
BUSH, GEORGE W.			NONEAD

(CHECK APPROPRIATE BLOCK AND COMPLETE AS APPLICABLE)

[X]	SUPPLEMENTAL SHEET TO RATING FORM WHICH COVERS THE FOLLOWING PERIOD OF REPORT	[ ]	LETTER OF EVALUATION COVERING THE FOLLOWING PERIOD OF OBSERVATION

FROM	THRU	FROM	THRU
1 May 71	30 Apr 71		

Precede comments by appropriate data, i.e. section continuation, indorsement continuation, additional indorsement, etc. Follow comments by the authentication to include: name, grade, AFSN, organization, duty title, date and signature.

ADDITIONAL INDORSEMENT

I concur with the ratings of the reporting and indorsing officials. Lieutenant Bush is an exceptionally fine young pilot and officer and is a credit to this unit. I have personally observed his participation, and without exception, his performance has been noteworthy.

BOBBY W. HODGES, Colonel, ████████ FG, 147th Ftr Gp, Commander, 26 May 1972

MICROFILMED 0 7 JUL '72

①

STATE (ING) TEXAS		AIR RESERVE FORCES RETIREMENT CREDIT SUMMARY									
BREAKS IN SERVICE (Include complete breaks and assignment to Inactive Reserve Status) none								DATE OF INITIAL ENTRY INTO SERVICE 27 May 68			
								ACTIVE DUTY PRIOR TO 1 JUL 49 none			
BUSH GEORGE W. FG								☐ WORLD WAR II ☐ KOREAN CONFLICT			
								DATE SERVICE FOR RETIREMENT BEGINS 27 May 68			
								ANNIVERSARY RETIREMENT DATE 27 May 68			

ALLOWABLE FEDERAL SERVICE	STATUS	ACTIVE DUTY POINTS A	IN-ACTIVE DUTY POINTS B	ECI POINTS C	GRATU-ITOUS POINTS D	TOTAL POINTS E	RETIRE-MENT POINTS F	SATISFACTORY FEDERAL SERVICE			SOURCE DOCUMENT OR POSTING AUTHORITY J
								YEARS G	MONTHS H	DAYS I	
PRIOR TO 1 JULY 1949											
DATES FROM — TO				ON OR AFTER 1 JULY 1949							
27 May 68 — 26 May 69	ANG	226	12	0	15	253	253	1	0	0	AF FM 190
CERTIFIED CORRECT *[signature]*							ROGER W. BIVENS, 1st Lt, NGANGPM, 21 May 70				
27 MAY 69 — 26 MAY 70	"	313	12	0	15	340	340	2	0	0	"
27 MAY 70 — 26 MAY 71	"	46	76	0	15	137	106	3	0	0	"
27 MAY 71 — 26 MAY 72	ANG	22	75	0	15	112	82	4	0	0	"

AF FORM 712 AUG 67   PREVIOUS EDITION OF THIS FORM WILL BE USED UNTIL STOCK IS EXHAUSTED

COPY: 1—MASTER PERSONNEL RECORD

147th Ftr Gp, TexANG, Ellington AFB, TX

A review of your record indicates that during the anniversary year ending 26 May 72 you have been credited with these points and federal services.

TO:

1ST LT GEORGE W. BUSH

PART 1 MPERR COPY

ANNUAL STATEMENT OF CREDITS
AF FORM 1353-3 MAR 67
PREVIOUS EDITION OF THIS FORM WILL BE USED UNTIL STOCK IS EXHAUSTED.

13 Jun 72	
ANNUAL REPORT OF TOTAL ALLOWABLE POINTS AND FEDERAL SERVICE	
ACTIVE DUTY	22
INACTIVE DUTY	75
CORRESPONDENCE COURSES	00
GRATUITOUS CREDIT	15
TOTAL POINTS	112

YEAR OF SATISFACTORY SERVICE FOR RETIREMENT

XX Yes ☐ No

FORWARD ANY CLAIM FOR POINTS, IN ADDITION TO THOSE LISTED ABOVE, TOGETHER WITH SUBSTANTIATION OF CLAIM, TO THE ABOVE PREPARING UNIT.

FIS

USAF RESERVE PERSONNEL RECORD CARD -- FOR RETENTION, PROMOTION, AND RETIREMENT

NAME (LAST, FIRST, MIDDLE INITIAL)	GRADE	SERVICE NUMBER	PERIOD COVERED		CARD NR
BUSH, GEORGE W.	1ST LT	SSAN	27 May 71 – 26 May 72		4
			YEAR FOR RETIREMENT BEGINS	YEAR FOR RETENTION BEGINS	
			27 May 68	27 May 71 (137)	

CODES FOR COLUMN HEADINGS
UTA - UNIT TRAINING ASSEMBLY APDY - APPROPRIATE DUTY
EQT - EQUIVALENT TRAINING TP - TRAINING PERIOD

DATE OF BIRTH 6 Jul 46   AERO RATING Plt On-fly

COMPUTATION OF SERVICE AND TRAINING POINTS

DATE	ACTIVE DUTY				INACTIVE DUTY TRAINING												TOTAL POINTS (ACROSS)	TOTAL POINTS (CUMULATIVE)
	FROM	TO	NR OF		UTA	APDY	EQT	TP	EXT COURSE		FLYING		INST		PREP INST			
	DAY	MO	DAY	MO	POINTS	PTS	PTS	PTS	PTS	CRS	HRS	PTS	HRS	PTS	HRS	PTS	HRS	PTS		
27 May 71									1										1	2
1 Jun 71																			2	4
12 Jun 71					2														2	6
13 Jun 71					2														2	6
15 Jun 71								1											1	8
19 Jun 71									1										1	9
29 Jun 71	29 Jun	29 Jun	1																2	11
10 Jul 71					2														2	13
11 Jul 71					2														1	14
12 Jul 71																				

TRANSFER ACTIONS

FROM (UNIT)	TO (UNIT)	EDCSA	ORDER NO.	PAR	HQ	DT OF ORDER
FROM (UNIT)	TO (UNIT)	EDCSA	ORDER NO.	PAR	HQ	DT OF ORDER
FROM (UNIT)	TO (UNIT)	EDCSA	ORDER NO.	PAR	HQ	DT OF ORDER
FROM (UNIT)	TO (UNIT)	EDCSA	ORDER NO.	PAR	HQ	DT OF ORDER

REMARKS

USAF RESERVE PERSONNEL RECORD CARD -- FOR RETENTION, PROMOTION, AND RETIREMENT

NAME (LAST, FIRST, MIDDLE INITIAL)	GRADE	SERVICE NUMBER	PERIOD COVERED	CARD NR
BUSH, GEORGE W.	1ST LT	SSAN ▮▮▮▮	27 May 71 – 26 May 72	4a

YEAR FOR RETIREMENT BEGINS	YEAR FOR RETENTION BEGINS
27 May 68	27 May 71 (137)

DATE OF BIRTH 6 Jul 46   AERO RATING Plt On-fly

CODES FOR COLUMN HEADINGS
UTA - UNIT TRAINING ASSEMBLY APDY - APPROPRIATE DUTY
EQT - EQUIVALENT TRAINING   TP - TRAINING PERIOD

COMPUTATION OF SERVICE AND TRAINING POINTS

DATE	ACTIVE DUTY FROM DAY MO	TO DAY MO	NR OF POINTS	UTA PTS	APDY PTS	EQT PTS	TP PTS	EXT COURSE CRS	HRS PTS	FLYING HRS PTS	INST HRS PTS	PREF INST HRS PTS	TOTAL POINTS (ACROSS)	TOTAL POINTS (CUMULATIVE)
														88
4 Apr 72							1						1	89
6 Apr 72							1						1	90
12 Apr 72	10 Apr	12 Apr	3										3	93
15 Apr 72				2									2	95
16 Apr 72				2									2	97
26 May 72	FOR RESERVE MEMBERSHIP FROM 27 MAY 71 THROUGH 26 MAY 72												15	112
	PERMANENTLY CLOSED												112	112
	22 34													

CERTIFIED CORRECT   RUFUS G. MARTIN, MAJOR, TEXANG

APPLICATION FOR RESERV. ASSIGNMENT

(If more space is need r any item, attach additional sheets indicating applicable item number)

INSTRUCTIONS

1. SUBMIT APPLICATION, IN TRIPLICATE, TO PRESENT UNIT OF ASSIGNMENT, (IF ASSIGNED TO ARPC (ORS, RRPS, MARS, ISLRS, ETC.), SUBMIT APPLICATION EITHER TO THE LOCAL AIR RESERVE UNIT OR TO THE UNIT WITH WHICH ASSIGNMENT IS DESIRED).
2. ALL APPLICANTS MUST ATTACH COMPLETED DD FORM 1844 (CHAP 32, AFM 35-3).
3. IF APPLICANT IS A CIVILIAN EMPLOYEE OF THE FEDERAL GOVT, ATTACH COMPLETED "CERTIFICATE OF AVAILABILITY FOR FEDERAL EMPLOYEE", (CHAP 32, AFM 35-3).

TO:
9921st Air Reserve Squadron
c/o Lt. Col. Reese H. Bricken
2704 Fairmont --- Montgomery, Ala.   36111

1. LAST NAME - FIRST NAME - MIDDLE INITIAL
Bush, George W.

2. DATE OF BIRTH	3. AFRES GRADE	4. DATE OF AFRES GRADE
July 6, 1946	1/Lt.	Nov. 1970

8A. SERVICE NUMBER	6B. SSAN	7. PRIMARY AFSC
▓▓▓▓	▓▓▓▓	1125B

5. ADDRESS AND TELEPHONE NUMBER (If different from permanent address, indicate both)

P. O. Box 4444
Montgomery, Ala. 36104
269-1841

8. ADDITIONAL AFSC'S	9. DATE AND TERM OF APPOINTMENT OR ENLISTMENT
none.	Sept., 1968

10. DRAWING DISABILITY COMPENSATION (If yes, state, percent)
☐ YES   ☑ NO   %

11. AERONAUTICAL RATING (Indicate if on flying status. If requested assignment will authorize flying duty, indicate flying experience by type aircraft and hours in each, date and type of instrument card now held, and date of last physical examination.)

Flying status

12. CIVILIAN EDUCATION (Indicate years completed, major subject and degree, if any)

16 years
Yale University - 1968
BA - History

13. CIVILIAN EXPERIENCE (In chronological order showing latest experience first, indicate pertinent experience to include employers, positions held, and duration.)

Red Blount For Senate - Campaign Management
Stratford of Texas - Assistant to Executive
                              Vice President - one year
George Bush For Senate - Surrogate Candidate

14. MILITARY SCHOOLS ATTENDED (Indicate date, course number or title, and location)

15. MILITARY EXPERIENCE (Indicate position title, level of command, DAFSC Highest grade and duration. List only those experiences that directly substantiate your qualifications for assignment requested.)

Pilot, Fighter Interceptor
squadron level 1125B, 1/Lt.

16. PRESENT ASSIGNMENT AND ATTACHMENT (Indicate unit and training category)

111th F.I.S. (TNG)
P. O. Box 34567
Houston, Texas 77034

17. ASSIGNMENT DESIRED (Indicate unit if any preferred, training category and pay group or description of type of training desired)

9921st Air Reserve Squadron
No pay, training category G
Reserve section MM

I CERTIFY THAT THE DATA CONTAINED HEREIN IS TRUE AND CORRECT TO THE BEST OF MY KNOWLEDGE, I ALSO ACKNOWLEDGE THAT UPON MY ASSIGNMENT TO THE READY RESERVE I AM RESPONSIBLE TO NOTIFY MY EMPLOYER OF MY READY RESERVE STATUS AND THAT AS A READY RESERVIST, I SHALL BE SUBJECT TO INVOLUNTARY ORDER TO ACTIVE DUTY IN TIME OF WAR OR NATIONAL EMERGENCY DECLARED BY THE CONGRESS, A NATIONAL EMERGENCY DECLARED BY THE PRESIDENT, OR WHEN OTHERWISE AUTHORIZED BY LAW.

DATE 24 May 72   SIGNATURE OF APPLICANT George W Bush

AF FORM 1288 JAN 66   PREVIOUS EDITION OF THIS FORM IS OBSOLETE.

atch 1

| TO: 1/LT GEORGE W. BUSH | FROM: 9921 Air Reserve Sq
2704 Fairmont Road
Montgomery, AL 36111 |

☒ APPROVED ☐ DISAPPROVED

REMARKS Your application for assignment to the 9921 Air Reserve Sq is acceptable and approved herewith. You already understand that this is a Training Category G, Pay Group None, Reserve Section MM proposition. XX XXX The continuation of this type unit is uncertain at this time and we may last 3 months, 6 months, a year or who knows! With this in mind, if you are willing to accept assignment under these circumstances, welcome! We're glad to have you.

| DATE | TYPED NAME AND TITLE | SIGNATURE |
| 26 May 72 | REESE H. BRICKEN, LTC, USAFH
Commander | *Reese W. Bricken* |

| TO: | FROM: |

☐ APPROVED (if approved furnish assignment data) ☐ DISAPPROVED

| 1. AUTH GRADE | 2. AUTH AFSC | 3. FUNCTIONAL CODE | 4. TRNG CATEGORY | 5. PAY GROUP |
| 6. UNIT OR TYPE OF ASSIGNMENT
☐ UNIT ☐ MA ☐ RD ☐ OTHER (Specify) | | 7. RESERVE SECTION CODE | 8. POSITION CONTROL NUMBER | |

REMARKS

| DATE | TYPED NAME AND TITLE | SIGNATURE |

NOTE: DO NOT INCLUDE ASSIGNMENT DATA IN SUCCEEDING INDORSEMENTS EXCEPT TO CORRECT ORIGINAL DATA.

| TO: | FROM: |

☐ APPROVED ☐ DISAPPROVED

REMARKS

| DATE | TYPED NAME AND TITLE | SIGNATURE |

| TO: | FROM: |

☐ APPROVED ☐ DISAPPROVED

REMARKS

| DATE | TYPED NAME AND TITLE | SIGNATURE |

REVERSE OF AF FORM 1288

GPO 970-538

1st Ind to AF Form 1288, 24 May 72, Application for Reserve Assignment
(Bush, George W., 1st Lt, ███████████)

147th Ftr Gp (Tng)/CBPO   2 JUN 1972

TO: AGTEX/AP
     ARPC/MM
     IN TURN

Recommend approval. Request this organization be notified on date of
appointment.

FOR THE COMMANDER

        SIGNED

RUFUS G. MARTIN, Major, TexANG
Personnel Staff Officer

2nd Ind

TAG Texas, P O Box 5218, Austin, Texas 78763 (APT)   5 June 1972

TO: ARPC/MM

Recommend approval.

FOR THE ADJUTANT GENERAL OF TEXAS

        For

CHARLES K. SHOEMAKE
Major, TexANG
Chief, Military Personnel (ANG)

DEPARTMENT OF THE AIR FORCE
HEADQUARTERS AIR RESERVE PERSONNEL CENTER
3800 YORK STREET
DENVER, COLORADO 80205

REPLY TO
ATTN OF: DPRMA

21 JUL 1972

SUBJECT: Application for Reserve Assignment, Bush, George W, 1st Lt, ▬▬▬▬,
USAFR

TO: TAG Texas

1. Application for Reserve Assignment for First Lieutenant Bush is
returned.

2. A review of his Master Personnel Record shows he has a Military
Service Obligation until 26 May 1974. Under the provisions of paragraph 30-6 a (4), AFM 35-3, an obligated Reservist can be assigned to
a specific Ready Reserve position only. Therefore, he is ineligible
for assignment to an Air Reserve Squadron.

FOR THE COMMANDER

GWEN L. DALLIN, Chief
Reserve Assignments Branch
Directorate of Personnel Resources

1 Atch
1. AF Fm 1288, 24 May 72 (2) w/atch

Cy to: 1st Lt Bush
147 Ftr Gp
9921 Air Reserve Sq

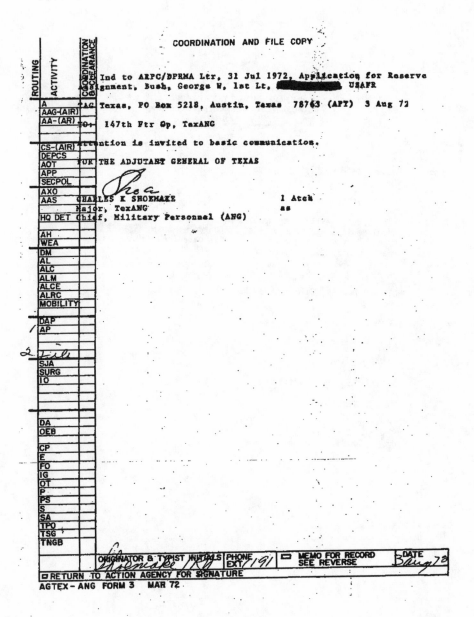

COORDINATION AND FILE COPY

ROUTING	ACTIVITY	COORDINATION CLEARANCE	

Ind to ARPC/DPRMA Ltr, 31 Jul 1972, Application for Reserve Assignment, Bush, George W, 1st Lt, ▓▓▓▓▓▓▓ USAFR

TAG Texas, PO Box 5218, Austin, Texas 78763 (APT) 3 Aug 72

To: 147th Ftr Gp, TexANG

Attention is invited to basic communication.

FOR THE ADJUTANT GENERAL OF TEXAS

CHARLES K SHOEMAKE
Major, TexANG
Chief, Military Personnel (ANG)

1 Atch
as

ORIGINATOR & TYPIST INITIALS   PHONE EXT /191   ☐ MEMO FOR RECORD SEE REVERSE   DATE 3 Aug 72

☑ RETURN TO ACTION AGENCY FOR SIGNATURE

AGTEX-ANG FORM 3   MAR 72

DEPARTMENT OF THE AIR FORCE
HEADQUARTERS 147TH FIGHTER GROUP (ANG)
P. O. BOX 34567
HOUSTON, TEXAS 77034

REPLY TO
ATTN OF: CC

5 September 1972

SUBJECT: Suspension From Flying Status

TO: 147th FG/CBPO

In accordance with paragraph 2-29m, AFM 35-13, failure to accomplish annual medical examination, 1st Lt George W. Bush, ▓▓▓▓▓▓▓, is suspended from flying status effective date 1 Aug 1972. Publish orders as directed in paragraph 2-28, AFM 35-13.

BOBBY W. HODGES, Colonel, TexANG
Commander

Cy to: 111th FIS/CC

1st Ind

147th Ftr Gp (Tng)

TO: AGTEX/APO

19 SEP 1972

Forwarded for your action.

FOR THE COMMANDER

RUFUS G. MARTIN, Major, TexANG
Personnel Staff Officer

2nd Ind to 147th FG (CC) Ltr, 5 Sep 72, Suspension from Flying Status

TAG Texas, PO Box 5218, Austin, TX 78763 (AOT) 20 September 1972

TO: NGB/XO

1. Forwarded for your appropriate action.

2. Recommend approval.

FOR THE ADJUTANT GENERAL OF TEXAS

E. C. HERBER
Lt Colonel, TexANG
Air Administrative Officer

DEPARTMENTS OF THE ARMY AND THE AIR FORCE
NATIONAL GUARD BUREAU
WASHINGTON, D.C. 20310

AERONAUTICAL ORDERS
NUMBER   87   29 September 1972

1. CAPT ELGIE H LUTES III, ▬▬▬▬▬, ANGUS (Not on EAD), CT ANG,
Hq 103 Tac Ftr Gp, Bradley ANG Base, Windsor Locks CT, whose flying
status orders terminated on 12 Jun 72, per para 2-13, AFM 35-13,
and who holds the aeronautical rating of Plt, is hereby required to
participate frequently and regularly in aerial flts in such rating
per Sec 102, EO 11157, 24 Jun 64 and para 2-5b, AFM 35-13. Reason:
Officer assigned to a position in the Reserve Forces requiring a
rated off as outlined in AFM 26-1. FSC Changed from FSC T to FSC 1.
Off will comply with para 2-10, AFM 35-13. Authority: Para 2-5,
AFM 35-13.

2. Each of the fol named offs, ANGUS (Not on EAD), orgn indc, is
granted the aeronautical rating of Comd Plt per para 1-14a, AFM
35-13. Authority: Para 1-7b(5), AFM 35-13:

GRADE, NAME AND SSAN	ORGANIZATION
LTCOL JOHN B CONAWAY KY	Hq 123 Tac Recon Gp, Standiford Fld, Louisville KY
MAJ ROBERT O BOARDMAN MA	102 CAM Sq, Otis AFB MA
MAJ EDWARD S MANSFIELD MA	101 Ftr Intcp Sq, Otis AFB MA
MAJ ROBERT J LAMB NE	Hq 155 Tac Recon Gp, Lincoln ANG Base, Lincoln NE
MAJ CLARK A ROSENBERGER NY	139 Tac Alift Sq, Schenectady Aprt, Schenectady NY
MAJ CRAIG R IVERSON UT	191 Mil Alft Sq, Salt Lake City MAP, Salt Lake City UT
MAJ GARY C NELSON UT	Hq 151 Mil Alft Gp, Salt Lake City MAP, Salt Lake City UT

3. Each of the fol named offs, ANGUS (Not on EAD), orgn indc, is
granted the aeronautical rating of Sen Plt per para 1-14b, AFM
35-13. Authority: Para 1-7b(5), AFM 35-13:

GRADE, NAME AND SSAN	ORGANIZATION
CAPT MARTIN E BEHRENDS IL	Hq 182 Tac Air Spt Gp, Greater Peoria Aprt, Peoria IL

AO 87, DAAF-NGB, dated 29 September 1972

74: 60: 72

CAPT BRIAN M LEIDING
IL

Hq 182 Tac Air Spt Gp, Greater
Peoria Aprt, Peoria IL

CAPT EDWARD L SHARP
IN

113 Tac Ftr Sq, Hulman Fld,
Terre Haute IN

CAPT WILBUR J LATHAM JR
IA

124 Tac Ftr Sq, Des Moines MAP,
Des Moines IA

CAPT JAMES H RENSCHEN
PA

103 Tac Air Spt Sq, Willow Grove NAS,
Willow Grove PA

4. Each of the fol named offs, ANGUS (Not on EAD), orgn indc, is
granted the aeronautical rating of Master Nav, per para 1-14d, AFM
35-13. Authority: Para 1-7b(5), AFM 35-13:

GRADE, NAME AND SSAN   ORGANIZATION

MAJ GENE J PETTY
NY

136 Ftr Intcp Sq, Niagara Falls
Intl Aprt, Niagara Falls NY

LTCOL CARL R BECK
PA

193 Tac Elect Warfare Sq, Olmsted
Fld, Middletown PA

5. CAPT DENNIS M HYATT, _____, ANGUS (Not on EAD), NY ANG,
136 Ftr Intcp Sq, Niagara Falls Intl Aprt, Niagara Falls NY, is
granted the aeronautical rating of Sen Nav per para 1-14e, AFM
35-13. Authority: Para 1-7b(5), AFM 35-13.

6. Verbal orders of the Comdr on 1 Aug 72 suspending 1STLT GEORGE W
BUSH, _____, ANGUS (Not on EAD), TX ANG, Hq 147 Ftr Gp, Ellington
AFB, Houston TX, from flying status are confirmed, exigencies of the
service having been such as to preclude the publication of competent
written orders in advance. Reason for Suspension: Failure to
accomplish annual medical examination. Off will comply with para
2-10, AFM 35-13. Authority: Para 2-29m, AFM 35-13.

7. Verbal orders of the Comdr on 1 Sep 72 suspending _____
, ANGUS (Not on EAD), TX ANG, Hq 147 Ftr Gp, Ellington AFB,
Houston TX, from flying status are confirmed, exigencies of the service
having been such as to preclude the publication of competent written
orders in advance. Reason for Suspension: Failure to accomplish
annual medical examination. Off will comply with para 2-10, AFM 35-13.
Authority: Para 2-29m, AFM 35-13.

BY ORDER OF THE SECRETARIES OF THE ARMY AND THE AIR FORCE

FRANCIS S. GREENLIEF, Major General, USA
Chief, National Guard Bureau

OFFICIAL

ALDO E. TIMM, Colonel, USAF
Executive, National Guard Bureau

DISTRIBUTION:
15 ea State for ea Off
1 AFMPC/DPMAJD
1 NGB-AD
25 NGB/DPM

September 5, 1972

Col. Jerry Killian
P. O. Box 34567
Houston, Texas   77034

Col. Killian:

I request permission to perform equivalent duty

with the

187th Tac Recon Group
P. O. Box 2584
Montgomery, Alabama   36105

This duty would be for the months of September,

October, and November.

Thank you for your consideration.

Sincerely,

First Lieutenant George Bush

1st Ind to Ltr, Lt Bush, 5 Sep 72, Permission to Perform Equivalent Duty with 187th Tac Recon Gp

111FIS/CC   6 Sep 1972

TO: 147FG/CC

Recommend approval.

JERRY B. KILLIAN, Lt Col, TexANG
Commander

2d Ind/CC   8 September 1972

TO: AGTEX-AAG, Air

Recommend approval.

BOBBY W. HODGES, Col, TexANG
Commander

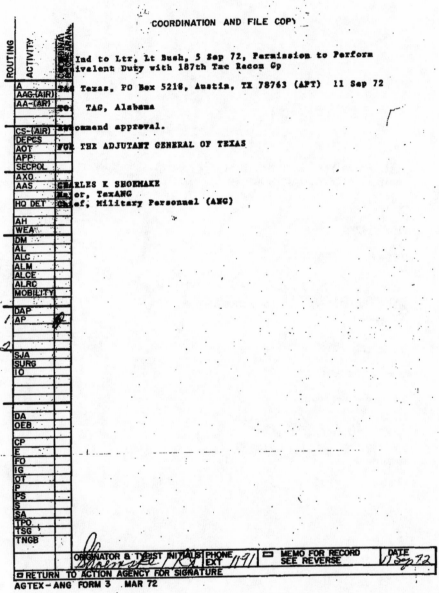

COORDINATION AND FILE COPY

ROUTING ACTIVITY

Ind to Ltr, Lt Bush, 5 Sep 72, Permission to Perform Equivalent Duty with 187th Tac Recon Gp

AG Texas, PO Box 5218, Austin, TX 78763 (APT) 11 Sep 72

TO: TAG, Alabama

Recommend approval.

FOR THE ADJUTANT GENERAL OF TEXAS

CHARLES K SHOEMAKE
Major, TexANG
Chief, Military Personnel (ANG)

ROUTING	ACTIVITY	COORDINAT/CLEARANCE
A	AAG-(AIR)	
	AA-(AIR)	
	CS-(AIR)	
	DEPCS	
	AOT	
	APP	
	SECPOL	
	AXO	
	AAS	
	HQ DET	
	AH	
	WEA	
	DM	
	AL	
	ALC	
	ALM	
	ALCE	
	ALRC	
	MOBILITY	
	DAP	
	AP	
	SJA	
	SURG	
	IO	
	DA	
	OEB	
	CP	
	E	
	FO	
	IG	
	OT	
	P	
	PS	
	S	
	SA	
	TPO	
	TSG	
	TNGB	

ORIGINATOR & TYPIST INITIALS | PHONE EXT 1191 | MEMO FOR RECORD SEE REVERSE | DATE 11 Sep 72

RETURN TO ACTION AGENCY FOR SIGNATURE

AGTEX-ANG FORM 3 MAR 72

5th Ind to 1Lt George Bush Ltr, 5 Sep 72, Permission to Perform Equivalent Duty with 187th Tac Recon Gp

Hq, 187th Tac Recon Gp (DPM)   15 September 1972

TO: TAG, AL (AL-AFAB)

1. Approved. Unit Training Assembly schedule is as follows:

          7-8 Oct 72   0730-1600
          4-5 Nov 72   0730-1600
September UTA was held on 9-10 Sep 72.

2. Lieutenant Bush should report to LtCol William Turnipseed, DCO, to perform Equivalent Training. Lieutenant Bush will not be able to satisfy his flight requirements with our group.

FOR THE COMMANDER

KENNETH K. LOTT, Capt, AL ANG
Chief, Personnel Branch

6th Ind

TAG Alabama (AL-AFAB)   19 September 1972

TO: TAG Texas

Forwarded.

FOR THE ADJUTANT GENERAL

DAVID E. McCUTCHIN, 2d Lt, AL ANG   Cy to: Hq 117 TRW
Air Admin & Tng Off

7th Ind

TAG Texas, P O Box 5218, Austin, TX 78763 (AP) 21 Sep 72

TO: 147th Ftr Intcp Gp, TexANG

Forwarded.

FOR THE ADJUTANT GENERAL OF TEXAS

CHARLES K. SHOEMAKE
Major, TexANG
Chief, Military Personnel (ANG)

1973

By 1973, George W. Bush is more absent than present in the Air National Guard's official records.

The one piece of hard evidence that Bush ever set foot at the 187th is Standard Form 603, Health Record/Dental, which recorded Lt. Bush's dental examination on January 6, 1973 (268). Yet Bush is supposed to have been back in Texas by the end of 1972; it's unclear why he would have been in Alabama in early January.

By May 1, Bush received a direct order (269) to report for Annual Active Duty Training on three upcoming weekends in May and June. The memo, from Billy Lamar of the Texas ANG, noted that "Rated personnel on flying status are authorized to participate in flying activities during the period covered by this order," but noted Bush's status as "non-flying."

Perhaps the most damning document revealed in early 2004 was Bush's Officer Effectiveness Report for 1972–3 (270–71), dated May 2, 1973. On this form—on which Bush had been rated so highly in previous years—his supervising officer, Lt. Colonel William Harris, checked "NOT

OBSERVED" in every category, and noted that "Lt Bush has not been observed at this unit during the period of this report." Harris appears to have believed that Bush had been "performing equivalent training in a non flying status with the 187 Tac Recon Gp, Dannelly ANG Base, Alabama."

So what service, if any, did Bush actually perform during the year 1972–73? The records are both slight and inconclusive. Bush's payroll records for 1973 (280–83) confirm that he was credited with scant duties that year. (For an exhaustive analysis of these challenging documents, see researcher Paul Lukasiak's series of essays on the subject, posted at www.glcq.com.) A Personnel Record Card – For Retention, Promotion, and Retirement (285), covering the period from May 1972 through May 1973, credits him with 56 points—barely enough to satisfy his requirement. These are shown as 9 active duty points and 32 UTA (Unit Training Assembly) points, along with 15 points "For reserve membership from 27 May 1972 through 26 May 73"—in other words, "gratuitous points" awarded simply for belonging to the Guard. His ARF Statement of Points Earned (287)[2] confirms that he was credited with only 41 actual duty points. There is still debate about whether Bush's service should be judged by the May-through-April years used to calculate his retirement points, or by the July-through-June fiscal year. As *U.S. News* reports, though, by neither standard did Bush meet specific requirements of 13 active and 44 inactive duty points per year. Even Reagan-era Assistant Secretary of Defense for Manpower and Reserve Affairs Lawrence Korb concurred that Bush "had not fulfilled his obligation," telling *U.S. News* that Bush "should have been called to active duty."

The U.S. Air Force was evidently dismayed by Lieutenant Colonel Harris's May Officer Effectiveness Report. In a report dated late June (288), Daniel Harkness of the USAF's Selection Boards Branch curtly stated that "Ratings must be entered on this officer [Bush]," despite Harris's lament that Bush had given them no basis for such a report. Harkness also observed, tellingly, that "This officer should have been reassigned in

---

[2] Two versions of the Statement of Points Earned are shown here: The first (286), which is torn at the upper left corner, became the subject of much speculation when it was first released. The complete statement (287), located and released later, included Bush's name and a complete list of dates. A third copy, annotated with the notes of Lietenant Colonel Albert C. Lloyd, is included in the Appendix (316).

May 1972 since he no longer is training in his AFSC or with his unit of assignment."

By July, Bush had apparently been located; in a statement he signed on the 30th (289) he noted that he had been "counseled . . . regarding my plans to leave my present Reserve of assignment due to moving from the area." Bush acknowledged that if he should do so without finding a suitable new placement, he would be "subject to involuntary order to active duty for up to 24 months"—a penalty he had first acknowledged back in 1968.

Soon thereafter, though, Bush appears to have "worked it out with the military," as he told Tim Russert in 2004. In a September 5 memo (290) he requested his discharge from the Texas Air National Guard "and reassignment to ARPC (NARS) effective 1 October 1973." His reason? "I am moving to Boston, Massachusetts to attend Harvard Business School." Bobby Hodges and Jerry Killian of the Texas ANG approved the request, and in a series of reports and memos Bush's discharge was formalized. In Bush's Report of Separation and Record of Service (292), which gives the date of his honorable discharge as October 1, 1973, Major Rufus B. Martin noted: "Officer has a six year service obligation . . . and has completed 5 years, 4 months, and 5 days toward this obligation."

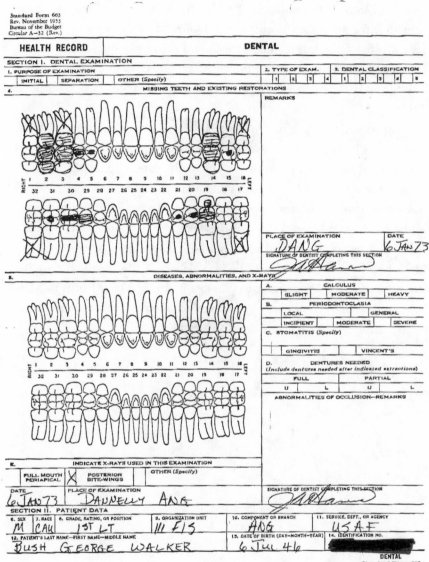

Standard Form 603
Rev. November 1955
Bureau of the Budget
Circular A—32 (Rev.)

HEALTH RECORD | **DENTAL**

SECTION 1. DENTAL EXAMINATION

1. PURPOSE OF EXAMINATION

| INITIAL | SEPARATION | OTHER (Specify) |

2. TYPE OF EXAM. | 1 | 2 | 3 | 4

3. DENTAL CLASSIFICATION | 1 | 2 | 3 | 4 | B

4. MISSING TEETH AND EXISTING RESTORATIONS

REMARKS

PLACE OF EXAMINATION   DANG   DATE 6 JAN 73

SIGNATURE OF DENTIST COMPLETING THIS SECTION

B. DISEASES, ABNORMALITIES, AND X-RAYS

A. CALCULUS | SLIGHT | MODERATE | HEAVY

B. PERIODONTOCLASIA | LOCAL | GENERAL | INCIPIENT | MODERATE | SEVERE

C. STOMATITIS (Specify)

GINGIVITIS | VINCENT'S

D. DENTURES NEEDED
(Include dentures needed after indicated extractions)
FULL | U | L
PARTIAL | U | L

ABNORMALITIES OF OCCLUSION—REMARKS

E. INDICATE X-RAYS USED IN THIS EXAMINATION

| FULL MOUTH PERIAPICAL | X | POSTERIOR BITE-WINGS | OTHER (Specify) |

DATE 6 JAN 73   PLACE OF EXAMINATION DANNELLY ANG

SIGNATURE OF DENTIST COMPLETING THIS SECTION

SECTION II. PATIENT DATA

| 6. SEX | 7. RACE | 8. GRADE, RATING, OR POSITION | 9. ORGANIZATION UNIT | 10. COMPONENT OR BRANCH | 11. SERVICE, DEPT., OR AGENCY |
| M | CAU | 1ST LT | 111 F15 | ANG | USAF |

12. PATIENT'S LAST NAME—FIRST NAME—MIDDLE NAME   BUSH GEORGE WALKER

13. DATE OF BIRTH (DAY-MONTH-YEAR) 6 JUL 46

14. IDENTIFICATION NO.

DENTAL
Standard Form 603
603-102

DEPARTMENT OF THE AIR FORCE
147TH FIGHTER INTERCEPTOR GROUP
ELLINGTON AIR FORCE BASE, TEXAS 77030

SPECIAL ORDER   1 May 1973
AE-226-IX

1. Fol named off and/or amn, orgns indicated, this station, are ordered
to attend Annual Active Duty Training at the Air National Guard training
site Ellington AFB, Texas for the period indicated: (Aero rating and fly
status as indicated). Personnel will report to their unit commander for
duty on effective date of training. Movement of dependents and household
effects at government expense not authorized. Per diem and TPC authorized
in accordance with JD 25-69 dated effective 9 July 1969. Rated personnel
on flying status are authorized to participate in flying activities during
the period covered by this order. Airmen within commuting distance (50mi)
are authorized basic allowances for subsistence at the rate of $2.57 per
day (Per diem not payable) when rations in kind not available per paragraph 30102c DODPM. The bearer being the agent of an Air Force Reserve
member on active duty in excess of 72 hours is authorized commissary privileges only for the period covered by these orders. Individuals not on
active duty in excess of 72 hours are not authorized commissary privileges.
P/A (Off) 5733850-563-4156-P521.01-S380000 (Amn) 5733850-563-4156-P521.07-
S380000. Trans: (Off) 5733850-563-4145-P521.14-408-S414502 (Amn) 5733850-
563-4145-P521.18-408-S414502. PD: (Off) 5733850-563-4145-P521.20-409-
S414502 (Amn) 5733850-563-4145-P521.24-409-S414502. Authority: ANGM 50-01.
Title 32, USC, Sec 503 (Formerly Sec 94, National Defense Act).

111TH FIGHTER INTERCEPTOR SQUADRON	NO DAYS	PERIOD
1ST LT GEORGE W. BUSH ▓▓▓▓▓▓▓▓▓▓▓	9	22May73 thru 24May73
PAFSC 1125D Non-F ▓▓▓▓▓▓▓▓▓▓		29May73 thru 31May73
		5Jun73 thru 7Jun73

2. SMOF 1, SO AE 176 IX, this hqs, dated 13 Apr 73, pertaining to
CAPT WAYNE E. WARE ▓▓▓▓▓▓▓ only as reads "NO DAYS": 6, PERIOD: 18
Apr 73 thru 19 Apr 73, 24 Apr 73 thru 27 Apr 73 is amended to read "NO
DAYS": 5, PERIOD: 18 Apr 73 thru 19 Apr 73, 24 Apr 73 thru 26 Apr 73.

FOR THE COMMANDER

BILLY B. LAMAR, CMSgt, TexANG   DISTRIBUTION
Asst Admin Officer   AE

AE-226-IX

I.	IDENTIFICAT	A (Read AFM 36-10 carefully before filling any item.)			
1. LAST NAME–FIRST NAME–MIDDLE INITIAL		2. SSAN	3. ACTIVE DUTY GRADE	4. PERMANENT GRADE	
BUSH, GEORGE W.		██████ FG	NONEAD	1st Lt	
5. ORGANIZATION, COMMAND AND LOCATION		6. AERO RATING	CODE	7. PERIOD OF REPORT	
111th Ftr Intcp Sq		C	2	FROM: 1 May 72 THRU: 30 Apr 73	
Ellington AFB, Texas		8. PERIOD OF SUPERVISION	9. REASON FOR REPORT		
TexANG (ADC)			Annual Report		

II.	PRESENT DUTY
PAFSC 1125D DAFSC 1125D	

Pilot, Fighter Interceptor, Squadron level. Pilots F-102 type aircraft and performs airborne intercepts as required by assigned missions.

III.	RATING FACTORS (Consider how this officer is performing on his job.)

1. KNOWLEDGE OF DUTIES — NOT ⊘ OBSERVED | SERIOUS GAPS IN HIS KNOWLEDGE OF FUNDAMENTALS OF HIS JOB. | SATISFACTORY KNOWLEDGE OF ROUTINE PHASES OF HIS JOB. | WELL INFORMED IN MOST PHASES OF HIS JOB. | EXCELLENT KNOWLEDGE OF ALL PHASES OF HIS JOB. | EXCEPTIONAL UNDERSTANDING OF HIS JOB. EXTREMELY WELL INFORMED ON ALL PHASES.

2. PERFORMANCE OF DUTIES — NOT ⊗ OBSERVED | QUALITY OR QUANTITY OF WORK OFTEN FAILS TO MEET JOB REQUIREMENTS. | PERFORMANCE MEETS ONLY MINIMUM JOB REQUIREMENTS. | QUANTITY AND QUALITY OF WORK ARE VERY SATISFACTORY. | PRODUCES VERY HIGH QUANTITY AND QUALITY OF WORK. MEETS ALL SUSPENSES. | QUALITY AND QUANTITY OF WORK ARE CLEARLY SUPERIOR AND TIMELY.

3. EFFECTIVENESS IN WORKING WITH OTHERS — NOT ⊗ OBSERVED | INEFFECTIVE IN WORKING WITH OTHERS. DOES NOT COOPERATE. | SOMETIMES HAS DIFFICULTY IN GETTING ALONG WITH OTHERS. | GETS ALONG WELL WITH PEOPLE UNDER NORMAL CIRCUMSTANCES. | WORKS IN HARMONY WITH OTHERS. A VERY GOOD TEAM WORKER. | EXTREMELY SUCCESSFUL IN WORKING WITH OTHERS. ACTIVELY PROMOTES HARMONY.

4. LEADERSHIP CHARACTERISTICS — NOT ⊗ OBSERVED | OFTEN WEAK. FAILS TO SHOW INITIATIVE AND ACCEPT RESPONSIBILITY. | INITIATIVE AND ACCEPTANCE OF RESPONSIBILITY ADEQUATE IN MOST SITUATIONS. | SATISFACTORILY DEMONSTRATES INITIATIVE AND ACCEPTS RESPONSIBILITY. | DEMONSTRATES A HIGH DEGREE OF INITIATIVE AND ACCEPTANCE OF RESPONSIBILITY. | ALWAYS DEMONSTRATES OUTSTANDING INITIATIVE AND ACCEPTANCE OF RESPONSIBILITY.

5. JUDGEMENT — NOT ⊗ OBSERVED | DECISIONS AND RECOMMENDATIONS OFTEN WRONG OR INEFFECTIVE. | JUDGEMENT IS USUALLY SOUND BUT MAKES OCCASIONAL ERRORS. | SHOWS GOOD JUDGEMENT RESULTING FROM SOUND EVALUATION OF FACTORS. | SOUND, LOGICAL THINKER. CONSIDERS ALL FACTORS TO REACH ACCURATE DECISIONS. | CONSISTENTLY ARRIVES AT RIGHT DECISION EVEN ON HIGHLY COMPLEX MATTERS.

6. ADAPTABILITY — NOT ⊗ OBSERVED | UNABLE TO PERFORM ADEQUATELY IN OTHER THAN ROUTINE SITUATIONS. | PERFORMANCE DECLINES UNDER STRESS OR IN OTHER THAN ROUTINE SITUATIONS. | PERFORMS WELL UNDER STRESS OR IN UNUSUAL SITUATIONS. | PERFORMANCE EXCELLENT EVEN UNDER PRESSURE OR IN DIFFICULT SITUATIONS. | OUTSTANDING PERFORMANCE UNDER EXTREME STRESS. MEETS THE CHALLENGE OF DIFFICULT SITUATIONS.

7. USE OF RESOURCES — NOT ⊗ ⊗ OBSERVED | INEFFECTIVE IN CONSERVATION OF RESOURCES. [MATERIEL] [PERSONNEL] | USES RESOURCES IN A BARELY SATISFACTORY MANNER. [MATERIEL] [PERSONNEL] | CONSERVES BY USING ROUTINE PROCEDURES. [MATERIEL] [PERSONNEL] | EFFECTIVELY ACCOMPLISHES SAVINGS BY DEVELOPING IMPROVED PROCEDURES. [MATERIEL] [PERSONNEL] | EXCEPTIONALLY EFFECTIVE IN USING RESOURCES. [MATERIEL] [PERSONNEL]

8. WRITING ABILITY AND ORAL EXPRESSION — NOT ⊗ ⊗ OBSERVED | UNABLE TO EXPRESS THOUGHTS CLEARLY. LACKS ORGANIZATION. [WRITE] [SPEAK] | EXPRESSES THOUGHTS SATISFACTORILY ON ROUTINE MATTERS. [WRITE] [SPEAK] | USUALLY ORGANIZES AND EXPRESSES THOUGHTS CLEARLY AND CONCISELY. [WRITE] [SPEAK] | CONSISTENTLY ABLE TO EXPRESS IDEAS CLEARLY. [WRITE] [SPEAK] | OUTSTANDING ABILITY TO COMMUNICATE IDEAS TO OTHERS. [WRITE] [SPEAK]

IV.	MILITARY QUALITIES (Consider how this officer meets Air Force standards.)

MILITARY QUALITIES — NOT ⊗ OBSERVED | BEARING OR BEHAVIOR INTERFERE SERIOUSLY WITH HIS EFFECTIVENESS. | CARELESS BEARING AND BEHAVIOR DETRACT FROM HIS EFFECTIVENESS. | BEARING AND BEHAVIOR CREATE A GOOD IMPRESSION. | ESPECIALLY GOOD BEHAVIOR AND BEARING. CREATES A VERY FAVORABLE IMPRESSION. | BEARING AND BEHAVIOR ARE OUTSTANDING. HE EXEMPLIFIES TOP MILITARY STANDARDS.

AF FORM 77 AUG 1972 PREVIOUS EDITION WILL BE USED.

COMPANY GRADE OFFICER EFFECTIVENESS REPORT

V.	OVER-ALL EVALU		§ (Compare this officer ONLY with officers o				s same grade.)			
SPECIFIC JUSTIFICATION REQUIRED FOR THESE SECTIONS								SPECIFIC JUSTIFICATION REQUIRED FOR THESE SECTIONS		
□	□	□	□	□	□	□	□	□		□
UNSATIS-FACTORY	MARGINAL	BELOW AVERAGE	EFFECTIVE AND COMPETENT			VERY FINE	EXCEPTIONALLY FINE	OUTSTANDING		

VI.	PROMOTION POTENTIAL	
1. DOES NOT DEMONSTRATE A CAPABILITY FOR PROMOTION AT THIS TIME. □	2. PERFORMING WELL IN PRESENT GRADE. SHOULD BE CONSIDERED FOR PROMOTION ALONG WITH CONTEMPORARIES.	□
3. DEMONSTRATES CAPABILITIES FOR INCREASED RESPONSIBILITY. CONSIDER FOR ADVANCEMENT AHEAD OF CONTEMPORARIES. □	4. OUTSTANDING GROWTH POTENTIAL BASED ON DEMONSTRATED PERFORMANCE. PROMOTE WELL AHEAD OF CONTEMPORARIES.	□

VII. COMMENTS

Lt Bush has not been observed at this unit during the period of report. A civilian occupation made it necessary for him to move to Montgomery, Alabama. He cleared this base on 15 May 1972 and has been performing equivalent training in a non flying status with the 187 Tac Recon Gp, Dannelly ANG Base, Alabama.

VIII. REPORTING OFFICIAL

NAME, GRADE, SSAN, AND ORGANIZATION	DUTY TITLE	SIGNATURE
WILLIAM D. HARRIS, JR.,Lt Colonel FG, 111th FIS TexANG (ADC)	Pilot, Ftr Intcp	SIGNED
	AERO RATING Command Pilot	CODE 1	DATE 2 May 1973

IX. REVIEW BY INDORSING OFFICIAL

I concur with the comments of the reporting official.

NAME, GRADE, SSAN, AND ORGANIZATION	DUTY TITLE	SIGNATURE
JERRY B. KILLIAN, Lt Colonel FG, 111th FIS TexANG (ADC)	Squadron Commander	SIGNED
	AERO RATING Command Pilot	CODE 1	DATE 2 May 1973

REVISED AF FORM 77

FOR OFFICIAL USE ONLY *(When Filled In)*
UNIFORM MILITARY PERSONNEL RECORD

```
FOR OFFICIAL USE ONLY (WHEN FILLED IN)
UNIFORM MILITARY PERSONNEL RECORD                     PAGE 1
1. NAME                     GRD  SOC-SCTY-NR           DATE
BUSH GEORGE W               1LT  ▮▮▮▮▮▮▮▮              73MAY10

2.************************* GRADE-DATA *********************
GRD  TYPE  DOR       EFF-DT      GRD  TYPE  DOR       EFF-DT
2LT   P              68SEP04
1LT   P    70NOV07   70NOV07
1LT   P    70NOV07   70NOV07




CURR-RES-OFF-WO-GR:
TYSD-PLSD: 68SEP04    PROM-CAT: LINE

3.************* CHRONOLOGICAL-LISTING-OF-SERVICE ************
EDOA      DAFSC      DUTY-TITLE-AND-DUTY-LOCATION
70JUN20   01125D     PILOT FTR INTCPT
                111 FTR INTERCEPT SQ ADC        ELLINGTON ANX TX
```

LAST-OER: 73APR30

```
4.******************* SPECIAL-EXPERIENCE *******************
SPEC-EXP-LAST:                  2ND:
3RD:                  4TH:                 5TH:
```

PREP FOR: RCD REVIEW   WC: RECORDS CBPO: L9 MAJCOM: ADC
AF FORM 1712   FOR OFFICIAL USE ONLY (WHEN FILLED IN)
AF FORM 1712
DEC 69

FOR OFFICIAL USE ONLY *(When Filled In)*
UNIFORM MILITARY PERSONNEL RECORD

```
FOR OFFICIAL USE ONLY (WHEN FILLED IN)
UNIFORM MILITARY PERSONNEL RECORD                    PAGE 2
1. NAME                      GRD   SOC-SCTY-NR        DATE
BUSH GEORGE W                1LT   ███████            73MAY10

5.******************* COMBAT-RECORD *********************
ACFT-DSTR:    MISSIONS: WW2-   KOREA-   N-VN-   SEA-




6.********* DECORATIONS *********    7. ****** AWARDS ********
DECOR  NR AUTH  HQ        YR TO DATE




                                     SAEMR




OTHER-US-DEC:     OTHER-US-AWD:
FOREIGN-DEC:      FOREIGN-AWD:        FOREIGN-UNIT-AWD:

8.****************** FOREIGN-SERVICE-TOURS ****************
DEPART    AREA           RETURN  TOUR  ADD-TOURS  ODSD-DEROS




NR-DA-PCS-TDY-SEA:        STRD: 65MAY
MAJCOM-AREA: US   ACCOM-STATUS:          UNACC-REAS:
OS-TOUR-LENGTH-CURR-LAST:
OS-AREA-CURR-LAST:
9. ***************** FOREIGN-SERVICE-TDY ****************
DEP-US   DAYS  AREA          DEP-US   DAYS  AREA




90-DA-ACCUM & DATE:
365-DA-ACCUM & DATE:

PREP FOR: RCD REVIEW          WC: RECORDS  CBPO: L9  MAJCOM: ADC
AF FORM 1712                  FOR OFFICIAL USE ONLY (WHEN FILLED IN)
AF FORM 1712
DEC 69
```

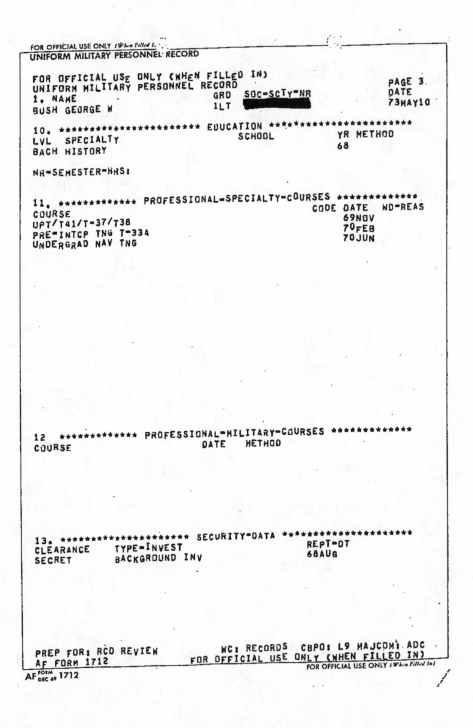

FOR OFFICIAL USE ONLY (WHEN FILLED IN)
UNIFORM MILITARY PERSONNEL RECORD   PAGE 3.
1. NAME   GRD SOC-SCTY-NR   DATE
BUSH GEORGE W   1LT ▮▮▮▮▮▮   73MAY10

10. ********************** EDUCATION **********************
LVL SPECIALTY   SCHOOL   YR METHOD
BACH HISTORY   68

NR-SEMESTER-HRS:

11. ************* PROFESSIONAL-SPECIALTY-COURSES *************
COURSE   CODE DATE WD-REAS
UPT/T41/T-37/T38   69NOV
PRE-INTCP TNG T-33A   70FEB
UNDERGRAD NAV TNG   70JUN

12 ************* PROFESSIONAL-MILITARY-COURSES *************
COURSE   DATE   METHOD

13. ******************** SECURITY-DATA ********************
CLEARANCE   TYPE-INVEST   REPT-DT
SECRET   BACKGROUND INV   68AUG

PREP FOR: RCD REVIEW   WC: RECORDS CBPO: L9 MAJCOM: ADC
AF FORM 1712   FOR OFFICIAL USE ONLY (WHEN FILLED IN)
AF FORM DEC 69 1712   FOR OFFICIAL USE ONLY *(When Filled In)*

```
  FOR OFFICIAL USE ONLY (When Filled In)
  UNIFORM MILITARY PERSONNEL RECORD

  FOR OFFICIAL USE ONLY (WHEN FILLED IN)
  UNIFORM MILITARY PERSONNEL RECORD                          PAGE 4
  1. NAME                        GRD   SOC-SCTY-NR           DATE
  BUSH GEORGE W                  1LT                         73MAY10

  14. ******************* TEST-INFORMATION *******************
  AFOQT-     PLT-    NAV-TEC-    OFF-     VERB-    QUAN-
  EDPT:      AFLAT:




  15. ******************* SERVICE-DATA ********************
                             PRIOR-AIRCREW-AFSC:
  SVC-OBLIG: 6 YEARS          DT-INTEGRATED:




  SVC-COMP:   ANGUS         SOURCE-OF-COMM:
  EAD-DT:           TAFMSD:        PAYDATE: 68MAY27
  ADSCO:            TAFCSD:        TFCSD:   68SEP04
  RES-AD-REAS:

  16. ******************* LANGUAGES ********************
       LANGUAGE         SPEAK     READ      WRITE     COMPR
  BEST:
  2ND:

  17. ******************** DER-DATA ********************
  PROJ-DER-DATE:    74APR30  PROJ-REASON: NO RPT 1 YR
  REPT-OFFICIAL:             DT-SUPVSN-BEGINS:    73MAY01






  18. ******************* AFSC-DATA ********************
  PAFSC:  011250  2AFSC:  00000   3AFSC:  00000
  DDA-AFS:        DDA-REASON:
  POSITION-NR:          PROJ-POS-NR:
  CLASS-UPGR-DT:               DDA-EXP-DATE:




  PREP FOR: RCD REVIEW          WC: RECORDS  CBPO: L9 MAJCOM: ADC
  AF FORM 1712             FOR OFFICIAL USE ONLY (WHEN FILLED IN)
  AF FORM 1712                 FOR OFFICIAL USE ONLY (When Filled In)
      DEC 69
```

FOR OFFICIAL USE ONLY (WHEN FILLED IN)
UNIFORM MILITARY PERSONNEL RECORD   PAGE 5
1. NAME   GRD   SOC-SCTY-NR   DATE
BUSH GEORGE W   1LT   ███████████   73MAY10

19.   ********* PERSONAL-DATA *********
DT-OF-BIRTH: 46JUL06   RELIGION: EPISC
PLACE-OF-BIRTH: CONN   SEX: MALE
HOME-OF-RECORD: LCMM   IN-SVC-LOAN:
LEG-RESIDENCE: TEX
LOCAL-ADDRESS: TX ZIP: 77005
HOME-PHONE: DUTY-PHONE:
OFFICE-SYMBOL:
MARITAL-STATUS: SINGLE   TOTAL-DEPN: DEPN-ADULTS:
DEPN-IN-SPONSOR-HOUSEHOLD:
DEPN-CHILDREN-(SEX-YOB):
NR-ADDITIONAL-CHILDREN: PASSPORT-EXP:
CITIZENSHIP: US-BIRTH   FORMER-CITIZENSHIP:
YR-NATURALIZED: NON-CONUS-RESIDENT:
MIL-STATUS-SPOUSE: CITIZENSHIP-SPOUSE:

20.   ********* HEALTH-AND-IMMUNIZATION *********
LAST-PHYSICAL: 71MAY   BLOOD-TYPE-AND-RH-FACTOR: 0   POS
PHY-EXAM/TEST: CR MEM ON FS   CLIN-EXAM/TEST:
TB-DETECTION-DATE: TB-DETECTION:
IMM-AREA: I   ADVERSE-REACTIONS:
ADENOVIRUS: TYPHOID-DT-AND-SEQ: 68JUL   3
INFLUENZA: 68   POLIO-DT-AND-SEQ: 73APR   3
SMALLPOX: 71JUN   TETANUS-DT-AND-SEQ: 6AJUL   3
YELLOW-FEV: 68JUL   CHOLERA-DT-AND-SEQ:
                              PLAGUE-DT-AND-SEQ   6AAUG   3

21.   ********* PAY-DATA *********
HAZARD-SPECIAL-DUTY-AND-DT:
FAM-SEP-ALW: COLA:

22.   ******** CAREER-AND-SEPARATION-DATA ********
DOS:
DOS-EXT/CURT-REAS:
PLACE-EAD:
PROJ-CAR-MOT-INTV-DT:
PROJ-SEP-DT: PROJ-PTI:
SON:
CHAR-OF-DISCH: SEP-AUTH:
REAS-AD-RET:

23.*REC-REV-DATA:* LAST-REC-REV: LAST-PHOTO: 70OCT13
PREP FOR: RCD REVIEW   WC: RECORDS CBPO: L9 MAJCOM: ADC
AF FORM 1712   FOR OFFICIAL USE ONLY (WHEN FILLED IN)
.-FORM 1712   FOR OFFICIAL USE ONLY *(When Filled In)*

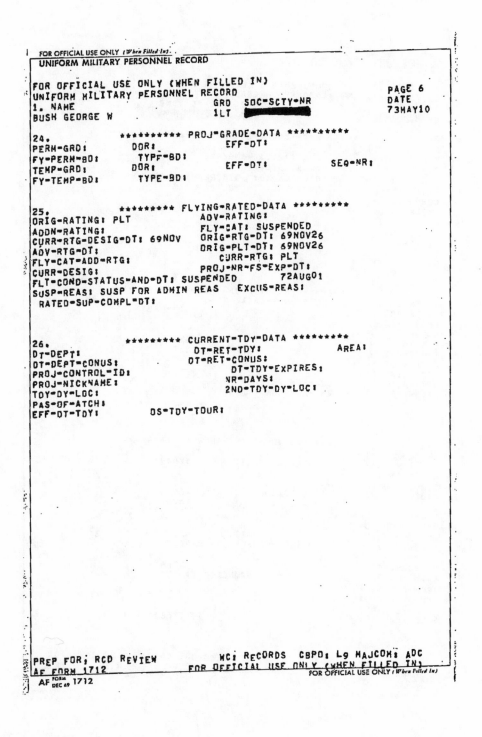

FOR OFFICIAL USE ONLY (When Filled In)
UNIFORM MILITARY PERSONNEL RECORD

FOR OFFICIAL USE ONLY (WHEN FILLED IN)
UNIFORM MILITARY PERSONNEL RECORD   PAGE 6
1. NAME   GRD   SOC-SCTY-NR   DATE
BUSH GEORGE W   1LT   ▓▓▓▓▓▓▓   73MAY10

24.   ********* PROJ-GRADE-DATA **********
PERM-GRD: DOR: EFF-DT:
FY-PERM-BD: TYPE-BD:
TEMP-GRD: DOR: EFF-DT: SEQ-NR:
FY-TEMP-BD: TYPE-BD:

25.   ********* FLYING-RATED-DATA *********
ORIG-RATING: PLT   ADV-RATING:
ADDN-RATING: FLY-CAT: SUSPENDED
CURR-RTG-DESIG-DT: 69NOV   ORIG-RTG-DT: 69NOV26
ADV-RTG-DT: ORIG-PLT-DT: 69NOV26
FLY-CAT-ADD-RTG: CURR-RTG: PLT
CURR-DESIG: PROJ-NR-FS-EXP-DT:
FLT-COND-STATUS-AND-DT: SUSPENDED   72AUG01
SUSP-REAS: SUSP FOR ADMIN REAS   EXCUS-REAS:
 RATED-SUP-COMPL-DT:

26.   ********* CURRENT-TDY-DATA *********
DT-DEPT: DT-RET-TDY: AREA:
DT-DEPT-CONUS: DT-RET-CONUS:
PROJ-CONTROL-ID: DT-TDY-EXPIRES:
PROJ-NICKNAME: NR-DAYS:
TDY-DY-LOC: 2ND-TDY-DY-LOC:
PAS-OF-ATCH:
EFF-DT-TDY: OS-TDY-TOUR:

PREP FOR: RCD REVIEW   WC: RECORDS CBPO: L9 MAJCOM: ADC
AF FORM 1712   FOR OFFICIAL USE ONLY (WHEN FILLED IN)
AF FORM 1712   FOR OFFICIAL USE ONLY (When Filled In)
DEC 69

UNIFORM MILITARY PERSONNEL RECORD

UNIFORM MILITARY PERSONNEL RECORD   PAGE 7
1. NAME   GRD SOC-SCTY-NR   DATE
   BUSH GEORGE W   1LT ▓▓▓▓▓▓▓▓   73MAY10

27.   ********** CURRENT-ASGMT-DATA **********
PAS: L9CMPY
DOLDS: FUNCT-CAT: ANG/RES
DAS: ASGMT-STAT:
FAC: 311000   RTD-POS-ID: AIRCREW (PILOT)
PEI: 5AP   DUTY-LOC: FWJL
CURR-AVAIL:
PREC-AVAIL:
LIMIT-1ST:
LIMIT-2ND:
LIMIT-3RD:
PERS-REL:
ORG-STRUCT:

28.   ********* PROJECTED-ASGMT-DATA *********
ACT-NR: LOS-FUNCT-CAT: RECLAMA:
ACT-REASON: GAIN-PAS:
LOSING-PAS: GAIN-AREA:
DAFSC:
PCS-ID: GAIN-DUTY-LOC:
FUNCT-CAT: EFF-DT-EDCSA:
EDCSA-CBPO-DIR:
CBPO-DIR-PAS:
GAIN-PTI: 1ST-REMARK:
LOSS-PTI: 2ND-REMARK:

29.   ********** ASGMT-PREFERENCE **********
LEVEL-1ST:
STATION-1ST: STATION-2ND: STATE:
CONUS-1ST:
CONUS-2ND:
MAJCOM: SAC   OS-1ST: TOUR:
                    OS-2ND: TOUR:
ASGMT-ACT-REASON: PREF-AFS:
D-REQ-REPT-DATE:
OS-VOL-STATUS: D-PTI:
INSTR-VOL: INSTR-QUAL-EXP: NONE
INSTR-QUAL-TYPE:
D-PROJ-DAFSC: D-PAS:
GAIN-DUTY-LOC: D-PROJ-FUNCT-CAT:
TECH-FLY-TNG:
TECH-FLY-2ND:
TECH-FLY-3RD:
SPEC-REQUEST: TYPE-ACFT:

PREP FOR: RCD REVIEW   WC: RECORDS CBPO: L9 MAJCOM: ADC
AF FORM 1712
AF FORM 1712

FOR OFFICIAL USE ONLY (When Filled In)
UNIFORM MILITARY PERSONNEL RECORD

AF FORM 1712
DEC 69

BUSH LTCMP746

| MGM | YR | 01 | 02 | 03 | 04 | 05 | 06 | 07 | 08 | 09 | 10 | 11 | 12 | 13 | 14 | 15 | 16 | 17 | 18 | 19 | 20 | 21 | 22 | 23 | 24 | 25 | 26 | 27 | 28 | 29 | 30 | JISCLI | ACM | UTAS | MF | G-L | COUNTERS |

JUL 72

AUG 72   99   0   0   00 IIIIIIIIPP

SEP 72

OCT 72   22 22 22 22   22 22   99   0   0   00

NOV 72

DEC 72

1ST. GTR 1973

1973 - 2cd QTR (1)

1973 3rd QTR
Page 2

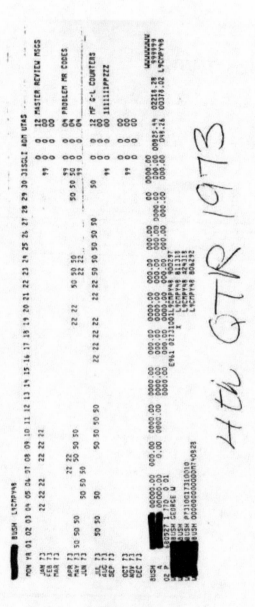

4th QTR 1973

26 90003 73

ARF RETIREMENT CREDIT SUMMARY

TO THE RESERVIST:

IF YOU DISAGREE WITH THIS STATEMENT, SUBMIT CORRECTION WITH DETAILED SUBSTANTIATION TO ARPC WITHIN 30 DAYS OF RECEIPT.

MAILING ADDRESS OF THE RESERVIST

1LT BUSH GEORGE W
2910 WESTHEIMER APT 4

HOUSTON   TX 77006

L9CMPY 48
EFF DATE: 730526
REASON FOR STATEMENT:
ANNUAL

NON-CREDITABLE SERVICE PERIODS

FROM DATE	TO DATE	REASON SERVICE NON-CREDITABLE

LEGEND FOR POINT TOTAL COLUMNS

A ADZACDUTRA
B INACDUTRA
C ECI

D GRATUITOUS
E TOTAL POINTS
F TOTAL POINTS FOR RETIREMENT

G SATISFACTORY SERVICE IN YEARS, MONTHS AND DAYS

TOTAL POINTS ACCRUED:	A	B	C	D	E	F	G
PRIOR TO 1 JULY 1949							
SINCE 1 JULY 1949 TO							
FOR THE CURRENT YEAR							
TOTAL POINTS ACCRUED TO							

TRANSFER ACTIONS

FROM (UNIT)	TO (UNIT)	EDCSA	ORDER NO.	PAR	HQ	DT OF ORDER
FROM (UNIT)	TO (UNIT)	EDCSA	ORDER NO.	PAR	HQ	DT OF ORDER
FROM (UNIT)	TO (UNIT)	EDCSA	ORDER NO.	PAR	HQ	DT OF ORDER
FROM (UNIT)	TO (UNIT)	EDCSA	ORDER NO	PAR	HQ	DT OF ORDER

REMARKS

_F?S_

USAF RESERVE PERSONNEL RECORD CARD... FOR RETENTION, PROMOTION, AND RETIREMENT

NAME (LAST, FIRST, MIDDLE INITIAL)	GRADE	SERVICE NUMBER	PERIOD COVERED		CARD NO
BUSH, GEORGE W.	1ST LT		27 May 72 – 26 May 73		5
		SSAN	YEAR FOR RETIREMENT BEGINS	YEAR FOR RETENTION BEGINS	
			27 May 68	27 May 72 (112)	

DATE OF BIRTH 6 Jul 46   AERO RATING Plt On-fly

CODES FOR COLUMN HEADINGS
UTA - UNIT TRAINING ASSEMBLY   APDY - APPROPRIATE DUTY
EQT - EQUIVALENT TRAINING   TP - TRAINING PERIOD

COMPUTATION OF SERVICE AND TRAINING POINTS

DATE	ACTIVE DUTY				INACTIVE DUTY TRAINING																TOTAL POINTS (ACROSS)	TOTAL POINTS (CUMULATIVE)
	FROM	TO	NR OF POINTS	UTA	APDY	EQT	TP	EXT COURS.		FLYING		INST		PREP INST								
	ALW	HR	RES	NC	FTS	FTR	PTS	PTR	CRS	HRS	PTS	HRS	PTS	HRS	PTS	HRS	PTS					
26 May 72				9	32																41	41
26 May 72	FOR RESERVE MEMBERSHIP FROM 27 May 72 THROUGH 26 May 72																				15	56
	PERMANENTLY CLOSED																					
				9	32																56	56
	CERTIFIED CORRECT							ROGER C. MARTIN, MAJ, TEXANG														

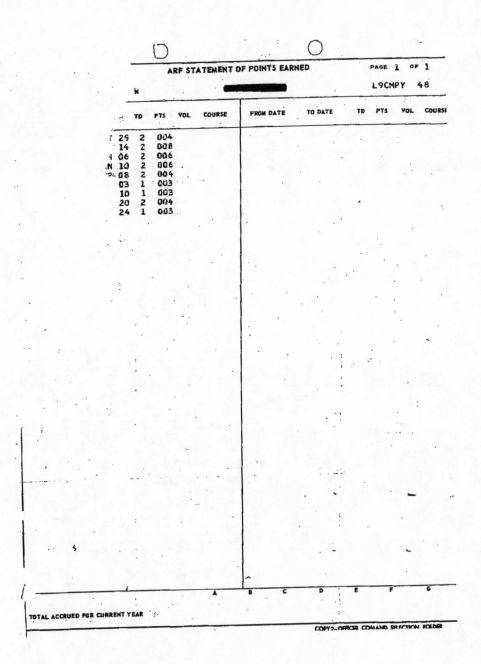

ARF STATEMENT OF POINTS EARNED

PAGE 1 OF 1

L9CMPY 48

	TD	PTS	VOL	COURSE	FROM DATE	TO DATE	TD	PTS	VOL	COURSE
29	2	004								
14	2	008								
06	2	006								
10	2	006								
08	2	004								
03	1	003								
10	1	003								
20	2	004								
24	1	003								

A   B   C   D   E   F   G

TOTAL ACCRUED FOR CURRENT YEAR

COPY 2—OFFICER COMMAND SELECTION FOLDER

ARF STATEMENT OF POINTS EARNED

PAGE 1 OF 1

LSCMPY 48

1LT BUSH GEORGE W

FROM DATE	TO DATE	TD	PTS	VOL	COURSE	FROM DATE	TO DATE	TD	PTS	VOL	COURSE
72 OCT 28	72 OCT 29	2	004								
72 NOV 11	72 NOV 14	2	008								
73 JAN 04	73 JAN 06	2	006								
73 JAN 08	73 JAN 10	2	006								
73 APR 07	73 APR 08	2	004								
73 MAY 01	73 MAY 03	1	003								
73 MAY 08	73 MAY 10	1	003								
73 MAY 19	73 MAY 20	2	004								
73 MAY 22	73 MAY 24	1	003								

A   B   C   D   E   F   G

TOTAL ACCRUED FOR CURRENT YEAR

NOTICE OF MISSING OR CORRECTION OF OFFICER EFFECTIVENESS/TRAINING REPORT		DATE 2 Jun 73	SUSPENSE DATE 6 Aug 73

1	TO	INFO	FROM
	NGB/DPMO		ARPC/DPABB

LAST NAME - FIRST NAME - MIDDLE INITIAL	GRADE	SSAN	UNIT
BUSH, GEORGE W.	1Lt	▓▓▓▓▓	111 FISq

ATTACHED REPORT IS RETURNED FOR CORRECTION. REPORTING PERIOD	FROM 1 May 72	THRU 30 Apr 73

CORRECTIVE ACTION REQUIRED AS INDICATED BELOW (Check applicable boxes)

	1. A rating factor has not been checked in Item ___, Section ___.		11. Period of report is incorrect, officer's last report closed on ___ ; therefore, this report must open on ___
	2. A more comprehensive job description will be entered in Section II.		
	3. Rating factors in Section III, Items 1, 2, 3, 4, 5, 6, 7 and 8; Sections IV, V and VI do not agree on all copies.		12. OER must be in one complete original and one complete carbon copy.
	4. OER will be reaccomplished due to erasure/correction in Section ___		13. Reporting and/or indorsing official has signed and dated the report prior to closing date.
X	5. DAFSC and/or duty title in Section II does not agree with Item 8, AF Form 11.	X	14. Returned for compliance with paragraph 6-7f(3) AFM 36-10.
	6. Period of supervision incorrect.		15. Request copy of Page 2, AF Form 11, IAW Para 4-1 f (2) AFM 36-10.
	7. Indorsing official must indicate his agreement/disagreement with ratings and comments of reporting official.	X	16. Returned for compliance with figure 6-25, AFM 36-10.
	8. OER is returned for additional indorsement by an official who meets the requirements of Rule ___, Table ___, AFM 36-10.		17. ___ official is junior to ___ official. Statement required by rule ___ Table ___, AFM 36-10.
	9. Returned for indorsement by an officer in the grade of ___ or higher, as prescribed by AFM 36-10.		18. Other (Specify)
	10. Reporting and/or indorsing official has not signed the report.	X	See Remarks

REMARKS (Reference item numbers)

Item 18. Ratings must be entered on this officer in Sections V & VI. An AF Fm 77a should be requested from the training unit so that this officer can be rated in the position he held. This officer should have been reassigned in May 1972 since he no longer is training in his AFSC or with his unit of assignment.

PLEASE RETURN ORIGINAL COPY OF THIS FORM WHEN RETURNING CORRECTED OER

TYPED NAME AND GRADE OF PERSONNEL OFFICER DANIEL P. HARKNESS, MSgt, USAF NCOIC, Selection Boards Branch	SIGNATURE	DATE 0 July	SUSPENSE Aug 73

2	TO TAC TEXAS	FROM NGB/DPMO		

REMARKS (If above suspense date cannot be met, furnish anticipated completion date.)

RETURN CORRECTED REPORT DIRECT TO ARPC

TYPED NAME AND GRADE OF PERSONNEL OFFICER	SIGNATURE Robert L Cole

(When additional indorsements or remarks are required use reverse or blank sheets.)

ARPC FORM 204 MAR 72   PREVIOUS EDITION DATED JUN 71 MAY BE USED.

STATEMENT

Date 3ᶜ Jᵤₗ 73

I have been counseled this date regarding my plans to leave my present Reserve of assignment due to moving from the area. I understand that:

a. If I disassociate from my current Ready Reserve assignment, it is my responsibility to locate and be assigned to another Reserve Forces unit or mobilization augmentation position. If I fail to do so, I am subject to involuntary order to active duty for up to 24 months under the provisions of AFM 35-3, chapter 14.

b. Moving outside the United States, its possessions, and the Commonwealth of Puerto Rico for any reason, does not relieve me of the possible consequences stated in paragraph a above.

_____
(Signature of Member)

Date 13 September 1973

1st Lt George W. Bush _____ has satisfactorily participated
(Name, grade, SSAN)
in his Ready reserve assignment while assigned to 111th Ftr Intcp Sq, Ellington AFB, Texas
(Unit and location)

_____
(Signature of Personnel Officer)

FROM: 111th Ftr Intcp Sq

SUBJECT: Application for Discharge   5 Sep 73

TO: 111th Ftr Intcp Sq/CC

I respectfully request my discharge from the Texas Air National Guard
and reassignment to ARPC (NARS) effective 1 October 1973. I am moving
to Boston, Massachusetts to attend Harvard Business School as a full time
student. I have enjoyed my association with the 111th Ftr Intcp Sq and
the 147th Ftr Intcp Gp.

GEORGE W. BUSH, 1st Lt
███████ FG

1st Ind   6 Sep 73

111th Ftr Intcp Sq/CC

TO: 147th Ftr Intcp Gp/CC

Recommend approval.

JERRY B. KILLIAN, Lt Col, TexANG
Commander

2nd Ind to 111th Ftr Intcp Sq Ltr, 5 Sept 73, Application for Discharge

147th Ftr Intcp Gp   18 SEP 1973

TO: AGTEX/APM

1. Recommend approval. The following information is furnished to facilitate discharge.

    a. Grade and name: 1st Lt George W. Bush

    b. SSAN: ████████████

2. Request officer be relieved from 111th Ftr Intcp Sq, Ellington AFB, TX 77030, Duty Title and AFSC: Pilot, Ftr Intcp, 1125D, UDL Grade Vacancy: 1st Lt, Functional Account Code: 3110, DOB: 6 Jul 46, HOR: Harvard Business School, Soldiers Field, Boston, Mass 02263 and Honorably Discharged from the TexANG effective 1 Oct 73. Request officer be assigned ARPC (ORS), 3800 York Street, Denver CO 80205 effective 2 Oct 73. AUTH: ANGR 36-05 (PTI 961).

BOBBY W. HODGES

BOBBY W. HODGES, Colonel, TexANG
Commander

DEPARTMENTS OF THE ARMY AND THE AIR FORCE
NATIONAL GUARD BUREAU

REPORT OF SEPARATION AND RECORD OF SERVICE IN THE AIR NATIONAL GUARD OF TEXAS
AND AS A RESERVE OF THE AIR FORCE
TYPE OF DISCHARGE HONORABLE
(No erasures or alterations in this entry valid)

1. NAME (Last, first, middle initial): BUSH, GEORGE W.	2. SERVICE NO	3. GRADE 1Lt	4. ARM OR SERVICE TexANG	5. TERM OF ENLISTMENT INDEF
6. ORGANIZATION 111th Ftr Intcp Sq HOME STATION Ellington AFB, Texas	7. DATE OF DISCHARGE 1 Oct 73	8. PLACE OF DISCHARGE Ellington AFB, Texas		
9. PERMANENT ADDRESS FOR MAILING PURPOSES 02263 Harvard Business School, Boston, Mass	10. DATE OF BIRTH 6 Jul 46	11. PLACE OF BIRTH New Haven, Connecticut		

12. CIVILIAN OCCUPATION (Include name and address of present employer, or if unemployed, the last employer)
Campaign Mgmt, Allison & Travalen, P. O. Box 4444, Montgomery, Ala 36160

| 13. RACE WHITE NEGRO OTHER (Specify) NA | 14. MARITAL STATUS SINGLE X MARRIED OTHER (Specify) | 15. U.S. CITIZEN YES X NO |
| 16. COLOR EYES Hazel | 17. COLOR HAIR Brown | 18. HEIGHT 5 FT 11 IN | 19. WEIGHT 175 LBS | 20. NO DEPENDENTS None |

MILITARY HISTORY

| 21. DATE AND PLACE OF ENLISTMENT 4 Sep 68, Ellington AFB, Texas | 22. MILITARY OCCUPATIONAL SPECIALTY AND NUMBER 1125D, Pilot, Ftr Intcp |

23. MILITARY QUALIFICATION AND DATE (i.e. Infantry, Aviation, Marksmanship Badge, etc.)

NONE

24. DECORATIONS, CITATIONS, MEDALS, BADGES, COMMENDATIONS, AND CAMPAIGN RIBBONS AWARDED OR AUTHORIZED (This period of service)

TAFMS   TAFCS

25. PRIOR SERVICE (Branch of service, inclusive dates, and primary duty with MOS)

(TexANG - 27 May 68 - 3 Sep 68, Enl, HG Amn, Prin Dy Apr Adm Spec, RES)

26. LENGTH THIS SERVICE		27. TOTAL SERVICE FOR PAY PURPOSES			28. EDUCATION (Years)			29. HIGHEST GRADE HELD
YEARS	MONTHS	DAYS	YEARS	MONTHS	DAYS	GRAMMAR	HIGH SCHOOL	COLLEGE	
5	0	28	5	4	5	8	4	4	1Lt

30. SERVICE SCHOOLS ATTENDED AND DATES
(UPT Crse5p-V4A-A, Moody AFB, Ga, 53 wks - Nov 69) (T-33 Preint Plt Tng, ANG112501 - 5Wks - 70 Feb) (F102 Intcp Plt Tng, ANG 112500D - 16wks - 70 Jun)

31. REASON AND AUTHORITY FOR DISCHARGE Officer is transferred to ARPC (ORS), 3800 York St, Denver, Colorado 80205 effective 2 October 1973. AUTH: ANGR 36-05 (PTI 961) SO ANG-A 158, AGTEX, 16 Oct 73.

32. REMARKS (This space for completion of above items or entry of other items specified in DO directive)

Officer has a six year service obligation under the provisions of the 10 USC 651, as amended, and has completed 5 years, 4 months, and 5 days toward this obligation. TFRSD: 4 Sep 68, THSD: 27 May 68, TTSD: 4 Sep 68, Security Clearance: Security Clearance: SECRET, BI, Hq USAF (AFISISA4I), Bldg T-K, Washington, D. C. 2 0333 (File Number: 10D51-1793)

| 33. SIGNATURE OF PERSON BEING DISCHARGED (Full name) NOT AVAILABLE FOR SIGNATURE | 34. SIGNATURE OF OFFICER AUTHORIZED TO SIGN RUFUS G. MARTIN, Major, 147th Cmbt Spt Gp. |

AGD FORM 22
15 JAN 58

1. Insert either Army or Air
2. Insert either Army or Air Force

REPLACES NGB FORM 72 DATED 15 NOV 49, WHICH IS OBSOLETE

1. LAST NAME	FIRST NAME	MI	AFSN	GRADE	157 Lt	'11 MAY 16
BUSH, GEORGE W.			FG3244754			

2. GRADE DATA

TEMPORARY	PERMANENT	EFF. DATE	DATE OF RANK
	2D Lt	4 Sep 1968	
	1st Lt	70 Nov 7	

OTHER GRADE DATA

3. FOREIGN SERVICE

DATE DEPARTED	LOCATION	DATE RETURNED

FOREIGN SERVICE SUMMARY | OASD

4. FORMAL EDUCATION

SCHOOL—COLLEGE—UNIVERSITY	DEGREE	YEAR
Yale University	BA(list)	1968

SPECIAL EDUCATION/QUALIFICATIONS

5. SERVICE SCHOOLS

TECHNICAL—FLYING TRAINING

SCHOOL, COURSE AND NUMBER	LENGTH	YEAR
UPT Crs/JP-Vld-1, Moody AFB Ga, AN011250	53 Wks	69Nov
T-33 Preintcp Plt Tnk, AN011250	5 Wks	70Feb
F102 Intcp Plt Tng, ANG 1125000D	16 Wks	70Jun

AWARDS
SAEBR (P)

PROFESSIONAL

COURSE

6. DECORATIONS AND AWARDS

DECORATIONS AND AUTHORITY

7. SECURITY DATA

TYPE	DATE	REPORT FILED
BI	20Aug66	Hq USAF W10D51-1793

OFFICER MILITARY RECORD
SUPPLEMENTS UNIFORM OFFICER RECORD

AF FORM 11 JAN 66   PREVIOUS EDITION WILL BE USED AS SPECIFIED IN AFM 35-9

LAST NAME	FIRST NAME	MI	AFSN	GRADE	PLACE OF BIRTH	DATE OF LAST OER	2
BUSH, GEORGE W.			FG32147754 ▆	1st Lt	New Haven, Conn.	73 APR 30	73 APR 30

CHRONOLOGICAL LISTING OF SERVICE

TDOA	DAFSC	BRIEF DESCRIPTION OF DUTY—ORGANIZATION AND STATION
27May68 to 3Sep68		Bhl, HQ Amn, Prin Dy Apr Adm Spec, RES (TexANG)
4Sep68	0006	Pilot Trainee, 111th Fighter Interceptor Squadron, Ellington AFB, Texas (TexANG)
26Nov68	0006	Stu Plt Tng P-V4A-A, 3550 Stu Sq, Moody AFB, Ga. (ATC)
		Total AD/ACDUTRA as of 26 May 69: 2d Lt, 226 days
69Dec29	0006	Pilot Trainee, 111th Fighter Interceptor Squadron, Ellington AFB, Texas (TexANG)
70 Jun 20	1125D	Pilot, Ftr Intcp, 111th Ftr Intcp Sq, Ellington AFB, Tx (TexANG)
		Total AD/ACDUTRA as of 70 May 26: 2d Lt 313 days
		Total AD/ACDUTRA as of 71 May 26: 2d Lt - 43 days, 1st Lt - 3 days
		Unit redesignated 111th Ftr Intcp Sq (TFR)
		Total AD/ACDUTRA as of 72 May 26: 1st Lt 22 days
1 Oct 73		HD TR TexANG Per ANGR 36-05, SO ANG-A 158, State of Texas AG Dept, Austin, Tx, and transferred to ARPC (ORS), 3800 York St, Denver, CO 80205 effective 2 October 1973. (DOS TexANG 1 Oct 73).

COMBAT REPORT

10. REMARKS Previous Service Numbers: AF26230538
Selective Service Number: 41-62-46-1480
Reserve Status Expires: 26 May 74   Code: AA
Civ Occupation: Student   Since:
Appointed TexANG 4 ... ANG 4 ...
Unif. Maint. Alwe. Entitlement: 72 May 25 Last Paid: 68 May 25
Next Payment Due: 72 May 25
Last Physical: May ...   Class: 73
TAFMS: 4/15 ...
TAFCS: 15/05 ...

STATE OF TEXAS
ADJUTANT GENERAL'S DEPARTMENT
Post Office Box 5218
Austin, Texas 78763

SPECIAL ORDER   16 October 1973
ANG-A 158

The verbal orders of the CinC, TexANG on 1 October 1973
directing the relief of FIRST LIEUTENANT GEORGE W BUSH,
▆▆▆▆▆▆▆, from Pilot, Ftr Intcp, AFSC 1125D, UDL grade
vacancy 1st Lt, FAC 3110, 111th Ftr Intcp Sq, PAS: L9CMPY,
Ellington AFB, TX 77030 and honorably discharged from the
TexANG effective 1 October 1973 are confirmed. Exigencies of
the service having been such as to preclude issuance of
competent written orders in advance. Officer is transferred
to ARPC (ORS), 3800 York Street, Denver CO 80205 effective
2 October 1973. DOB: 6 Jul 46, HOR: Harvard Buiness School,
Soldiers Field, Boston, Mass 02263. Authority: ANGR 36-05 (PTI
961).

BY ORDER OF THE GOVERNOR

OFFICIAL   THOMAS S BISHOP
                                      Major General, TexARNG
                                      The Adjutant General

E. C. HERBER   DISTRIBUTION
Lt Colonel, TexANG   15 - AGTEX-APM
Chief, Air Guard Branch.   1 - AGTEX-A
                                      16 - Total

DEPARTMENTS OF THE ARMY AND THE AIR FORCE
NATIONAL GUARD BUREAU
WASHINGTON, D.C. 20310

SPECIAL ORDER
NUMBER 256M   24 October 1973

1. By order of the SAF announcement is made of the ext of Fed recog to the fol ANG offs in grade, State and on date indc, such offs having qual under the provisions of 32 USC 305 and 307:

GRADE	NAME	SSAN	UNIT	STATE	DATE OF FED RECOG
CAPT KENNETH J STROMQUIST JR			179 FISq	MN	17 Oct 73
CAPT MICHAEL R MICKELSON			106 TCSq	UT	21 Sep 73
1STLT MARION G PRITCHARD JR			167 TASq	WV	16 Oct 73

2. By order of the SAF announcement is made of the withdrawal of Fed recog from the fol ANG offs, in grade, State and on date indc, by reason of having trnsfr to the AFRes:

GRADE	NAME	SSAN	STATE	EFF DATE
CAPT ROBERT W HUTCHINS			AZ	17 Oct 73
COL ROBERT L FULLER			DE	23 Mar 73
MAJ(NC) LORRAINE J SKINNER			DE	23 Mar 73
CAPT RAY W KIMICK			GA	3 Oct 73
CAPT JAMES C ROSSITER JR			GA	20 Oct 73
CAPT EDWARD J WHITE			GA	3 Nov 73
CAPT ROBERT G ZEPECKI			IL	16 Oct 73
LTCOL LESTER A ROBERTS			IN	10 Nov 73
CAPT RICHARD N KRIEPS			NY	1 Sep 73
CAPT EDWARD T MCCAFFERY			NY	18 Aug 73
1STLT(DC) NEIL NEUGEBOREN			NY	31 Aug 73
MAJ ROBERT W WINTERS JR			NY	1 Sep 73
CAPT JEFFREY M MILLER			SD	10 Oct 73
→ 1STLT GEORGE W BUSH			TX	1 Oct 73

3. SMOP 1, DAAF-NGB SO 246M, cs, pertaining to the ext of Fed recog of CAPT JOSE A GOYCO, JR, _____, 140 AC&WSq, PR, as reads "CAPT JOSE A GOYCE JR" IATR "CAPT JOSE A GOYCO JR".

BY ORDER OF THE SECRETARIES OF THE ARMY AND THE AIR FORCE:

FRANCIS S. GREENLIEF, Major General, US
Chief, National Guard Bureau

JOHN T. GUISE, Colonel, USAF
Executve, National Guard Bureau

DISTRIBUTION:
5 ea State for ea Off
6 ARPC (DPAA)
1 ARPC (DPFDE)
1 AFMPC(DPMAJB1E)

1 AFMPC (DPMAJB1); 1 NGB-IS
40 NGB/DPMO

OFFICIAL

MICROFILMED 7 DEC '73   APDS PROCESSED   238

LAST NAME-FIRST NAME-MIDDLE INIT.	SSAN	ACTIVE DUTY GRADE
BUSH, GEORGE W.	☐☐☐☐ FG	NONEAD

(CHECK APPROPRIATE BLOCK AND COMPLETE AS APPLICABLE)

☐ SUPPLEMENTAL SHEET TO RATING FORM WHICH COVERS THE FOLLOWING PERIOD OF REPORT	☐ LETTER OF EVALUATION COVERING THE FOLLOWING PERIOD OF OBSERVATION
FROM	THRU	FROM	THRU

Precede comments by appropriate data, i.e. section continuation, indorsement continuation, additional indorsement, etc. Follow comments by the authentication to include: name, grade, AFSN, organization, duty title, date and signature.

Not rated for the period 1 May 72 through 30 Apr 73.

Report for this period not available for administrative reasons.

[signature]

RUFUS G. MARTIN, Major, ☐☐☐☐ FG, 147th Cmbt Spt Sq, Chief, CBPO, 12 Nov 73

AF FORM 77a PREVIOUS EDITION OF THIS FORM WILL BE USED UNTIL STOCK IS EXHAUSTED.   SUPPLEMENTAL SHEET TO AF FORMS 77, 707, 909, 910, 911 AND 475

2nd Ind to ARPC Form 204, 29 Jun 73, Notice of Missing or Correction
of Officer Effectiveness/Training Report (1LT George W. Bush, ▮▮▮▮▮▮

147th Ftr Intcp Gp/CBPO

1 3 NOV 1973

TO: AGTEX/APM

Basic communication complied with.

FOR THE COMMANDER

RUFUS G. MARTIN, Major, TexANG
Personnel Staff Officer

1 Atch
AF Fm 77a

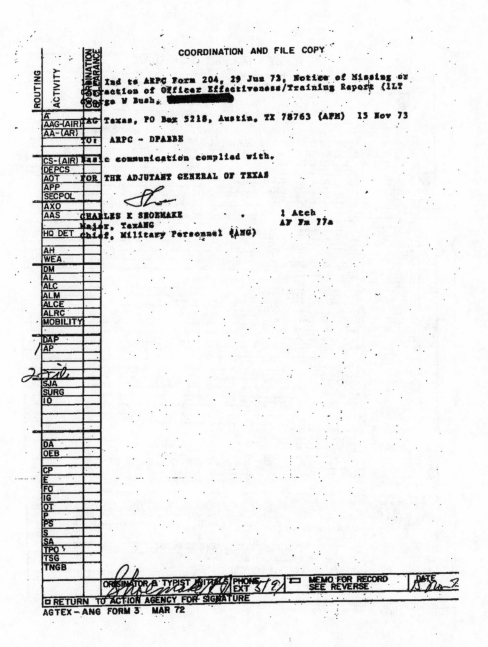

COORDINATION AND FILE COPY

1st Ind to ARPC Form 204, 29 Jun 73, Notice of Missing or Action of Officer Effectiveness/Training Report (1LT George W Bush,

AG Texas, PO Box 5218, Austin, TX 78763 (APM)   13 Nov 73

TO: ARPC - DPABBE

Basic communication complied with.

FOR THE ADJUTANT GENERAL OF TEXAS

CHARLES K SHOEMAKE
Major, TexANG
Chief, Military Personnel (ANG)

1 Atch
AF Fm 77a

ORIGINATOR & TYPIST INITIALS   PHONE EXT

☐ RETURN TO ACTION AGENCY FOR SIGNATURE

☐ MEMO FOR RECORD SEE REVERSE   DATE

AGTEX - ANG FORM 3 MAR 72

R ORDS TRANSMITTAL/REQUEST
(Use reverse for remarks)

☐ TRANSMITTAL ☐ REQUEST ☐ OTHER

TO: *(Consult PAS directors for address of CBPO)*

ARPC - ORS

FROM:

TAG Texas

BASIC IDENTIFICATION OF INDIVIDUAL

LAST NAME—FIRST—MIDDLE INITIAL	GRADE	SSAN
BUSH, GEORGE W 460-	1LT	

FORM TITLE (Check)

X	AF 4/10	AIRMAN/OFFICER UNIT PERSONNEL RECORD GROUP
	AF 7/11	AIRMAN/OFFICER MILITARY RECORD
	AF 175	HOMETOWN NEWS RELEASE DATA
	AF 186	INDIVIDUAL RECORD—EDUCATION SERVICES PROGRAM
	AF 185/195A	INDIVIDUAL MANDATORY CLOTHING CHECK (Male & Female)
	AF 229	LEAVE BALANCE LISTING (Reassignment)
	AF 324	RETENTION INTERVIEWS
	AF 452	SERVICEMAN'S STATEMENT CONCERNING APPLICATION FOR COMPENSATION FROM THE VETERANS ADMINISTRATION
	AF 513	RECORD OF CAREER INFORMATION AND COUNSELING
	AF 572	GENERAL MILITARY TRAINING RECORD
	AF 623	CONSOLIDATED TRAINING RECORD
	DD 722	HEALTH RECORD
	DD 722-1	DENTAL FOLDER—HEALTH RECORD
	AF 889	RELIGIOUS INTERVIEW GUIDE
	AF 1295	TRAFFIC SAFETY RECORD
	AF 1296	DRIVER BACKGROUND EXPERIENCE SURVEY
	DD 1360	OPERATOR QUALIFICATIONS AND RECORD OF LICENSING, EXAMINATION & PERFORMANCE
	DD 1495	CRYPTOGRAPHIC MAINTENANCE TRAINING EXPERIENCE RECORD
	AF 1710	LEAVE—AUTHORIZATION BALANCE RECORD
	AF 1710-3	LEAVE—AUTHORIZATION BALANCE RECORD
	AF 1711	HEALTH—IMMUNIZATION RECORD
	AF 1714-2	UOR SOFT COPY (Pertains to members returning from overseas for separation)
	AF 1717-2	UAR SOFT COPY (Pertains to members returning from overseas for separation)
		UAR/UOR FORMAT 4
		PERSONAL CLOTHING AND EQUIPMENT RECORD GROUP
		FINANCIAL DATA FILE
		INDIVIDUAL FLIGHT RECORD
		UNIFORM MILITARY PERSONNEL RECORD (Abbreviated)

AIRMAN SELECTION FOLDER
☐ MAILED SEPARATELY ON
☐ RETAINED FOR PROMOTION PURPOSES.

MILITARY PAY RECORD:
☐ HANDCARRIED IN SEPARATE CONTAINER ☐ WILL BE MAILED BY AFO
APR: ☐ BEING PREPARED AND WILL BE FORWARDED. ☐ NOT REQUIRED

RECEIPT AND CERTIFICATION FOR HANDCARRIED RECORDS

I ACKNOWLEDGE RECEIPT OF RECORDS CHECKED ABOVE AND CERTIFY THAT AIRMAN PERFORMANCE REPORTS FOR THE PERIOD

CLOSING DATE OF INITIAL APR	CLOSING DATE OF LAST APR IN FILE

ARE PRESENT
AND AF FORMS 229 LEAVE BALANCE LISTING, FYS. IN MY AF FORM 4, WITH THE EXCEPTION EXPLAINED IN REMARKS, ON REVERSE. I UNDERSTAND THAT I AM TO TURN THESE RECORDS OVER TO THE APPROPRIATE PROCESSING ACTIVITY UPON ARRIVAL AT MY NEW STATION, THAT I AM RESPONSIBLE FOR SAFEGUARDING THESE RECORDS ENROUTE; AND THAT I AM NOT AUTHORIZED TO OPEN THE SEALED ENVELOPE IN WHICH THESE RECORDS ARE BEING TRANSMITTED.

DATE	TYPE OR PRINT NAME AND GRADE	SIGNATURE

VERIFICATION BY LOSING CBPO/GSU

DATE	TYPE OR PRINT NAME AND GRADE	SIGNATURE
15 Nov 73	CHARLES A SHOEMAKE, MAJ, TexANG Chief, Military Personnel (ANG)	

VERIFICATION BY GAINING CBPO/GSU

DATE	TYPE OR PRINT NAME AND GRADE	SIGNATURE

AF FORM 330 SEP 69 PREVIOUS EDITIONS WILL BE USED

Dear Sirs.

I am writing to receive information regarding my status with the Air Reserve. I would like to discharge from standby reserve. My unit is or section is S70IFIX6RB. I would appreciate knowing how and when such action may be taken.

Please send the mail to 373 Broadway
                        Cambridge, Mass 02138

Thank you for your consideration

George Bush

George Walker Bush 1/LT

Standby reserve number

410062461480

1974

Despite his discharge in October 1973, the arrangement Bush made with the military appears to have allowed him to retain a kind of pro forma affiliation with the Air Force until November 1974—without any further pretense of completing his service obligations to them, which he had begun ignoring back in May 1972. The final documents in the available military files, his ARF Retirement Credit Summary for 1973–74 (305)* and ARF Statement of Points Earned (306), credit him with 19 points of active duty and 16 points of inactive duty, all of it supposedly performed between May 29 and July 30, 1973; this would correspond roughly, though not exactly, with the period when he was under direct orders (269) to report to Ellington for service. Yet even with the five gratuitous points awarded him on his Retirement Credit Summary, his total of 40 points remains—for the second year in a row—well below the minimum service requirement he had pledged to the Guard in 1968.

George W. Bush had been let off the hook.

---

* A different scan of the same document, showing the notation "TRANS AFR 2 OCT 73," appears on 307.

183 APR 10 74   ANG-A-158 16 OCT 73

ARF RETIREMENT CREDIT SUMMARY

170 APR 8 74

TO THE RESERVIST:

IF YOU DISAGREE WITH THIS STATEMENT, SUBMIT CORRECTION WITH DETAILED SUBSTANTIATION TO ARPC WITHIN 30 DAYS OF RECEIPT.

DATE PREPARED : 74/01/30

MAILING ADDRESS OF THE RESERVIST

1LT BUSH GEORGE W
2910 WESTHEIMER APT 4

HOUSTON   TX 77006

L9CMPY 48
EFF DATE: 730915
REASON FOR STATEMENT:
INACTIVE STATUS

NON—CREDITABLE SERVICE PERIODS

FROM DATE	TO DATE	REASON SERVICE NON—CREDITABLE

LEGEND FOR POINT TOTAL COLUMNS

A. AD/ACDUTRA   D GRATUITOUS   G SATISFACTORY SERVICE IN YEARS, MONTHS AND DAYS
B INACDUTRA   E TOTAL POINTS
C ECI   F TOTAL POINTS FOR RETIREMENT

TOTAL POINTS ACCRUED:		A	B	C	D	E	F	G
PRIOR TO 1 JULY 1949		0	0			0	0	000000
SINCE 1 JULY 1949 TO	730526	0	0	0	0	0	0	000000
FOR THE CURRENT YEAR		19	16	0	5	40	38	000319
TOTAL POINTS ACCRUED TO	730915	19	16	0	5	40	38	000319

ARF STATEMENT OF POINTS EARNED   PAGE 1 OF 1

1LT BUSH GEORGE W   L9CKPY 48

FROM DATE	TO DATE	TD	PTS	VOL	COURSE	FROM DATE	TO DATE	TD	PTS	VOL	COURSE
73 MAY 29	73 MAY 31	1	033								
73 JUN 05	73 JUN C7	1	003								
73 JUN 23	73 JUN 24	2	004								
73 JUL 02	73 JUL G3	1	002								
73 JUL 05	73 JUL C5	1	001								
73 JUL 09	73 JUL 12	1	004								
73 JUL 16	73 JUL 19	2	008								
73 JUL 21	73 JUL 22	2	004								
73 JUL 23	73 JUL 27	1	005								
73 JUL 30	73 JUL 30	1	001								

	A	B	C	D	E	F	G
TOTAL ACCRUED FOR CURRENT YEAR	19	16	0	5	90	38	000319

TRANS AFR 2 Oct 73
183 APR 10 74 ANG-A-158 16 OCT 73
1 PD AR 87

ARF RETIREMENT CREDIT SUMMARY

0 THE RESERVIST:

IF YOU DISAGREE WITH THIS STATEMENT, SUBMIT CORRECTION WITH DETAILED SUBSTANTIATION TO ARPC WITHIN 30 DAYS
OF RECEIPT.

DATE PREPARED : 74/01/30

IAILING ADDRESS OF THE RESERVIST

```
1LT   BUSH GEORGE W                              L9CMPY  48
2910 WESTHEIMER APT 4                   EFF DATE: 730915
                                        REASON FOR STATEMENT:
HOUSTON            TX  77006            INACTIVE STATUS
```

NON-CREDITABLE SERVICE PERIODS

FROM DATE   TO DATE   REASON SERVICE NON-CREDITABLE

LEGEND FOR POINT TOTAL COLUMNS

A AD/ACDUTRA   D GRATUITOUS   G SATISFACTORY SERVICE IN YEARS, MONTHS AND DAYS
B INACDUTRA   E TOTAL POINTS
C ECI   F TOTAL POINTS FOR RETIREMENT

TOTAL POINTS ACCRUED:	A	B	C	D	E	F	G
PRIOR TO 1 JULY 1949	0	0			0	0	000000
SINCE 1 JULY 1949 TO 730526	0	0	0	0	0	0	000000
FOR THE CURRENT YEAR	19	16	0	5	40	38	000319
	19	16	0	5	40	38	000319

DEPARTMENT OF THE AIR FORCE HEADQUARTERS AIR RESERVE PERSONNEL CENTER 3800 YORK STREET, DENVER, COLORADO 80205	PERSONNEL DATA CHANGE ORDER 90 MAR 2974

RESERVE ORDER N— D 1704	DATE 7 MAR 74

```
┌                                        ┐
   1LT  GEORGE W BUSH
   5000 LONGMONT APT 8
   HOUSTON  TX 77027
└                                        ┘
```

ASSIGNMENT

[X] ARPC   [ ] RETIRED RESERVE

Announcement is made of the following personnel data change-

RESERVE STATUS AND STANDBY SCREENING CODE

NEW PRIMARY AFSC

7021 EXECUTIVE SUPPORT OFFICER

NEW SECONDARY AFSC

NEW TERTIARY AFSC

REMARKS

Authority — AFM 35—1

FOR THE COMMANDER:

AUTHENTICATION

OFFICIAL
AIR RESERVE PERSONNEL CENTER

R. R. KOSTELNY, JR. Capt, USAF
Assistant Director
Directorate of Administration

DISTRIBUTION

Q

ONLY ITEMS CONTAINING ENTRIES APPLY

ARPC FORM 286   REPLACES MAR 68 EDITION WHICH WILL BE USED
MAR 73

RESERVE ORDER
HB-001484

DEPARTMENT OF THE AIR FORCE
HEADQUARTERS AIR RESERVE PERSONNEL CENTER
3800 YORK STREET
DENVER, COLORADO 80205

01 MAY 74

1LT BUSH GEORGE W
HARVARD BUSINESS SCHOOL
BOSTON, MA . 02163

ABOVE NAMED RESERVIST IS REASSIGNED AS INDICATED BELOW:

FROM: HQ ARPC (NARS-B) THIS CENTER

TO: HQ ARPC THIS CENTER
        INACTIVE STATUS LIST RESERVE SECTION (ISLRS)
        RESERVE SECTION: RB   RESERVE STATUS: STANDBY B

EDCSA: 27 MAY 74

AUTHORITY: CHAPTER 10, AFM-35-3

FOR THE COMMANDER:

R. R. KOSTELNY, JR. Capt. USAF
Assistant Director
Directorate of Administration .

DISTRIBUTION:
.K

DEPARTMENT OF THE AIR FORCE
HEADQUARTERS AIR RESERVE PERSONNEL CENTER
3800 YORK STREET
DENVER, COLORADO 80205

135ZC 307:

RESERVE ORDER
CB-6892

21 NOV 1974

1ST LT BUSH GEORGE W
373 BROADWAY
CAMBRIDGE MA 02138

By direction of the President the above named officer is relieved from assignment indicated and honorably discharged from all appointments in the United States Air Force. DD FORM 256AF will be furnished.

ASSIGNMENT	HQ ARFC (ISLRS) THIS STATION PAFSC: 7021
EFFECTIVE DATE 21 NOV 1974 FOR THE COMMANDER:	**AUTHORITY** AFR 35-41

DISTRIBUTION:
B

R. R. KOSTELNY, JR. Capt, USAF
Assistant Director
Directorate of Administration

C/3

THE LATE-BREAKING
RECORDS

In September 2004, as this book was in its final stage of production, a series of records was made available to the public by the Pentagon in response to a Freedom of Information Act lawsuit filed by the Associated Press. At first released only to some members of the press in CD-ROM form, on September 21 they were finally shared with the public via the Pentagon's Web site.

Among these documents, the one that first attracted headlines was a letter from Bush's father, then-congressman George H. W. Bush, to Air Force Major General G. B. Greene, Jr., of Lackland Air Force Base in Texas (313). Bush was writing in response to a letter Greene had written on August 27, which for some reason was not released by the Pentagon, and his comments bolstered the impression that Bush had received special treatment in his early days in the Guard: "That a Major General in the Air Force would take interest in a brand new Air Force trainee made a big impression on me," the congressman wrote.

Also included in this batch of documents were complete versions of three 1970 Texas ANG press releases (314–19); the first page of the first such release had been made available earlier (196), but it appears again here as part of the complete set. The new pages show Lieutenant Bush admitting "I've got a hell of a lot more to learn. . . . I've got to learn to respect the airplane and its capabilities, as well as my own abilities," and telling his interviewer, "Flying, the whole thing, is kicks" (315).

More important to a real understanding of Bush's service record were a more complete set of his payroll records (320–43), and especially his flight logs (346–58). As mentioned in the introductory essay, the flight log for the first half of 1972 (354) recorded that after several years of flying the more challenging F102A fighter, Bush began returning to his training jet, the T-33A, and on two occasions in February and March it took him multiple passes to land the F-102. His Mission Design Summaries from mid-1972 to December 1974 (355–8) confirm that after mid-1972 Bush never again logged flight time with the Guard.

GEORGE BUSH
7TH DISTRICT, TEXAS

MEMBER:
WAYS AND MEANS
COMMITTEE

WASHINGTON OFFICE:
LONGWORTH HOUSE OFFICE BUILDING

DISTRICT OFFICE:
FEDERAL OFFICE BUILDING
HOUSTON, TEXAS 77002

Congress of the United States
House of Representatives
Washington, D.C. 20515

September 11, 1968

Dear General Greene:

I was surprised and very, very pleased to receive your
letter of August 27th.

That a Major General in the Air Force would take interest
in a brand new Air Force trainee made a big impression on
me.

Naturally, as a father I was pleased to read your comments
about George. He is anxiously looking forward to going to
flight school and with parental pride, I do have the feeling
that he will be a gung ho member of the U.S. Air Force. I
think that he will make a good pilot as well.

When he came home, he was full of the training that he had
received, and particularly enthusiastic about the dedication
of the men he met. I'll never forget the way he kept us up
that first night telling about Sgt. Henry Onacki, who apparently was his first instructor. It did my heart good to hear
him describe Onacki's love of country and dedication to the
Air Force. I know that the Air Force through men like Sgt.
Onacki helped awaken the very best instincts in my son. In
this day and age when it has become a little bit fashionable
to be critical of the military, I was delighted to see him
return to our house with a real pride in the service and with
a great respect for the leaders that he had encountered at
Lackland.

General Greene, this is a personal letter but I did want to
write to you from the heart and thank you for what you, Sgt.
Onacki and the others are doing, and obviously doing well.

Yours very truly,

George Bush, M.C.

Major General G. B. Greene, Jr., USAF
Commander
Headquarters Lackland Military Training Center (ATC)
Lackland Air Force Base, Texas 78236

Office of Information
147th Combat Crew Training Group
Texas Air National Guard
Houston, Texas 77034

FOR IMMEDIATE RELEASE
spl to The Houston Post
and The Houston Chronicle
w/art

ELLINGTON AFB, Tex., March 24, 1970---George Walker Bush is one member of the younger generation who doesn't get his kicks from pot or hashish or speed. Oh, he gets high, all right, but not from narcotics.

Bush is a second lieutenant attached to the 111th Combat Crew Training Squadron, 147th Combat Crew Training Group, Texas Air National Guard at Houston.

Lt Bush recently became the first Houston pilot to be trained by the 147th and to solo in the F-102 Fighter Interceptor, a supersonic, all-weather aircraft.

In January, the 147th's mission was changed from active air defense of the Texas Gulf Coast to a new mission--to train and make combat-ready all Air National Guard F-102 fighter pilots in the United States.

Lt Bush was the first member of the 147th to be trained by people he will be working with in the future.

After his solo, a milestone in the career of any fighter pilot, Lt Bush couldn't find enough words to adequately express the feeling of solo flight.

"It was really neat. It was fun, and very exciting", he said. "I felt really serene up there   It's exciting to be alone in such a big aircraft and it's a real challenge to fly such a powerful airplane by

MORE

ADD ONE
BUSH

yourself".

Fighter planes are Lt Bush's "thing". He says he has no ambition
to fly any other type of aircraft.

"Fighters are it. I've always wanted to be a fighter pilot and
I wouldn't want to fly anything else", he said. "You have such speed,
such power in a fighter, that it's just fantastic. And the F-102 is
really a good-looking, well-constructed aircraft. It's a really stable
airplane".

Despite the fact that he's flown the F-102 solo for the first time.
Lt Bush isn't letting it go to his head.

"I've got a hell of a lot more to learn," he said. I've got to
learn to respect the aircraft and its capabilities, as well as my own
abilities."

Lt Bush is the son of U.S. Representative George Bush, who is a
candidate for the U. S. Senate seat of Senator Ralph Yarborough. The
elder Bush was a Navy fighter pilot. Lt Bush said his father was just
as excited and enthusiastic about his solo flight as he was.

Lt Bush, who is 23, is due to complete his pilot training June 23.
He will then be released from active duty and assume reserve status in
the Air National Guard. He plans to fly as much as possible with the
Air Guard and work in his father's campaign. Beyond that, he hasn't
any plans.

As far as kicks are concerned Lt Bush gets his from the roaring
afterburner of the F-102.

"Flying, the whole thing, is kicks," he said. "But afterburner
is a real kick."

-30-

PREPARING FOR SOLO FLIGHT under the watchful eyes of an instructor pilot, 2Lt George W. Bush gets himself squared away in the cockpit of his F-102. Lt Bush, son of U.S. Congressman George Bush, is the first "hometown" student to undergo instruction at the Texas Air National Guard's 147th Combat Crew Training Group, Houston, Texas.

Capt Charles W. Whitsett, a Combat Ready F-102 pilot and Delta Airlines pilot, watches the procedures for correctness.

NEWS RELEASE

Ellington AFB, Tex., 29 Jul 70 - The 147th Fighter Group, Texas Air
National Guard, Houston, commanded by Lt Col Bobby W. Hodges, has just
completed a successful deployment to Tyndall AFB, Florida firing missiles
and rockets from their F-102 aircraft. The deployment required members
of this unit to depart Ellington for Tyndall AFB, Panama City, Fla.,
fire the missiles and rockets in a maximum of 5 days and return to
Ellington. An unusual problem was added this year as Hurricane "Becky"
came out of the Gulf, headed for the Florida Panhandle, on Tuesday,
which required evacuation back to Ellington by the unit personnel. After
the storm passed, the unit redeployed to Tyndall to complete the firing
within the five day limit.

Another unusual fact on this deployment was that the unit sent
four new Lieutenants, of the 12 pilots on this deployment, and each
fired a missile, all scoring exceptionally well. The fact that the
Lieutenants did so well attests to the training conducted by the 147th
Fighter Group's daily mission of Combat Crew Training.

Several Houstonians were cited for their outstanding contributions
to the highly successful deployment. They were: SMSgt Alton K. Curry,
SMSgt Jimmy L. Jackson, MSgt Dale M. Brenneman, MSgt Walter W. Huehlefeld,
MSgt Lindsey T. Smith, TSgt Billy B. Beck, TSgt William E. Chapman,
TSgt James A. Craig, TSgt William J. Grant, Jr., SSgt Charles E. Brant,
SSgt Donald B. Haig, SSgt David E. Howard, Jr., Sgt Harris H. Beyer, Jr.,
Sgt Kenneth R. Kana and Sgt William G. McKeown, all members of the
147th CAMRON, commanded by Lt Col David K. Barnell.

MORE

PAGE 2
147th Fighter Group

The four Lieutenants firing missiles from the F-102 aircraft for the first time were: Fred E. Bradley, George W. Bush, Jr., Lee M. Honeycutt II, and Dean A. Roome, all members of the 111th Fighter Interceptor Squadron, commanded by Lt Col Jerry B. Killian.

- 30 -

FOR IMMEDIATE RELEASE
Date _____

Office of Information
147th Combat Crew Training Group
Texas Air National Guard
Houston, Texas 77034

ELLINGTON AFB, Tex.---2Lt George Walker Bush, 23, of Houston today graduated from the 147th Combat Crew Training School, taking his place among the operationally-ready F-102 pilots of the Air National Guard.

Lt Col Bobby W. Hodges, Commander, 147th Combat Crew Training Group, Texas Air National Guard, presented Lt Bush with his certificate of completion, signifying an ending--and yet a beginning.

Although Lt. Bush has completed a tough and very intense period of training in flying the fighter-interceptor, his training and learning will continue throughout his flying career.

The graduation of Lt Bush signifies a first for the 147th--he is the first hometown graduate of the 147th Combat Crew Training School since the school was established.

He will now assume his duties as a fighter pilot with the 147th, joining the other pilots assigned to the 111th Combat Crew Training Squadron, and will eventually be putting other student pilots through their paces.

Lt Bush is a 1968 graduate of Yale University. Included among his decorations and awards are the Small Arms Expert Marksmanship Ribbon, the Air Force Outstanding Unit Award and the Presidential Unit Citation.

-30-

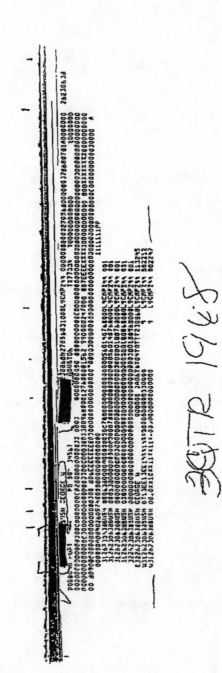

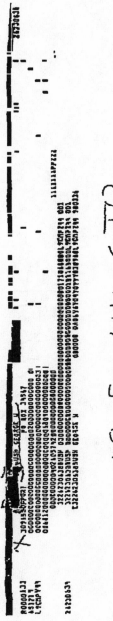

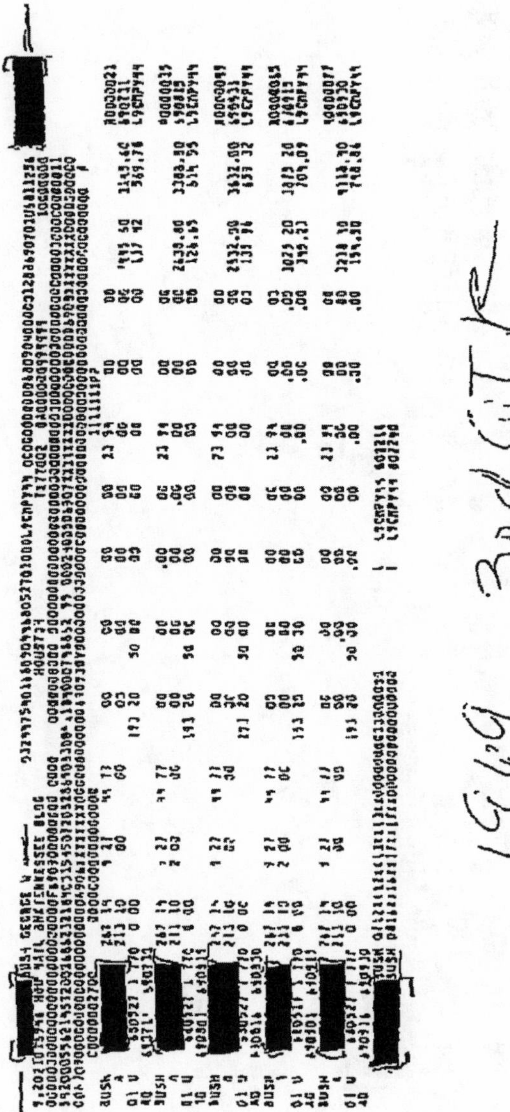
BUSH GEORGE W
HOU NATL BK TENNESSEE BLDG
HOUSTON
1969 3rd QTR

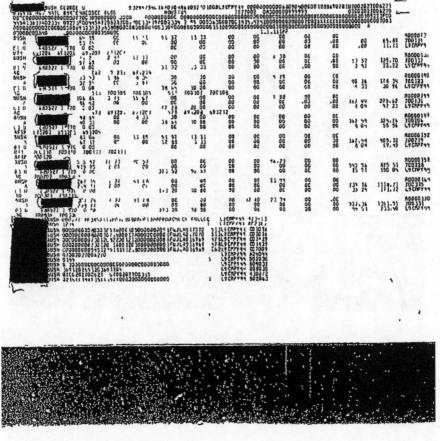

1970 - 1st QTR

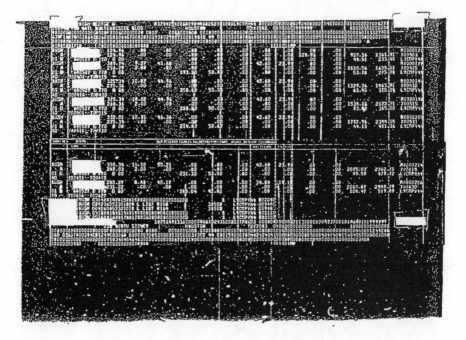

1976 2nd QTR

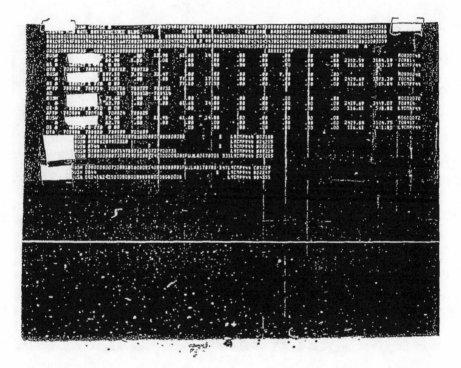

1st QTR 1971

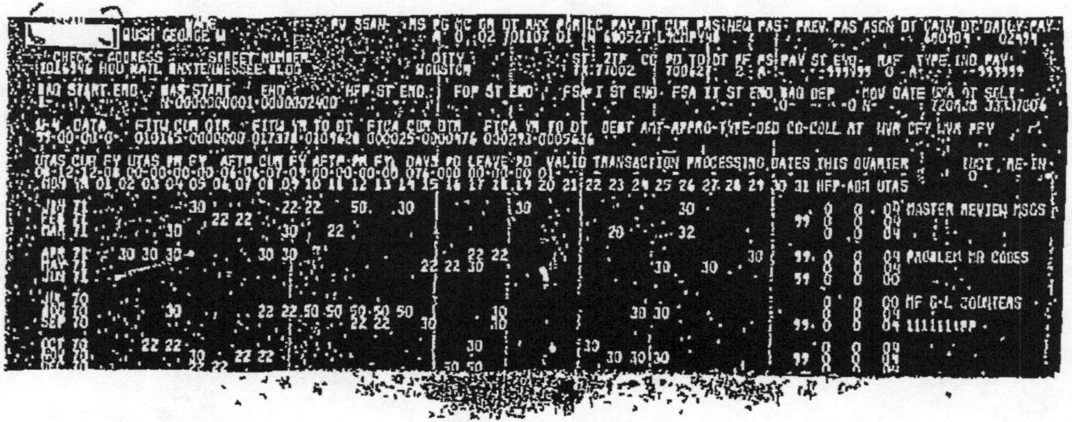

BUSH GEORGE W

CHECK ADDRESS STREET NUMBER CITY ST ZIP

HOU NATL HOUSTON TX 77002

FICA CUR QTR FICA YR TO DT

UTAS CUR FY UTAS PR FY AFTP CUR FY AFTP PR FY DAYS PD LEAVE PD VALID TRANSACTION PROCESSING DATES THIS QUARTER

01 02 03 04 05 06 07 08 09 10 11 12 13 14 15 16 17 18 19 20 21 22 23 24 25 26 27 28 29 30 31 HFP-ADM UTAS

MASTER REVIEW MSGS

PROBLEM MR CODES

MF G-L COUNTERS

1971-2nd QTR

1971
3RD GTR

1971   4th GTR

Page 1 — 1972 1st Qtr

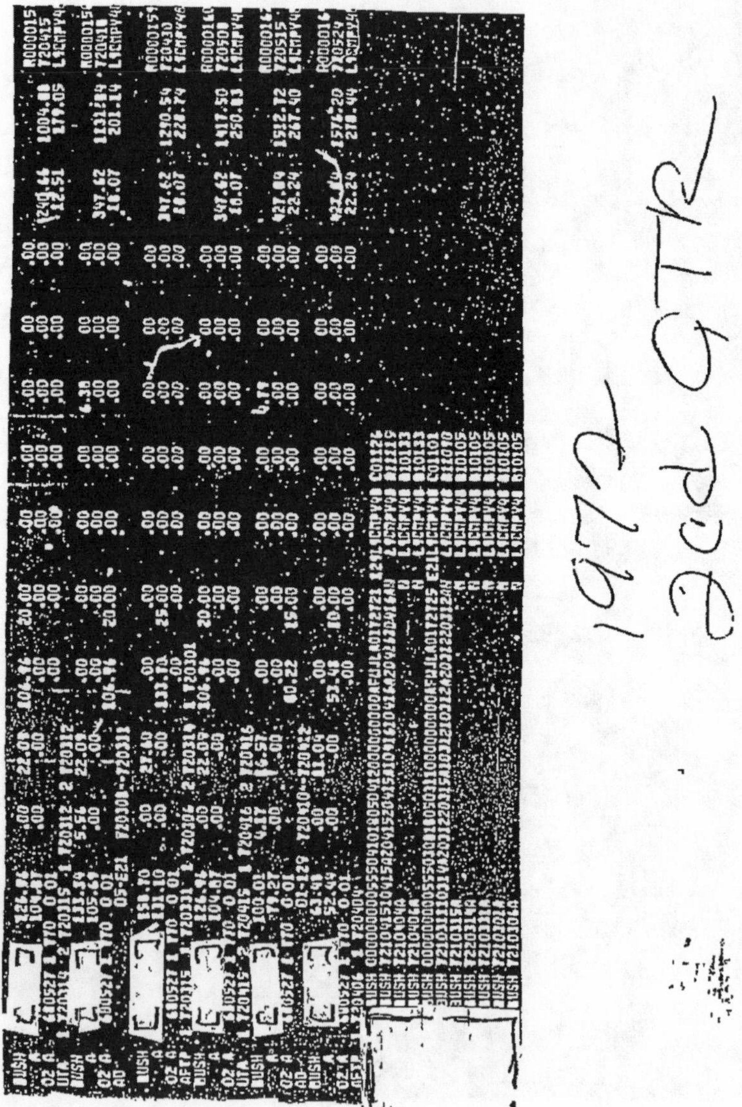
1972
2nd QTR

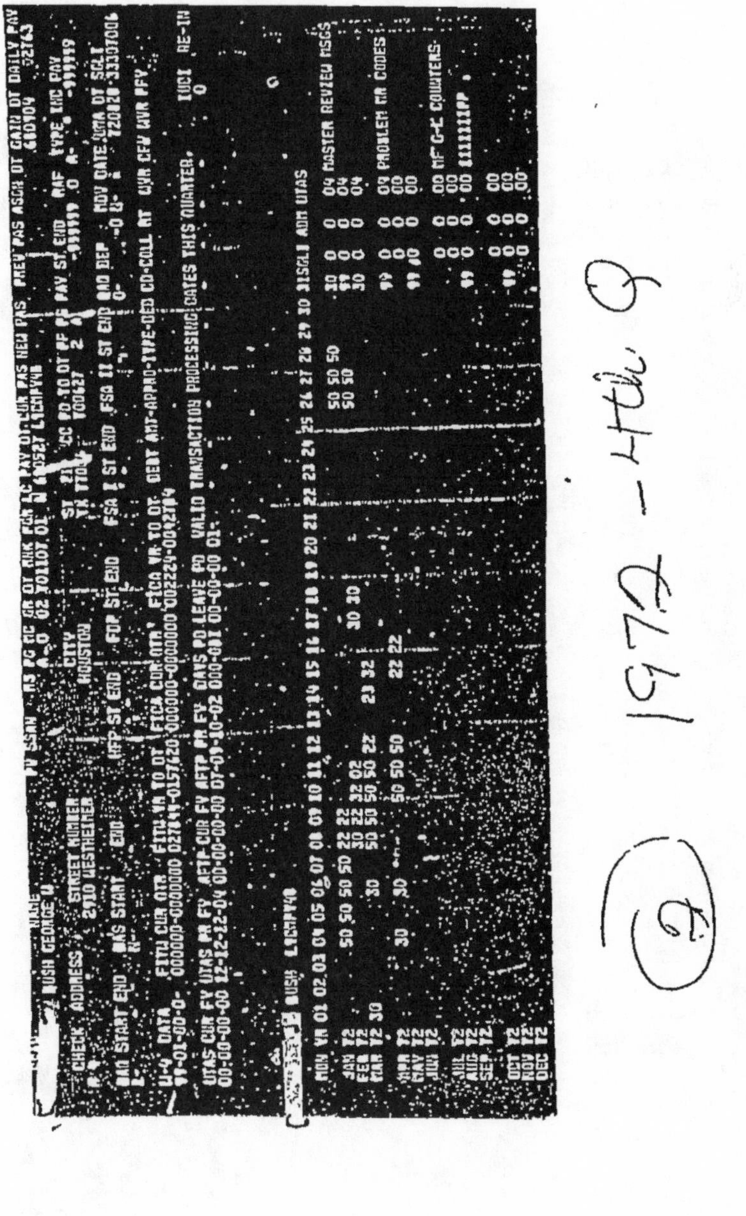

```
NAME                         PV SSAN  MS PG MC GR DT MHK PGN LC PAY DT CUR PAS NEW PAS  PREV PAS ASGN DT GAIN DT DAILY PAY
BUSH GEORGE W                         A 0  02 701107 01  N 680527 L1CMPY40                        680904    02763
CHECK  ADDRESS    STREET NUMBER          CITY           ST  ZIP  CC PD TO DT PF PG PAY ST END   RAF  TYPE INC PAY
                  2910 WESTHEIMER        HOUSTON        TX  770        720627  2  A      -999999 0 A-        -999999
RAD START END  RAS START   END     HFP ST END   FDP ST END   FSA I ST END  FSA II ST END RAD DEP   MDV DATE UMA DT SGLI
                                                                                     0-       -0          720820 33307006
W-4 DATA   FITW CUR QTR   FITW YR TO DT   FICA CUR QTR   FICA YR TO DT   DEBT AMT-APPRO-TYPE-DED CD-COLL AT  WVR CFW WVR PFY
99-01-00-0-  000000-0000000 027849-0157620 000000-0000000 002224-0092704
UTAS CUR FY UTAS PR FY  AFTP CUR FY AFTP PR FY  DAYS PD LEAVE PD  VALID TRANSACTION PROCESSING DATES THIS QUARTER.   IUCI  RE-IN
00-00-00-00 12-12-12-04 00-00-00-00 07-09-10-02 000-001 00-00-00 01-                                                  0

BUSH  L1CMPY40
MON YR 01 02 03 04 05 06 07 08 09 10 11 12 13 14 15 16 17 18 19 20 21 22 23 24 25 26 27 28 29 30 31SGLI ADM UTAS
                                                                              50 50 50      30  0  0  04 MASTER REVIEW MSGS
JAN 72          50 50 50 50 22 22                                             50 50         99  0  0  04
FEB 72                      30 22 32 02                        30 30                        30  0  0  04
MAR 72 30              30   50 50 50 50 22    23 32
                                                                                            99  0  0  09 PROBLEM MR CODES
APR 72       30    30          50 50 50             22 22                                        0  0  00
MAY 72                                                                                      99  0  0  00
JUN 72
                                                                                                 0  0  00 MF G-L COUNTERS
JUL 72                                                                                           0  0  00
AUG 72                                                                                      99   0  0  00 11111111PP
SEP 72
                                                                                                 0  0  00
OCT 72                                                                                      99   0  0  00
NOV 72                                                                                           0  0  00
DEC 72
```

1ST. GTR 1973

1973 - 3cd QTR   (1)

CHECK ADDRESS   STREET NUMBER   CITY   ST ZIP CC PO TO DI PF PS PAY ST END   RAP TYPE INC PAY
                        2910 WESTHEIMER   HOUSTON   TX 77006 7G0627   2   A   999999   0   A*   -999999

GSO START ENG   GAS START   ENG   HSP ST END   FOF ST END   FSA I ST END   FSA II ST END BAV DEP   NOV DATE UTA DT SCL I
                                                                                                  0   0   N*   730828 33337006

U A DATA   FTIL CIX ATP   FITU YR TO DT FIC1 DUE DTE   FICA YR TO DT   DEBT AMT AFPRO TYPE GED CO CELL RT   UTE CFV NYR PFY
44 01-00 0   01010 0000000 0379.32 022162? 002759 007169 004324-0082549

UTAS CIX F / UTAS SR F /   SFTP CIA FY   FIE 99 F /   DAYS PG LEAVE FD   VALID TRANSACTION PROCESSING DATES THIS QUARTER   IUCI AE IN
12 00 00 00 00 12 12 12 00 00 00 00 00 00 00 025 049 00 00-00 33 0703 0724-0303-0407   0

BUSH L %CMPY44

MON YR OC 02 03 04 05 06 07 08 09 10 11 12 13 14 15 16 17 18 19 20 21 22 23 24 25 26 27 28 29 30 31 SCLT ABM UTAS

JAN 73   22 22 22   22 22 22   99   0   0 12 MASTER REVIEW MSGS
FEB 73   0   0 00
MAR 73   0   0 00

APR 73   22 77   99   0   0 04 PROBLEM MA CODES
MAY 73 50 50 50   A 50 90   22 22   50 50 50   50 50 50 0   0 04
JUN 73   50 50 50   22 22   99   0   0 04

JUL 73   50 50   50   50 50 50 50   22 22 22 22   2c 22 50 50 50 50 50   50   0   0 12 PF D L COUNTERS
AUG 73   0   0 0C
SEP 73   99   0   0 00 LLLLLLPP

OCT 72   2c 22 22 22   22 22   0   0 04
NOV 72   99   0   0 04
DEC 72   L   0 0L

BUSH   02211 15 005 2 403* 25 C117 32 003 00 C000 0C 000 00 L04 7*   00   0000 00   AG000059
02 A   01 70 72   0 00 0000 03 00 0003 000 00 0000 00 000 00 000 00 0000 00 000 CL C0342 70 01 441 24   730705
UT A 1 730623 2 730623   1 730624 2 730627   04 22h 730605 730707   2035 44 000 00 0000 00 000 00 000 00 000 00 C00 00 029 35 00252.13 L %CMPY44

BUSH   00211 53 012 01 0035 25 0000 00 000 00 000C 00 00G 06 011 12   00   000C 00   AG000061
02 A   00 14 71   1 50 0000 00 0000 00 0CC 00 000C 00 000 00 000 00 000 00 000 CC 04740 54 01447 49   730731
UT A 1 730527 1 730   1   04 41 3 730102 730101   028 34 000 00 000 00 000 00 C0C 00 000 00 037 12 00281.38 L %CMPY44

BUSH   00221 30 004 82 0043 32 0117 52 000 00 0000 00 00G 00 000 06   00   0000 00   AG000064
02 A   00214 31   0 00 0000 00 0000 00 000 00 000 00 000 00 000 00 000 00 00 00799.95 01952 96   730807
UT A 1 730721   01 462 730721 2 730722   0147 40 000 00 0000 00 C00 00 000 00 000 00 000 00 046.59 C0332.70 L %CMPY44

BUSH   00244 72 001 72 0043 32 0235 44 000 00 000C 00 C00 00 001 40   00   0000 00   AG000067
02 A   00219 44   0 CL 0000 00 0000 00 000 00 000 00 000 00 000 00 000 00 00 C0829 44 02216.28   730813
UT A 1 730527 1 730718 2 730718 1 730718 1 730717 2 730717   0029 44 000 00 0000 00 000 00 000 00 000 00 000 00 044 26 00374.02 L %CMPY44

BUSH 000000000 9550 730170 PoFU JFVUCUCUCUDUDUDUCCUOFV U A AG1 73731 4ISL %CMPY44 C0121A
BUSH 000000000 7300 730171 PoFU J7UUCUDUDUDUD0UONFV U A AG1 73731 7131 %CMPY44 C0121A
BUSH 730 092210 71 AN20 972.07 LAV10 42 71 7071 7420 92 33071 XNN   L %CMPY44 81121A
BUSH 730 09219 10 71 AN20 A1 A20 71 6A310 41 7131 7420A1 92071 XNN   L %CMPY44 81121A
BUSH 730 72 71 07 2 N20 72 2 A20 71 7121 722N20 N72 72072 N   L %CMPY44 81121A
BUSH 000000000 3330 730 2170 UDUD0UCUDUDUD0UDV U A AG1 73731 4ISL %CMPY44 C01201
BUSH 000000000 3330 70 05 4070 07 05 UDUDUDUD0 UDV U A AG1 73731 7171 %CMPY44 C01201
BUSH 000000000 354 U 071 AV 0U0 UDUD0UDUDUDV U A AG1 71731 72AL %CMPY44 C0121AC
BUSH 730 062 71 A62 730202 L 0421 7170 7 2 H2A 7020 42 A2A2 72A   L %CMPY44 81121A

1973 3rd QTR
Page 1

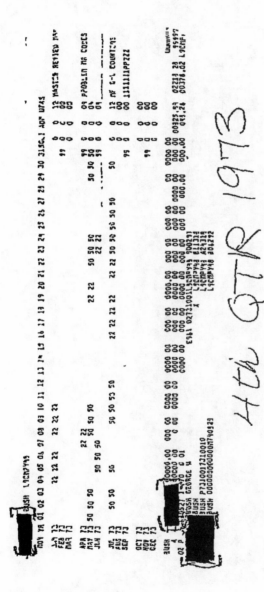

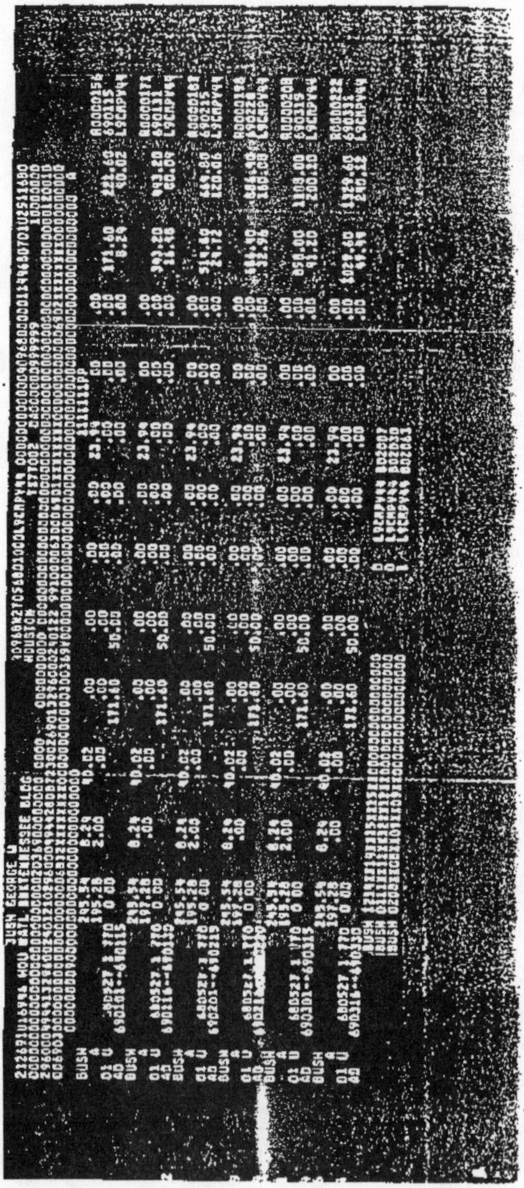

BUSH GEORGE W

CHECK ADDRESS STREET NUMBER 2910 WESTMINER CITY HOUSTON ST ZIP TX 77006

BUSH L9CMPY48

SUMMARY RECORD OF TRAINING (FLYING)

1. LAST NAME - FIRST - MIDDLE INITIAL				2. GRADE	3. SEX	3. NATIONALITY	6. TRAINING BASE
BUSH GEORGE W.				2/LT	Male	U.S.	Moody AFB, GA

4. DATE OF BIRTH	5. EDUCATION		APTITUDE			10. OTHER AFSC'S	11. SOURCE	12. COMMAND	14. PREVIOUS BASE
6 JUL 46	BA	OBS	OFF	PLT	15 PAFSC 0006	NONE	ANG	ANG	ANG - TEXAS

9. COURSE TITLE	18. COURSE NR	16. QUAN	12. DATE ENT.	14. CLASS DESIGNATION	18. AERO RATING	18. FLT. STATUS	21. TYPE OR SOURCE
Undergraduate Pilot Training (T41/T37/T38)	P-V4A-A	1	26 Nov 68	70-04	NONE	No	ANG - 1928 YALE UNIV

ACADEMIC TRAINING RECORD

SUBJECT OR PHASE	12B. PRESC. HOURS	12C. EXAM. GRADES		12D. SUBJECT GRADE
		4ND PHASE	FINAL	
Airmanship	11.0		88	88
Aviation Physiology (T-37)	29.0		98	98
Physiological Support	10.0	Comp	Comp	Comp
T-37 Systems Operations	17.0		93	93
Principles of Flight	10.0		93	93
Flight Instruments	13.0		98	98
IFR Navigation	34.0	100	100	100
CFR Navigation	25.0		93	93
Aural Code	10.0	Comp	Comp	Comp
Flying Safety	6.0	Comp	Comp	Comp
Weather	30.0	93	96	95
Aviation Physiology (T-38)	5.0	Comp	Comp	Comp
Instrument Procedures & Radio Aids	17.0		97	97
T-38 Systems Operations	17.0		100	100
Applied Aerodynamics	19.0		100	100
Flight Planning	32.0	90	88	89
Radar	8.0	Comp	Comp	Comp
Electronic Warfare Fam (Secret)	10.0	Comp	Comp	Comp

GRADES IN PARENTHESIS INDICATE GRADES MADE ON REMARK EXAMINATIONS	32E.	REG. FINAL ACADEMIC THE GRADE
32F. TOTAL HOURS:	303.0 300.0	94.95
32L. TOTAL HOURS COMPLETED:	300.0	
ACADEMIC CLASS STANDING:		1

OFFICER TRAINING RECORD

SUBJECT OR PHASE	23B. PRESCRIBED HOURS	23C. HOURS COMPLETED	23D. GRADE
Orientation & Processing	28.0		Comp
Career Planning	6.0		Comp
Counterinsurgency	7.0		Comp
Physical Conditioning & Developing	125.0		Comp
Marksmanship	6.0		Comp
23E. TOTAL HOURS:	172.0	172.0	

RECORD OF CLASS CHANGE(S)

24A. MELDOVER TO CLASS	EFFECTIVE DATE	24C.	24B. REASON FOR MELDOVER

DISPOSITION OF STUDENT

33A. GRADUATED WITH (Class and Date) CLASS 70-04 26 Nov 69

33B. ELIMINATED FROM (Class, Date, and Reason for Elimination)

33C. TRANSFERRED TO (Command, Organization and Location) ANG, 111th FIGHTER GP, ELLINGTON AFB, TX

32D. AUTHORITY (S.O., Para, and Date) ANG-T-1103, 16 OCT 68, TK & AUTH'T GENERAL OFFIC, AUTH'T 7 HQ 3550AH FLT TNG WG (ATC) MOODY AFB, GA 31602

ATC FORM 240
NOV 67

PREVIOUS EDITIONS ARE OBSOLETE.

Bush

FLYING TRAINING RECORD

Subject or Phase	Type Acft and/or Eqpt	Total Hrs Presc	Flying Hrs Presc	Flying Hrs Rec'd (Dual)	Flying Hrs Rec'd (Solo)	Flying Hrs Rec'd (Total)	Check Grades	Grad
Policies and Procedures	T-41	5.0						Com
Contact (Type)	T-41	60.0	-	24.0	6.0	30.0	87	88
Policies and Procedures	T-37	12.7						89
Contact	T-37	109.4	54.7	38.0	17.0	55.0	88(94) 93	89
Instrument	T-37	41.6	20.8	21.9		21.9	97	97
Navigation	T-37	18.6	9.3	9.4		9.4		97
Formation	T-37	10.4	5.2	4.6		4.6		Com
Synthetic Trainer	T-37	22.5	(21.6)	-		(21.6)		98 97
Policies and Procedures	T-38	28.0						Com
Contact	T-38	71.4	35.7	19.6	13.6	33.2	88	88
Instrument	T-38	59.0	29.5	30.8		30.8	94	96
Navigation	T-38	31.6	15.8	17.1	3.7	15.8		97
Formation	T-38	72.8	36.4	29.1	11.1	40.2	93	94 93
Synthetic Trainer	T-38	31.9	-	-	-	(29.4)		96 96
		5749	237.4	187.2	51.4	240.6		92.6

GRADES IN PARENTHESIS INDICATE A REPEAT

TOTAL HOURS AND FINAL
FLYING TRAINING GRADE

FLYING TRAINING CLASS STANDING: /

OVERALL CLASS STANDING: /

REMARKS:

AUTHENTICATION (Signature)
ALEXANDER J FALCINELLI, Capt, USAF, Administrative Officer, Deputy Commander for Operations

		COMPUTATION OF FLYING AND ACADEMIC RANK ORDER							
CORRELATION FLY/ACAD = .28				CLASS 70-04		TRAINING BASE MOODY AFB, GA 31601			
STUDENT	TOTAL FLYING HOURS	FLYING HOURS			OVERALL RANK	FLYING RANK	ACADEMIC RANK	AIRCRAFT ASSIGNMENT	
		T-41	T-37	T-38					
	228.0	18.0	90.0	120.0	1	4	1	F-102	3
	235.0	30.0	90.0	115.0	2	1	23.5	T-29	22.5
	240.0	30.0	90.0	120.0	3	9	2	F-106	7
	240.2	30.0	90.2	120.0	4	6	7.5	F-100	1.5
	228.4	18.0	90.0	120.4	5	15	4.5	A1E	10.5
	238.1	30.0	90.0	118.1	6	11	11.5	C-141	.5
	228.3	18.0	90.0	120.3	7	7	15.3	F-4	8.5
	240.9	30.0	90.5	120.4	8	14	11.5	PIT	2.5
	225.2	18.0	90.0	116.1	9	16	18	C-47	8
	240.0	30.0	90.0	120.0	10	12	15.5	USMC	7.5
	228.0	18.0	90.0	120.0	11	25.5	7.5	PIT	18
	240.4	30.0	90.0	120.4	12	10	18	USMC	5
	237.0	30.0	90.0	117.0	13	27	7.5	F-102	19.5
	236.8	30.0	90.3	116.5	14	17.5	13.5	C-141	4
	240.5	30.0	90.0	120.5	15	30	7.5	C-130	20.5
	235.9	30.0	90.0	115.9	16	17.5	21	C-141	3.5
	240.5	30.0	90.0	120.5	17	3	34.5	FOREIGN	31.3
	240.0	30.0	90.0	120.0	18	2	36.5	USMC	34.5
	240.0	30.0	90.0	120.0	19	33	10	F-4	23
	228.0	18.0	90.0	120.0	20	38	4.5	OLE	33.5
	223.0	18.0	90.0	115.0	21	19	26.5	C-130	7.5
BUSH G	240.6	30.2	90.6	120.0	22	20	26.5	F-102	6.5
	297.2	100.1	90.0	117.2	23	16	29	C-141	13
	240.2	30.0	90.0	120.2	24	28	23.5	KC-135	4.5
	235.4	30.0	90.0	115.4	25	22	30	C-141	8
	240.6	30.0	90.0	120.5	26	21	31	C-141	10
	223.9	18.0	90.8	115.1	27	42	13.5	C-130	28.5
	240.0	30.0	90.0	120.0	28	5	49.5	FOREIGN	44.5
	240.9	30.0	90.9	120.0	29	41	18	OLE	23
	240.5	30.0	90.3	120.2	30	39	21	USMC	18
	228.7	18.0	90.0	120.7	31	40	21	C-141	19
	235.0	30.0	90.0	115.5	32	8	48	C-141	40
	242.8	30.0	91.2	121.6	33	25.5	34.5	FOREIGN	9.0
	235.8	30.0	90.0	115.8	34	24	36.5	C-141	12.5
	235.0	30.0	90.0	115.0	35	23	42	B-52	19
	241.0	30.0	90.0	121.0	36	29	42	KC-135	13
	223.0	18.0	90.0	115.0	37	32	42	C-130	10
	240.5	30.0	90.0	120.5	38	24	32.5	KC-135	11.5
	233.0	20.0	90.0	123.0	39	47	25	KC-135	22
	240.1	30.0	90.1	120.0	40	34	45	C-130	11
	242.1	30.0	90.0	120.1	41	31	47	OLE	16
	230.2	30.0	90.0	120.0	42	37	42	C-130	5
	240.0	30.0	90.0	120.0	43	35	46	OLE	11
	241.6	30.0	90.6	121.0	44	49	32.5	KC-135	16.5
	233.3	19.4	90.0	123.4	45	51	3	B-52	48
	242.7	30.0	90.0	122.7	46	46	38.5	C-47	7.5
	230.9	30.0	90.0	120.9	47	36	52	B-52	16
	234.8	18.7	90.0	123.9	48	45	51	KC-135	6
	243.5	30.0	90.4	120.1	49	48	49.5	B-52	15
	240.5	30.0	90.1	120.1	50	50	42	OLE	12
	240.3	30.0	90.0	120.3	51	52	28	B-52	24

08/28/2004 15:20 FAX 3018370293   NARA GENERAL COUNSEL   ☒005

COMPUTATION OF FLYING AND ACADEMIC RANK ORDER									
CORRELATION FLY/ACAD =				CLASS		TRAINING BASE			
STUDENT	TOTAL FLYING HOURS	FLYING HOURS			OVERALL		FLYING	ACADEMIC	AIRCRAFT ASSIGNMENT
		T-41	T-37	T-38		RANK	RANK	RANK	
	241.9	30.0	90.6	121.3		53	43	53	B-52	10
	240.0	30.0	90.0	1200		53	53	385	O1E	14.5

ATC FORM JAN 66 471

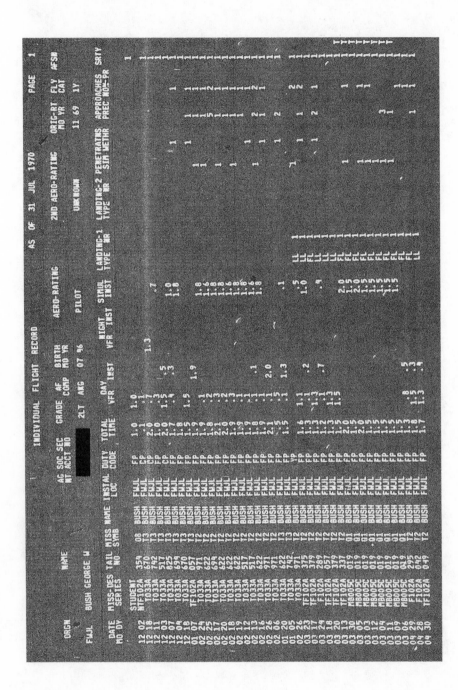

INDIVIDUAL FLIGHT RECORD   AS OF 31 JUL 1970   PAGE 2

ORGN · NAME · AG SOC SEC · GRADE AF · BIRTH · AERO-RATING · 2ND AERO-RATING · ORIG-RT · FLY AFSN
NT ACCT NO · COMP · MO YR · MO YR · CAT

FWJL · BUSH GEORGE W · 21T · ANG 07 46 · PILOT · UNKNOWN · 11 69 · 1Y

INDIVIDUAL FLIGHT RECORD AS OF 31 JUL 1970 PAGE 3

ORGN	NAME	AG SOC-SEC NT ACCT NO	GRADE	AF COMP	BIRTH MO YR	AERO-RATING		2ND AERO-RATING	ORIG-RT MO YR	FLY CAT	AFSN
FWJL	BUSH GEORGE W	▮▮▮▮▮	2LT	ANG	07 46	PILOT		UNKNOWN	11 69	1Y	1

DATE MO DY	MISS-DES SERIES	TAIL NO	MISS SYMB	INSTAL NAME LOC	DUTY CODE	TOTAL TIME	DAY VFR INST	VFR INST	NIGHT VFR INST	SIMUL INST	AERO-RATING PILOT	LANDING-1 TYPE NR	LANDING-2 TYPE NR	PENETRATNS STN WETHR	APPROACHES PREC NON-PR	SRTY
06 19	TF102A	336	T2	BUSH	FWJL	FP	1.5	1.2			.3		FL 1		1		1
06 23	F102A	295	T2	BUSH	FWJL	FP	1.7	1.0	.7				FL 1			2	1
06 22	F102A	188	T2	BUSH	FWJL	PO	1.8	1.8								5	1
06 19	TF102A	336	T2	BUSH	FWJL	FP	1.7	1.0	.7				FL 1				1
06 12	TF102A	339	T2	BUSH	FWJL	FP	1.7	.9	.8			FL 1		1	2	1
06 11	F102A	042	T2	BUSH	FWJL	FP	1.7	1.6	1.0	.1			FL 1			2	1
06 10	F102A	042	T2	BUSH	FWJL	FP	1.7	1.7					FL 1				1
06 09	F102A	042	T2	BUSH	FWJL	FP	1.7	1.7					FM 1				1
06 07	F102A	259	T2	BUSH	FWJL	FP	1.3	1.3	.7				FL 1				1
06 04	F102A	042	T2	BUSH	FWJL	FP	1.4	1.4					FL 1				1
06 10	TF102A	206	T2	BUSH	FWJL	FP	1.6	1.6					FL 1		1	1	1
06 08	F102A	049	T2	BUSH	FWJL	FP	1.5	1.5					FL 1				1
06 03	TF102A	049	T2	BUSH	FWJL	FP	1.5	1.5	.5				FL 1				1
06 02	TF102A	337	T2	BUSH	FWJL	FP	1.5	1.5					FL 1				1
06 05	F102A	079	T2	BUSH	FWJL	PP	1.7	1.7					FL 1				1
07 19	TF102A	336	T3	BUSH	FWJL	FP	2.0	2.0			1.5		FL 1		1	2	1
07 10	TF102A	205	T3	BUSH	FWJL	FP	1.5	1.5	.2				FL 1				1
07 20	F102A	049	T3	BUSH	FWJL	FP	1.5	1.5	.5				FL 1				1
07 24	TF102A	206	T3	BUSH	FWJL	FP	1.5	1.5					FL 1				1
07 23	F102A	289	T3	BUSH	FWJL	FP	2.0	2.0	.7				FL 1				1
07 23	F102A	206	T2	BUSH	FWJL	FP	1.0	1.0					FL 1				1
07 31	TF102A	057	T2	BUSH	FWJL	FP	1.9	1.9			.4		FL 1				1
07 22	F102A	057	T3	BUSH	FWJL	FP	2.1	2.1	.6				FL 1			1	1
07 21	F102A	289	T3	BUSH	FWJL	FP	1.8	1.8	.5				FL 1		3	1	1
07 14	F102A	289	T3	BUSH	FWJL	FP	1.2	1.2			.2		FL 1			2	1
07 16	C05GC	507	S2	BUSH	FWJL	CP	2.0	1.9	.6				FL 1			1	1
07 19	TF102A	049	T3	BUSH	FWJL	VP	2.9										1

INDIVIDUAL FLIGHT RECORD AS OF 31 JUL 1970 PAGE 4

ORGN	NAME	AG SOC SEC NT ACCT NO	GRADE	AF COMP	BIRTH MO YR	AERO-RATING	2ND AERO-RATING	ORIG-RT MO YR	FLY CAT	AFSN
FWJL	BUSH GEORGE W	▮▮▮▮	2LT	ANG	07 46	PILOT	UNKNOWN	11 69	1Y	

MISSION / DESIGN SUMMARIES

MISS-DESM SERIES	MDS CODE	TOTAL HOURS	PILOT	INSTRUCT	CO-PILOT	COMMAND	AC-CMDR	OTHER RATED	LAND-INGS	SORTIES	LAST-FLOWN YR MO	FRST-FLOWN YR MO
CO F 102	110	101.9	101.9						64	68	70 07	69 12
T 33	454	35.9	30.8		5.1					20	70 05	69 12
C 54	504	.9			.9					1	70 07	70 07

FLYING HOUR CAREER TOTALS

RATED FLYING TIME	138.7	JET-TIME	137.8
CIVILIAN - OVER 450 HP			
FOREIGN MILITARY		COMBAT	
OTHER U.S. MILITARY	240.0	COMBAT-SUPPORT	
STUDENT			
TOTAL HOURS	378.7		

IN BALANCE WITH BASE CAREER TOTAL RECORD

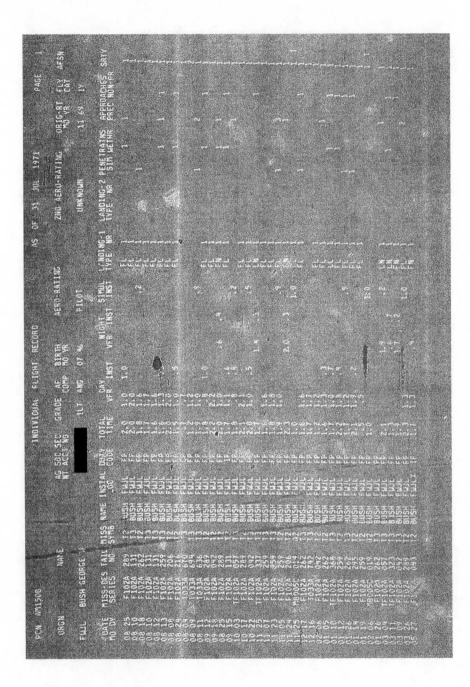

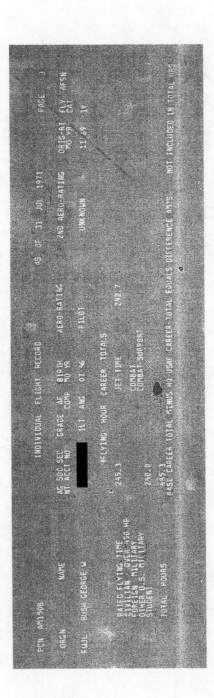

PCN AM1506B

INDIVIDUAL FLIGHT RECORD   AS OF 31 JUL 1971   PAGE   3

ORGN   NAME

FWJL   BUSH GEORGE W

AG SOC SEC   GRADE AF   BIRTH   AERO-RATING   2ND AERO-RATING   ORIG-RT FLY AFSN
NT ACCT NO   COMP MO YR   MO YR   CAT

                      1LT ANG 07 46   PILOT   UNKNOWN   11 69   1Y

FLYING HOUR CAREER TOTALS

                                JET TIME   252.7

                                COMBAT
                                COMBAT Support

RATED FLYING TIME   245.3
CIVILIAN
FOREIGN MILITARY
OTHER U.S. MILITARY
STUDENT

TOTAL HOURS   240.0

                                   452.3
FLIGHT CAREER TOTAL MINUS MAJ USAF CAREER TOTAL EQUALS DIFFERENCE AMTS.   NOT INCLUDED IN TOTAL HRS

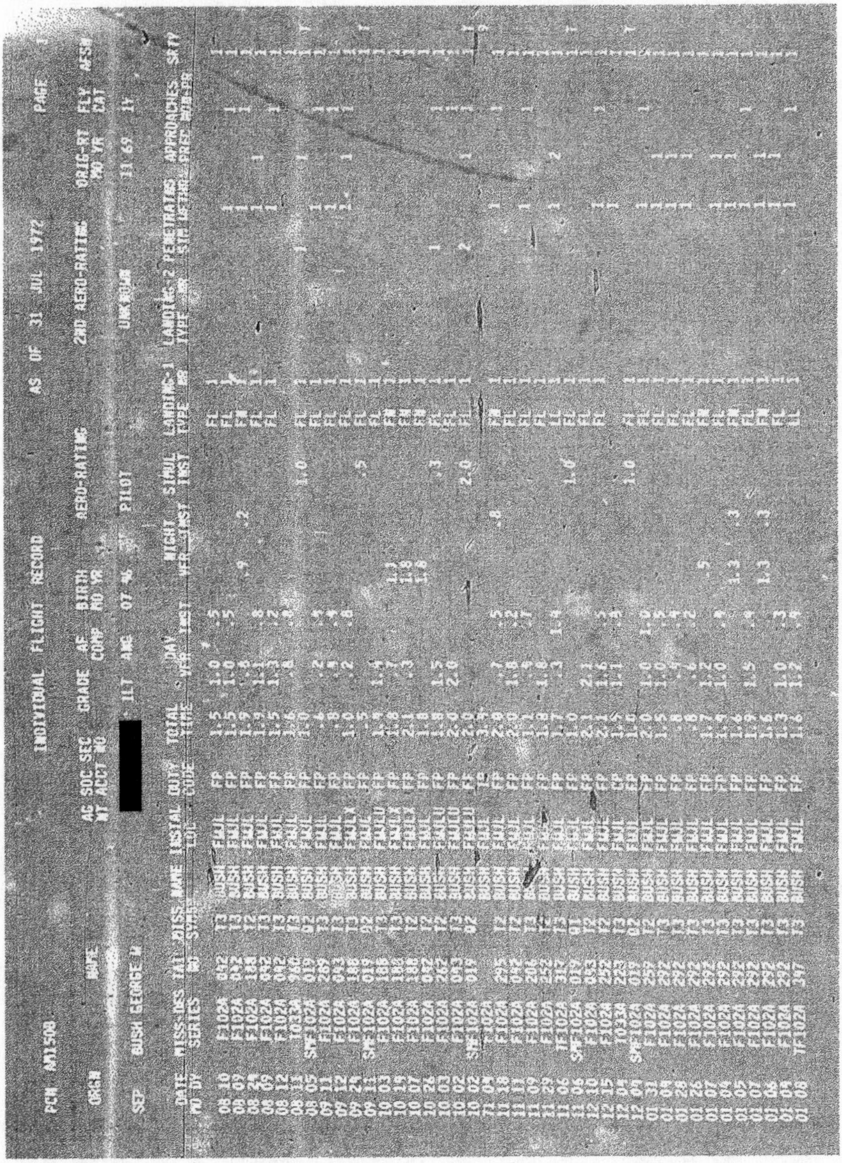

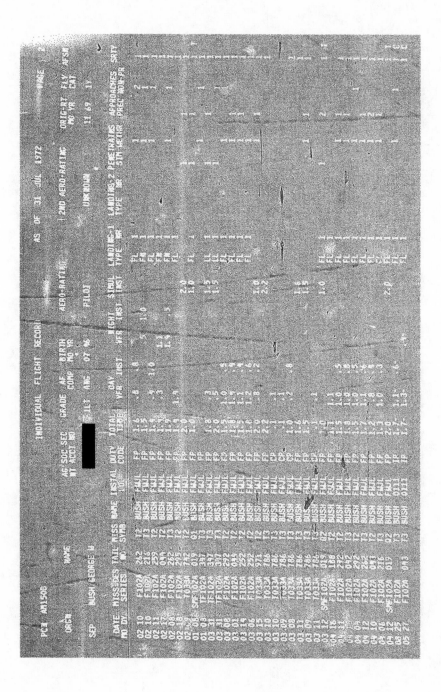

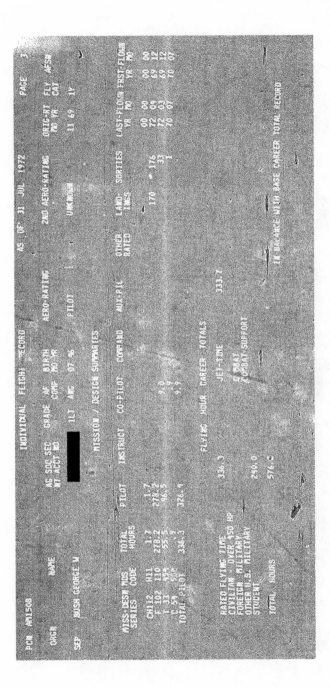

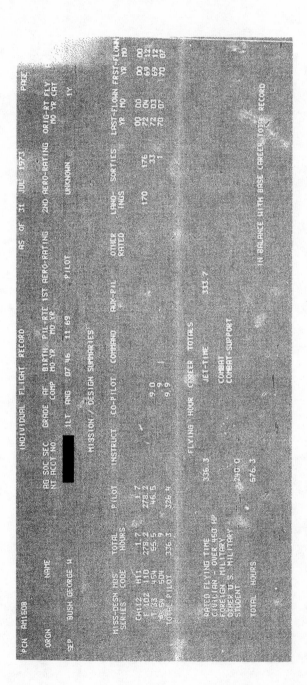

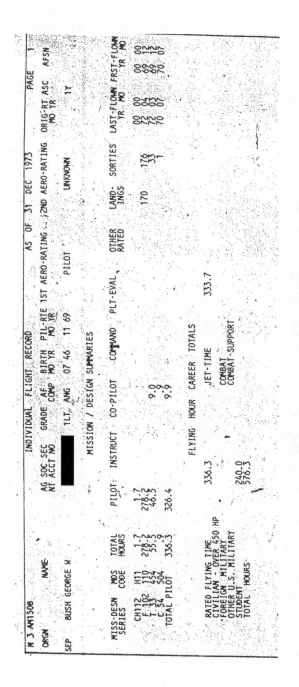

B 4 AN1308

INDIVIDUAL FLIGHT RECORD AS OF 31 DEC 1974 PAGE 1

ORGN NAME AF SOC SEC GRADE AF BIRTH PIL-RTE 16T AERO-RATING 2ND AERO-RATING ORIG-RT ASC AFSN
NT ACCT NO COMP MO YR MO YR MO YR MO YR

SEP BUSH GEORGE W 1LT ANG 07 46 11 69 PILOT UNKNOWN J 1Y

MISSION / DESIGN SUMMARIES

MISS-DESN SERIES	MDS CODE	TOTAL HOURS	PILOT	INSTRUCT	CO-PILOT	COMMAND- PLT-EVAL	OTHER RATED	LAND-INGS	SORTIES	LAST-FLOWN YR MO	FRST-FLOWN YR MO
CH112	H17	1.7	1.7							00 00	00 00
F 102	110	278.2	278.2					170	176	72 04	69 12
T 33	454	55.5	46.5		9.0				33	72 03	69 09
C 54	504	9.9			9.9				1	70 07	70 07
TOTAL PILOT		336.3	326.4		9.9						

FLYING HOUR CAREER TOTALS

PLT-EVAL 333.7

JET-TIME
COMBAT
COMBAT-SUPPORT

RATED FLYING TIME 336.3
CIVILIAN OVER 450 HP
FOREIGN MILITARY
OTHER U.S. MILITARY
STUDENT 240.0
TOTAL HOURS 576.3

I. IDENTIFICATION DATA (Read AFM 36-10 carefully before filling out any item)

1 LAST NAME—FIRST NAME—MIDDLE INITIAL	2 AFSN		3 ACTIVE DUTY GRADE	4 PERMANENT GRADE
BUSH, GEORGE W.	SSAN	YO	NON-RAD	2d Lt

5 ORGANIZATION COMMAND AND LOCATION	6 AERO RATING	CODE	8 PERIOD OF REPORT	
111th Ftr Interceptor Sq	Pilot	1	FROM: 4 Sep 68	THRU: 26 Nov 69
Ellington AFB, Texas (TexANG)	7 ACADEMIC PERIOD		9 REASON FOR REPORT	
	366 days		[X] FINAL [ ] ANNUAL [ ] DIRECTED	

10 NAME AND LOCATION OF SCHOOL OR INSTITUTION

3550th Pilot Training Wing, Moody AFB, Georgia

11 NAME OR TITLE OF COURSE	12 LENGTH OF COURSE
Undergraduate Pilot Training T-41/T-37/T-38	53 weeks

II. REPORT DATA (Complete as applicable)

1 COURSE HOURS COMPLETED	2 COURSE HOURS FAILED	3 AFSC AWARDED	4 AERO RATING AWARDED	5 DEGREE AWARDED
719.4	0	11112	Pilot	

6 COURSE SUCCESSFULLY COMPLETED (Final report only)

[X] YES [ ] NO (If 'No,' state reason)

7 TITLE OF THESIS	8 ACADEMIC FIELD

III. COMMENTS

DAFSC: 0006

IV. REPORTING OFFICIAL

TYPED NAME, GRADE, AFSN AND ORGANIZATION	DUTY TITLE	SIGNATURE
JERRY C. SMITH, Captain	Training Officer	
FR		DATE
3550th Stu Sqdn (ATC)		1 Dec 1969

AF FORM 475 PREVIOUS EDITION OF THIS FORM WILL BE USED UNTIL STOCK IS EXHAUSTED.   TRAINING REPORT   GPO 860-834

JERRY C. SMITH, Captain
JERRY C. SMITH, Captain
Training Officer DATE

APPENDIX

When questions began arising again about Bush's record of service in early 2004, the White House asked retired National Guard Lieutenant Colonel Albert C. Lloyd, Jr., to prepare an analysis of Bush's earned service points. His memorandum, included here (363), credits Bush with 56 points for 1972–3 and again for 1973–4. Yet his math for the latter year does not add up: By any standard, 19 plus 16 plus 15 equals 50, not 56.

This wasn't the first time Lloyd had been enlisted on Bush's behalf. During the 2000 campaign the now-defunct *George* magazine obtained Bush's points record for 1972–3, annotated with handwriting that has since been identified as Lloyd's (365); the clean and intact original can be found at 287.

The final document reproduced here is the Pentagon's "Military Biography of George W. Bush," released in 2004. It makes no mention of Bush's purported service in Alabama.

MEMORANDUM

I have reviewed the following documents:

      1. SO AE-108-TX, 147th FIG, 23 Apr 73
      2. SO AE-226-TX, 147th FIG, 1 May 73
      3. AF Form 526, 1LT George W. Bush, May 72 - May 73
      4. AF Form 526, 1LT George W. Bush, May 73 - May 74

Members of the Air National Guard/ Reserve are required to have 50 points per retirement year in order to have a satisfactory year for retirement/retention. Points are earned as follows:
      1 point for each day of active duty (denoted by 1 in the TD column of the 526)
      1 point for each 4 hour period of inactive duty (denoted by 2 in the TD column)
      15 points per year for guard/reserve membership

Looking at the AF Form 526 for the period May 72 - May 73 George W. Bush accumulated 9 points for 9 days of active duty and 32 points for 32 periods of inactive duty plus the 15 points for his guard/reserve membership for a total of 56 points for that year. LT Bush did in fact have a satisfactory year for retirement/retention.

Looking at the AF Form 526 for the period May 73 - May 74 George W. Bush accumulated 19 points for 19 days of active duty and 16 points for 16 periods of inactive duty plus the 15 points for his guard/reserve membership for a total of 56 points for that year. LT Bush did in fact have a satisfactory year for retirement/retention.

This clearly shows that 1LT George W. Bush has satisfactory years for both 72-73 and 73-74 which proves that he completed his military obligation in a satisfactory manner.

Albert C Lloyd Jr.
ALBERT C. LLOYD, JR., LTC (Ret)

I served in various Military Personnel positions from Squadron to Numbered Air Force level during the period Jul 1956 until my retirement in Aug 1995. During this time I performed many short tours in support of the Air Force and the National Guard Bureau, among these tours was the validation of service dates for all Air National Guard professional officers, assisting in writing many personnel directives, and developing of personnel data systems and programs for use nationwide. In addition I served as an original member of the three person Air National Guard's Transition Team for the implementation of the Reserve Officer Personnel Management Act (ROPMA).

January 72	4,5,6,7,8,9,26,27,28,31
February 72	9,10,11
March 72	1,6,8,9,10,11,12,14,15,31
April 72	4,6,10,11,12,15,16
October 72	28,29
November 72	11,12,13,14
January 73	4,5,6,8,9,10,
April 73	7,8
May 73	1,2,3,8,9,10,19,20,22,23,24,29,30,31
June73	5,6,7,23,24
July 73	2,3,5,9,10,11,12,16,17,18,19,21,22,23,24,25,26,27,30

No 1974 data, Separated October 1, 1973

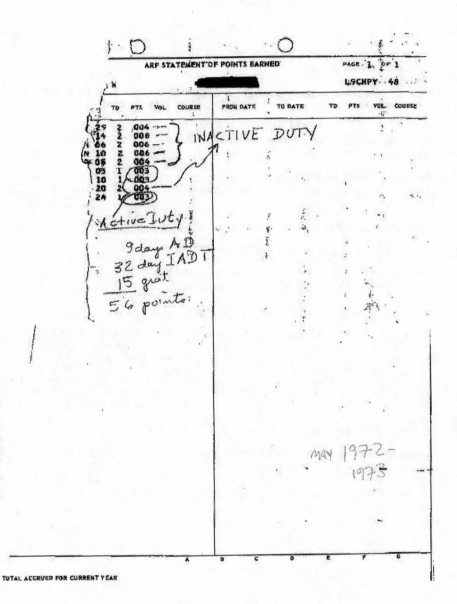

MILITARY BIOGRAPHY

OF

GEORGE WALKER BUSH

The following information is releasable under the Freedom of Information Act. It is an outlined military history of Mr. George W. Bush

DATE OF ENTRY: Enlisted in the Texas Air National Guard at Ellington AFB TX on 27 May 1968.

OFFICER APPOINTMENT: Discharged from enlisted status 3 Sep 1968 and commissioned in the Texas Air National Guard on 4 Sep 1968.

PROMOTIONS: First Lieutenant effective: 7 Nov 1970.

Air Force Specialty Code (AFSC):

    70230 - Apr Administrative Specialist (Enlisted)
    1125D - Pilot, Fighter Interceptor

PAST DUTY ASSIGNMENTS and LOCATIONS:

27 May 68 - 13 Jul 68	147th Cmbt Spt Sq	Ellington AFB TX
14 Jul 68 - 25 Aug 68	3724 BAMILTRARON	Lackland AFB TX
26 Aug 68 - 3 Sep 68	147th Cmbt Spt Sq	Ellington AFB TX
4 Sep 68 - 20 Nov 68	111th Ftr Intcp Sq	Ellington AFB TX
21 Nov 68 - 29 Nov 69	Pilot Trainee, 3550 Stu Sq, Moody AFB GA	
30 Nov 69 - 1 Oct 73	111th Ftr Intcp Sq	Ellington AFB TX
2 Oct 73 - 21 Nov 74	HQ ARPC (ORS)	Denver CO

INITIAL ACTIVE DUTY: 14 Jul 1968 - 25 Aug 1968

PROFESSIONAL MILITARY EDUCATION: Basic Military Training, Undergraduate Pilot Training

DATES OF SERVICE: 27 May 1968 to 21 November 1974

MILITARY AWARDS AND DECORATIONS:

Small Arms Expert Marksmanship Ribbon
National Defense Service Medal

PLACE OF INDUCTION: Ellington AFB Texas

PLACE OF SEPARATION: Denver Colorado

ACKNOWLEDGMENTS

I'd like to thank my editor, Calvert Morgan, at ReganBooks. Without his skill and judgment, this book would not have been possible. I'd also like to thank those reporters who have worked for months and years to uncover the truth about President Bush's military record. Too often their Herculean efforts go unnoticed by partisans. But it's hard, thorough work, and many of them do it extraordinarily well.

To the researchers who graciously offered their assistance, I say thanks.

Finally, to the honorable men and women who serve or who have served in our nation's military, I extend my deepest appreciation and thanks. Perhaps this controversy will help bring additional attention to all those who defend and protect our country with honor and courage.